Praise for *Money in One Lesson*

'Delightful and deep, *Money in One Lesson* is a superb account of the strange connections between money and economics'
Tim Harford, author of *How to Make the World Add Up*

'This is a highly illuminating, well-researched and beautifully written book on one of humanity's most important innovations. People both love and hate money. But mostly, they fail to understand it. Such ignorance is not bliss. Happily, this book will go far to cure it'
Martin Wolf, chief economics commentator, *Financial Times*

'A lucid exposition of a widely misunderstood topic, liberally illustrated with nuggets of intriguing information'
John Kay, economist

'Gavin Jackson has written that rarest of things: an intellectually rigorous and informative book on a technical subject that is also a pleasure to read. Anecdotes, stories and history bring money to life'
Duncan Weldon, author of *Two Hundred Years of Muddling Through*

'A lucid and at times very funny history of money'
Stephen Bush, *Financial Times*

Money in One Lesson

Gavin Jackson is an economics correspondent at *The Economist*, writing about climate change and specializing in economics, business and public policy. He is an emerging voice on the economy and has appeared on BBC Radio and TV. *Money in One Lesson* is his first book.

Money in One Lesson

And Why it Doesn't Work the Way
We Think it Does

Gavin Jackson

PAN BOOKS

First published 2022 by Macmillan

This paperback edition first published 2023 by Pan Books
an imprint of Pan Macmillan
The Smithson, 6 Briset Street, London EC1M 5NR
EU representative: Macmillan Publishers Ireland Ltd, 1st Floor,
The Liffey Trust Centre, 117–126 Sheriff Street Upper,
Dublin 1, D01 YC43
Associated companies throughout the world
www.panmacmillan.com

ISBN 978-1-5290-5185-8

3 5 7 9 8 6 4 2

A CIP catalogue record for this book is available from the British Library.

Typeset in Janson Text by Palimpsest Book Production Ltd, Falkirk, Stirlingshire
Printed and bound by CPI Group (UK) Ltd, Croydon, CR0 4YY

Visit **www.panmacmillan.com** to read more about all our books
and to buy them. You will also find features, author interviews and
news of any author events, and you can sign up for e-newsletters
so that you're always first to hear about our new releases.

For my father

Contents

Introduction

People have all sorts of strange ideas about money. Tradition has it that when you make a wish at the Trevi Fountain in Rome you must always toss a coin into the water over your left shoulder. Only if you follow this rule exactly are you guaranteed to return to the Eternal City. In Britain pushing a small coin into the bark of certain 'wishing' trees is supposed to cure you of any illness – although the practice often kills the tree. We learn as children that the Tooth Fairy will exchange any baby teeth we leave under our pillows for money.[1]

There really is something magical about money. Despite only being a set of representative tokens – although often decorated with obscure symbols and phrases in dead languages – money can still build cathedrals, send us to space, or cause someone to sacrifice what they thought were their most valued principles. Few other things can have done so much to transform the world and our lives, despite being so inherently worthless.

Despite this magic, money comes with a fairly dry set of associations – conjuring up visions of a miserly Ebenezer Scrooge-like figure in counting houses, stacking up his coins and ignoring the needs of his employees. Money is meant to signify calculation and rationality, indifference and impersonality. The world of money is supposed to be one of figures and facts, without any room for folklore and superstition. The mysteries of money are cloaked by technical, mathematical language obscuring the fact that, as this book will show, money is always deeply human and interpersonal.

It is partly this social nature that has meant economists have struggled to cope with money. The starting point of the discipline is often – though not always – individuals who make choices based on what is in their best interest,[2] but there is nothing, on the surface, rational or self-interested about the ritual at the Trevi Fountain, or really anything about the way we invest money with symbolic value.

Money is communal rather than individual. It is a shared fiction; it is a story we believe in so long as others act as if it is true. As a headline in the satirical US newspaper *The Onion* has it: 'US economy grinds to halt as nation realizes money just a symbolic, mutually shared illusion'.[3] Money's power comes solely from the fact that we all treat that power as if it is really there. Insisting that seashells are money would not get you very far today, but there have been plenty of times when you would have been absolutely right. It is context that gives money its value.

Myths and folklore like the Tooth Fairy can therefore serve a deeper truth, or a purpose at least. In the words of one historian writing on the subject, money circulates among a faith-based community.[4] Through these exchanges – whether tossing coins in wishing wells or giving up our baby teeth – we are reasserting and reaffirming money's value. The superstitions reinforce the metaphor at the heart of money that the tokens are really worth something.

Money seems to have been getting stranger in recent years. Our faith in it has been shaken: the story we are telling is becoming surreal. When banks failed in the 2008 financial crisis, many of us took, maybe for the first time, a deeper look at money and wondered exactly what we were looking at. The economic chaos that followed called attention to banks' role in our monetary system and how much we depend on them. Debt both public and private seemed to have proliferated without limit. Government money-printing policies known as 'quantitative easing' caused us to question how money could keep its value when it could be created so easily at the touch of a button; and why, we asked, were governments so concerned to repay their debt if they faced only an artificial shortage of cash?

Technology, too, has called our attention to how money may not be all as it seems. What we thought it was – metal coins and paper notes – is disappearing and now we can pay just using our fingerprints, for example. Then there are new types of money appearing out of nowhere: cryptocurrencies that seem to rocket in value one day and plunge the next, attracting acolytes convinced they will transform society, as well as plenty of speculators just looking to make a quick buck.

This book aims to demystify money, explaining where the faith that we have in it comes from, how it is sustained, what it allows a society to do and what more we could do with it in the future. It should, hopefully, make the story a bit easier to understand.

That economics struggles with money might sound surprising. But when modelling how businesses, consumers and governments interact, economists have often got rid of money entirely. The nineteenth-century economist and moral philosopher John Stuart Mill once wrote that there could scarcely be a less important thing than money[5] – it only mattered when it became disordered.

This is because he, like many economists, saw money as just a means to an end. Money itself was not important; what mattered was what it stood in for: real goods and services. People only wanted it because they could exchange it for the things that were actually useful or brought them happiness. Money, sterile and pointless if others would not accept it, was not desired for itself: only collectors seek coins or banknotes purely for their aesthetic value. What mattered was how production related to consumption – how easy it was to make goods and services, how desired they were. Money just helped us answer these questions by providing a common scale for costs and benefits and a means of trading without resorting to barter.

Think about the book you are holding in your hands, or perhaps listening to on your phone. To buy it you may have paid some money, but to earn that money you had to do some work, perhaps an hour's worth. Money represents that hour of your time and allows you to trade it for something else. Instead of looking at the monetary price, we could dispense with money and look at the relative rate of exchange between goods and services. An hour of your time paid for this book but maybe it could have bought a meal instead. Thinking about it in this way allows us to understand the actual trade-offs we are making and the actual costs we as a society face between working, reading and dining.

The neglect of money, however, was the source of one of economics' big intellectual failures in the run-up to the 2008 financial crisis. Much of traditional macroeconomics – studying national economies in aggregate – had decided that money and banking could be dispensed with. They were assumed to work just fine. The sole goal of monetary policy – controlling the supply of new money – was to keep prices stable.

This book argues that money is very important. To do that it uses insights from economists and the debates they have had over the role that money plays: whether that is preventing depressions, funding government spending or destabilizing prices. It introduces a number of famous economists, some of whom are household names like the twentieth-century British economist John Maynard Keynes or the Scottish Enlightenment philosopher Adam Smith. Others may be slightly more obscure.

It also borrows insights from sociologists, anthropologists and historians, as well as a few philosophers and plenty of journalists. This is because money is not only about commerce but about lots of other things as well. Money is powerful: the rise and fall of empires has been reflected in their money. It is social: it affects how we treat each other and what sort of society we live in. As much as you might want to, you cannot avoid money.

And while money is often an abstraction, it is always governed by particular people and organizations. By the end of this book you should, hopefully, know, among other things, what a central bank is, what the International Monetary Fund does and the important differences between the dollar and the euro. When you watch the news you will be able to put stories about finance and economics into context: you will know what it means when the dollar is up or why central banks are raising interest rates in response to strong employment figures.

This means that this is a political book. It has to be: money is always political. The way it is managed, as we will see, determines who gets what – it influences the distribution of wealth and income in our economies. Different views on how it behaves, and even what it is, have influenced how our societies work and who is in charge. It has often been a symbol of political power itself. Look at the money in your pocket, if you have any, and you will see symbols and images chosen by the state that issued it in order to communicate particular ideas.

Understanding money is not only about being a good, well-informed citizen but also a practical skill to have. There are plenty of people who would like to separate you from whatever amount you do have. While this book is by no means a guide to personal finance or avoiding fraud, plenty will try to use the fact that money is so mysterious to trick you, promising that its seemingly arcane properties mean they can, in some counter-intuitive way, create more for you.

The first four chapters of this book focus on the basics – what money is, how it is produced, what it costs and what determines its value. Hopefully you could just read these chapters, leave the rest, and still have a pretty good idea about money. They also contain some of the more technical ideas in the book, as we look at banking and theories of where interest rates come from. These topics are complicated, so you might want to return to them again as you read the later chapters.

The middle four chapters look at some perennial policy debates, like the international monetary system, how to finance government spending, the impact of borrowing from abroad and money's potential impact on prosperity. These are topics you will be seeing people debate forever – partly because they are inherently related to social conflict, which group pays and which one receives. These chapters contain potted histories of economic thought and show how it is constantly adapting and being re-evaluated in terms of the recent performance of the economy. They touch on much of the last century or so of economic history, at least in rich countries, from the Great Depression in the 1930s through Japan's lost decades starting in the 1990s to the eurozone crisis in the 2010s.

The final four chapters look at some more recent debates, including how financial markets work and what purpose they serve, how technology is changing the nature of money, money's role in fighting climate change and, finally, whether it is making our societies unequal. These debates are happening as I write, and their contours will be changing even as you read this book. The principles set out here, however, will help you understand exactly what people are arguing about and why.

This book's title is inspired by a 1946 volume by Henry Hazlitt, a leader writer at the US business newspaper the *Wall Street Journal*, called *Economics in One Lesson*. Beyond the title and the fact that I do the same job for the UK-based *Financial Times*, there is not much overlap. In fact, we disagree pretty intensely about the impact of money.

Hazlitt's book is centred on a parable about a broken window. In the story a brick is thrown through a baker's window. As shards of glass lie amid the pastries, a crowd gathers and, after some commiseration, tells the baker not to be too distraught. In fact, the crowd say, the broken window is something to be welcomed: it has created work for glaziers. Fixing the window might be a cost for the bakery but that extra spending will benefit workers in the glass trade. That will, in time, create more employment and a higher income that those workers will be able to spend, perhaps on baked goods – in fact the broken window has made us all better off.

This is supposedly a fallacy.[6] If the window costs $25 to fix – this was $25 that the baker could have spent on a new dress instead. Whatever the glaziers have gained, the seamstresses have lost. The total amount of spending has remained the same, but instead of the community getting a new dress it now has to labour just to restore the window it had in the first place – just as much work needs to be done but nothing is truly gained for all the effort. Stripping away money lets us clearly see what has happened: the baker will have to trade some of their work for some work from the glazier instead.

Hazlitt's lesson, and it is a good lesson, is that we must be mindful of the things that we do not see as well as those we do. When the crowd sees the broken window, they see all the economic activity and employment that fixing it could create. They do not see what has been prevented, like the dress that could have been bought with the money instead. We should, he says, remember all the effects that ripple out through the economy, not just the obvious.

Yet the arguments of this book will show why the parable is not the fallacy it first appears. A key assumption behind the lesson is that all the resources of the economy are fully employed. What this means is that everything, including workers' time, is being used to the best of our abilities – when the baker pays the glazier for a new window it takes up time the glazier could have spent doing something else. The act of vandalism just shifts resources from a better use to the fundamentally pointless task of fixing something that did not have to be broken.

For Hazlitt, money is a 'veil' over the real economy of physical things. When the baker exchanges some money for a new window they are really exchanging some of the goods they produced themselves for the goods someone else produced – the baked goods for the window. Money is a symbol that stands in for these trades. In a world without money – the one economists sometimes imagine when trying to understand our world – the act of buying and selling are one and the same. If a baker wanted to pay a seamstress for a dress they would have to give them some cakes or bread.

Money, however, gets in between to mean that sometimes not everything is sold, and that means not everyone who wants a job is employed. The baker can sell cakes without ever having to buy anything, storing the proceeds of the sale in cash. In the broken window parable, there was no guarantee the baker would have spent the $25 – it could have sat as coins in a jar on top of the fridge or been stuffed as notes under a mattress.

As much as we might want to strip away money to see what is going on underneath the surface, we cannot get rid of it. It has an independent power over the economy, not only because we can hoard it, but also because more can always be created. To fix the broken window the baker could have paid using borrowed money – getting into debt may not always be wise but it does allow us to spend more. To understand the consequences of the broken window for employment we need to understand how money works and how people use it.

Hazlitt argues that whether the baker had spent the money or not, someone else would have. If they had no good use for the cash, then by depositing the $25 in the bank, the bank could have lent the money to someone else and then that person would have in turn found a better use. When we save, that means someone else invests and there is exactly the same amount of spending in the economy.

Money does not work like he thought, however. It is elastic and can be newly created by banks without someone else saving it first. This is the lesson of this book: money matters. And to understand why, the first question we will need to answer is what exactly money is.

1. What is money?

Money is best understood with a few beers. Buying and selling ale is a great prism for seeing how money works. A bartender running a tab – tracking clients' bills, extending credit to the regulars and ensuring debts are eventually settled – is doing the same kind of work as a banker who deals solely in the more abstract world of money.

This was undeniable in Ireland in 1970.[1] That summer, Ireland ran out of money when staff at the six largest banks went on strike. On their side, so they believed, was control over the lifeblood of the economy. Without their labour, shoppers could not get the cash to buy goods from businesses, which in turn would be unable to pay wages. Quickly, the striking workers expected, management would bow to public pressure and meet their demands.

Yet, contrary to predictions, Ireland's economy survived unscathed,[2] for the most part, and in the process became a parable for understanding how modern money works.

Cheques were adopted as the main means of payment. Shops and businesses had stockpiled cash before the strike but this was not enough to get by. Instead, ordinary people just wrote out what they owed to each other, ready to be cashed when a bank reopened. What turned these cheques into a substitute for money, however, was that they could circulate beyond the initial buyer and seller, just like a banknote.

One British economist who had visited Ireland during the strike called his bank when he returned home. He found that when the cheque he had written, claimable on an open British bank, had been cashed, it had come with signatures on the back. Each person in Ireland signing that they had transferred the debt to someone else.[3]

Here is where the beer is necessary. Ireland's network of pubs stepped up and replaced the banks as the main institutions responsible for clearing debts, allowing customers to exchange these IOUs for cash.

Suppose Albert wanted to pay Brenda for a day's labour, he could simply write Brenda a cheque for £100. This would, however, leave Brenda with a problem. If she wanted to buy something for £50 she could not use the cheque. As the banks were closed, she could not deposit it in her account and withdraw £50 in cash. Even if she wanted to pay someone £100, they might not know Albert and wouldn't be willing to trust the cheque would hold its value when the banks reopened.

The pubs proved the solution. As the proprietor of a cash business, a pub's landlord would see huge volumes of notes and coins pass over their bar every day, so they would often have the resources necessary to exchange the cheque into something that could be used for payment. Publicans, like bankers, were not doing this out of the goodness of their hearts – they would only accept cheques if they thought they were going to be repaid. Fraud skyrocketed during the strike. Although sometimes it worked out, one enterprising racing fan wrote out a cheque for a horse, then used its winnings to repay the debt.[4]

In fulfilling this role landlords had an advantage. The manager of the local pub already knew how likely people were to pay them back, thanks to their previous experience of letting customers run up tabs for a night of drinking. Knowledge about their clientele meant that they had a good idea about the quality of the IOU and how much cash to give out if they wanted to stay in business. As we will see throughout this book, money is intimately connected with information and risk.

There are two key lessons from the Irish banking strike. The first is that debt is a kind of money: you can use the fact that someone owes you to pay other people. A transferable promise of payment can itself be payment. This can be created from nothing – anyone can write out an IOU.

However, the second lesson is critical. Money relies on trust. Without trust that it will be repaid, the debt is not worth anything. Cheques could indeed be created from nothing, but they were worthless if you did not think the person writing them would pay you back. Pubs played this credit monitoring role, keeping record of who was a high-quality borrower and who was not.

In effect cheques and pubs, as well as other businesses like corner shops which also cleared debts, created a monetary system without banks. There were two kinds of money within this system: the first was credit, promissory notes like cheques that could circulate around the economy. They had value because people expected the debt to be repaid when the banks eventually reopened.

The second was cash, the amount of physical money in the tills of businesses and the wallets of their customers. The total amount of money was a combination of the two and could fluctuate even as the amount of cash remained fixed. There was a monetary base of cash and a total money supply including both the cash and the cheques. Cheques were eventually settled in hard currency, but they worked fine as money themselves when the other kind was not available. In fact, when cheque-books were used up Irish shoppers made their own. One bank worker recalled seeing them written on toilet paper.

Money's ancient origins

The example of the Irish banking strike only gives us half the picture. To understand money fully, we need to go right back to its debut in the ancient world.

When the British Museum decided to tell the story of money's origins it similarly turned to beer.[5] One of the oldest objects in its collection, alongside Swedish copper plate money and the giant stone money of the island of Yap, is a clay tablet from ancient Mesopotamia detailing the daily beer rations owed to workers. This description of a debt is now seen as one of humanity's earliest records of money.

This was not always the accepted story of money's invention. The version included in *The Wealth of Nations*[6] by Adam Smith, the founding text of modern economics, goes that humans used to rely on barter to get what they wanted. In a 'primitive economy' a hunter might trade their bison for some fruit. If they did not want fruit, they would then have to find someone else who did. Money was invented, goes the story, so that we would not have to rely on this 'coincidence of wants'.

No anthropologist or sociologist has ever found a real example of the kind of barter economy described by Smith.[7] Most of the pre-monetary economies they observed were gift economies. In these societies, gifts are exchanged, creating an expectation of reciprocity.[8] Instead of bartering, a hunter might simply give the gatherer and the fisher some meat in anticipation that the others would return fruit and fish when the hunter went hungry.

In effect this creates a kind of debt.[9] The hunter's gift of meat would mean that the fisher has to repay it with a gift of fish. If the fisher does not help out when it is their turn, they would lose face and social status.[10]

This exchange of gifts is not necessarily altruistic and can be competitive. One society in Papua New Guinea – which did include the Australian dollar as part of the gift-giving – considered it very bad form to only repay the gift, usually pigs, you received at a ceremony. Instead, it was essential to give back more than you got in the first place. A 'big man' would be the person who gave away the most; everyone else would owe him and he would become the most powerful figure in the tribe.[11]

These sort of norms are enforceable in small-scale societies where everyone knows each other. Think of a group of friends where one person develops a reputation for never getting their round in. They will be shunned and no longer able to take part in the economic system, having essentially defaulted on their debt and violated the system of reciprocal gifts.

Instead, what is needed in an economy composed of thousands of transactions between strangers is a measure of how much society at large owes you. The total volume of goods and services you can request, and then receive, from other people. In our economy this means money: present a note worth £10 to someone and they will swap it for £10 worth of goods.

Money is effectively a symbol representing what we are owed by the economy. Imagine our hunter in the gift economy. They bring back a bison from the hunt and share it with the fisher and the fruit gatherer. They may think to themselves, 'Okay, now I am owed three fish and five fruit for the food I brought back.' They might add them both together and think, 'I am owed ten fruits' worth of stuff in total.'

This is how it works in our monetary economy: we work and we get our bank account credited with a number – our wages. The wages are measured in money rather than fruit, but they are still a measure of what we are owed for the labour we have supplied. We can then go and redeem that debt for fruit if we wish, or for something else. The key innovation is to create a standard unit that allows us to compare the value of an hour of our time to the goods we can buy with it. A universal measure of economic value.

Debts were not quantified in this way in gift economies. Instead the hunter was likely to think that they were 'owed back' by the community rather than that they were entitled to a specific amount of resources. These debt relationships would be wrapped up with other social forces too. Think of the tension in our societies about who pays the restaurant bill on a date. The gift from your date, if they pay for the whole thing, is not understood in terms of a particular monetary amount, but is wrapped up in all sorts of expectations and ideas about chivalry, sexuality and power. The gift is often not purely selfless either.

The key move of quantifying these debts in terms of a 'money of account', the universal measure that allows us to compare the value of very different things, appears to have happened first in ancient Mesopotamia – the land between the Euphrates and Tigris rivers that includes parts of modern-day Iraq, Syria and Turkey. The clay tablets in the British Museum are some of the earliest records of these debts becoming measured in a standard unit rather than the general sense of an obligation to mutual support.

Mesopotamia played host to what is now known as the Sumerian civilization, which contained some of humanity's earliest cities. This movement of people into cities meant there were now frequent economic interactions between strangers. According to some scholars, this meant there was a need for a new way of distributing goods rather than the reputation-based gift economy.[12]

As far as we know, these urban economies were based on central planning, with the temple as the key institution coordinating production and distribution. Archaeologists think the temple's accountants would use small clay tokens to represent these commodities: tiny vases and cylinders representing oil, wool or herbs. Perhaps many tokens could be sealed within a clay cylinder and marked with a stamp similar to a signature, essentially representing a contract to be fulfilled.

Eventually, these tokens were represented in cuneiform script – humanity's earliest form of writing was used for accounting, not storytelling – such as the rations of beer owed to workers. This meant the first money appears as an abstraction on the clay tablets too, just as modern money mostly remains on silicon chips. Later Babylonian scribes would use these tablets to keep astronomical records. And along with the daily positions of the planets, the scribes would list the prices of six important commodities: barley, dates, cuscuta (a type of herb), cardamom, sesame and wool. Each was given a price in terms of a fixed weight of silver – known as a shekel.[13]

Many currency names – pound, peso and shekel – come from words originally used for a measure of weight. The Kazakh tenge descends from a word meaning 'scales', and like scales a standard unit allows us to draw an equivalence between very different goods: one kilogram of oranges weighs as much as one kilogram of lead. Similarly a standardized concept of economic value lets us compare the price of commodities and services on a single scale. Instead of comparing sesame to wool, wool to cardamom, cardamom to barley and so on, each commodity only needs to be expressed in terms of silver. The silver worked as a 'unit of account' for all other products.

Sumeria lacked much silver of its own. Most of the precious metal had to come from its trade partners, or possibly colonies, in Anatolia in modern Turkey. Often this scarcity meant the silver on the tablets was just a number used in accounting, allowing the temple bureaucrats to perform calculations and produce economic forecasts without going through all the steps. Likewise, some scholars doubt that Sumerians actually weighed out this silver in the marketplace and assume vendors let their customers pay on credit. The metal was a means of keeping track of the size of the debt, just like a bar tab.[14]

This unit of account was eventually given physical existence when the first coins were minted in the kingdom of Lydia, in Anatolia, where the famously rich Croesus ruled.[15] They were nuggets of electrum, a naturally occurring alloy of gold and silver, and not coins as we understand them, of fixed size and shape. Instead they were of fixed weight. To prove that each one weighed the same, they were imprinted with a lion's head, the guarantee of the king.

By turning the abstract 'money of account' into a physical token, money became more accessible and useful. Shoppers and merchants would no longer have to weigh out the amount of silver necessary to complete a transaction. The 'gift economy' based on personal relationships and reputations could shrink and the monetary economy, of quantification and commerce, could expand.

The functions of money

Money has at least three purposes.[16] It is a medium of exchange, a unit of account and a store of value. The cheques written during the Irish banking strike worked as a medium of exchange, but they were denominated in the state-created unit of account: the Irish pound. In Lydia, the coins were a medium of exchange but the unit of account was a given weight of silver.

For something to be money, however, it also has to store value. It is not only essential that you get repaid the money that you lend, but also that it is worth the same – at least roughly – when you get it back. Few people would want to deposit money in the bank if there was a risk that it would be worthless in terms of actual goods and services when the time came to spend it.

So, economists distinguish between what they call the 'real' and the 'nominal' prices of goods. The 'real' price attempts to adjust for the changing value of money. In the gift economy example, a fruit was worth three-fifths of a fish; in a monetary economy the equivalent 'nominal' price might be 60p for fruit and £1 for the fish. In 'real' terms this would be no different from £6 and £10: fruit's relative price in both examples is 60 per cent of a fish.[17]

The ratio of the two prices is the same even though the monetary price is higher – you have to give up three-fifths of a fish to get one fruit. Money mediates that transaction, but the nominal price does not change the real price.

Inflation is a change in the overall price of goods relative to money and not a change in the price of goods compared to each other. For example, suppose the price of fish rose to £1.20 but fruit stayed at 60p. A piece of fruit has become cheaper relative to fish – it's now half the price. This is a change in relative prices. If both fruit and fish prices rose by an equivalent amount – say 20 per cent in monetary terms – then that would be inflation. The value of £1 has become less relative to all goods and services available for purchase, rather than the value of fruit falling relative to fish.

Hyperinflation, when the value of goods relative to money spirals out of control, is one way in which monetary systems fail. When Zimbabwe experienced hyperinflation[18] in the late 2000s, it was cheaper to take a bus in the morning than in the afternoon because of the speed by which prices rose.[19] The eventual solution was to abandon the Zimbabwean dollar and switch to foreign currency entirely: people preferred money they could trust to keep its value.[20]

The Zimbabwean dollar worked as a medium of exchange and a unit of account, but because it could not store value it failed as money. A currency needs to do all three to work effectively.

Historically people have often solved the problem of ensuring money keeps its value by using precious metals, such as gold and silver. The metal embedded in the coin guarantees the coin's value: a silver shekel was worth a certain amount of silver because that was exactly what it was. This theory, that countries should adopt a currency linked to a precious metal in order to protect its value, is known as 'metallism'.

Plenty of other forms of 'commodity money' have been used, including bars of salt in Ethiopia and whelk shells for trade among indigenous North Americans and colonists. One famous case is detailed in R. A. Radford's classic 1945 paper, 'The economic organisation of a prisoner of war camp', which describes how cigarettes became the standard medium of exchange.[21] Another example is in the US prison system today, where tins of mackerel are used as payment. The fish was adopted as money by prisoners in 2004 after smoking was banned.[22]

The view most commonly contrasted with metallism is known as 'chartalism', which is said to get its name from a Latin word for ticket: *charta*. Chartalism holds that ultimately all money is a creation of the state. The government can use its power to demand that certain tickets are accepted as payment for private debt and also, more importantly, the debt the government imposes on the public – taxes. It is this legal order that preserves the value of money and not the metal embedded in it. We all need to pay our taxes, so we will accept whatever the government declares as money.[23]

For a demonstration of how this works, we can look to the

Mexican revolutionary Pancho Villa. The larger-than-life Villa partly contributed to the stereotype[24] of a Mexican bandit that would appear in American Western films: he had a thick bushy moustache, cultivated a macho image and stole from the rich to give to the poor. Before he became a revolutionary he was already an outlaw. A canny operator, he signed a deal with a Hollywood studio to film his battles and used the royalties to finance his revolutionary campaign.[25]

In 1913, as the provisional governor of the northern Mexican state of Chihuahua, Villa began printing his own currency across the border in the United States. He was able to use his military control to get the peso notes accepted within his territory: those discriminating against his currency were given sixty days in jail, for example. Most importantly for the civil war effort, however, American banks over the border in Texas accepted them as worth 89 cents of a dollar.[26] This granted Villa the foreign currency necessary to buy weapons and supplies from the colossus to the north.

At that point Pancho Villa was seen as a safe bet by the American banks. He was an extraordinary general, famed for his tactics; he was winning battles and the war was going the way of the Constitutionalists his División del Norte fought for. Foreign companies bought the Villa pesos in anticipation of his victory: they believed that when the fighting was done they would need it to pay Mexican taxes. With this money and American support at his back General Villa was able to advance from his northern stronghold and defeat the military government of President Victoriana Huerta.

Victory at the Battle of Zacatecas in 1914 was the peak for Villa, however. Like in so many revolutions, victory led to division, and Villa fell out with his allies. He retreated north to his home state of Chihuahua, and then decided to try his luck again.

He was a legendary revolutionary and a successful general: he would be able to win against the odds once more.

The printing presses continued to churn out more and more of his paper money. This time, however, the Texan banks no longer expected him to win. In search of stability, the American government was now backing Villa's rivals. His pesos, which had fallen to 30 US cents a few months before, were now worth just 1.5 cents. His failure as a revolutionary was given a brutal financial assessment.

Without trust in his ability to win the war, Pancho Villa's money was not worth as much to the American banks. His cash was really another form of IOU: if he had won then US companies would have been able to use the Villa pesos in Mexican territory. The ability to wield power within a given territory means you get to decide what tokens can be used to settle debts and pay taxes within that economy. That, among other reasons, means people accept these worthless slips of paper as if they have intrinsic value.

The difference between the two schools of thought – metallism and chartalism – was illustrated when the Knights Hospitaller ran out of gold and silver during the 1565 siege of Malta. The Knights printed coins made out of copper instead, each bearing the legend 'not bronze but trust'.[27] The value was not in the metal but in the bearers' opinion of the knightly order and whether or not they would be able to guarantee the value of the coin on the other side of the siege. Money's value is bound up in the power of the sovereign: the Knights Hospitaller won and so their tokens kept their value; Villa lost, so his were worthless.

Gold, silver and even cigarettes do not really have any intrinsic value either, beyond the fact we desire them. Gold has historically been sought after because people want it and recognize it as valuable, in exactly the same way as the US dollar is seen as valuable today. The prisoner-of-war camp may have used cigarettes as currency, but any value they had could have disappeared overnight if the POWs had all collectively given up smoking.

Mackerel, according to one prisoner, worked as money precisely because only the bodybuilders in search of protein actually wanted to eat it.[28] It had value solely because the other prisoners believed it had value. Money, like language, is social: it gets its meaning from everyone using the same one.

Modern money

Money today is no longer backed by precious metals or any other commodities. Instead it is what is called 'fiat currency', getting its value from the government declaring it has value: hence the name – it has worth by government fiat, or decree. The state also accepts it as payment for taxes, although not everything we use as a means of payment can be used to pay taxes. In the UK you cannot pay your tax bill with a personal credit card, for example. Nevertheless we can certainly reject metallism, at least as an explanation of how money works today.

But chartalism has not always been a universally accurate description either. Governments being able to declare what is the sole currency within their territory is a more recent innovation than you might expect,[29] as we will see in a later chapter. It needed the development of a certain amount of administrative capacity and perhaps even political legitimacy for governments to ensure they, and only they, got to decide what money is.

For example, in the French colony of Upper Volta, present-day Burkina Faso, the colonial government consistently failed to displace traditional monies in the early twentieth century, despite imposing a 'head tax' that had to be paid in francs.[30] Traditional seashell forms of currency, ones the colonizers saw as primitive, were exchanged into francs only at tax-paying time, the metal money was not used universally. Local traders preferred the shells. As well as rejection of the metal money being an act of resistance to colonialism, the currency was unfamiliar and did not fit into pre-existing ideas of what money should be.

Further east, in the south of Nigeria, a British colony at the time, manillas, horseshoe-shaped bits of copper or bronze, circulated alongside the colonial currency for decades.[31] When dealing with the imperial administration many Nigerians exchanged manillas for the metal coins, but imposing a tax paid in British money did not make it accepted right throughout the economy. Local merchants would still demand manillas, much to the annoyance of Europeans, who had to use them to buy food and so on but were paid in the colonial currency. The colonial government only managed to eradicate the manilla in 1948[32] – after fifty years of trying – by buying up stores at above market rates.

Money is a sort of collective agreement. So long as we all recognize the same thing as money, it works – precious metal and taxes have played their roles in different societies of maintaining that compact but neither metallism nor chartalism has been essential everywhere. Perhaps it even works at an unconscious level: we have become habituated to seeing certain things as money and it takes a significant amount of effort to stop – many economists have puzzled why even in the face of hyperinflation communities still stick for so long to the money they are used to.

In Latin *credo*, the origin of the word credit, means 'I believe' and the credit theory of money holds that all money is ultimately debt. For commodity monies, like shells or tins of mackerel, this is a metaphor. Mostly we think of a debt as being between two distinct people – Albert promises to pay Brenda £100, for example – but money is a debt that can be redeemed by anyone, simply by accepting it as a means of payment. Money is a symbol of what we are owed by society at large, whether that society is a prison or a nation. The debt is repaid in-kind by the goods and services we get in exchange for the coins, the tins of mackerel or the shells.

For the vast majority of modern money, however, calling it credit is not a metaphor. The overwhelming bulk of money in our societies is literal debt: a debt from banks to their depositors. In 2020, in the US, only around 10 per cent of the total money stock consisted of notes and coins, most of the rest was bank deposits.[33] These are debts, essentially IOUs from the banks to us. If my account has a balance of £100, that means my bank owes me £100 and promises to repay me as soon as I ask for that money. I can then transfer that debt to someone else to pay for something. Banks are usually trusted, so there's no need for the seller to take a view on how reliable I am.[34]

Normally I do not even have to ask for the physical cash. When I buy something in a shop with a debit card, my bank reduces the amount I am owed by however much I have spent and creates a new debt to my shopkeeper's bank of equal value, transferring the debt within the banking system. A bank deposit is like the cheques from the Irish banking strike: it is debt that we can transfer to someone else.

Bankers keep track of the payments their clients make and their constantly changing balances like a landlord running a bar tab. And we can borrow from them, like a tab, allowing us to pay for things even when we do not have the cash available. Banks can create new money, in the same way as Irish shoppers and businesses could just write cheques to one another. Unlike the bar tab, however, bank deposits are a generally accepted means of payment – anyone will accept them. You cannot use your bar tab to pay at the supermarket, but you can use a bank overdraft.

While this private credit system is controlled by the banking sector, it critically depends on a government agency known as a central bank. This is the banker to the banking system, lending them the resources they need to stay in business and provide the money we use day-to-day. The economist John Maynard Keynes,[35] who we will meet in more detail later, called the central bank the sun about which the planets of the private banks orbit. Generally, they inhabit very grand buildings in the capital or the main financial centre of a country, and have names like the People's Bank of China, the European Central Bank or the Reserve Bank of Australia.

Central banks lend the private banks something called 'reserves' to ensure the banks can settle their own debts to one another. This money that remains inside the banking system is the foundation of our monetary system – forming the monetary 'base', like the cash during the Irish banking strike underpinned the value of the cheques. It is itself a debt from the central bank to the private banks. Our monetary system is all based on nothing but promises of one sort or another.

Central banks have the job of making sure that money keeps its value. Because they lend to the private banks, and decide how much the private banks have to pay to borrow, they can decide how expensive or not it is for the private banks to get hold of reserves. Using this control over interest rates in the interbank market, they can influence the growth of bank deposits, and the availability of money.[36] Usually the unelected head of a central bank – essentially a very senior civil servant – is given a mandate by elected politicians. This generally involves some target for the rate of inflation, most commonly 2 per cent a year, and an instruction to consider the effect of their policies on economic growth and unemployment.

Despite the apparent complication of this system it remains very simple. At its heart is trust. Sometimes money has been a golden nugget, other times an IOU, or a cigarette. While it has changed its public face, it has always had the same fundamental nature: it is a representation of social trust. Everyone has to recognize the same thing as money, believe it will keep its value, and trust that everyone else will at the same time. The colonial powers in Burkina Faso or Nigeria tried to use violence and taxation to get their money accepted but they could not create a trusted means of payment without widespread cooperation.

The main form of money used in our economies is a promise from banks: we have invested our trust in them. But when we are no longer convinced that they will keep our money safe, or if we think others might no longer accept the money we keep in our bank, then the whole system might come tumbling down as the foundations are kicked away.

Shutting down the banks did not stop Ireland's economy from functioning; instead a new system of private credit was invented. During the financial crisis of 2008, however, a catastrophic loss of trust in the banks plunged the global economy into recession. Understanding why that happened – and how money works in a modern credit-based system – means taking a look directly at the inner workings of banks.

2. How do banks work?

On the surface the hawala brokers who gather in the courtyard of the Kabul currency market, piles of banknotes stacked beside them,[1] do not look much like the hordes of besuited bankers who pile into glass-and-steel offices in Hong Kong, Frankfurt and New York every morning. Appearances, however, are misleading. The two groups are doing the exact same kind of work: making private debts into a publicly accepted means of payment.

The chief distinguishing feature of money is that you can pay with it immediately.[2] Other ways of storing wealth – classic cars, shares in a company, government bonds – will let you buy goods and services eventually, once they have been sold, but the defining feature of money is that it is instantly exchangeable for something else. Money flows easily from pocket to pocket. For this reason other financial assets are often classed by how 'liquid' they are, or how easily they can be exchanged for money,[3] in other words into a means of making payment.

Banks exist, partly, because of this link between money and time. They lend us money to use now – paying our bills and buying the things we need – and we give them funding because we need to store our money safely for the things we will want to buy tomorrow. There might be no need for bank deposits if all our bills were due on the same day we got paid.[4]

Originally, however, banks were there to move money not through time but across space. Kabul's hawala brokers are part of what is probably the world's oldest banking system, dating back to the eighth century.[5] Hawala, meaning 'transfer' in Arabic or 'trust' in Hindi,[6] relies on a network of dealers who use honour, reputation and debt to move money vast distances. Often today's clients are migrants to rich countries from central Asia or the Horn of Africa, who want to send funds home cheaply.[7] Much of the remittances – money from overseas migrants – that are so critical to the war-torn Afghani economy still arrive through this millennia-old network.[8]

Understanding how the hawaladars, as the brokers are known, transfer this money across borders can help illuminate the seemingly more obscure activities of traditional banks. To do this we can use the example of a pair of brothers, both of whom were hawala brokers, one in Melbourne, Australia and one in in Jalalabad, eastern Afghanistan, who were profiled in a 2001 report by the World Bank.[9] The World Bank did not give their real names, so let's call the one in Melbourne Mustafa and the one in Jalalabad Jamil.

Clients of the two brothers could use their relationship to transfer money between Australia and Afghanistan. Suppose someone wanted to move $1,000 from Melbourne to Jalalabad. Mustafa could then just tell his brother to give $1,000 to the intended recipient. If both parties to the transaction were in the respective dealers' rooms at the right time it could happen instantly,[10] as one client would pay Mustafa in Australia and the other would immediately receive the money from Jamil in Afghanistan. Alternatively, the client could share a secret code, like a password, over the phone, that would let the recipient pick the money up from Jamil whenever it was convenient. As we will see when we look at the future of money, establishing your clients' identities is a vital part of banking.

No money actually needed to cross borders, but instead a debt would be created – Mustafa would now owe Jamil $1,000. The transactions between the clients would be mirrored by debts created between the brokers. This is exactly how more formal banking systems work too: when we transfer money to each other or pay for things with credit or debit cards, the banks enable this by creating new debts to each other. There is no security van full of armed guards moving money between the banks – they simply change their records.

Banks supply money. Using their debts allows this supply to be elastic, meaning it can expand or contract based on public need. There is no fixed amount of money in a modern economy, but banks can and will create more so long as they think it is in their business interests to do so. So if we want to understand how much money is created, we need to understand the costs banks face in extending credit. One of the key questions they and the hawala brokers face is how expensive it is to get hold of sufficient resources to make good on their debts: in other words, how hard it is to get what is known as the 'means of settlement'.

Monetary systems are hierarchal. There are lots of different methods of payment, many of which are forms of debt. But not all of them are equal. Consider a credit card. You can go to a shop or a website and use your credit card to pay for things. But you will eventually need to pay off that debt with some other more fundamental money, the 'means of settlement'. In the Irish banking strike example from chapter 1, cheques were a means of payment but they were settled in Irish pounds. There are other examples – within a Las Vegas casino betting chips work as a means of payment, but they are settled in dollars.

The two brothers in the hawala business would wait until the end of the month to settle their accounts. If the flows between

Australia and Afghanistan were of equivalent value over the month then there would be no need to pay each other anything: if someone wanted to send $1,000 to Melbourne, that would cancel out the $1,000 heading to Jalalabad.

If the flows were not the same size, however, then some other method of clearing the debts was needed. In that case Mustafa would travel from Australia to Japan and buy second-hand cars, which would then be exported to Afghanistan where Jamil could sell them for profit. Debts the other way were harder to clear. Jamil would either have to use a Pakistani bank account to transfer the money via Japan, or he would buy and export Afghani carpets. Goods of these kinds – cars and carpets – were the 'means of settlement' between the two hawaladars.

Banks settle their debts at the end of every day[11] but, rather than cars and carpets they transfer central bank reserves to one another – these are the means of settlement within the banking system, discharging all debts. Like the hawaladars, the banks only have to transfer the net balance that their customers have transferred over the day, just as the two brothers did at the end of the month.[12] This creates liquidity – it is easier to transact – but also risk. One of the banks in the system might be unable to make good on all debts, creating trouble for all those who have dealt with them.

If a dealer in the hawala network runs away without repaying, then their career is over. The whole network will eventually hear of their dishonesty and they will no longer be able to transfer money. It is the same for the banks – they need to remain liquid and solvent, able to pay their debts to the other banks.

How they manage all these debts is the key to determining their success or failure. Just like for the hawaladars, a bank that cannot repay what it owes will fail and be cut off from the system. But because the debts of the banking system are the main means of payment in our economies, the failure of a bank can mean failure of a significant part of our economies: businesses may find themselves unable to buy or sell. This makes the private debts of the banks a very public problem.

Balance sheets

Banking today is mostly about transferring money in time, not space.[13] Some people need to spend money right now that they will only receive later, and a loan lets them pull that liquidity – the ability to pay – from the future into the present. Others have money that they currently have no need for but would like to store for tomorrow – they can lend this liquidity to the bank and earn interest in exchange.

Because banking is so bound up with time, it inevitably has to cope with uncertainty.[14] We do not know what the future holds. People may claim they will pay us back but they could be lying, or just unable to due to unforeseen circumstances. Others may decide to withdraw their money from a bank and thereby deprive it of the funding it needs. To be able to repay their debts to each other and remain solvent and liquid, the banks need to protect against these possibilities.

The main tool that banks can use to manage the risks is known as a balance sheet, originally invented in Renaissance Italy.[15] It was often a physical book kept open by moneylenders at a mercantile fair. A balance sheet, in electronic or physical form, is just a ledger describing everything an institution owes to others and others owe to it. On one side are the liabilities: the loans made to the institution. On the other side are the assets, what it owns. Very often these assets would be what it has lent to others; one person's debt can be another's wealth.

An economy is a set of interlocking balance sheets, records of what we owe to each other and what others, in turn, owe to us. Governments and businesses have balance sheets detailing their debts and all their assets, whether bundles of cash or blocks of flats. For you, personally, your liabilities might include a loan to buy a car, while your assets would be the car itself and perhaps a savings account. If you need cash to pay off your debts, you rely on your assets: you can sell your car or draw down your savings. Your net worth is the difference between your assets and liabilities – whatever will make the two sides of the balance sheet balance.

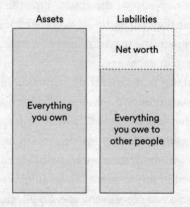

Understanding a bank's balance sheet, at least roughly, is vital to understanding where money comes from. A bank's assets and liabilities are the opposite way round to what you might expect. Deposits are not cash that the bank keeps in a vault, but a promise to its depositors that it will return their cash, when asked. Your 'money in the bank' is not actually in the bank, it's a record of what the bank owes to you – it is the bank's debt or liability. A loan, meanwhile, is a promise from you to the bank and therefore part of the bank's assets.

To understand how this works and why it can create so many

problems we can take a trip to seventeenth-century Sweden, which brought both paper money to Europe and central banking to the world.[16]

At the time, Sweden had a huge monetary problem, literally: its money was huge. It used what is called a mixed-metal standard, in that some of the daler, its currency, was made from silver, but the rest was copper – Sweden did not have much in the way of precious metal, but it had plenty of copper mines.

There was one, very big, flaw. For the standard to work, the value of the two types of money had to be kept at a fixed ratio. But, unfortunately, the productivity of Sweden's mines kept increasing. With more and more copper unearthed, the value of the bronze-coloured metal plunged. So, to keep the two coins worth the same, the copper version had to get bigger and bigger.

By 1644, Sweden had produced the largest coin ever in existence: a 20kg behemoth that was completely impractical for commerce.[17] One story has it that the coins were so heavy[18] a group of thieves were unable to lift their haul above their knees. These 'coins' look like no others. The only thing about the giant metal slabs that resembles normal money is a set of five circles, the kind used to stamp coins, one in each corner and one in the centre.

It was a Latvia-born merchant and former burgher of Amsterdam – calling himself Johan Palmstruch after a spell in jail for defaulting on his debts – who came up with the solution: a bank. By the seventeenth century, banking had spread north in Europe from Italy to Amsterdam, which had become the leading commercial and financial centre of the time.

Palmstruch would, in turn, bring these Dutch ideas to Sweden. Living and working in Stockholm and Riga, then part of the Swedish empire, he had his plan for a chartered bank rejected several times before it was finally backed by the new king, Charles X Gustav. Founded in 1656, while the king was on campaign invading Poland, it ensured a steady flow of credit that was as vital to military success for the imperialist king as it was, centuries later, for the revolutionary Pancho Villa.

The idea behind the scheme, called Stockholms Banco, was that Swedes could deposit their copper coins in the bank's vaults instead of having to carry them. In exchange they would get a paper certificate recording this deposit. This certificate – a banknote – could circulate independently of the coin and move around the economy easily. It was essentially an IOU from the bank to whoever held it, promising the return of a copper daler if presented at Stockholms Banco. These banknotes were a debt from the institution to its depositors.

These notes, Europe's first paper money, were on the liability side of the bank's balance sheet. If anyone wanted their copper money back they would receive a coin in exchange – the bank had to repay them what they were owed. For everyone else, however, the notes were an asset, part of their wealth, recording their ownership of the daler. These debts of the bank could circulate as money and be transferred to others as a means of payment – helpfully the government accepted them for taxes. The paper notes were a 'means of payment', while the copper coins were the 'means of settlement'.

Stockholms Banco could create brand new money even more efficiently than the copper mines: a single metal coin could back more than one of the notes. So long as the flow of copper into the bank's vaults from new depositors roughly matched the flow out, then the amount of notes it printed could safely increase: there would be sufficient metal to exchange for the paper money. Today this is known as fractional reserve banking, a bank keeps reserves worth only a fraction of its liabilities. A bank does not actually have enough cash to repay all of the depositors their balance – it is effectively gambling that not everyone is going to ask for the 'means of settlement' at the same time.

Fractional reserve banking

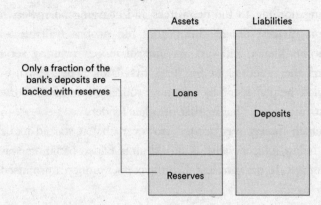

When someone borrowed from Stockholms Banco both the asset and liability side of the balance sheet could grow. The bank would lend out the new money it created, increasing its liabilities, but the loan would be an asset for the bank, increasing the other side of the balance sheet too.[19] Just as a debt from your bank to you – the balance of a savings account, for example – is part of your wealth, so too are your debts to the bank part of its wealth.

A bank makes a profit by ensuring it earns a higher rate of interest on its assets than it does on its liabilities. To do this, it does what is called 'maturity transformation'.[20] In other words, they earn an income by moving money through time. They borrow short-term from depositors – your money in the bank must be returned instantly whenever you demand – but they lend for longer. A car loan might have to be repaid over three or five years, for example.

This means they can usually pay less interest on the liability side of the balance sheet than they earn on the asset side. In the 1950s and 1960s, US banking was said to operate on a '3-6-3' model: bank managers should borrow at 3 per cent, lend at 6 per cent and make it to the golf course by 3 p.m.[21]

Paying nothing to the depositors and charging borrowers 6 per cent interest meant there were big profits available to Stockholms Banco, and vast amounts of money printing soon followed the founding of Sweden's first bank. The crown, in particular, helped itself to this new source of funding – the interest rate was far below that of other lenders.

So much money was printed, however, that it started to be priced below its face value. A Stockholms Banco banknote was now worth 8–10 per cent less than the copper money it promised in exchange.[22]

Savvy Swedes would buy the notes and exchange them at the bank for the coins – earning the 10 per cent discount as profit. To meet these withdrawals copper money started flowing out, undermining the financial basis of the bank.[23] In these circumstances a bank holding reserves worth only a portion of its liabilities has a problem. Most of the bank's assets are illiquid – the loans cannot be handed over as repayment. A bank that does not have enough reserves risks being illiquid, meaning it is unable to repay all its creditors the cash they are owed[24] when they are owed it.

Stockholms Banco was experiencing what is known as a 'bank run'.[25] These, memorably dramatized in the films *It's A Wonderful Life* and *Mary Poppins* with crowds of clamouring depositors demanding their money back, happen when lots of people try to get the bank to settle its debts all at once. Because the bank does not keep sufficient cash on hand to repay all its creditors – remember, only a fraction of deposits are backed by reserves – it risks failure: it does not have sufficient liquid assets on hand to repay its debts. The bank's liabilities are equivalent to cash but its assets are not: its loan book is illiquid, it cannot be easily converted into the means of settlement.

It makes sense for depositors who think a bank is on the brink of failure to rush to have their deposits repaid as soon as possible.[26] If you are late then there is a chance that there will be no money left by the time you get to the front of the queue. But this becomes a self-fulfilling prophecy: it is precisely because people are rushing to take their money out of the bank that there could be none left over. When trust starts to crumble, it can quickly vanish all at once.

During a bank run the elasticity of the money supply goes into reverse – like an elastic band suddenly, and painfully, snapping back. Once trust in the means of payment evaporates, people want to get hold of the ultimate means of settlement. In the case of Stockholms Banco, this was copper coins, but it is any kind of money that has value irrespective of trust in that particular bank. If the bank fails, its promises to you are worthless, although nowadays many governments will insure banks' deposits to make sure there is never a need to run on a bank.

A royal inquiry was launched into Stockholms Banco's conduct, recommending that it call in all its loans to try to stay afloat. This meant the monetary expansion the bank had enabled went into reverse: credit crunched. The value of the paper money even began to recover as more notes were taken out of circulation. It was too late, however, and the bank could not satisfy so many creditors demanding their money back at the same time. Stockholms Banco had failed.

The founding of Sweden's first bank led, very swiftly, to Sweden's first bank bailout.[27] The Swedish parliament, the Riksdag, took over and liquidated the bank. The inquiry found some missing funds and Palmstruch was imprisoned for false bookkeeping – he blamed it on the chaos and the stress, saying it was due to errors rather than theft. These excuses were not believed and he would die in a Stockholm jail within three years, aged sixty. Nevertheless, he was a pioneer, for unleashing a financial revolution in Europe not only as one of the first to beat what is now, after three and a half centuries of fractional reserve banking, a familiar path for bankers – of financial crises, fraud allegations and jail time.

Stockholms Banco had most of the features of a modern bank. Its liabilities were to the depositors who lent their coins to the bank in exchange for a more convenient means of payment – exactly the same as most commercial banks today. Its assets consisted of its reserves and the loans it made, again the same as banks today. There was one crucial component missing, a component that might have helped Stockholms Banco stay afloat. Johan Palmstruch did not provide the bank with any capital.

Capital, in this context – and the word will unfortunately be used in different ways throughout this book – is the difference between a bank's assets and liabilities. It is a measure of the bank's net worth, everything that would be left over after creditors are repaid. You can think of it as the owner's money that is given to the bank – a fund that allows it to do its job.

A bank which has no capital is on the precipice of failure. Like Stockholms Banco, its liabilities are worth more than its assets and it cannot repay its creditors even if it sells every single thing it owns. If a bank has no capital there is no reason to trust it with your money and it can no longer do its job,[28] it is a sign that it has promised too much to too many people. This lack of capital and the attendant fear the bank will go bust is often what provokes a bank run.

A simplified bank balance sheet

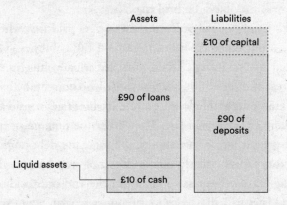

The more capital a bank has as a proportion of its assets, the more easily it ought to survive an economic downturn.[29] When workers lose their jobs and cannot repay their mortgages or car loans, this reduces the value of the bank's assets and so its capital. If, rather than repaying £10,000, someone defaults after £5,000, that leaves the bank £5,000 down, but capital can absorb that loss so the bank still has enough to repay its depositors. If the capital disappears altogether and the bank cannot raise additional funding, it will go bust.

This is exactly what happened to Stockholms Banco. Even after calling in all its loans it still did not have enough money to repay its depositors – its debts were now worth more than its assets.

In a sense, what ultimately backs a lot of our money – bank deposits are the main means of making payment – is banks' assets and, therefore, a lot of the time, housing. When people lose their jobs and cannot repay their mortgages, capital takes a hit and people may start panicking that their deposits will not be repaid if the bank becomes insolvent. This can create financial instability as all the people the bank has made promises to – businesses, governments and other banks, as well as depositors – fear those promises will inevitably be broken.

A bank's liabilities are ordered by who gets paid first when it fails. The order these creditors appear on the liabilities side is determined by 'seniority'. Depositors are usually first in line, then the rest of its creditors (such as those who bought the bank's bonds, a kind of tradable loan). Senior creditors get repaid first, junior creditors get repaid last. The earlier the debt gets repaid in any restructuring or bankruptcy, the safer the debt ought to be. This (on paper) orderly queue does not stop bank failures from being extremely messy affairs, like the end of Stockholms Banco, and lawyers will make a lot of money working out exactly who is owed what and whether the now-failed bank has made contradictory promises.

Bank's shareholders are always the most junior and they get whatever is left after everyone else is repaid. This means the share price of a bank is intrinsically bound up with the amount of 'capital' in the bank. If a bank has capital of £10 then, in a very simplified way, its outstanding shares ought to be worth around £10. In reality this is more complicated – a bank can, for example, trade at far below its 'book value' because investors think its assets are worth less than the bank claims they are. If a bank needs more capital, it has to raise it from its shareholders, so when a bank's share price falls to nothing, that is a judgement by investors that it is likely to be insolvent and not worth anything.

This, then, is the basic model of a bank. The reality can be a lot more complicated, but it still follows the principles set out here. Banks are based around a balance sheet with assets on one side and liabilities on the other. Loans are the bank's assets, while the money you imagine sitting in a vault – its customer's deposits – is actually the bank's debt.

Banks need to remain able to repay their creditors, the depositors, and so they need to keep a certain amount of their assets as reserves. But the risks inherent in lending also mean they need some capital as a kind of buffer in case the loans – their assets – go bad. So long as they do this, then they can retain public trust and, through some clever accounting, create the vast majority of the money in our economy.

How banks create money

Banks create new assets by lending[30] in exactly the same way as Stockholms Banco. They might not print a new banknote for the loan, as the Swedish bank did, but they do create the digital equivalent.

Consider a car loan. You go to your bank and ask to borrow £10,000. When the bank lends the money it creates a new asset for itself: you now owe it £10,000. At the same time the bank creates a new liability of the exact same amount: it gives you a deposit with the bank to the value of the loan. The £10,000 comes from nowhere. The bank has just changed its records to say it now owes you an additional £10,000.

The two sides of the balance sheet cancel each other out. The asset side has increased by £10,000 (the loan) while the liabilities side has also increased by £10,000 (the deposit). This deposit is money which can then be used to pay the car company: by lending, the bank has created the money necessary to buy goods and services.

**Balance sheets showing creation of money
by new lending**

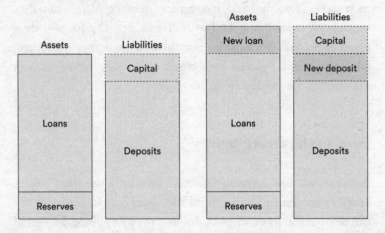

It is worth saying this again because it is fundamental to how money works and quite hard to get your head around. More money has been created by the act of lending. This is because the bank's debt is a kind of money, a transferrable IOU like the cheques from the Irish banking strike. The bank can get into more debt because the loan is also a new asset – the balance sheet remains in balance.

You could withdraw your deposit and pay for the car in cash, but most likely you would just use a bank transfer. This is simple if the car dealer uses the same bank as you: the bank's liabilities remain exactly the same and it just switches them from one depositor to another. But if the car company uses a different bank, then your bank's liability would be to another bank rather than its own client.

Follow the money: first it is created by your bank, Bank A, when you borrow the money, then it is transferred to the car dealer's bank, Bank B, to pay for the car. Bank A has a new asset, the car loan, and a new debt, the money it owes to Bank B. Bank B likewise has a new asset, the money owed to it from A, and a new debt, which it owes to its client, the car dealer.

Balance sheets showing the payment and the effect on capital

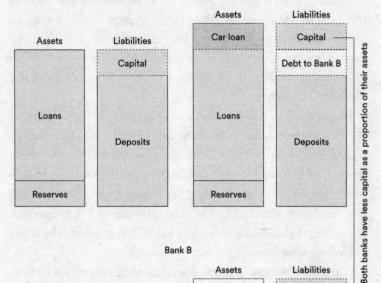

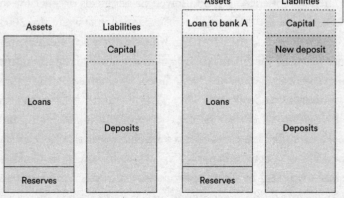

This is similar to how the hawaladars transfer money across the world: money is transferred from you to the car dealership and at the same time a debt is created between the two banks that mirrors the transactions between their clients. Payments between individuals are facilitated by debts between the banks.

But, like all businesses, the amount they produce – in this case by lending – will depend, partly, on their costs. Banks face all the normal expenses of running a business: staff, premises, branding, software and so on. But they also need to consider how expensive it is to safely expand their balance sheets. This will depend on the cost of capital and the cost of acquiring the means of settlement.

Banks need to remain solvent and liquid.[31] If banks increase the size of their balance sheets without increasing their capital, then the amount of capital falls as a proportion of the whole thing. If a bank's assets turn out not to be worth as much – people stop repaying their loans – then the value of the capital will fall as it effectively absorbs the loss. Too little capital as a proportion of assets and the bank will have to worry about going bust when borrowers stop repaying.

The 2008 financial crisis followed on the heels of a decade in which the banks' balance sheets expanded massively. In 2003 Lehman Brothers, the US bank whose failure led to the most acute phase of the financial crisis, had assets worth $312bn. Just four years later, before the bank failed, its total assets had more than doubled to $691bn.[32]

This diluted Lehman Brothers' capital. As it lent more and more, the bank's liabilities increased much faster than its capital. The ratio of assets to capital – known as 'leverage' in banking jargon – was 30.7 by 2008, up from 23.9 in 2004.[33] And Lehman Brothers was by no means alone. All of its peers had increased their leverage in the run-up to the financial crisis – Lehman was actually less leveraged than its peers Morgan Stanley, Merrill Lynch and Bear Stearns at the time of its failure.

A synonym for debt, leverage gets its name because it magnifies both the gains and losses for investors – like a lever allows a small amount of force at one end to become more powerful at the other.[34] Suppose you make a bet with a lot of borrowed money and a little bit of your own. You win and you can turn your small stake into something far bigger. If you lose, however, not only do you lose the little you started with, but you now need to find the money to repay your creditors.

The potentially disastrous consequences of leverage have been shown in countless gangster movies and TV shows, not least the anxiety-inducing 2019 thriller *Uncut Gems*, in which Adam Sandler plays Howard Ratner, a basketball-obsessed gambling addict who must wheel, deal and scheme to repay his mob-connected loan shark former brother-in-law.[35] Bet on a basketball match with $10 and perhaps you can make $20, depending on the odds. But if you borrow an additional $90 and bet with that as well, you could turn the $10 you started with into $200. If you lose, on the other hand, you need to repay the $90 and if, like Ratner, you do not have the ability to settle your debts you can be in deep, deep trouble, especially if you borrowed from gangsters.

For the banks the financial crisis[36] was similarly nerve-shredding. They had been betting with borrowed money, just as Ratner did, financing the huge growth in their balance sheets without raising new capital from their shareholders. Leverage helped juice up profits – and their share prices – before the moment of crisis. But when the mortgages started to go bad they had to find the money necessary to repay those from whom they had borrowed. So many banks had behaved similarly that it created a particularly vicious cycle. To get cash quickly they were forced to sell their assets, but this only exacerbated the problem: the mortgages on their books fell even further in value and capital was eroded even faster.[37]

Trust in the banks disappeared. In 2007, depositors started queueing up in the streets outside branches of Northern Rock, a Newcastle-based bank in England. The depositors wanted their money back immediately: it was a bank run. But Northern Rock did not have sufficient cash on hand to repay them all, and so it had to go to the central bank to obtain the means of settlement necessary to repay its debts.[38]

This shows the other constraint, as well as solvency, facing banks when they create new money: liquidity.[39] In *Uncut Gems*, Ratner faced the exact same problem. He had an asset that he believed would net him the money necessary to repay his creditors and leave him with some profit: a rare Ethiopian black opal. The trouble he faced, alongside his gambling addiction, was turning this illiquid asset into the means of settling his debts. He might have been solvent but it was useless without liquidity. Similarly, as a bank's balance sheet grows, the fraction of its liabilities backed by reserves falls. This reduces the proportion of assets which are liquid and there's a greater risk that the bank may not have enough on hand to repay its creditors.

Howard Ratner's inability to pay his debts caused all sorts of problems for those around him – his estranged wife, his much-younger girlfriend, his father-in-law – but even so it was still a very private set of problems. When the banks got into trouble, however, it had much wider consequences as their failure led to a cascading cycle of other businesses failing and mortgagors losing their homes. The money creation that leverage enabled went into reverse and a long, deep recession followed.

To try to prevent this from ever happening, governments and banks' own internal risk management processes impose rules on how much capital and reserves the banks must have as a proportion of their balance sheets – these requirements have been toughened up since the 2008 financial crisis. But while banks can create money in the form of deposits, they are not able to create capital or reserves. Banks may create money, but not in the circumstances of their choosing.

The costs of getting hold of more capital and more reserves are the chief constraints on how quickly the banks can expand their balance sheets and how cheaply they can create money.[40] So it is these costs facing banks that determine exactly how elastic the money supply is.

Banks can raise additional capital from the stock market,[41] selling more shares in their business in exchange for cash or reserves. This appears as an asset – cash is equivalent to reserves – but there is no additional liability, so the value of their capital, meaning the difference between assets and liabilities, increases. This process dilutes the ownership of the existing shareholders and can be expensive, especially if the bank is not seen as a good bet compared to investing elsewhere. The new shareholders might demand a sizeable portion of any future profits in exchange for investing.

Even if the bank does not sell more shares to raise capital, it still needs to think about the opportunities it misses. If it lends a lot to people who want to buy cars, then there is less capital, as a proportion of assets, for mortgage lending. If it wants to do both, and not sell shares, the only alternative is to become more leveraged,[42] which means taking on more risk or falling foul of regulations.

The cost of getting new reserves, meanwhile, depends on the money markets. Banks can turn to these and borrow reserves from their fellow banks – or shadow banks – who currently have more than they need. Alternatively, they can turn to the central bank.[43]

The role of the central bank

Central banks are the only institutions that can create reserves.[44] These once used to be exchangeable for gold, or in Stockholms Banco's case copper, but are nowadays just accounting entries on the central bank's balance sheet. They are still, however, the ultimate means of settlement[45] within the banking system, just like cars and carpets were the means of settling the debts between the Afghani hawala dealers. Central banks, handily, also print banknotes, so these reserves can be transferred into cash on demand. There is never any need to worry about the liquidity of a central bank.

The private bank's ultimate clients, ordinary depositors like you or me, never see reserves, just like Mustafa's clients never saw the goods used to settle the debt to his brother. Reserves stay within the banking system at all times and never leave. Banks cannot make or destroy them, only swap them with one another.

A central bank is based around a balance sheet, just like a private bank. In fact, it acts as the banker to the rest of the banking system, taking deposits from them and lending them the money they need to pay each other. Reserves and banknotes are both liabilities of the central bank but can be assets for the banking system in the same way that a deposit with a private bank is a liability for them, but an asset for you or me.

Look at a British ten-pound note and you will see the words 'I promise to pay the bearer on demand the sum of ten pounds'. That note is the central bank's debt. It is a legacy of the time when the banknotes were convertible into gold and the Bank of England would exchange the paper money for metal,[46] but now it is more philosophical: a banknote is a debt that is settleable by itself. All the private banks have accounts with the central bank and these deposits, rather than cash in vaults, are their most liquid asset.

The assets of a central bank are many, including loans made to the government. Central banks emerged from the wars between European powers in the seventeenth century and were often bankers to the sovereign:[47] the first was founded from the ashes of Stockholms Banco, with the Swedish parliament providing the capital[48] for the newly renamed Bank of the Estates of the Realm.

The second, and the one which came to define what a central bank did, was in London. The Bank of England was founded in 1694 after the country's Glorious Revolution – when parliament asserted its supremacy over the monarchy by backing a Dutch coup – to help fund the new king's wars against France. A consortium of investors lent £1.2m to the government and the newly created Bank of England earned the right to issue paper notes backed by this debt.[49] Think about this just as a grander version of the cheques from the Irish banking strike. A promise to pay can become money; a promise from the king of England was particularly good.

During the day, private banks essentially have overdrafts with the central bank, borrowing reserves for free[50] so that money can stay liquid and easily travel around the economy.

But at the close of business the banks need to make sure they have sufficient reserves to repay the central bank. They can either get these from the interbank market – borrowing them from other banks – or from the central bank itself in the exact same way. The private banks swap some collateral with the central bank in exchange for reserves, in an arrangement known as 'repo', agreeing to repurchase the collateral at a fixed price on a future date – essentially like a financial pawn shop.

This repo agreement is arithmetically equivalent to an ordinary loan but the pledge of collateral protects the lender. Collateral replaces trust; it means you do not need to take a view on the reliability of the borrower and can look only at the quality of what they have pledged. If the borrower runs away without paying, then the lender, the central bank, can just sell the collateral. Much of the interbank lending market – where the private banks and other financial institutions lend reserves to each other – works the same way.

Central banks set the price of these reserves – the overnight interest rate – as well as deciding what sort of assets they are willing to accept as collateral. Normally these are government bonds, a kind of standardized tradeable loan to the government, making the state's debts an extremely liquid asset. So the overnight interest rate is effectively the price banks have to pay to bring new reserves into the system. If the banking system in aggregate has increased the volume of its lending during the day and there are not enough reserves to borrow in the interbank market, then a private bank will have to pay the central bank rate for new reserves.

This is the last piece in our model of how banks work and, therefore, the production of money in a modern economy. Banks provide the main means of payment in our economy but their willingness to do so depends on the costs they face: the price of capital in the stock market and the price of reserves in the money markets – the cost of the means of settlement.

The central bank sets the limits on interest in the money market through its borrowing and lending rates, and the competitive forces of the market do the rest of the job in controlling the money supply. If the committees of economists who manage monetary policy – as setting interest rates and so on is known – believe that inflation is getting out of hand they raise interest rates; if they think the economy is in trouble and deflation is a possibility, they lower them.

The other main function of a central bank is to be the 'lender of last resort' to the financial system, heading off the destructive spirals of financial collapse that can follow the failure of a private bank. When a private bank gets into trouble and its depositors rush to demand their money back, the central bank can always step in and provide more liquidity.

The Victorian economist and journalist Walter Bagehot,[51] who popularized the idea, described the job of a central bank during a financial panic as lending freely to any solvent institution, against good collateral and at punitive rates. Making sure they are solvent protects the central bank's shareholders, today meaning the government and behind them the public, from the private bank's failure costing them even more, as does requiring good collateral.[52]

Bagehot's call to lend at punitive rates is designed to guard against something called 'moral hazard'. If the central bank were to lend to private banks cheaply when they were about to fail, there would be less of an incentive for them to be run properly, since they could be assured of making a profit even when they got into trouble. Lending at a higher rate of interest than everyone else is designed to pressure the banks into making sensible choices, ensuring the central bank remains the very last resort, an insurance policy and not the normal way of doing things.

The most important point, however, is to lend freely. Bagehot quotes a director of the Bank of England[53] dealing with a financial panic in the nineteenth century: 'We lent [reserves] by every possible means and in modes we had never adopted before; we took in stock on security, we purchased Exchequer's bills . . . in short by every possible means consistent with the safety of the Bank, and we were not on some occasions over-nice. Seeing the dreadful state in which the public were we rented every assistance in our power.'

The goal is to restore the liquidity of the banking sector and trust in money; to stop a full-scale panic from bringing down the whole of the financial system. Because the debts of the banks are the main form of money today, their collapse can undermine the very foundations of our economy.

When the banks collapsed during the financial crisis of 2008, central banks once again stepped in and fulfilled this role as lenders of last resort. While many banks could access emergency loans from the Federal Reserve, the US central bank, Lehman, did not. Those in charge of the central bank believed Lehman was not solvent.[54] Critics claim this was just cover to disguise that the real reason Lehman was allowed to fail was political and the desire to avoid further, controversial, bailouts.

Nevertheless, after the chaos the bank's failure unleashed in the financial markets and, eventually, the wider economy, the central banks launched a vast programme of lending to stabilize the financial system.[55] They began by slashing the cost of borrowing to close to zero: the Federal Reserve, America's central bank, lowered the rate at which it would lend to banks to just 0.25 per cent from 6.25 per cent in 2006.

These interest rates, at the time seen as extraordinarily low, were not enough. Central banks in the US and the UK swiftly followed them up with what is known as 'quantitative easing' (QE). This arcane term refers to large-scale programmes of asset purchases using reserves created at the stroke of a button to buy government debt. Quantitive easing is similar to the repo transactions, where the central bank temporarily buys government bonds from the private banks, but permanent – the central bank never agrees a date to sell it back to the bank. This meant the size of the Fed's balance sheet ballooned from $870bn in 2007 to $4.5tn[56] by 2015, as the central bank did its best to flood the financial system with more and more liquidity.

As banks create new money in the form of deposits when they lend, the unravelling of the financial system in 2008 ended this monetary growth and pushed the global economy into a deep recession. The decisions of the central bankers to try to stimulate the economy through quantitive easing and low interest rates were controversial – many thought the increase in reserves would eventually lead to hyperinflation but it was counterbalancing a much greater deflationary force in the economy: when banks retrench, so does the money supply.

The hyperinflation never turned up. In fact, there was barely any inflation at all in the next decade, much to the puzzlement of the central bankers who kept interest rates at historic lows. Further bouts of QE, essentially money printing, were announced in a bid to try to stimulate the rich economies out of their malaise. Some economists began to despair that the world had now changed for good, that it was an era of constant stagnation and that growth would never return.

What had happened, they told each other, was that the 'natural rate of interest' had fallen. There was nothing they could do.

3. Why do we pay interest?

What is possibly the world's most popular savings product,[1] has four legs, produces milk and, as every child knows, says 'moo'?

In many parts of the world, particularly the Indian subcontinent and sub-Saharan Africa, those living in rural areas without bank branches or ATMs can use cattle as a means of preserving surplus funds.[2] Like a savings account, they provide a regular income, although in the form of milk and dung for fuel rather than interest payments. While you might not be able to withdraw your money from a cow, you can always sell or eat them.

This is nothing new: humanity's oldest economic model may have been based on cows.[3] A roughly 4,000-year-old Sumerian tablet discovered at Drehem in modern-day Iraq describes the growth of an idealized herd over ten years. Like many such models, it relies on unrealistic assumptions: no cows ever die and each pair always has a calf. Nevertheless, the accountants of Sumeria may have used this tablet to forecast the value in terms of silver of the milk and cheese produced by such a herd over ten years. Archaeologists believe the Drehem tablet was probably an investment plan. The initial number of cows increases exponentially in the same way as adding interest to savings compounds the value over time.

The cows are used as assets, stores of value. Interest payments, and other forms of income, are flows: the amount someone receives over time. If some portion of income is saved – say the Sumerians keeping their cows' calves instead of eating them – it adds to the stock of assets, like a stream flowing into a reservoir and topping it up.

The idea of a herd of livestock naturally growing in number may be where the Sumerians got the idea to charge each other interest. If a farmer lends a neighbour his herd, not only would he expect to get back what he lent – the principal – but also the income produced by the assets, in this case the calves. The longer the borrower has the cows, the more the lender should get back. It is no surprise that the Sumerian word for interest is *mash*, which also means 'calves'.

The English word 'capital' has a parallel, though unrelated, origin. Cattle were, similarly, a key store of wealth and a fundamental plank of trade in medieval Europe. Then, as now, the amount of livestock was referred to as heads of cattle. The Latin for head, *capita*, would then gradually start to refer to wealth more generally and, eventually, specifically a fund of money used by merchants. Nowadays 'capital' is used for any stock of assets or money advanced to a business – such as, as we saw in chapter 2, the permanent resources of a bank.[4]

These days economists draw a distinction between capital goods and financial capital. Actual things – a business's premises, software and equipment – would all be capital goods, just like a herd of cattle. They are commodities used to produce other commodities – an oil rig gives you oil; a cow gives you milk. This physical capital can be lent to a business, like money. A company might lease laptops for its staff, and whoever owns the laptops would earn a monthly fee for letting the company borrow them.

Similarly, a business will need financial capital: the money its shareholders and creditors lend it. Just like capital goods, this is needed before production can take place: workers will need to be paid and capital goods will need to be bought or rented, and that requires money. Imagine you set up a bakery. You will need physical capital – a location, ingredients, some ovens – but you will also need money. You will need to pay your staff and sustain yourself while you get set up, especially before any revenue starts coming in.

We could think of lending money the same way the Sumerians thought about lending cattle. Borrow a herd and they will produce calves; lend someone the money to run a business and they can make a profit. This profit can then be divided up between the entrepreneur and their investors. Economists refer to the bit that goes to those who provided the capital as interest – whether the investment was in the form of a loan or otherwise. In the simplified world of economic models, workers get wages, land owners get rent, entrepreneurs get profit and capital gets interest.

The distinction between physical and financial capital allowed Knut Wicksell, a Swedish economist writing in 1898, to distinguish between what he called the 'natural rate of interest' and the monetary interest rate.[5]

As well as being an economist Wicksell was a radical[6] pamphleteer, concerned to reduce poverty and, controversially for the time, advocated the use of birth control. His common-law wife Anna Bugge was a noted feminist, lawyer and suffragette – what was called in her time the 'Wicksellian discovery' referred not to any of her partner's economic theories but to a loophole in tax law that she uncovered which permitted certain married women to vote.[7] Bugge would eventually become a Swedish delegate to the League of Nations. In a letter to her former headmaster explaining her unusual marriage – her future husband wanted no wedding and only contracts covering child maintenance and inheritance – she described Wicksell as 'the best person in the world'.

Nevertheless, the practically minded Bugge sometimes found her husband's provocations of established authority and obstinacy frustrating. She refused to support him in his self-sabotaging reluctance to write 'Your Majesty's most obedient servant' in an application to the king for a grant, but stood by him when Wicksell was sentenced to two months in prison for blasphemy after a lecture satirizing the virgin birth.[8] Despite his unorthodox lifestyle and views, his death prompted a funeral worthy of a statesman, where the red banners of the country's labour movement featured prominently, according to his biographer.

Nowadays the radical Wicksell's work on the 'natural interest rate' is the bedrock of much of the conventional view of how an economy works and how central banks should conduct monetary policy. For Wicksell, interest tended towards a natural rate over time, representing what the owners of capital would earn in a world without money. In that world, interest would be paid with the actual stuff that could be produced. Someone lends you cows and you give back calves, for example.

This set a limit on the monetary rate of interest, based on how productive the use of the financial capital could be. If an entrepreneur gave back more than they produced, they would swiftly find their business failing. If they gave back less, then more competitors would get into the industry until profits returned to normal. Say it only cost you £100 to borrow the money necessary to set up a business that earned £200 in profit, you would quickly find yourself swamped with competitors. This was the idea, at least.

Wicksell knew that banks created the vast majority of money in our economies and wanted to know what the limits were to this process.[9] In other words, why did the banks not create so much money that prices simply spiralled out of control? His answer was that there was some rate of interest, a price, that would balance the supply and demand for funds that could be used for investment, keeping the economy in a stable equilibrium. We saw in the previous chapter that the banks' willingness to create new money would depend on the costs they faced – partly determined by the central bank. This is the other half of the picture: the potential revenues they can earn by lending.

Economists tend to think of the world in terms of supply and demand, with prices matching the two. Central banks, private banks and similar institutions supply money, as we saw in the previous chapter – the availability of financial capital to the public depends on them. The demand, to Wicksell, would depend on the opportunities for profitable investment: the rate of return on physical capital.[10] If the two were not matched, then the economy would be out of balance until prices rose – through inflation – to bring it back towards some sort of stability.

He wrote that if money was loaned at the natural rate of interest then it was 'nothing more than a cloak to cover a procedure which, from the purely formal point of view, could have been carried on equally well without it.'[11] Lenders could have lent the actual capital goods, and received in return the fruit of those goods – like lending someone cows and receiving calves. It was only when the monetary and natural rate were out of sync that money would have an impact on the economy.

For Wicksell, and many modern economists, this is the key influence on the speed at which an economy expands. He thought that if the central bank set its policy rate below the natural rate, then prices would have to rise until the two interest rates were once again brought into balance. In the Wicksell-inspired framework that still dominates monetary policymaking today, it is the difference between the interest rate on money and the return

on 'real assets', meaning capital goods, that determines the inflationary pressure in the economy. Sometimes this is called the
neutral rather than natural rate.[12]

This is why today's central bankers often do not believe they
really set interest rates.[13] The long-term natural rate of interest,
in this theory, is independent of the short-term rates at which a
central bank lends overnight. As central bankers target a particular
rate of inflation they will adjust their policy rate to either stimulate the rate of price growth or cut it back. Bank borrowing costs
will then depend on a combination of the central bank's estimates
of this natural rate[14] and their inflation target.

Think of it like a car going up a hill: as the road gets steeper,
the driver has to press harder on the accelerator to maintain the
same speed. Central bankers want to keep inflation stable, so as
the natural rate changes they adjust the policy rate to deliver
more or less stimulus. In this framework it is not them setting
interest rates but natural forces in the economy; they are just
reacting to the changes in the road.

Time is money

Still, there is a puzzle about where the interest on money actually comes from. Unlike cows, money does not produce anything;
it bears no offspring. Yet when you lend it to someone else it
can still multiply – you could get more of it back than you
initially lent. Similarly, if you borrow it, you have to repay more
than you got. Money, puzzlingly, breeds more money.

The supposedly dry topic of where interest comes from is a
much more controversial one than you might expect. In fact, it
gets to the heart of one of the most contentious debates in human
history: the morality of making money from money. All the way

back in ancient Greece, the philosopher Aristotle wrote that interest was 'unnatural'.[15] Money, unlike cows, is barren, in Aristotle's words, and produces nothing itself. Earning more money by lending was unethical and parasitical – interest, he theorized, must come from the creditor extracting some of the debtor's wealth.

Christian philosophers later justified the Church's prohibition on usury on similar grounds as Aristotle. In Dante's *Inferno* both 'sodomites' and moneylenders occupy the same circle of hell. Both, Dante thought, sinned against nature, sodomites by having sex that would not produce children and moneylenders by making something (money) breed without sex.

Arguments about the source of interest have remained controversial. In fact, disagreements about it have been at the heart of one of the great ideological battles of the twentieth century – the clash between communism and capitalism.

By the middle of the ninteenth century – before Wicksell was writing about the natural interest rate – the idea that interest was parasitical had found another standard bearer. The radical journalist, activist and political philosopher Karl Marx was originally born in Germany but, after being exiled from France after the failure of the revolutions of 1848, scribbled his theories of the origin of the return on capital in London. The work, known as *Capital*, would be unfinished at the time of his death in 1883 – only the first volume was completed – and it was left to his long-time collaborator Friedrich Engels to compile the final two volumes from Marx's notes. Nevertheless the tome would provide the justification for communist revolutions across the world during the next century.

Marx argued that capitalism was always exploitative – and had to be for capital to earn interest. What is fundamental about the economic system, he wrote, is that capitalists can make money solely by having money. When they invest, capitalists swap money and goods back and forth – they invest in some commodities and then use these to produce more commodities, aiming to make a profit. By doing this, capitalists were somehow able to create a surplus and increase the amount of money they had. They could make money breed: 'It brings forth living offspring,' Marx wrote, 'or, at the least, lays golden eggs.'

Imagine our cattle farmer is not the owner of his own herd but is the employee of a meat company. The owners of the company have swapped their money for some cows, and now expect a return from this investment. Simplified to its basic elements, this is an exchange going money to commodity to more money, M-C-M' in Marx's notation. Owners of Meat Inc. would not only be able to keep their original investment but grow it thanks to the profit they earned. Marx labelled this increase 'surplus value', roughly similar to what we have been calling interest.

Labour[16] in Marx's theory was the ultimate source of all value, and the surplus value, the capitalist's interest, was taken from the workers. Our farmer does all the work – the capitalists just own the cows – but the workers do not get the full fruit of their labour. The reason why M' is more than M is because it includes a bit of the farmer's labour power – the capitalist's interest comes from the unpaid work of labourers.

Thanks to a historical process of European peasants having common land taken away from them and colonization in the rest of the world, there were two classes of people: one with nothing to sell but their labour and the other that owned both physical and financial capital, the means of production. The class that owned capital, the bourgeois, was able to accumulate more thanks to the exploitation of the other class, the proletariat. Marx compared capital to a vampire that lives by sucking the life out of labour,[17] 'and lives the more, the more labour it sucks'.

This is not, as you might expect, the theory of interest's origins that influences central bankers when they set interest rates. They do not try to keep their policy rates close to what they believe to be a natural rate of exploitation based on the ability of capitalists to extract the value that workers create. Instead it finds its origin in the theories of a different German-speaking economist who, similarly, wrote a multi-volume opus on the concept of capital: Eugen von Böhm-Bawerk.

Böhm-Bawerk was a very different character than the two more radical economists we have already met in this chapter. The much more conservative, albeit still liberal, Böhm-Bawerk combined his stints in academia with periods as the Austrian finance minister – actually putting his world-view into practice.[18] His portrait – slightly balding, bearded and with round wire-rimmed glasses – featured on the Austrian 100-schilling note before the country adopted the euro. Today, outside his homeland, he is mostly remembered as a critic of the much more famous Marx.

At the core of the disagreement between Böhm-Bawerk and Marx, as well as their contemporary followers, is the concept of value. Marx – along with others in a group known as the 'classical economists' that includes the much more pro-capitalist Adam Smith – believed all economic value was created by labour in conjunction with the natural world: prices reflected the amount of work done to produce something.

It is easy to see the labour theory of value as the economic equivalent of the belief that the sun orbits the earth, rather than the other way around: outdated and naive at best and obviously silly at worst, only of historical interest. This would be a mistake. There are too many problems with the theory for it to work as an explanation of what determines prices, but it does contain an important germ of truth: everything that is bought or sold was made by someone. Even naturally occurring commodities like diamonds or wild berries had to be mined or harvested. Humanity started out with nothing but nature and now, thanks to workers, many of whom are long dead, we have skyscrapers and smart-phones.

The decisive break between classical and more modern economics came when a group known today as the Austrian School – although not all of their members were actually Austrian – rejected this theory and argued instead that economic value was ultimately subjective. The price of goods and services depends not on how they are made, but on how much they are desired. One work of art is worth more than another not because there is more labour involved in producing it but solely because people believe it to be worth more. There is no objective standard of value; it is all based on our individual needs and desires. It is our hunger that means we pay for food and not the work of the farmer.

And generally, Böhm-Bawerk wrote, people favour the present over the future. We value things not only because of what they are, but also because of when we get them, especially money. The sooner the better: most of us would rather have £100 today than £105 in five years' time. Money's worth depends not only on 'how much' but also 'when'.

Because we are impatient, weak-willed and may die before we ever see it, we usually discount the future relative to the present. We give in to temporary temptation and have a cigarette, a drink or some other indulgence that will do long-term harm, because present pleasures are so much nicer; or perhaps we put off some embarrassing conversation even though delaying will just cause more unpleasantness. These are slightly adapted examples that Böhm-Bawerk used of how we systematically value present enjoy-ments over the future.

In Marx's model of the economy there was no time,[19] Böhm-Bawerk said, but in reality when the capitalist exchanges money for commodities and back to money, these exchanges do not happen instantly. The shareholder has to wait, and give up their ability to spend today to get it. It is this waiting – this time – rather than exploitation, that allows capitalists to transform money today into more money in the future.

People who have different subjective time preferences can trade money in the same way that people who have different aesthetic tastes can trade artworks. This creates an interest rate: someone who is willing to lend £100 for five years can make £5 in interest. Böhm-Bawerk argued that the surplus value Marx identified is really the counterpart to the subjective rate of discount we apply to the future. As he pointed out, lending for consumption comes with an interest rate just as much as lending for production – the return could not purely be due to exploitation, as Marx said, nor how useful capital goods are, as many earlier liberal economists had suggested.

There is nothing particularly moral or unjust about the origins of interest, Böhm-Bawerk argued. It is not a reward for thrift as others had suggested – a view that was mocked by socialist thinkers for implying that wealthy capitalists living in luxury were actually the height of parsimony – but neither did it always come from exploitation. Instead it was just the reflection of a psychological regularity; people prefer the present to the future, so those who can enable that profit.

And what's more, he noted, spending some time today can produce greater benefits for tomorrow. Böhm-Bawerk called this 'roundaboutness'.[20] If less direct methods of production are used – a cattle farmer fermenting milk to become cheese rather than selling it immediately – then more or more valuable products can be made. While humanity may have needed the natural world and labour to get smartphones and skyscrapers, it also needed time.

Capitalists' savings pay the wages of workers while these processes are taking place, and the return on capital comes from the higher value that is created over time. A group of workers could band together to form a cooperative, say, and gain all the value for themselves but it would mean not getting paid until the very end. For most workers, lacking any savings, this is not an option but, Böhm-Bawerk argued, even if wealth were divided equally there would be still be a difference in value between the present and the future, and so there would always be interest for someone or other, even under communism.

The dominant theory of the origins of interest eventually became a modified version of Böhm-Bawerk's, as some of the rough edges were smoothed off, especially by the American economist Irving Fisher, whom we will meet in more detail in the next chapter. You will not see the term 'roundaboutness' in contemporary discussions of interest rates.[21] Nevertheless the core idea is still that there is a market for savings and investment. The supply of savings, people's willingness to give up their present ability to consume, depends on their time preference, the subjective discount they apply to the future. But the demand for investment depends on the productive uses that their savings could be put to, in other words the investment opportunities on offer. Interest rates would then adjust to balance the two.

A rather unusual Italian bank can help demonstrate how interest rates do this. Credito Emiliano, located in the region of Italy that makes the Parmigiano-Reggiano cheese that you might better know by the generic name parmesan, serves a lot of dairy farmers. Parmesan, like fine wine or whisky, becomes more valuable as it ages – a wheel of the cheese is initially floated in a bath of salted water, which helps form the rind. It then takes two years for the salt to reach the centre of the cheese.[22] As salt crystals form, it becomes more delicious and so the subjective value it has to cheese aficionados increases.

Suppose you are a parmesan maker. Every year you leave the cheese to mature, it becomes just a little bit more valuable, but by a lower proportion each time – so if you leave it for a year the price doubles, but leave it a year more, it only increases by half.

At some point, the higher price the cheese would fetch will not be worth the wait. Say, after having left it for two years, it will only increase in value by 5 per cent in another year. At that point you might rather have the money straight away than the current price plus 5 per cent in a year's time and so would sell it. In this way, an individual should balance the extra return earned by waiting just a bit longer with their personal rate of time preference – how much they discount the future.

But, in a competitive market economy, what matters is not your own preferences for money now or money later but the prevailing market interest rate. Even if you wanted to sell the cheese this year and take the money now, it might still be best to leave it to age – depending on the interest rate. If it was 4 per cent you could borrow the money for a year, then repay the loan by selling the cheese once it had matured. You would have the money today and still make a 1 per cent profit by investing. But if the interest rate on money rose to 10 per cent, then you would obviously be better off selling the cheese immediately rather than waiting. The profit could just be put in a bank account and earn more over the next year than the 5 per cent profit on offer from leaving the cheese to mature.

When Credito Emiliano, the Italian bank, makes a loan to the farmers it often takes the wheels of Parmigiano-Reggiano cheese as collateral.[23] Partly it provides a warehousing service, storing the cheese, and rotating and brushing it every fifteen days for the first year of maturation, as is required. But it also lets farmers make these sorts of trades: the bank treats the young cheese as if it is worth the value of fully mature cheese, letting the farmers realize their gains immediately at the expense of paying the bank the market interest rate. If interest rates go up, it makes sense for the farmers to take their cheese out of the bank and sell it straight away; if they go down, they should wait longer.

Most investment is not like leaving cheese to mature. It usually involves someone, even if not the investor, doing a lot more work than just waiting. It still, however, requires time. If you are in the business of making capital goods, whether that is building a bread oven for a baker or writing a film script – both of which are used in the production of other goods and services – you are spending time in the present making something that will hopefully be useful at some point in the future.[24]

But because you are making something that will only pay off later – perhaps years later – someone else must provide you with the means to survive while you are working. I was only able to write the book you are reading because my publisher provided me with an 'advance' while I wrote it. Lending money in this way can give someone the time to produce things and as the monetary interest rate changes it becomes more or less attractive to do so.

So if central banks routinely set their policy rate below the investment returns available on 'real assets' then prices would spiral out of control as more and more people borrowed money to invest. This would create more money until hyperinflation resulted, some new form of money was adopted and the natural rate was eventually restored. Time preference and the productivity of capital, rather than the choices of central bankers, will always end up determining how much interest we have to pay.

Liquidity preference

It is an elegant theory but there is at least one big problem. Time brings with it uncertainty: none of us knows what the future holds. And it was this uncertainty that made the British economist John Maynard Keynes conclude in the middle of the twentieth century that, in fact, the interest rate would not always do the job of balancing the total amount of saving and investment in an economy.

Keynes himself is a fascinating figure.[25] Witty and bright, he was the epitome of a certain sort of English intellectual, possessing an acid tongue along with a determination that the world could be made a much better place through the application of his prodigious intellect. He loved the arts and was part of the Bloomsbury Group of artists and writers that included the novelists Virginia Woolf and E. M. Forster. Keynes, along with the rest of his set, rebelled against stuffy Victorian conventions: most of his early romantic adventures were with men before he met and married Lydia Lopokova, a Russian ballerina[26] – his other great affair was with the painter Duncan Grant.

In his career, he combined the radical energies of Wicksell with the government experience of Böhm-Bawerk. As well as criticizing the actions of Winston Churchill, the country's finance minister prior to the Great Depression – notably in *The Economic Consequences of Mr Churchill* – he would also periodically work for the British state. And not only as an economist: he bought art for the nation after the First World War[27] and during the Second World War was chair of the Arts Council, which ensured funding for the arts even as the government was forced to cut back elsewhere.[28] His greatest contribution to the conflict was negotiating war loans with the US, although the Americans often found his manner infuriating.

Keynes made his name warning that treating Germany badly after the First World War could lead to a second and devastating European conflict. He had worked for the British government as part of the delegation that negotiated the Treaty of Versailles, setting the terms of Germany's surrender after the war, but resigned his position and wrote about his experience in a 1919 book called *The Economic Consequences of the Peace*. There was no way Germany would ever be able to repay the sums demanded by France and Britain, he said,[29] which seemed more driven by a destructive desire for vengeance rather than preserving the hard-won peace.

Today Keynes is seen as the father of macroeconomics – analysing the behaviour of the economy in aggregate rather than particular markets. He is most famous for his writings during the Great Depression in the 1930s on why recessions happen and what can be done to stop them. His ideas are referenced today when someone advocates higher government spending to combat a downturn, often called Keynesian stimulus.

He began his career as a civil servant in Britain's India Office[30] in the early years of the twentieth century. This was a time when the hot topic in economics was whether currencies should be pegged to silver, gold or a mixture of both. The Indian rupee had been made out of silver since it was first coined in the mid-sixteenth century in the Suri empire of northern India – the word rupee derives from a Sanskrit word meaning 'wrought silver'.[31]

The debate about whether the US dollar should be backed by gold or silver is said by some critics[32] to have been immortal-ized in the 1900 book *The Wonderful Wizard of Oz* (eventually a film) – 'oz' being the symbol for ounces, which were used to measure the weight of gold.[33] They argue that the author, L. Frank Baum, advocated the use of silver, and in the book version Dorothy wore silver (not ruby) slippers as she travelled down the yellow (gold) brick road. The whole time she was able to free herself from the land of Oz by clicking together her silver heels. She was, however, unaware of their power.

In this reading the Scarecrow represents the farmers, who were said to be too dumb to see they would benefit from a silver standard, the Tin Man was the alienated urban working classes who supposedly lacked the heart to join with the farmers, and the Cowardly Lion stood in for the politicians who would not stand up to the financial interests on the East and West coasts – interests represented, in turn, by the Wicked Witches of the East and the West. All along the farmers, working men and politicians had the necessary requirements to build a better society, they just did not know it. Others, however, suggest this allegorical reading is more accidental than anything else, as the author was not an overly political man[34] – personally I think it would require far too many coincidences not to be deliberate.

Most countries at the time, not just the US, had their currencies pegged to gold. This was a problem for India. In the late nineteenth century, the price of silver was falling relative to the yellow metal, weakening the rupee compared to currencies on the gold standard, particularly the British pound. As the price of silver fell the colonial government in Delhi had to pay more and more rupees to London.

It was a similar problem that led the so-called populists in the US to advocate silver: farmers' debts were denominated in dollars linked to gold and as the price of the metal rose the cost of servicing these debts would increase, driving many – like Dorothy's aunt and uncle – into poverty. Deflation – prices falling year after year – may sound attractive but it can be disastrous for those in debt.[35] Not only do consumer prices fall relative to money, but so do incomes: the prices the farmers' crops would get at the market dropped but their mortgage payments would remain unchanged.

In 1893 the Indian government suspended free coinage – they would no longer mint any silver brought to them into rupees; instead they exchanged silver rupees into gold sovereigns at a fixed rate of 15Rs to £1. Keynes in his book on the subject described the rupee as a 'note printed on silver',[36] its value being unrelated to the metal content of the coins but solely based on the value assigned to it by the Indian government. It was, he said, an artificially valued token, exactly like paper money.

Writing in 1913, after he had stopped working at the India Office, Keynes thought this would be an optimal kind of currency for the whole world – though printing it on silver rather than paper was wasteful – and he urged the Indian government not to go onto a gold standard. Within India, he argued, the value of money could depend on the needs of the domestic economy, while those who needed the international currency, gold, could still get hold of it. Policymakers could not only manage the domestic money supply as they saw fit but also fix its price in terms of the international currency.

Keynes would champion these kinds of managed currencies his whole life. He was an outspoken critic of the gold standard, describing it in another of his books as a 'barbarous relic'. Similarly, *The Economic Consequences of Mr Churchill*, published in 1925, predicted that Britain's return to the gold standard would be a mistake – the fact that wage cuts and unemployment followed only enhanced Keynes' reputation as an economist of unique genius. Keynes' greatest contribution to economic thought, however, came from his attempt to understand the origins and potential solutions to an ever deeper crisis: the Great Depression.

The Great Depression gets that name for the same reason

the First World War is called the Great War: it was not great – quite the opposite – just so big, and so destructive, it over-shadowed all that came before or after. It was not quite as bad in Keynes' native Britain as in the US[37] where images of bread lines and destitute farmers in the 'dustbowl' still shape the popular imagination of the period, but unemployment in the UK reached two million for the first time ever. Unemployed and hungry ship-workers from Jarrow, in the north-east of England, marched the 300 miles or so to London to ask for help. This was just one of dozens of 'hunger marches' as unemployed workers protested they could not find enough work to feed their families.

For Keynes, getting money right could prevent such slumps. This was the subject of his most influential book, written in 1936: *The General Theory of Employment, Interest and Money.*[38] The name referenced Albert Einstein's general theory of relativity that, in physics, had overturned the previous paradigm based on Isaac Newton's theories – no one would ever accuse Keynes of being excessively humble.

The General Theory is dense and difficult in places but at its core is an idea of how, because the future is uncertain, an economy that uses money is prone to falling into recessions. Like Wicksell, Keynes believed that the level of investment spending is dependent on the relationship between the interest rate on money and the returns available on investment. However, Keynes stressed that what matters for investors was what they expect to earn, rather than the actual return they end up getting. The confidence they had in the future, or what Keynes referred to as 'animal spirits', would influence the total amount of invest-ment spending.

Keynes' key insight, however, is that when you try to save using money it is not like the parmesan example from the previous section: there is no automatic link between one person deciding not to spend and another person deciding to invest. In the monetary economy we actually live in, rather than Wicksell's world without it, a saver does not need cows, parmesan or any other capital goods – just money. This means that all the different spending plans in the economy can be inconsistent; there is no guarantee that savers will be able to put as much of their income aside as they intend.

Keynes argued that, ultimately, spending provides the funds necessary for saving, rather than the other way around. One person's spending is another's income. If businesses think new investment will be profitable then they will spend more – hiring workers to make the capital goods they want. Workers' incomes will then rise, meaning the workers will be able to save more. If that business investment does not take place, they will find themselves unable to save.

So, the amount of employment adjusts to balance saving and investment, rather than the interest rate. If everyone tries to save at once then total spending falls, workers are laid off and the attempts to increase saving fail. Later followers of Keynes would call this the 'paradox of thrift':[39] saving might make an individual wealthier but if everyone tries to do it at once they will get poorer.

There was another wrinkle: savers would face a choice between keeping their funds in money or actually buying other assets. In other words, between hoarding 'liquidity' or investing in capital. This was because it was not 'time preference' that mattered for determining interest rates but a preference to keep savings in money rather than another asset. In other words, once we have decided to save some of our income we need a reason to choose money rather than, for example, buying shares or building a house.

Keynes came up with three reasons why someone would want

money. First, the desire to carry out transactions: you need money if you want to buy something. Second, for speculation: you might want to hold on to some money because you think it will go up in value. Third, and most important, you would want to hold on to money in case something goes wrong. Keynes called the relative preference for money over other assets 'liquidity preference'.

Crucially, in terms of his theory of recessions, Keynes understood that money was trust. In times of difficulty people would flock to a store of value they could rely on and demand for money would rocket. People wanted to be certain they could pay their bills and wanted to hoard whatever was the material in which they could do so. Even in normal times, uncertainty about the future means we want to keep money by just in case. To give up this 'liquidity premium', as Keynes called it, they needed to be compensated by interest payments.

'Our desire to hold money as a store of wealth is a barometer of our distrust of our own calculations and conventions concerning the future,' he wrote in a later paper clarifying the *General Theory*. Unlike shares in a company – or cows, for that matter – money provides you with no income, it cannot produce anything. Instead, what money offers is reassurance:[40] if things go very wrong you want the most liquid asset available, something you can rely on to buy things and pay off your debt. If you are afraid of losing your job you want to make sure that you will have the means to pay your rent and buy food and that will always mean money.[41] Interest was the 'premium which we require' to give up this sense of safety.

The collapse in confidence that accompanies a recession would increase the demand for money and, without some action by the central bank to offset it by increasing the supply of money, would lead to higher interest rates. To make things worse, the expected return on investment would collapse – fewer people buy very expensive parmesan during a slump, for example – and the 'animal spirits' of investors were dampened. This uncertainty meant that with an inelastic money supply – for example if the central bank was determined to defend the currency's value in terms of gold – the rate of interest on money would increase far above the expected return of investment in a recession, and the economy would get stuck in a deflationary trap.

In Wicksell's original version of the natural interest rate theory, a fall in wages would restore the economy to full employment: lower wage costs meant potential profits increased and a higher natural interest rate would lead to more investment, bringing unemployment back down again. Keynes argued that the effect of falling wages was uncertain, it depended what effect it had on total spending. Perhaps it could restore employment if profit expectations increased and stimulated investment but, on the other hand, it could just lead to lower consumer spending. Anyway, he added, 'it can only be a foolish person who would prefer a flexible wage policy to a flexible money policy'. In other words, cutting wages rather than interest rates.

Negative interest rates

Towards the end of the *General Theory*, Keynes wondered about what the future might look like if his theories were used to inform economic policy. He looked forward to the point where, thanks to governments keeping interest rates at the level consistent with full employment, there would be no more 'rentiers', meaning investors who simply collected interest without taking any risks. There would be such an overabundance of physical capital that all the best opportunities for investment would already be taken. It would no longer be possible to take advantage of capital's scarcity to gain a high income, in the same way as landlords take advantage of the scarcity of land to earn a rent.

This would be a happy death, a 'euthanasia of the rentier', as many of the most objectionable features of capitalism would be banished. Keynes, unlike Marx, did not want to overthrow capitalism, he wanted to save it from itself; the poverty it produced as well as the periodic slumps.

Keynes' vision would, eventually, come true but not in the way he would have wanted. After the 2008 financial crisis, interest rates did fall to a level where rentiers struggled. As part of their efforts to lift economies out of the recession, many central banks cut their policy rates to only slightly above zero.

In fact some went even further: in 2009 the Swedish central bank, the Riksbank, was the first to charge private banks for keeping overnight reserves.[42] They were followed by the European Central Bank in 2014[43] and the Bank of Japan in 2016.[44] Eventually some private banks would pass these costs on to their customers and begin to charge businesses who deposited large amounts of cash, eroding the value of their savings the longer they lent it to the bank.

These negative interest rates allowed some governments and corporations to be paid to borrow. In 2019 Germany's government debt yielded minus 0.4 per cent[45] – in other words, investors lost 0.4 per cent of their investment every year they lent it to the German government. Similarly, the manufacturing conglomerate Siemens sold bonds with an interest rate of around minus 0.3 per cent in 2019.[46] Investors would pay for the privilege of lending to trusted borrowers. Many even said they were disappointed to miss out on the chance to pay to lend to Siemens.

The central banks had cut their policy interest rates so low for a reason. Shortly after Keynes' work was published, there was an attempt to synthesize it and make it consistent with what he called the 'classical' theory. In 1937 the economist John Hicks, in a highly influential paper,[47] wrote that interest rates simultaneously had to balance the supply and demand for liquidity – as Keynes suggested – but also the supply and demand for savings. Interest rates would do both jobs at once.

What's more, the amount of employment would affect not only the amount of investment spending but also the demand for money. A richer society would mean more money was needed to carry out transactions. In other words, faster growth means more buying and selling, and this as well as liquidity preference would influence the interest rate.

In this so-called neo-classical synthesis, the level of employment and the interest rate are jointly determined – neither dominates the other. Most of the time competitive forces would push interest rates until both money markets and the capital markets were in balance. If there was completely full employment then this would simply be the 'natural rate' of Knut Wicksell: any cut by the central bank below this level would just lead to inflation. If the economy was operating with 'spare capacity' then the central bank cutting interest rates could push it back towards equilibrium. In the model, the economy works on Keynesian terms in recessions and classical ones in normal times.

This synthesis, which is still taught in undergraduate economics degrees today, provided a version of Keynes' theories that could then become a workhorse model for policymakers. Some of the subtleties were lost in translation but it was, as the saying goes, 'good enough for government work'. Many of those in central banks will have an adapted version in their heads[48] when they set interest rates.

In this theory it is possible for an economy to fall into what is called a 'liquidity trap',[49] where the rate of interest that would simultaneously match both Keynes' liquidity preference and the market for saving and investment is below zero. The desire for money is so high and the expected profitability of investment is so low that only a negative interest rate could stimulate the economy out of the slump.[50] Money markets and capital markets cannot simultaneously be balanced and there is a permanent shortfall of investment.

In traditional economic theory, however, negative interest rates are meant to be impossible – in the jargon, there is a zero 'lower bound' on interest rates.[51] Savers always have the option of withdrawing their money from bank accounts and hoarding cash; indeed, sales of safe deposit boxes rocketed after negative interest rate policies were introduced in Germany[52] and Japan.[53] If it costs too much to keep your capital then it is easy to just get rid of it. This was one of the motivations behind the policy – central bankers wanted people to spend and not save. They wanted to flip Böhm-Bawerk's theory on its head and make waiting more expensive than spending today.

Negative[54] rates were meant to encourage the banks to get rid of any excess reserves as quickly as possible and for their big business clients to spend rather than keep their money at the banks where it was gradually eroding in value. Quantitative easing – buying up government debt with newly created central bank reserves – was a long-shot attempt to flood the economy with so much money that liquidity preference was satiated.[55] The money markets and the capital markets would then be brought into balance again and the economy lifted out of its recession.

Being paid to borrow was not as popular as you might think: many groups rely on waiting to earn their income. Banks complained negative rates eroded their margins and actually made lending less likely; they struggled to pass on the rates to depositors due to competitive pressures.[56] Pension funds and life insurance companies found it harder to meet their obligations with little income from their assets.[57] Some suggested that their clients would have to save even more because they were earning so little on their savings – they needed to accumulate more wealth to maintain the same income.[58]

The central bankers countered that the natural rate of interest had fallen, it was not their choice.[59] They had a point in that the low rates did not bring back anything close to an economic boom. It was like the accelerator pedal was not attached to anything. Growth and inflation did not return as predicted after the 2008 financial crisis; economies remained sluggish despite the cheap-money policies of the central banks; and the central banks largely undershot their inflation targets.[60]

Why this happened provokes intense debate. For many the problem was that the productivity of capital had simply fallen. The natural interest rate was lower because investment was providing lower returns. So interest rates had to be lower because of this structural shift in the economy. This unexplained and sudden fall in productivity growth became known as 'the productivity puzzle'.[61]

Other explanations focused on the 'time preference' part of the traditional explanation for interest rates: arguing there was a glut of global savings[62] thanks to changing central bank practices after the Asian financial crisis in the late 1990s, which we will look at in chapter 7, and ageing populations who only wanted to put their retirement pots into super safe assets. One economics paper labelled it 'the murder-suicide of the rentier', in reference to Keynes' speculation at the end of the *General Theory*.

Keynes' theories provide an alternative lens. With no automatic method for an economy to return to full employment after a crisis, Keynes suggested the government should take over where the private sector failed.[63] Endemic uncertainty meant that business could not be relied on to invest enough. This meant not only that slumps were self-sustaining but also that there would be a permanent shortfall of investment, even in the good times. If instead governments spent, then they would create full employment, and higher tax receipts from a booming economy would cover the costs.

This did not happen after the financial crisis. Instead, governments across the world cut public spending and raised taxes in order to try to restore their budgets after the expense of the crisis. As austerity removed the demand for goods and services from government there was no longer so great a return on capital to be had by waiting and investing.

Either way, for the central bankers the natural rate of interest had fallen – they had to press much harder on the accelerator to maintain the same speed. One of the implications of the natural rate theory is that the technocrats in charge of the central banks do not have much power, even over interest rates. The 'natural rate of interest' is an outcome of forces beyond their control, and if they try to resist these forces it will inevitably lead to missing their inflation targets. Whatever else this theory has to recommend it, you can see why it appeals to the central bankers: money is enormously powerful and the theory absolves them of responsibility. It suggests the power of money ultimately lies elsewhere.

4. Where does inflation come from?

In the middle of the eighteenth century, a swathe of West Africa including parts of present-day Nigeria, Benin and Ghana went through the Great Inflation.[1]

Inflation, meaning the rate at which the overall level of prices increases, is generally a problem if it either gets too fast or goes into reverse. Contracts are usually made for nominal amounts of money – the dollar, pound or yen value, for example – so when prices increase faster than expected, the value of what was agreed changes. For workers it means that as they get further away from annual pay negotiations they can buy less with their wages – the 'real' value decreases. Most critical, however, is the effect on debt and savings: deflation makes it harder to repay debts while inflation erodes the value of savings.[2]

Over time a little modest inflation can help an economy.[3] Not only does it provide a kind of economic lubricant – businesses find it much easier to adapt to straitened circumstances by increasing wages by less than inflation, a real-terms pay cut, than to slash headline wages – but it is also an indicator of an economy's overall health. Inflation suggests businesses are having to compete for workers by paying higher wages, which end up being passed on to shoppers through higher prices. Very high inflation, however, makes it harder to plan for the future: the returns from a potential investment could be entirely eradicated by an unexpected bout of inflation.[4] Extreme inflation – hyperinflation – can utterly destroy an economy.

For these reasons keeping inflation stable ought to be a key goal of policy. So theories of where it comes from and how to control it play a big role in determining how our economies are managed. The case of West Africa's Great Inflation demonstrates one of these theories. It is an example of what many economists would describe as the chief cause of inflation: too much money chasing after too few goods.

Since the fourteenth century, the humble cowrie shell – the smooth, white home of a species of sea snail – had been one of the most important currencies in the region[5] and, since it was first used in Bengal in the middle of the first millennium, one of the most important currencies in the world. The shell itself is a smooth dome on one side and flat on the other, with a narrow aperture for the snail's foot. In Italian the cowrie was known as *porcellana*, reputedly for its resemblance to a sow's vulva; the shells would lead the explorer Marco Polo to name the white pottery he encountered in China porcelain.

From the point of view of West Africa, cowrie shells were as good as gold. They were durable, of regular size and shape and, most importantly, rare. The shells were originally brought from their home in the Indian Ocean by Arab traders in exchange for gold, textiles and slaves. This meant the amount in circulation only fluctuated slightly, since they had to travel halfway around the world. For something to be money it has to be scarce enough that it keeps its value but not so scarce that no one can actually use it to trade – cowrie shells met the brief perfectly.

That they were used in West Africa meant the shells would eventually become the dominant currency of the transatlantic slave trade.[6] Starting in the Maldives, where the shells were almost exclusively harvested, the Dutch and English East India

Companies would buy them from markets in Bengal and Sri Lanka and then ship them to London and Amsterdam. Slave traders from all over western Europe would then buy the shells at auction – weighing a total of 25 million pounds or 10 billion shells over the eighteenth century, according to auction house records[7] – and use them as ballast for the journey to Africa's Atlantic coast.

There the shells would be replaced with a human cargo. The tradition among the local traders was that around a fifth to a third of the value of a slave shipment had to be paid for with cowrie shells – although when cowries were particularly expensive European traders tried to substitute other goods like guns, alcohol or textiles. This meant a greater and greater demand for the shells and more were brought to West Africa than ever before: the price of a slave quadrupled from around 100 lb of the shells in 1694 to 400 lb in 1772, or about 160,000 individual shells.[8]

Historic inflation data for West Africa are hard to come by, but it is likely the exact same trends were seen in domestic prices. In Ouidah, a port city that is today part of Benin, a chicken cost between 50 and 67 cowries in 1694, but by the middle of the eighteenth century this had risen to around 270–330 cowries.[9] Over fifty years that works out at an inflation rate of 3 to 4 per cent a year – reasonably high but by no means extreme.

For much of the next century, as the pace at which the shells were imported slowed, the price of a chicken remained roughly stable. The abolition of the Atlantic slave trade by the British in 1807 and the enforcement of its ban by the Royal Navy ended the shipments of cowrie shells. Without any increase in the supply of money there was little inflation in the cowrie zone. The value of the shells, too, fell by an estimated 70 to 80 per cent[10] following the Abolition Act, probably prompting a recession in the Maldives as demand for one of their main exports dried up.

Imports of shell money into West Africa enjoyed a second lease of life, however. By 1820 palm oil was greasing the wheels of the industrial revolution and was becoming the new, booming commodity out of West Africa. The cowries were still used as money in the region and European merchants needed some means to pay. Exports of the shells from Britain – the Dutch having gone into decline as an imperial power – surged to the highs seen during the era of the transatlantic slave trade, although the East India Company, mired in scandal, had lost its monopoly and cowrie shipping was opened to all comers.

This new demand for cowries would eventually prove almost fatal to the currency. The culprit was an enterprising merchant called Adolph Jacob Hertz,[11] originally from the port of Hamburg on Germany's North Sea coast. In his bid to undercut the competition, Hertz went to the source. But, for the most part, he failed to buy the shells from the Maldives – the islanders did not sell directly to Europeans after some disappointing early experiences with the Portuguese. Bengalese merchants monopolized the trade, providing the Maldives with rice in exchange.

Hertz did manage to buy a small stock of cowries from the locals though, reportedly having to sweeten the deal by including in the trade one of his ship's wheelbarrows that took the fancy of the island's sultan. He would, however, eventually find another option that proved the making of his fortune, but nearly led to the downfall of the cowrie.

There are at least 250 species of cowries but only two of their shells have routinely been used as currency in West Africa: the money cowrie and the ring cowrie. The ring cowrie, *Cypraea annulus*, bears a yellow circle on its domed top, unlike the money cowrie, *Cypraea moneta*, which is plain white.

Hertz had found huge volumes of the ring cowrie, a seemingly untapped source, on the island of Zanzibar,[12] off the coast of Tanzania in East Africa. There the ring cowrie could be bought for roughly a tenth of the price of the money cowrie. So, if anyone on the other side of the continent could be persuaded to accept it as payment for palm oil, there were huge potential profits to be made – Hertz would effectively be able to buy palm oil at a tenth of the price.

Others had tried this trick before, so it remains a puzzle why Hertz found just the right time to begin his experiment. Some speculate that the boom in palm oil had made the money cowrie too expensive. Whatever the reason, by the middle of the nineteenth century he was able to buy palm oil not with *Cypraea moneta* but with the much more common and plentiful *Cypraea annulus*. Huge hauls of the ring cowrie were shipped from East to West Africa to pay for the palm oil.

Hertz would eventually lose his dominance of the trade to an even cannier German merchant: William O'Swald. Originally Wilhelm Oswald, he had changed his name to sound Scottish due to his admiration for the works of the historical novelist Sir Walter Scott.

In total O'Swald and Hertz, along with a few other German and French merchants, shipped 79 million pounds of ring cowries to West Africa between 1851 and 1869. This was roughly triple the weight slave traders had brought during the entirety of the eighteenth century. The ring cowrie for palm oil trade was so profitable that the Germans labelled their cargo as 'kaffee' to keep what they were actually shipping hidden from prying eyes.[13]

In an example of Gresham's law – 'bad money drives out the good' – areas that did not accept the ring cowries still saw a huge increase in the money supply as the money cowries from other areas were displaced. In Abomey, a city about 100km from Ouidah, the price of a chicken had risen to 2,000 cowries by 1864, from 280 in 1850: this more than sevenfold increase in prices works out at an inflation rate of close to 15 per cent a year.

This was by no means hyperinflation – in Weimar Germany inflation reached an annual rate of 29,500 per cent, and at the start of 2018 in Venezuela prices were increasing at 979,790 per cent a year, according to the International Monetary Fund. The Great Inflation was, however, enough to substantially reduce the usefulness of the shells. By 1895, cowries were worth only a tenth of the value they had in 1850: the costs of feeding porters to transport them inland was now more than their monetary value.[14]

When Hertz and O'Swald exported tons of the ring cowrie into West Africa, the supply of money surged and, without any change in the economy's ability to absorb it, inflation was the result. This is what economists mean by 'too much money chasing after too few goods'. It might seem obvious that if there is too much money, its value will inevitably fall.

What counts as too much is another question altogether. To answer it, economists historically turned to what is known as the quantity theory of money and the arcane concept known as the velocity of money.

The velocity of money

In the 1920s the British economist Dennis Robertson[15] used a parable to explain the quantity theory of money. Two men, Bob and Joe, travel to the horse races with a barrel of beer, intending to sell it for a profit. Bob, who has a single threepenny coin, gets thirsty and buys a pint off Joe. Then, after they walk a little further on, Joe gets thirsty and buys a pint from Bob using the same coin. On their journey to the races they proceed to drink the whole barrel dry and earn no profit whatsoever, the single threepenny coin underpinning all the transactions.

The quantity theory of money is a relatively simple bit of mathematics that relates the amount of money in an economy to the level of prices, and therefore to inflation. The relationship is mediated by two different features of the economy, its size – and so the number of transactions – and what economists call the velocity of money.

Velocity is how frequently a dollar, a cowrie shell or anything else is used in transactions, the speed at which it moves through the economy. It is quite a strange idea, emerging from the truism that what something costs is the money that is paid for it. By definition the total amount of spending is always equal to the amount of money and how quickly it is spent.

In Robertson's example, assuming Joe and Bob were using a standard imperial size barrel, then the number of pints costing 3d each would be 288. Overall that's 864d of total spending, but the amount of money changing hands was only ever 3d. The velocity of the threepenny piece is therefore 288 transactions over the course of the afternoon. That the two apparently made it to the races is a miracle.

Suppose there were two barrels instead – effectively doubling the size of this toy economy. So long as the two men kept drinking for the whole afternoon, there would be twice as many transactions and so velocity would double as well. Alternatively, if Bob started with two threepenny coins, doubling the 'money supply' along with the size of the economy, then velocity could stay the same – 288 transactions per threepenny piece – if Bob keeps one of his coins in his pocket, for example.

But if there were an increase in the 'money supply' without a change in the size of the economy there would be two possible outcomes: either velocity would halve or Bob and Joe could charge each other twice as much, raising the price of a beer to sixpence. In other words, inflation. If there is an increase in the amount of money in the economy, without any increase in the number of goods and services for sale or any change in velocity, then inflation will result. So understanding how velocity behaves, whether it is fixed or changeable, is key to working out where inflation comes from.

Understanding velocity means understanding the demand for money. In chapter 2, when we looked at banks, we examined the money supply: how is money created and why. Now we need to think about the demand for money: what do people want money for and what do they do with it? If, when more money is supplied to the economy, most people just hoard it, then velocity will collapse and increasing the money supply will not lead to inflation. But if money 'burns a hole in your pocket', as the idiom goes, and its velocity increases, then inflation will inevitably result.

This is not a question solely of interest to economic theorists. Inflation is at the heart of many social conflicts. Remember *The Wonderful Wizard of Oz* from chapter 3? How American farmers at the start of the twentieth century were harmed by deflation, lowering their incomes relative to their debt? This was not so bad for their bankers who made the loans. Indeed, they often advocated a more tightly controlled supply of money – debtors may be happy for the money they have to repay to be worth less but creditors want to make sure, when they lend, that it keeps its value. Extreme inflation or deflation is in no one's interest but, at the margin, creditors and debtors have a different tolerance for changes in the value of money.

Eventually the farmers' push to leave the gold standard dissipated as more gold mines, especially in South Africa, came on stream. The increase in the supply of gold helped alleviate the deflation. In fact, the US then faced the opposite problem – inflation. It was in this context that an American economist, Irving Fisher, revitalized the quantity theory of money, asking how government could keep prices stable.

Fisher's puritan upbringing – his father was a pastor – and a bout of tuberculosis when he was forty were major influences on his life. He was an advocate of healthy living, promoting vegetarianism and the prohibition of alcohol. In his lifetime he was better known as a health adviser than an economist, rising every day at 7 a.m. for a jog and doing callisthenics before bed: very odd behaviour at the turn of the century.

He asked, in one of his most famous books, *The Purchasing Power of Money*, what would happen to prices if the amount of money in circulation, both currency and bank deposits, was doubled.[16] The answer? Increasing the quantity of money could lead to an increase in trade only if the trade itself was associated with money. In Fisher's time this meant goldsmiths and so on. Doubling the numbers on every banknote could not make anybody more productive or goods arrive out of nowhere.

Neither, in the long run, would it change the speed at which money travelled through the economy, which, Fisher thought, depended on technological and geographical factors like the spread of the railways or how densely populated an area was. In the short run velocity might increase, as people tried to get rid of the new money they had been given, but this would soon settle down once they were back at the level they started with: just increasing the amount of money in circulation should not change the proportion of their wealth people wanted to keep in their bank accounts.

Eventually the effect of the change in money would be 'neutral', only affecting the price level and not the real amount of economic activity going on. Velocity would be based on slowly changing features of the economy,[17] he thought, and an increase in the money supply would inevitably lead to a roughly proportional increase in prices.

Fisher's theory of inflation depends on a 'transactions theory' of currency demand. People want money in order to spend it; as the economy grows and more transactions take place they need more money. The job of whoever controls the money supply (the US did not have a central bank in Fisher's time) is to keep the two growing in tandem. No one wants to hoard money in this economy, they just want to get rid of it as soon as possible and exchange it for goods and services. Increasing the amount of money available just means you spend it faster so you can get more stuff – money burns a hole in your pocket.

The conclusion from Fisher's theory was that the growth rate of the money supply should ideally be matched by the growth in the economy and so the number of transactions. If the amount of money increases by 20 per cent, but production only increases by half that, then the price level must increase, meaning inflation. Central banks, or whoever controls the money supply, need to make sure changes in the money supply match changes in productivity – economic growth – to keep prices under control.

Unless the size of the economy somehow increased in response, growth in the money supply would lead to higher inflation – just like when the ring cowrie shells were imported into West Africa by Adolph Hertz.[18] More shells could not increase the volume of palm oil being produced – palm trees take around four years to bear fruit. Too much money chased too few goods and inflation was the result.

In the century or so prior to the end of the transatlantic slave trade in the early 1800s, the impact of the mass import of cowrie shells on inflation in West Africa is less conclusive, partly due to a paucity of data. If the reports of only moderate annual increases are representative, however, it suggests one of two things happened: either the speed with which cowrie shells were spent fell or the size of the economy increased.

Both are plausible. Cowries were not only used as money, they were also used as decoration and in artworks – just like the Europeans at the time were covering churches, artworks and cutlery in the same gold and silver they used as money. Many shells ended up in hoards, were employed in divination[19] – think about how Europeans were flipping coins to make decisions or tossing them into wishing wells – or used to make jewellery. If more were used for non-monetary purposes it might have been enough to slow their circulation and offset the increase in the money supply.

The alternative is that the number of transactions in the cowrie zone increased. There are two reasonable hypotheses for this. Either the domestic West African economy was expanding – there are some reports of increased internal trade and plantations being established in Africa[20] in the decades before the formal end of the transatlantic slave trade; or the borders of the cowrie zone were pushing outwards, bringing new areas into the currency area and increasing the number of transactions using the shells.

The quantity theory of money can help us make sense of West Africa's Great Inflation but it probably is not the best lens to understand a modern economy. Fisher's 'transactions' theory[21] of currency demand stands in contrast to Keynes' view, which emphasized the precautionary and speculative motives. Keynes argued that one reason why people want money is to have it just in case something goes wrong, even if they never intend to spend it. In effect, his liquidity preference theory argues that the velocity of money is unstable, and that changes in the demand for money ultimately show up in interest rates.[22] The implication of Keynes' theory is that velocity falls in recessions because we are nervous about the future.

Keynes argued that the quantity theory of money, while true (it has to be because of how velocity is defined), was the wrong way to approach monetary matters. Because the future is incalculable, we must think instead about money's price, the interest rate, rather than the total amount of money.[23] For the same money supply there could be very different levels of demand, raising its price and therefore the amount of economic activity that takes place. Money is not neutral but affects the rate of economic growth itself.

The Great Depression eventually cemented Keynes' reputation but it devastated Fisher's.[24] Shortly before the stock market crash of 1929, Fisher, by then a popular commentator on financial matters, had said that stocks had reached a 'permanently high plateau',[25] partly due to the salutary effects of alcohol prohibition on workers' productivity – as you might expect from the health-conscious Fisher.

He recommended investment in the stock market all through what are now seen as the 'bubble years', investing his own money in them too. The crash destroyed his reputation and much of his personal wealth. Most devastatingly, he had bought stocks[26] with borrowed money, and so spent the rest of his life deep in debt and had to rely on his wealthy sister-in-law to bail him out.

The Keynesian revolution in macroeconomics, however, would eventually face its own failure. This was due not to anything Keynes said, but to something he missed out. His *General Theory* lacked a fully fleshed-out theory of the supply side of the economy.[27] Instead Keynes had focused on aggregate demand and, for their model of how the economy would react to this demand, his followers would come to rely on what became known as the Phillips curve.

The Phillips curve

For more than six decades economists have been obsessed with the shape of an imaginary line. The Phillips curve, named after the New Zealand economist Bill Phillips, summarizes a hypothetical relationship between unemployment and inflation.[28] Looking at UK figures from 1861 to 1957, Phillips found there had been a relatively stable relationship between the rate of unemployment and increases in wages: periods of low unemployment were associated with high wage growth and vice versa.

Phillips thought this correlation represented the aggregate labour market. When few workers were unemployed businesses had to raise wages to attract them into jobs, and this, in turn, led to higher consumer prices, since labour is the most important input to production. Businesses would therefore raise their selling prices to try and maintain their profit margins. When there were more unemployed workers, by contrast, wages would not grow as fast and so price growth similarly slowed down.

An increased cost of imports, such as during the American Civil War, was also sometimes enough to increase inflation. Industrial relations – the relative strength of workers and bosses in pay negotiations – could influence growth too. For example, Phillips saw the creation of employers' federations – the bosses' equivalent of a trade union[29] – in the 1890s as contributing to slower increases in wages during that decade. But the most important and overwhelming factor, according to his analysis, was the rate of unemployment – the supply of labour.

A sensible policymaker, using the tools that Keynes supplied, was supposed to be able to pick a point on the Phillips curve.[30] Unemployment too high? Lower interest rates, raise government spending and boost growth. Inflation too high? Do the reverse. The *General Theory* had explained aggregate demand; the Phillips curve promised to provide a model of aggregate supply.[31] With both, the Keynesians believed they could usher in a better world after the poverty of the Great Depression and the horrors of the Second World War.[32] Rather than focusing on keeping the amount of money growing in line with the overall size of the economy, the idea was that monetary policy should focus on keeping the total amount of spending in line with the economy's capacity to meet that demand.

The Phillips curve provided the model of the available capacity in the economy. When there was 'slack', meaning unemployed workers, prices would fall. But when the overall level of demand for goods and services outstripped the capability of the economy to supply them, prices would rise – businesses were having to compete to attract staff. The Keynesians distinguished between two causes of inflation: 'demand pull' of this sort, and 'cost push', when the trade-off between unemployment and inflation shifted thanks to an increase in some other costs, like fuel or imports. This displaced the quantity theory of money as the main means of understanding, and controlling, inflation.

In Europe, at least, the post-war policy paradigm – a coordinated vision of capitalism with high investment and cooperation between unions and bosses – did help deliver record economic growth and near full employment.[33] In France, the years between 1945 to 1975 are still known as *les trente glorieuses*, meaning 'the glorious thirty', and in Germany as the *Wirtschaftswunder* or 'economic miracle'.[34] Employment was high, inequality was low, wages were growing and living standards were steadily rising. Compared to the economic disaster between the wars it was, truly, a glorious time.

Inflation brought the era to an end. In the US and UK, where Keynesianism was dominant, inflation started to steadily increase from around 1 per cent at the start of the 1960s to closer to

6 per cent in the US[35] and around 7 per cent in the UK by the decade's close.[36] Much worse was to come in the 1970s. Today the decade is associated with 'stagflation', referring to simultaneously high inflation and high unemployment. This combination of economic stagnation and inflation was supposedly ruled out by the Phillips curve.[37] The experience of the 1970s was not a trade-off between unemployment and inflation, but both at the same time – in America this is known as its own Great Inflation.

Debates about what caused the problems are still ongoing. For many it was the so-called 'oil shock' when, as punishment for supporting Israel during the Yom Kippur war, Arab oil-producing countries embargoed imports to the US and Europe[38] – this would be 'cost push' inflation in the Keynesian framework, representing non-wage cost increases.

For others, particularly the American economist Milton Friedman, it was the fault of misguided monetary policies.[39]

Milton Friedman was Keynes' inverse, he was similar but reversed. Even their heights were opposite: Keynes was 6 foot and 7 inches tall while Friedman stood at only 5 feet. They were, however, both brilliant and enormously clever, dominating the economic debates of their times. For Keynes that meant the deflationary 1930s, when the Great Depression brought with it falls in wages and prices, and for Friedman it was the stagflation of the 1970s. Like Keynes, Friedman was a public intellectual. As well as providing advice to governments, he presented a ten-part TV series on his views in 1980, while his 1962 book on his libertarian philosophy, *Capitalism and Freedom*, sold over a million copies.[40]

But while Keynes was the doyen of the technocratic liberal left, providing an explanation of why and how the economy should be managed, Friedman has often been the favourite of the free market right with his counterarguments that such government control would usually turn out to be harmful in the end.

For Friedman it was this kind of failure of macroeconomic management that caused the inflation of the 1970s. After president Richard Nixon unpegged the dollar from gold altogether in 1971 – the Bretton Woods system, which we will see in more detail in the next chapter, had come to an end – the currency was unmoored. Its value could fluctuate based on whatever factors the US government chose. Nixon, paranoid at the best of times, wanted the Federal Reserve to target full employment rather than inflation; he believed that overly tight monetary policy and the resulting slowdown in the US economy had cost him the 1960 election against John F. Kennedy.[41]

The Nixon tapes, secret recordings of the president's meetings with officials revealed during the Watergate scandal, showed that the president put considerable personal pressure on the Fed chair Arthur Burns to keep the money supply growing,[42] especially in advance of the 1972 presidential election. Nixon leaked to the press that he was considering expanding the Fed's board to allow him to appoint more pliant members, as well as that Burns had requested a pay rise – all intend to intimidate the central bank into doing exactly what he wanted. In an early meeting with Burns ahead of his Senate confirmation Nixon had openly laughed about the 'myth of the autonomous Fed'.[43]

Those who defend the Fed's actions point to the high interest rates the central bank maintained during the 1970s, but after adjusting for inflation these were quite low, even negative. With inflation running at 11 per cent in 1974,[44] if you saved at an interest rate of 10.5 per cent – the average central bank rate that year – you would get 0.5 per cent less back in terms of your spending power. There was every incentive to spend rather than save.

The mistake that policymakers had made, according to Friedman,[45] was forgetting that money was trust. The dollar was no longer anchored to anything, and those people responsible for negotiating wages – often the trade unions – would need some other way to form their expectations about the future and demand higher wages. The simplest way of predicting what inflation would be tomorrow was to look at what it was today and so higher prices would be incorporated into these expectations and then into trade unions' demands.

Friedman argued in a speech in 1968 that while there may be a temporary trade-off between inflation and unemployment as described by the Phillips curve, there was no such trade-off in the long run.[46] Instead, if unemployment was kept permanently below a 'natural rate' then inflation would continually accelerate, gradually getting out of control as expectations of price growth kept rising.

The problem with the original Phillips curve, he argued, was that it failed to take into account the difference between real and nominal variables. An increase in the money supply could, for a while, produce an increase in employment and nominal wages, but companies would then raise their prices. Eventually inflation would leave the real purchasing power of wages unchanged – workers' incomes would go no further; their pay cheques were higher but prices in the shops were higher too.

Those workers who were tempted to find jobs because of the higher wages would then leave the labour market again. A further increase in money would be needed to attract them back, but now they would expect higher inflation and demand even higher wages to compensate for the fall in the purchasing power of their wages. The pattern would continue with wages and prices spiralling out of control until a sharp deflation and a period of high unemployment was needed to bring inflation back down.

This was neither 'cost push' nor 'demand pull' but a change in inflation expectations feeding off itself.

Central banks could not target any 'real' variables like employment, Friedman argued.[47] The amount of money could not influence the natural rate of unemployment that the economy would reach in equilibrium, when wages and prices are on a stable path reflecting changes in technology and so on. Like Fisher, Friedman believed the world of physical stuff – workers, factories, offices – and the rules and regulations governing an economy could not be changed by increasing the amount of money or lowering its price.

This concept of the 'natural rate' of unemployment (to match a natural rate of interest) would become essential to economic management over the next few decades. The idea was that there was only one rate of unemployment that was consistent with stable inflation – attempts to push the economy beyond this point would lead to accelerating price growth, while holding the economy below it would lead to deflation.[48] Estimating this rate became vital to assessing what monetary policy should be doing.

What's more, this natural rate of unemployment might be far below full employment, for several possible reasons. Workers might not be well-suited to the jobs available, for example, having received the wrong training. Or it could be that some combination of unions, minimum wages and monopolistic competition among companies meant that not everyone who wanted a job at the going wage could find one.

The key to increasing employment, then, was improving these 'supply side' features of the economy rather than using Keynesian demand management. The best that central bankers could do was not targeting a 'real' goal like full employment, but fixing money in terms of a 'nominal' value like prices, inflation or an exchange rate to keep expectations under control.

To understand how this works, think about types of measurement. Historically, measures used in the metric system, like weight, distance or volume, were tied to physical artefacts kept in an underground vault in Paris. Starting in 1889, weight was defined by an object officially known as the international prototype kilogram, but unofficially as *le grand K*.[49] One kilogram meant the weight of this metal block. In 2019 the definition of the kilogram was changed and the International Bureau of Weights and Measures, which manages the metric system, adopted a new standard based on one of the fundamental constants of the universe, as discovered by physicists.

Money is a unit of measure too – remember one of its three functions, a unit of account – but unlike the kilogram, or the metre, it cannot be defined in terms of anything physical. Dollars, for example, only really exist as a shared illusion; there is no concept of value in nature. Neither are there any universal constants we can use to define what a unit of money is worth. So instead central banks try to keep the purchasing power of money, the collective dollar we all imagine in our heads, fixed in terms of some 'nominal anchor', a measure of price.

During the classical gold standard this anchor was a fixed quantity of gold, and one troy ounce of gold cost £4.25; under Bretton Woods, the dollar was fixed at a price of $35 to a troy ounce of gold. For countries that maintain a fixed exchange rate today, like China, the currency is usually kept stable in terms of value proportionate to the dollar. The goal of monetary policy is to preserve this anchor, in the process keeping the purchasing power of money fixed[50] and inflation expectations under control.

For most advanced economies nowadays the anchor is an inflation target. Inflation is measured using a representative basket of goods. Statisticians gather price data on thousands of different items and then weight them according to how much a typical family spends on them. For the Harmonized Index of Consumer Prices, for example – the measure of inflation used by the European Central Bank – food makes up 15 per cent of the basket, hotels and restaurants 10 per cent, clothes 6 per cent and healthcare 5 per cent, among other categories.[51]

You can think of this basket of goods as the monetary equivalent of the international prototype kilogram. Just like the kilogram was defined by the metal weight, the euro is fixed to this basket of goods: an abstract unit of measurement is tied to something else. If the ECB is to keep to its mandate for controlling inflation, the purchasing power of the euro in terms of this basket must fall by at most 2 per cent each year. Imagine a set of scales: on one side is the euro, on the other the basket of goods used to measure inflation, and it is the ECB's job to keep the two balanced.

In the early 1980s, when Milton Friedman's theories were starting to become dominant and politicians were looking for a way to bring inflation down, the anchor that central banks targeted was the quantity of money. Friedman had, shortly before, argued that while the velocity of money was not stable, as Fisher had thought, it did react in fairly predictable ways.[52] In a 1956 article he revived the quantity theory of money,[53] not by treating velocity as constant but by specifying a formula that described the demand for money.

Keynes was right that velocity was not fixed, Friedman argued, but he was wrong to present it as a 'will o' the wisp shifting erratically and unpredictably with every rumour and expectation'. Instead the demand for money – while not as rigid as Fisher thought – did have a relatively stable relationship to changes in other features of the economy. Friedman[54] wrote that the relationship between an increase in the quantity of money and an increase in prices was so predictable and so uniform it was the closest thing that economics had to a law of nature, just like those ones that scientists would eventually be able to use to replace *le grand K*.

The Volcker shock

Economics, as you might have noticed by now, proceeds by failure. The mass unemployment of the Great Depression led Keynes to develop his theories of how to manage the macro-economy. Then the rising inflation of the 1960s and 1970s led Friedman to respond with a restatement of the quantity theory of money. Friedman's theories, known as monetarism, displaced the Keynesian paradigm; and while the Federal Reserve was not replaced with a computer that mechanically increased or decreased the amount of money in the economy, as Friedman suggested at one point,[55] it did adopt money supply targets in its attempt to control inflation.[56]

Friedman's theories, however, would soon fail too. The Fed chair between 1979 and 1987, Paul Volcker, was a giant figure in economics. Both literally – at 6 feet 7 inches he towered over his contemporaries and was nicknamed 'Tall Paul'[57] – and fig-uratively, since his crusade against inflation in the early 1980s created the new economic status quo in which we still live today.[58]

Iran's Islamic Revolution had contributed to rising fears of another spike in inflation, because of worries that it would contribute to higher oil prices,[59] and on 6 October 1979, Volck-er announced the Federal Reserve would now, as Friedman suggested,[60] target the amount of money in the economy. Over the next few years Volcker would run an extremely tight monet-ary policy in the face of often rising unemployment and slowing growth. This bitter medicine brought inflation down from about 13.5 per cent in 1980 to around 3 per cent in 1983.[61]

But this came at a high price: unemployment rose from around 6 per cent to 10 per cent.[62] Angry unemployed builders mailed Volcker planks of wood as a protest. Car dealers sent him the keys to cars they would never sell.[63] The impact of these high interest rates became known as the 'Volcker shock'.

The Fed, however, was not alone in the shift to monetarism. West Germany had been the first to adopt money supply targets in 1975,[64] after the end of Bretton Woods, and its relative success in controlling inflation through the 1970s[65] had provided other central banks with evidence that the policy could work.[66] It also contributed to the difficulties of maintaining Europe's currency snake system of exchange rates we will meet in the next chapter.

Switzerland and Canada followed with their own money supply targeting in 1975, then France and the UK in 1976,[67] although in many of these countries the policy was only half-heartedly followed. After 1979, however, it was embraced with gusto. An intellectual revolution on both sides of the Atlantic helped spread the ideas: monetarism fit with the free market world-view espoused by British prime minister Margaret Thatcher and US president Ronald Reagan,[68] while the public, for its part, was plain fed up with relentless inflation.

On one level these policies were a success. The dragon of inflation was slain, and the world has not repeated the inflation shocks of the 1970s.[69] Where inflation has risen – for example when oil prices spiked in the late 2000s – it has, so far at least, not lead to sustained growth in consumer prices but quickly faded back to a more modest level.[70]

However, the theory behind monetarism was discredited by the experiment. The goal was not achieved in the way that

Friedman, or his followers, had anticipated. The targets for the amount of money were usually missed, or changed.[71] The concept of the money supply, which had seemed so clear at the start, became much murkier: coming up with a coherent taxonomy of money in a modern credit-based economy is a lot harder than delineating between the ring cowrie and the money cowrie.

The biggest problem for the theory was that, at almost the exact moment when Friedman's theories began to inform policy, the velocity of money started to behave differently.[72] New banking systems, ATMs and the growth of credit cards had all changed how people interacted with money. Banks started offering interest rates on current accounts, possibly because this would exclude these deposits from some central banks' monetary supply targets.[73] Economics would once again have to rebuild from failure.[74]

How, then, did the new policies manage to reduce inflation? Some argue the circumstances of the 1970s were so unusual they were not likely to be repeated. Oil prices peaked in 1980 and spent the rest of the decade falling. Others say that it was the adoption of a more confrontational attitude towards the labour unions: workers were not as able to argue for higher wages following legal changes brought in by Reagan and Thatcher that reduced their bargaining power. The mass unemployment that the high interest rates brought about reduced the power of workers further – perhaps the higher unemployment after the 1980s meant there was some permanent 'excess capacity' in the economy.

Monetary targeting might not have worked in one sense, but it did offer central bankers a place to stand and argue back against those who called for looser policy. Michael Mussa, a member of Reagan's council of economic advisers, argued that 'to establish its credibility, the Federal Reserve had to demonstrate its willingness to spill blood, lots of blood, other people's blood'.[75] The unemployment and shuttered factories that accompanied what became known as the 'Volcker shock' convinced workers and investors that the central bank was committed to reducing inflation and helped change expectations. It restored trust in money, even if it did not do so in quite the way Friedman had predicted.

Money supply targets have nevertheless been abandoned. Today central banks use interest rates and their estimates of the Phillips curve to control inflation but, following Milton Friedman, they want to keep the public's expectations of inflation anchored, maintaining the credibility they paid for with 'other people's blood'. The theory goes that if expectations of inflation get out of hand, and the central bank's commitment to keeping it under control at all costs is doubted, then it could set off a 'wage-price spiral'. Workers would demand higher pay, businesses would then raise their prices, and so on, until consumer prices spiralled out of control and a period of high unemployment would be necessary to bring it back down: a second dose of the bitter medicine provided by the Volcker shock.

So, to prevent this, the central banks closely monitor employment and wage growth – as well as surveying the public about their inflation expectations. They begin raising interest rates when they think the labour market is getting 'tight'; in other words when the unemployment rate is low and wage growth may soon start to increase. Achieving full employment has been retired as a macroeconomic goal. Unlike during *les trente glorieuses*, some level of joblessness is permanently tolerated as the cost of keeping inflation stable and inflation expectations anchored.

Cracks have begun to appear in this consensus. Since the 2008 financial crisis the problem central banks have faced is how to generate inflation rather than bring it down. Despite everything they tried to do to lift economies out of their post-crisis malaise – printing money, negative interest rates – the inflation rate barely troubled their targets.

This led many economists to suggest that the Volcker shock went too far. In the attempts to bring inflation under control workers lost too much power: the 1980s were fundamentally a class war and labour lost too much – investors were reassured that their assets would hold their value but workers lost faith that their own living standards would improve as they once did. Indeed, wage growth has been relatively modest in the US and Europe since. This time, some economists argue, rebuilding economies will mean changing how and in whose interests money is managed.

5. What is the power of money?

London is, ceremonially at least, two separate cities. The one in the west, appropriately called Westminster, contains the institutions of formal power: the Houses of Parliament, Buckingham Palace where kings and queens live, and Westminster Abbey where they are crowned. In the east is the City of London: a forest of glass-and-steel skyscrapers playing host to insurance brokers, bankers, lawyers, and all the others who manage money.[1]

This square mile of land, uniquely for a city in Britain, is run by a self-governing corporation.[2] It is a democracy, but an unusual one: those who own property within the City get a vote alongside the residents, as do major workplaces. Most years, for the past eight hundred or so, the Lord Mayor of the City of London, which has fought and negotiated to retain this autonomy against multiple kings,[3] leads a procession to swear an oath of loyalty to the crown in Westminster,[4] a relic of the uneasy compromise between commercial interests and the sovereign.

Outside of ceremony, the world of money cannot be neatly separated from the domain of political power. It was the institutions of the temple and the palace which gave birth to the first money in Mesopotamia.[5] The first coins in Lydia were stamped with a lion, the mark of the king,[6] and the names of many currencies and coins still show this heritage: the Danish krone, meaning 'crown'; the Spanish real, for 'royal'; and British gold sovereigns.

On the other hand, those same kings and queens who reigned in Westminster and whose faces appeared on these coins relied on the bankers in the City. A government that needs to borrow money to finance its spending – and does not want to print more – will depend on the good opinion of its lenders, or it will need to find some other means to take their money against their will. For instance, when Britain's Bank of England was created in 1694 to be a new bank to the government, memories were still fresh of when the previous king, Charles II, just twenty-two years before, had repudiated his debts to the City of London's goldsmiths,[7] the previous bankers to the state.

Conflict between the two has nowadays given way to at least some cooperation. Modern monetary systems are essentially public–private partnerships.[8] Reserves are entirely creations of the state and government debt is the most important form of collateral within the private financial system. Meanwhile banks, which produce the vast majority of the money we use day to day, are private profit-making companies, supervised by the state but with their own agenda. Neither the state nor business has complete control over money – they are in a constant state of give and take.

Every part of this arrangement is controversial. Many left-wingers object to the role of banks in controlling money, believing this power has been undemocratically stolen by businesses who are more interested in making money than promoting the public good. The profit motive encourages risk-taking, and so financial crises. A financial system that depends on speculation is one of the chief reasons why capitalism is unstable, the argument goes.

For a number of right-wingers it is government that is destabilizing, distorting the true value of money and debasing currencies in the name of funding ultimately unsustainable social programmes. Regulation of finance and control of money is a usurpation of adults' basic liberty to enter into any sort of contract they want. Politicians distrustful of postmodern abstraction and social constructivism call for a return to the gold standard, a straitjacket that would rein in big government's spending habits.

It was no accident that a proposed bill to audit the Federal Reserve, the US central bank, was introduced to the Senate by the self-described socialist Bernie Sanders[9] and to the House of Representatives by the libertarian Ron Paul in 2009.[10] Both ends of the political spectrum distrust the way in which money is managed, and for good reason: currency is an enormously powerful tool. If you want to change the world, you probably want to change how money works too.

It is not only at home, however, where the power of money is keenly felt but also internationally: world history is financial history. As different countries have become more and less powerful, so too has their money. This, in turn, allows them to influence the world in new ways – shaping it in line with their interests and their values.

But, because of the importance of private enterprise, a state's control over money is never absolute. In fact, as government control over money becomes a greater burden, banks and financial companies can offer a chance to escape this power. Which is how the City of London, that great capitalist centre, was given a helping hand by the Soviet Union.

At the turn of the twentieth century, when much of the world used the pound sterling – pegged to gold – for trade and international finance, London was the most important financial centre in the world, just as the British Empire was the dominant geopolitical power. British capital was exported everywhere: newly independent European and South American countries would call on London bankers to raise funds; Canadian railway companies would tap British savers; and British-owned companies, which financed themselves by listing on the London stock exchange, would run cattle farms in the US or tea plantations in Sri Lanka.[11]

Two world wars put an end to all that.[12] The UK had to raise vast funds to pay for munitions and food, mostly from the US and the countries of the British Empire. This turned the world's biggest creditor into the world's biggest debtor. The cattle farms and tea plantations were sold off to buy wheat and steel, and instead of exporting domestic funds to build railways and mining operations, British savings went towards repaying war debt. Much of the overseas investment of the previous century was nationalized by new socialist or nationalist governments.[13] London faded as the premier financial centre and the mantle passed to New York.

In 1956, however, the USSR helped revitalize the City. The Hungarian uprising that year had panicked the Soviet leadership. They worried that their suppression of pro-democracy protestors would lead to a backlash from the US, who would freeze the Soviet Union's accounts with American banks.

To escape the regulatory power of its chief rival during the Cold War, the USSR moved some of its dollars to Moscow Narodny Bank,[14] a London-based but originally Russian bank that had incorporated itself as a British company during the 1917 Russian Revolution. Moscow Narodny Bank then lent the balance out via a London merchant bank. Some was taken by a similarly Soviet-owned bank based in Paris called the Banque Commerciale pour l'Europe du Nord. Its handle in the international communication system, Eurbank, gave the name 'eurodollars' to these dollar bank deposits outside the reach of the US authorities.

Eurodollars may have been a communist innovation but they were swiftly embraced by capitalists.[15] London became the centre of the trade in the 1950s and 1960s – although it was often the

London offices of US and Japanese banks that were the biggest players. They were helped along by the Bank of England's[16] permissive attitude towards new financial ideas, which had developed when London was the premier financial centre and persisted even as it played second fiddle to New York.

The rise of the eurodollar market would help re-establish London as an important money market and banking centre,[17] although now it was another country's money offered for sale. Britain was no longer a particularly powerful country itself, but the private companies resident there could provide an outlet for those chafing under the new top dog: the United States. The Federal Reserve's Regulation Q, which fixed the interest rate that banks could pay to depositors, meant that many moved their money to London instead. The US-based banks were then forced to replace this lost funding by borrowing the eurodollars back. Other regulations and taxes gave a further incentive for Americans to keep their money outside their own country.[18]

The creation of the offshore dollar market meant that London would remain an important financial centre but based on the US currency and not so much the pound. Eurobonds – dollar loans sold outside the US – became big business:[19] Belgium borrowed several tens of millions of dollars in London in the early 1960s.[20] This role persisted: for decades dollar loans worldwide were priced using Libor – the London Inter-bank Offered Rate – until its manipulation by the UK-based Barclays bank in the 2010s forced the world to find an alternative.

Eurodollars were so important because of the unique position of the US in the world's financial system.[21] Dollars do a similar job to reserves in a banking system: they were and still are the ultimate means of settlement for international debts, much like gold was during the era of the gold standard. Commodities like oil and copper are priced in dollars, as are much of the world's manufacturing supply chains[22] – a Japanese electronics company buying a semiconductor manufactured in Taiwan may pay in dollars. When the Soviet Union bought and sold commodities in the 1950s it used dollars too.[23]

Critically the dollar is the currency of international finance.[24] The US is the largest – and deepest – financial market in the world. If you want to borrow dollars you can be relatively sure that someone else will want to lend them; it is far harder to find someone to lend you Ethiopian birr or Bulgarian lev. At the end of 2019 there were roughly \$22.6tn of outstanding international debt securities and cross-border loans priced in dollars – equivalent to 26 per cent of the world's total income and half of all international debt. This reinforces the dollar's use in trade: businesses want to transact in a currency that it is easy to borrow.

Many dollars end up in the twilight world of 'offshore', a mix of different legal jurisdictions that offer even more protection from regulatory oversight. Sometimes, through financial engineering, managing to combine the secrecy of Caribbean[25] shell companies with the low corporation tax in Ireland or Luxembourg, or even the 'onshore–offshore' of US states like Delaware, Nevada and Utah that offer relative secrecy for companies registered there. This stateless money is even more free from regulation, taxation or any form of oversight than the original eurodollars.

Because of the dollar's global role, when the first wave of the coronavirus pandemic shut down international trade in 2020 it created a shortage of the US currency.[26] Whenever a US company buys oil or manufactured goods from other countries they send dollars out into the rest of the world. When US tourists fly to Thailand or Mexico they bring dollars with them. Measures taken to stop the spread of the virus also stopped international trade and tourism which, in turn, interrupted the flow of dollars to everyone else in the world.

Businesses and countries still needed dollars to buy things or to repay their dollar debts. But they could no longer access them in the normal way and so the price of dollars in terms of other currencies rocketed[27] as companies and banks tried to hoard the now scarce greenback. Something very similar to a bank run was happening behind closed doors in international financial markets.[28] Poorer countries, which tended to export the now much cheaper commodities, as well as relying more on tourism, were hit the hardest and investors sent vast flows of funds rushing out of them in fear.[29]

Ultimately, this left the Federal Reserve as the lender of last resort to the world economy. The Fed very quickly extended the scope of its pre-existing swap lines – loans between central banks – to the United States' closest allies and most important financial centres: the Bank of Canada, the European Central Bank, the Bank of England, the Bank of Japan and the Swiss National Bank. This was swiftly followed up by loans to the central banks in the next tier of importance, to the US at least: Sweden, Norway, South Korea, Brazil, Australia, Denmark, Mexico, Singapore and New Zealand.[30]

Those who were not US allies, however, were left on their own. When the Federal Reserve had set up similar swap lines during the 2008 financial crisis the list of countries that would get access to dollars was jointly approved by the Treasury and the State Department.[31] Russia and China, for example, were out, while western Europe was in – despite the overwhelming importance of China to the global economy and financial stability. The list in 2020 was very similar to the list in 2008.[32]

Control over the world's reserve currency, which former French president Valéry Giscard d'Estaing famously labelled America's 'exorbitant privilege',[33] affords the US economic benefits – it costs America virtually nothing to produce the dollars for which foreigners sell them real goods and services in exchange – but it also offers political power. Not only can they help allies in times of economic stress, like during the early stages of the coronavirus pandemic, but they can deploy the dollar as a weapon, cutting off countries and individuals from the international financial system.

In 1979, when Iranian students seized the US embassy in Tehran and took its employees hostage, the dollar was one of the most powerful tools that US president Jimmy Carter had in his arsenal.[34] President Carter froze all the assets the Islamic republic had in the US, and even extended this to dollars outside the country's borders. This included eurodollars, which turned out to be far less free of US control than anticipated: most were transferred via banks in New York, under the jurisdiction of the US, and the branches of the American banks may have been based in London but they were still unwilling to go against their government back home.

These powers were used even more aggressively in the 2010s by President Donald Trump. While the UK, France and Germany all wanted to abide by a 2015 agreement with Iran over its nuclear programme, the US's departure from the treaty in 2018[35] meant the deal was effectively dead. It was the position of the dollar that gave the American government this power: the importance of the currency prevented the European nations from being able to conduct an independent foreign policy.

The introduction of US sanctions meant that any banks that used dollars would simply not deal with Iran.[36] European companies who were legally allowed to keep trading and investing in the country stopped completely. They did not want to take the risk of being cut off from the dollar banking system. When Iran did manage to sell oil, it accepted gold as payment to sidestep the sanctions.[37]

The US can use these powers against individuals too. In 2020 Carrie Lam, the chief executive of Hong Kong, revealed that she kept piles of cash around her house.[38] Because of her role in a controversial national security law that would increase the Chinese mainland's control over Hong Kong she was put under sanctions by the US government. This meant no banks would serve her, and like a criminal she was forced into the purely cash economy.

For the US, the world's most powerful country, money is a force multiplier. The importance of the dollar in international finance and trade means that other countries need to think about their access to it when they make strategic decisions. For many other countries – poorer ones in particular – money is experienced very differently: rather than a tool that can be used to achieve what they want, it seems more like a kind of debtors' prison, keeping them trapped in poverty.

Bretton Woods

Although it was already rivalling the British pound between the world wars, the US dollar became the undisputed premier international currency at the same time the country became the world's number-one military power.[39] In 1944, as the Second World War was ending, finance ministers of the victorious Allies met at the Mount Washington Hotel in Bretton Woods, New Hampshire.[40] Their goal was to create a new international financial system, one that would avoid the economic failures between the wars when the straitjacket of the gold standard pushed the world into the Great Depression and, as the Allies saw it, helped fuel the rise of fascism.

Those who were members of what became known as the

Bretton Woods system – the Soviet Union declined to join, aware that the world was already breaking into capitalist and communist blocs – pegged their currencies to the dollar, their value being allowed to fluctuate by about 1 per cent against the US currency. The dollar itself was linked to gold, convertible at a rate of $35 per troy ounce.[41]

If that sounds similar to Keynes' view of what the optimal monetary system would look like from his writings on India, it is no accident. The two most significant figures at the Bretton Woods conference were Harry Dexter White, of the US Treasury, and Keynes, working for the British government.[42]

The two men made a sharp contrast. While the British economist was a dazzling product of the elite English institutions of Eton and Cambridge, a renowned wit and already world famous for his theories, the American was a career civil servant who had come from a modest working-class background in New York state, the youngest son of Lithuanian Jewish émigrés. The world's media at Bretton Woods were obsessed by the celebrity Keynes and his ballerina wife. Even the US Treasury secretary was afraid that Keynes would overshadow him and Harry Dexter White was just the secretary's assistant.

At Bretton Woods, however, Keynes was outmatched. Partly it was that he was playing a bad hand – Britain's war debt to the US and the London government's drive to keep its preferential trading system with its empire gave Keynes little room for manoeuvre. Creditors, like the US, often get to dictate the terms to needy debtors, like the UK. But White was far cleverer than the British gave him credit for. A rhyme going round had it that 'in Washington Lord Halifax once whispered to Lord Keynes, it's true they have the money bags but we have all the brains'.

They had also not counted on White's grit. Little-liked but unanimously considered doggedly intelligent by his colleagues,

White was not swayed in any way by Keynes' high-handed academic manner. The British economist's charm played far better in Cambridge seminars than in an American negotiating room. Keynes often relied on browbeating his opponents with his intellect and ridiculing them with his vituperative wit – techniques that worked far better when demolishing an academic rival than in a negotiation with an important creditor. And so White was the true author of what became known as the Bretton Woods[43] system.

Perhaps history does not remember White as fondly because this author of the new international monetary system, one that aimed to save capitalism from totalitarianism, was also a source for Soviet intelligence. White passed along information about the goings-on at the US Treasury. It is not entirely clear why. His Soviet handler once wondered what had motivated him to bother – White's economic philosophy was very similar to that of the liberal Keynes, though White did express admiration for the Soviet system in private.[44] It may also have been that White saw the Soviet republic as a better potential partner for the US after the Second World War than its other main wartime ally: the imperialist monarchy of Britain.

Either way, the anti-communist tilt in US attitudes that followed the end of the wartime alliance with the Soviets and the advent of the Cold War did irreparable damage to White's legacy. He successfully defended himself at the infamous House Un-American Activities Committee, run by Senator Joseph McCarthy, but died of a heart attack three days later.[45] Nevertheless, the accusations of Soviet espionage were revived half a decade later when President Harry Truman was called in front of the committee to defend his attempted appointment of White as the first ever managing director of the International Monetary Fund.[46]

This fund, devised at the Bretton Woods conference and

reflecting White's and Keynes' ideas of a managed international economic system, still exists today.[47] The IMF was intended to monitor countries and provide finance to those who got into trouble. Its sister organization, the International Bank for Reconstruction and Development, now known as the World Bank, provided loans at favourable rates to poor countries, intended to help their development and pay for investment.

The creation of these institutions would enhance the US's power further: they are both based in Washington, DC, and the US is their largest shareholder and funder, although by tradition the head of the IMF is always a European while the head of the World Bank is an American[48] – a gesture by the Americans perhaps to save embarrassment from having to put forward a Soviet mole to head up the IMF[49] – failure to nominate White, the most prominent candidate, would have only led to further questions. This 'gentlemen's agreement' between the US and Europe may not last much longer as Asia, particularly China, gets richer and more powerful.

It took fifteen years to get the system functioning as intended and even then it only lasted from 1959 until 1971. The big problem was the role of the dollar as the reserve currency. In order to supply sufficient dollars to the rest of the world the US needed to run a current account deficit, buying more imports from other countries than it exported to them.

Originally the US provided the ruined economies of western Europe with currency through the Marshall Aid programme that paid for reconstruction, but over time the US started to run a deficit – exporting dollars in exchange for trade goods. This allowed other countries to get the currency they needed, but it meant the volume of dollars in the rest of the world was gradually increasing. And all of those dollars had to be exchangeable for gold at a rate of $35 per ounce.

Gradually the US became a debtor rather than a creditor: by 1960 there were more dollars abroad than the Federal Reserve[50] could exchange at that price. If the other countries all demanded gold, it would effectively be a run on the US currency; the Fed would not have enough reserves to meet the requests. In 1965 French president Charles de Gaulle – always uncomfortable with the disproportionate power of the US – demanded gold in exchange for France's dollars.[51] On that occasion he was the only one. Meanwhile, US spending on the Vietnam War was building resentment: the overvaluation of the dollar worsened and Europeans did not want to import inflation into their domestic economies in order to finance American belligerence.[52]

While America was, and still is, in debt to the rest of the world this did not mean its power evaporated. As the saying goes: 'If you owe the bank £100, it is your problem. If you owe the bank £100bn it is the bank's problem'. If someone else's debt is a significant part of your wealth then if they become poorer you become poorer too – the City and Westminster are inter-dependent.

As the dollar was the foundation of the Bretton Woods system, actions by the US would reverberate through the system. Other countries' monetary policy had to adapt to what was happening in the US to keep their currencies stable against the dollar.

Starting in 1968, the same year as protesting Parisian students were manning the barricades, the problems became undeniable. The long-foreseen run on the dollar – as well as the British pound, the first line of defence for the dollar as the Americans saw it – came to pass. Germany left the Bretton Woods system first, allowing the Deutschmark to float. Pressure mounted on the US to devalue the dollar. In August 1971, President Richard Nixon did exactly that, allowing the dollar to float. This course of action, Nixon said, was to prevent the US being taken advantage of in international trade.

Bretton Woods was no more, but the two international institutions the system had given birth to – the IMF and the World Bank – are still with us, as is the World Trade Organization, which emerged from an agreement on international trading standards that followed in 1947. The goal behind all these organizations was to prevent a repeat of the disorderly disintegration of the global economic system between the world wars when countries responded to the Great Depression with economic nationalism and trade barriers.[53]

International cooperation, however, did not mean everything would be tranquil, and IMF bailouts remain enormously controversial. When the tensions between borrowers and lenders come to a head, whether it is Westminster and the City, the UK and the US at the Bretton Woods conference, or the IMF and its borrowers, creditors often want the rules to be strict and to get back as much of their money as possible, hopefully at a favourable interest rate.

As conditions of its loans, the fund demands countries follow a package of structural reforms, opening up the domestic economy to international companies and deregulating labour markets. The IMF often forces private creditors to accept that they will not get back all the money they lent, but it also mandates strict austerity programmes, requiring governments to cut back on social spending and raise taxes. Critics suggest the cuts are counterproductive, particularly to health and education; it's hard for poor countries to become more prosperous without healthy and educated workers.

Others suggest that the IMF is just another tool of US foreign policy,[54] helping spread its idea of capitalism and advancing the interests of its financial institutions – ensuring they get paid whatever the human cost. In this reading, it is just one of the many institutions that maintain a system of neocolonialism, with a rich 'global north' extracting wealth from the poor 'global south'. Just as the UK had to accept US demands for the loans, it needed to survive the Second World War, so the IMF's debtors have to do what it says to get the credit they need.

Defenders, meanwhile, point out that the reason the IMF lends to countries is because they are already in trouble: without its loans austerity would have to be even harsher and financial crises even deeper.[55] The organization lends out public money and so needs to offer loans with strings attached in order to maintain good value for those taxpayers who, ultimately, fund its programmes. Some even argue the fund is not harsh enough: it is because countries know they can get a bailout that they get into such trouble in the first place.[56] From this viewpoint the IMF prevents unreliable borrowers from facing the full consequences of their mistakes.

Creditors and debtors

At their core debts are promises: when we take on a debt we make a promise to repay someone, at a given time, the money we borrowed from them. These promises can be made in good faith, we can have every intention of repaying, but events intervene and we are unable to do so, breaking our bond. When that happens, if we are lucky, negotiations follow. If we are unlucky it can be something far worse.

Different societies have had very different attitudes to what ought to happen when these promises are broken. In many societies, such as, historically, the Ashanti of West Africa,[57] or in pre-colonial Cambodia,[58] those who defaulted on debts could become slaves[59] of their creditors. Until 1833 debtors in the US could be imprisoned[60] for failure to repay their debts. In some states, before the American Revolution, bankrupts had their palms branded with a 'T' for thief and would have a nail driven through their ear before it was sliced off.[61]

Today the US is much more understanding, at least to businesses. In some parts of the country, like the tech hub of Silicon Valley, corporate bankruptcy can be seen as a waypoint on the journey to success: going bust means you took risks and only risk-takers make a profit. Businesses owned by former president Donald Trump, including casinos and hotels, went bankrupt six times before voters elected him to their country's highest office.[62]

It is understandable that the law aims to protect creditors from fraud. Asking for a loan with no intention to repay it really is just another way of stealing.[63] But it is also possible that through no fault of your own you are unable to meet your obligations: a farmer who borrows from the bank in expectation of a decent harvest can be ruined by a flood or hurricane. Other cases are more murky. The difference between the over-optimistic entrepreneur who failed to make good on their promise and the charlatan who swindled lenders is often one of perspective.

Debtors' prisons were abandoned partly because of their cruelty but mainly because they were counterproductive: an imprisoned debtor had no way of ever being able to repay their creditors.[64] As the law and finance became more sophisticated, there were more efficient ways of enforcing contracts – secured loans, where the lender can repossess your car or house; credit scoring in which default is permanently recorded and priced into future loans; and the possibility of 'garnishing' wages, where a portion of a worker's income is given straight to their creditors.

Even with these more humane means of enforcing debt contracts, when you cannot repay you still lose control. For an individual that can be devastating: a missed payment can see you lose your house, your family and much else. After a personal bankruptcy it can be almost impossible to get a mortgage or a car loan – credit companies screen for those who have previously been unable to repay their debts and it can take decades to rebuild your reputation as someone who keeps their promises.

For the countries which turn to the IMF it means they lose sovereignty. They lose their ability to decide for themselves what policies they follow, instead having to negotiate and get permission from their creditors. This is still a vast improvement over what has happened to many countries after defaulting on debt. For example, in the 1930s the heavily indebted Newfoundland was pushed by the British into a union with Canada;[65] the customs houses of the Dominican Republic[66] were taken over in the early twentieth century by the US government to ensure debts to a private company were repaid;[67] and, in the middle of the nineteenth century, the French emperor Napoleon III used unpaid debts as a pretext to invade Mexico and try to establish a client state.[68]

While the era of debt contracts enforced by gunboats is long gone, many countries' experience of borrowing is still one of powerlessness. Since Argentina joined the IMF in 1956 it has been in one or another of the fund's various programmes for thirty-four years. The South American country has received, in total, twenty-one bailouts from the IMF, including in 2018 the largest in the history of the fund. Each bailout has left recriminations in its wake – Argentina has had to follow austerity policies to reduce its debt. Losing control of money has frequently meant that Argentina has lost control of its own destiny.

This loss of power has not been limited to the IMF. Private sector borrowers have similarly been able to shape Argentina. The country's 2001 default and the long, drawn-out negotiation with creditors that followed can help illuminate the power that money still holds today to take away a country's ability to decide its own affairs and make it dependent on outsiders.

In the 1990s Argentina was the model student of the 'Washington Consensus'. This was a set of ideas, identified with the political philosophy of neoliberalism, which argued that the basis of prosperity was deregulation, privatization and free-flowing capital. The Washington Consensus got that name because it was advanced by the IMF, the World Bank and the US Treasury, all based in Washington, DC.

The term is controversial as it suggests that the turn to the free market in 1990s Latin America was imposed from the outside, although the region had plenty of its own neoliberals. Including the Argentine finance minister Domingo Cavallo, who in a bid to end the country's regular monetary troubles had pegged its currency to the dollar in 1991, taking away the ability for governments to print more.[69]

Under this scheme the value of the peso was fixed to be exactly the same as the US dollar. The *peso convertible*, as it was known, worked for a time. Inflation fell, international investors trusted the government and financial capital flowed in.[70] The country experienced one of the highest rates of economic growth in Latin America during the 1990s.[71]

Critically for what would come later, the one-to-one equivalence of the peso and dollar meant that many Argentinians, as well as the government, could borrow in dollars while earning in pesos.[72] It was cheaper to borrow the US currency but, so long as the peg was maintained, the two were worth exactly the same. A fall in the value of the peso relative to the dollar, however, would increase the cost of their interest payments while leaving Argentinians' incomes unchanged – that is, if they kept their jobs.

The Brazilian crisis of 1999 dealt a crippling blow to the

convertible peso.[73] Brazil was Argentina's main trading partner, and after it was forced to abandon its own dollar peg due to an economic crisis, Argentina's exporters began to lose competitiveness as the prices of their products rose for Brazilian consumers.[74] The US dollar was rising in value too and Argentina's exports plunged. This all helped push Argentina into a recession.

The country turned to the IMF for help,[75] borrowing $1.6bn in 2000 and then $8.2bn in 2001[76] to help calm investors worried that the country would either be unable to maintain the value of the peso or repay its debts or both. The IMF loans are intended to stop these concerns from becoming self-sustaining – lending in sufficient volumes could head off a financial crisis in the first place.

That time it was not enough. Fears that the government would prevent Argentinians from being able to take their money out of the country led to a bank run. This, in turn, prompted Cavallo to introduce what became known as the *corralito*, meaning a 'little enclosure', on 1 December 2001. In an attempt to protect the value of the peso relative to the US dollar, all bank accounts were frozen for ninety days, and withdrawals were restricted and limited to peso-denominated accounts.

These policies led to an immediate public backlash. Unions declared a general strike and riots spread across the country, leaving dozens of people dead. President Fernando de la Rúa and Cavallo resigned in response but this did nothing to alleviate the shortage of cash. The new interim government instituted what became known as the *corralón*, the 'big enclosure', as they forcibly swapped all dollar bank accounts for pesos and peso-denominated bonds. The Argentinian Great Depression had begun.

Argentina went through five presidents in just ten days. The third, President Rodríguez Saá, announced that Argentina would not be repaying debt it owed to foreigners. He said, to chants of 'Argentina!' from the Argentine National Congress: 'The gravest thing that has happened here is that priority has been given to foreign debt while the state has an internal obligation to its own people.'[77]

It may have started with nationalist chanting but the saga ended in humiliation for Argentina. For the next fifteen years, the country would remain in negotiations with international creditors over this debt. The twists and turns would, in 2012, see an Argentine naval vessel impounded in Ghana and president Cristina Fernández de Kirchner taking private jets around the world for fear that if the presidential jet landed at the wrong airport it would be seized.[78] A country of around 40 million people was acting like a bankrupt hiding from the bailiffs.

The injunction that impounded the ship – ironically named the *Libertad*, meaning 'freedom' – had been issued on behalf of a hedge fund named Elliott Management. Elliott had managed to find a way to sue for the repayment of government debt and seize the few assets[79] that travelled outside of Argentina – since the 1970s the principle of sovereign immunity, that governments cannot be taken to court, has been relaxed in the UK and US,[80] where many government bonds are sold.

Elliott, run by the American billionaire Paul Singer, had purchased the debts at a steep discount – cents on the dollar – after Argentina defaulted and there seemed little prospect of being repaid.[81] The hedge fund's strategy was to sue the country for repayment in full. Ownership of the naval vessel was given to the hedge fund in lieu of money that courts in the US and UK had ruled the South American country owed the fund.[82]

Having a naval ship impounded may be embarrassing, but the real problem was the difficulty Argentina faced in borrowing new funds – losing a court judgment in New York locked it out of the US financial market, the world's most important source of funding, and the government resorted to printing money to finance its deficit.[83] Sovereign default is so painful because the government's failure to borrow can spill over to the private sector,[84] raising the costs for businesses and so on to get funding and provoking a wider economic crisis.[85]

Foreign and domestic lenders are often entwined in the same way as governments and their creditors. While it may be satisfying and politically appealing for politicians to repudiate the debts they owe to foreign billionaires – especially billionaires who have no say in how the country is run or many domestic friends – there are costs to doing so. The City and Westminster may be interdependent but so are the City and Wall Street, America's financial district. And so, in turn, are downtown Buenos Aires and Wall Street.

While governments often want their country to repay its debts as a matter of principle, these incentives were likely one reason why, in 2016, the new president Mauricio Macri would come to terms with these holdouts,[86] including Paul Singer's hedge funds and groups of small Italian investors – Italians had been among the biggest lenders to Argentina after the European country's banks had marketed Argentina's bonds as a savings product. Macri wanted to reform the economy, rescue it from high inflation and normalize its relations with the outside world.

Peace did not last long. In 2018 Argentina had to ask for another IMF bailout, President Macri's attempts to reform the country's economy having come to naught.[87] Argentina would then default in 2020 for the ninth time since its independence from the Spanish empire and enter into renegotiations with creditors[88] – although this time in less acrimonious circumstances, since both sides knew the coronavirus pandemic was beyond anyone's control.

Argentina's persistent inability to pay its own way in the world places it on the other end of a spectrum, alongside many other poor countries, to the US. While the dollar allows the US to project power outside its borders – controlling the actions of both individuals and states – other countries' financial weakness means they must negotiate with not only investors but also international organizations like the IMF and richer countries. What's more, these monetary troubles make a government such as Argentina's weaker and unable to carry out the domestic reforms that could help it grow. Debtors' lack of money often means they also have no power.

The euro

There is just one significant rival to the dollar's international hegemony.[89] The euro – an almost uniquely transnational currency – is the only one with the size and weight in the international economy to work as an alternative.[90] If the world had to coordinate and pick a single money to use for trade and investment, then the euro has a lot to recommend it: it is managed based on a clear set of rules written in international treaties and, for good or ill, the EU is often more reluctant than the US in extending its values beyond its borders.

Perhaps one day China, already in some measures the world's largest economy and one of its biggest creditors, may see its currency, the renminbi or yuan[91] (the terms are used much as the British currency is referred to both as sterling and the pound), become the dominant international money. For the moment, however, it faces an uphill struggle.[92] The renminbi is tightly controlled by the Chinese government and is much harder to borrow internationally than the dollar or euro – a market meltdown in 2015 led the People's Bank of China to clamp down on the offshore market, mainly based in Hong Kong, in a way the US did not do for the eurodollars.[93] Geopolitics play a role too: an increasingly combative relationship between the US and China has led many Western investors to fear that their money will get trapped in the People's Republic.[94] For the moment the renminbi remains firmly in the second tier of international currencies, alongside the Japanese yen, the British pound and the Swiss franc.

There are two main reasons, however, why the euro has so far failed to topple the United States' financial supremacy – first, the bloc has less deep and liquid financial markets.[95] In Europe most financing comes from bank loans, while in the US bond markets matter more.[96] This prevents the euro from being the currency of international finance, as it is far harder to borrow euros than dollars[97] – large loans often require a personal relationship with a bank, while bonds are anonymous and standardized. Companies do not want to make contracts in currencies they might struggle to borrow.

The more fundamental problem for the euro is that the individual countries that make up the eurozone do not particularly trust each other:[98] they do not want to share responsibility for government borrowing. The internal divisions between north and south – the creditors and the debtors – are a source of fragility for the currency. That is, the countries in the north that are more in the position of the US and those in the south that are more like Argentina – although the inequality between eurozone members is nowhere near as large[99] as between the two American nations.

This lack of trust may, in fact, be no different than in other monetary blocs. Perhaps the states of India and the US would be unwilling to help each other if they had the choice. But unlike these other continent-sized monetary unions, the euro is an unfinished revolution:[100] the eurozone has a single currency without a single government. When crisis hits the bloc it launches a sequence of politically fraught summits to try to come to an agreement on what to do,[101] improvising as it goes.

Like the dollar's international dominance, the roots of Europe's single currency go back to the Second World War: western Europe took its first steps towards monetary union during the Bretton Woods period. Between 1950 and 1958 a European Payments Union was set up to help alleviate the war-torn economies' chronic dollar shortage.[102] Instead of having to find US currency to pay for intra-European trade the members would create credits and debits at the EPU. At the end of the month they would clear only the net amount they owed each other with dollars or gold – a very similar system to the hawala international money transfers.

After the collapse of Bretton Woods, the European Economic Community tried its own system of managing exchange rates. The first version was known as the 'currency snake'. The countries belonging to the EEC at the time (and later joined by Denmark, Ireland and the UK) pegged their currencies to each other. Their value compared to the other currencies could fluctuate within a band, like the wriggling of a snake.[103]

Within Europe, Germany informally played the role that the US officially played for the rest of the world.[104] Its currency was the most important one within the bloc and decisions on how to manage the Deutschmark would have repercussions far beyond its borders. But while the supremacy of the dollar was established by US military success, trust in Germany's currency came from a very different source: the reputation of the Bundesbank. The German central bank was seen as a stalwart fighter of inflation.

Many speculate that Germany's attitude to debt is a legacy of its traumatic twentieth-century history.[105] The successive hyper-inflation and deflation of the Weimar Republic are thought to have helped create fertile ground for the rise of the Nazi party.[106] Others think it has roots in the German language, where the words for debt and guilt are virtually identical: analysis of German-speaking cantons in Switzerland find they have higher rates of saving than the French- or Italian-speaking areas.[107]

A 2018 exhibition at the German Museum of History called *Saving: History of a German Virtue* suggested it ultimately comes from nineteenth-century German nationalism.[108] The nationalists agitating for the disparate German-speaking states to unify would call on their fellow citizens to deposit their cash into the new savings banks where it could be channelled into financing the country's industrial transformation. Savings were also seen by these liberal nationalists as a defence against socialism: workers with a little bit of wealth would probably be much less likely to support revolution.

Wherever the attitude to fiscal and monetary discipline came from, it served West Germany well and even became a source of national pride for West Germans.[109] The country's relatively swift recovery compared to other European countries after the Second World War helped cement their faith in national economic institutions. 'Not all Germans believe in God,' quipped European Commission president Jacques Delors in 1991, 'but they all believe in the Bundesbank.'[110]

The problem for all these international monetary systems – whether the euro, Bretton Woods or the snake – was what happened if a country could not clear its debts.[111]

Some countries export more goods and services to others, building up credit in foreign currencies, while others routinely find themselves in deficit and build up debts.

If one country exports more to the rest of the world than it imports, then, to pay for its exports, the trading partners need to borrow from it to make up the difference. These sort of international transactions are known by economists as the balance of payments. At the Bretton Woods conference Keynes had proposed an international clearing union that made the surplus countries partially responsible for adjusting their economic policies; but the US, at the time consistently running trade surpluses, wanted only for the deficit countries to have to become more competitive.[112]

Under both Bretton Woods and the snake system, there were measures the surplus countries could take to prevent deficit countries from having to devalue their currencies and protect them from speculative attacks.[113] The US government, which wanted to shore up the economies of western Europe and Japan as a bulwark against communism during the Cold War, cooperated with foreign governments and central banks to ensure they could get sufficient dollars. In the early days of the Bretton Woods system it was aid from the US – in the form of the Marshall Plan in Europe and the Dodge Line in Japan – that allowed other countries to participate. Eventually formal swap lines were set up as the Federal Reserve agreed to lend dollars to other central banks, partly to stop them demanding gold.[114]

The snake failed much quicker than Bretton Woods. One of the main culprits was a lack of European cooperation.[115] The Bundesbank was, during the late 1970s, too worried about the inflationary consequences to lend new Deutschmarks to help out other members of the system, while others were unwilling to accept the constraints on their own domestic policy that could help the bloc converge economically – chronically weak Britain was forced to leave the snake almost immediately, followed by Italy and then, temporarily, France.

Nevertheless, the European Community was on the road to

economic and monetary union. The snake was replaced by the European Monetary System in the 1980s, then the Exchange Rate Mechanism, and finally by a single currency in 1999: the euro.[116]

The euro may have come about thanks to one of Germany's few remaining geopolitical aims: the desire for reunification.[117] Upon hearing of Chancellor Helmut Kohl's 1989 declaration to combine West and East Germany, the French president François Mitterrand was incensed. The German government had decided to redraw the post-war borders of Europe without consulting its closest ally. While there was never a formal agreement, as its price for French consent to reunification – Mitterrand warned Kohl that Germany would find itself as isolated as it was in 1913 – the French president pushed Germany to stop dragging its feet over the introduction of a single currency.[118]

The typical eurozone country is small and heavily integrated with its neighbours' economies. Having relatively stable exchange rates was helpful to reducing the cost of trading with one another, but the previous attempts to keep Europe's currencies moving in tandem – the snake, the EMS, the ERM and so on – had not worked out. It was hard for the economically weaker countries to keep up with the strength of Germany. The euro was the solution, allowing all eurozone members to share in the Deutschmark and the Bundesbank's success while having a seat at the table. 'Without a common currency we are . . . already subordinate to the Germans' will,' Mitterrand said.[119]

It would, however, take a significant offer to get Germany to give up its national currency. In the words of one French official, 'we may have the nuclear bomb, but the Germans have the Deutschmark'.[120] German reunification would turn out to be the price. Such compromises and negotiations are frequent in the history of the eurozone: the European Central Bank is located in Germany's financial centre, Frankfurt, close to the Bundesbank, but of the four people who have helmed the organization so far, two have been French and none have been German.[121]

When the global economy went into recession after the 2008 financial crisis the old problems of how creditor and debtor countries could get along rose to the surface.[122] One of the advantages of national money is that nations imagine themselves to be a single community and this helps facilitate solidarity – welfare states are usually national.[123] When Texas is in crisis it can count on support from California, and vice versa, because as well as being a currency union the US is a fiscal union: taxes are gathered by the federal government from the more prosperous states and transferred to poorer ones.

European solidarity has often been less reliable. Historically the individual nations of the EU have looked to themselves when they get into trouble rather than to the union. When the deficit countries were facing a debt crisis during the 2010s, the surplus countries were slow to take the necessary steps to bail out their weaker neighbours. Often they relied on unkind national stereotypes: German tabloids depicted Spanish, Portuguese and Greek workers as sleepy, workshy tax dodgers.[124]

A decade later, however, things looked very different during the coronavirus pandemic, when the bloc agreed to borrow and spend as a collective – sharing the risk.[125]

This may have been due to political changes in Germany – Chancellor Angela Merkel, who had, just eight years earlier, said that common eurozone debt would never happen 'as long as I live',[126] was on her way out of office and more concerned with building a legacy than public opinion. It was much harder, too, to blame individual Spaniards and Italians for their countries' economic trouble: the pandemic was obviously a collective problem. So the largest eurozone member swung behind the idea of a common pool of resources to help protect the eurozone economy. In 2020, the twenty-seven members of the EU finally agreed to borrow as a collective to support each other.[127]

The amount was not large but it was highly symbolic, since economic risk was now shared across the bloc. The richer countries would extend solidarity to the poorer ones and transfer money from north to south. Many asked if this was Europe's Hamiltonian moment[128] – named after the point when the American nationalist Alexander Hamilton, after the country's Revolutionary War, had the US federal government adopt the debts of the individual states, creating a single monetary union and binding them into becoming a single country.

That probably goes too far. First, the total amount was small, only about 0.5 per cent of the EU's national income. Second, its design reflected the still unfinished European project: the currency bloc lacked the economic institutions of a finance ministry, a budget or a civil service. Even so, the 'recovery fund', as it was known, could become, or not, the next plank in the development of a fully fledged European state. It could also provide the foundation for the euro to begin to rival the dollar.

In the development of the euro as well as all the other cases looked at in this chapter – the US and eurodollars; Bretton Woods; Argentina and the IMF – those with the money have had enormous power to decide the direction of the world. Chancellor Merkel's decision to respond to the coronavirus by backing common eurozone debt will, no doubt, change the direction of world history.

Often, but not always, these divisions fall along the lines of borrowers and lenders. The differing interests of these two groups, whether inside or outside the country, will play a big role in the next few chapters as we turn to discussions of government borrowing and international finance where the way in which money is managed can redistribute between the two groups. They also, as we have seen in this chapter, can have differing abilities to shape the world according to those interests, especially when the borrowers want to keep borrowing.

The power of money should not be overstated, however. The dollar became the premier international currency because the US was the only major economy that was left standing after the destruction of the Second World War; Argentina lost control because its politics and economy were a mess; Germany decides the direction of the eurozone because it is the most populous and productive country in the bloc. But money is always there in the background, reinforcing these existing hierarchies and as a tool for those who are already powerful to extend their reach even further.

6. Why don't governments just print money?

For Vladimir Ilyich Ulanov, known to history by his pen name Lenin, not repaying Russia's national debt was a matter of principle. Why, he asked, should its citizens have to return money to the mostly French[1] investors who had financed the cossack whip and sword that had kept them oppressed for so long under the tsarist regime? If it had not been for those bondholders, then the Romanov dynasty would have been out of power and the citizens of the Russian Empire free from tyranny maybe thirty years earlier.[2]

So, in 1918, just a few months after the October Revolution that had brought Lenin's Bolshevik party to power, Russia defaulted. Lenin may not have wanted to repay out of principle but it was probably inevitable – the country had only been able to pay its way through the First World War thanks to its allies in the UK and France.[3]

The new communist government, instead of relying on capitalist finance, reached for the printing presses. Initially, after the revolution, the employees of the State Bank went on strike[4] and refused to cooperate with what they saw as nothing but a group of terrorists. A pamphlet from the striking bank workers exhorted the public: 'CITIZENS! The money in the State Bank is yours, the people's money, acquired by your labour, your sweat and blood. CITIZENS! Save the people's property from robbery, and us from violence, and we shall immediately resume work.'[5]

Here – albeit in particularly stark colours – you have a picture of a conflict common to many societies. Governments that want unopposed control over money against the central bankers who, as they see it, want to protect the public's savings. This is ultimately what stops governments from just printing money: they have placed it beyond their control by handing power to central banks. Generally this has been done to put temptation out of reach, as financing government through printing money has often led to hyperinflation.[6]

This is exactly what happened in Russia. Eventually, the Bolsheviks took control of the State Bank. The Cheka, the first version of the Soviet secret police, arrested officials and ransacked apartments until the new regime had all the keys to the bank's safes. The initial resistance overcome, by the time of the default the employees of the renamed People's Bank had little option but to cooperate.[7] In 1920 the central bank was abolished altogether but reestablished the year after as part of the People's Commissariat for Finance.[8]

To pay for the civil war that followed the revolution, the Bolshevik regime then printed vast amounts of both roubles and what they called sovznaks, meaning 'Soviet tokens'.[9] The increase in the quantity of money led to inflation, which reached a rate of more than 7,000 per cent a year by 1922.[10] While some in the communist leadership saw this as a good thing, helping to eradicate capitalist money and usher in a new socialist society, the Kronstadt Rebellion of 1921 persuaded enough[11] that if they could not improve living standards for ordinary Russians the revolution would soon come to the same sort of end as the Romanovs.

The Soviet leadership embraced a degree of economic

orthodoxy.[12] The first step to restoring the stability of the currency was to balance the government budget by raising taxes. Hyperinflations have usually been accompanied by large government deficits[13] – the government spending more than it collects in taxes – and this one was no exception.[14] The second was to create a new currency, in this case known as the chervonetz[15] after an imperial-era gold coin. These initially circulated alongside the sovznaks until the worthless tokens were abolished altogether.

To manage this money, Gosbank, the newly recreated state bank, was given a degree of autonomy. This, the Soviet Union's central bank, was eventually given control over money printing: the chervonetz were in part backed by gold too.[16] Once socialism had achieved its worldwide victory, gold would just be used to build public toilets, Lenin wrote, a fitting monument to the cause of world wars and untold human misery. For the time being, however, 'when you live with wolves you have to howl like a wolf'.[17]

The only constraints on a government's ability to print money are institutional:[18] the independence of central banks and their ability to deny the requests of finance ministries. Usually the political constraints are self-imposed – few would doubt that the murderous Joseph Stalin,[19] Lenin's successor, could force Gosbank to do whatever he wanted. Accepting these institutional constraints, however, helps maintain trust in the value of money. Ideally, this not only prevents too much inflation but also allows governments to finance themselves more cheaply in the long run.[20] Those who lend to them can be reassured that their investments will not be eroded by inflation.

Governments which control their own money supply, meaning those that do not fix the value of their currency to another, or to gold, always have the option of funding their domestic spending by creating more.[21] One of the services that central banks can offer is an overdraft facility, so that when the government needs to pay the wages of teachers, the latest instalment on an aircraft carrier or the interest on its outstanding debt, it can be certain the central bank will always produce the necessary funds.

Normally these facilities lie dormant. The US government, for example, makes sure to keep a balance worth at least five days of spending in its account with the Federal Reserve to stop it going overdrawn.[22] In this way, governments act as if they are unable to print money, and instead borrow it from private investors – usually pension funds, insurance companies, banks and other savers – instead.

Accepting these self-imposed constraints means monetary policy and fiscal policy are the responsibility of separate institutions. The technocrats at the central bank focus on monetary matters and leave the politicians in finance ministries to concentrate on tax and spending.[23]

Since the financial crisis in 2008 these institutional boundaries have been blurred. Central banks have been handing money to governments, albeit not directly. The quantitative easing programmes launched after the crisis involve buying up vast quantities of government debt with newly created central bank reserves.[24] In these schemes central banks are usually prohibited from buying debt in the 'primary market' – where the government initially auctions bonds to investors – but must buy in the secondary one, where the bonds are traded; essentially central banks can buy debt second-hand but not brand new.[25]

These restrictions mean that the money creation process is separated, at least in principle, from the sale of government debt. Bond traders, however, know that the central bank will always be a large buyer in the secondary market and they may be able to quickly flip any bonds they buy in the auctions.[26] QE might not be the same as just handing fresh banknotes to a finance minister, but in practice it works out very similarly.

There are two important differences. The first is motivation. QE is not intended to fund the government but to keep long-term interest rates low.[27] To encourage growth, employment and inflation – some of the signs of a healthy economy – central banks have tried to lower these interest rates and push investors out of relatively safe government debt and into more risky, but potentially productive, investments instead.[28]

The other difference is that central banks receive government bonds in exchange for the reserves. Central banks say this swap is temporary.[29] When the economy has recovered, QE will be unwound as they sell the government's debt back to private investors – this will reduce the amount of reserves in the system, the same way as the quantitative easing process created them. At that point the state will need to borrow money from savers again rather than getting cash from the central bank. Quantitative easing is meant to be a short-term increase in the money supply rather than a permanent one.

The central banks have now been saying that for close to a decade and a half. It will only be possible to tell how temporary quantitative easing was with hindsight. The original loan that established the Bank of England, for example, was only repaid in 1994, three hundred years after the central bank was set up.[30] It did not last forever, but from the perspective of monetary policy it was pretty damn close.

Debt dynamics

Ask anyone in the street what happens when governments begin funding themselves by printing money and they will tell you the exact same thing that happened in Soviet Russia: hyperinflation. The amount of money spirals out of control until it becomes worthless. They might be able to point to examples as well: previous chapters of this book have referenced Weimar Germany, Zimbabwe and Venezuela.[31] While the reality is more complex, they do have something of a point: in all these cases governments funded themselves through printing money rather than through tax, and in all of them the money supply surged. Hyperinflation was the result.

But as we know, that has not happened with quantitative easing. The quantity of reserves in the banking system rocketed but velocity collapsed.[32] There was little to no sign of inflationary pressure in rich countries following the financial crisis. As we saw in chapter 4, the connection between the amount of money and inflation is by no means as clear-cut as it first seems. Sometimes it might lead to inflation but other times it does not.

Most economists now think the amount of unused capacity in the economy – as described by the Phillips curve – as well as expectations of inflation are better predictors of inflationary pressure than the quantity of money. After the 2008 financial crisis there was substantial 'slack' in the labour market and inflation expectations remained 'anchored' at the central bank's targets. This meant the increase in reserves caused by the quantitative easing programmes did not provoke anything like hyperinflation, in fact quite the opposite as most central banks undershot their targets.

Yet at the same time as governments seemingly discovered this magic money tree, they became terrified of the possibility of defaulting on their debt.[33] Government deficits exploded after the 2008 financial crisis thanks to a combination of the collapse in tax revenues and the need to keep spending to stop income falling even further.[34] As it so often is, the increase in deficits on its own was enough to promote panic about the possibility of governments going bankrupt.

The fear of default meant that austerity policies – cutting deficits by reducing spending – were swiftly launched in the 2010s before the global economy had properly recovered.[35] Politicians in the US and across Europe attempted to reduce borrowing from investors by cutting public investment and social welfare programmes and by raising taxes.

In some places these fears came true. For most of the 2010s it was Greece[36] that provided the cautionary tale.[37] In 2009, the recently elected Greek prime minister George Papandreou revealed the country's budget deficit – the difference between what it spent and what it received in tax – was double officially published estimates. According to the rules of the eurozone, member states were limited to borrowing just 3 per cent of their national income a year,[38] but Greece had borrowed an estimated 12.5 per cent in 2009[39] – although at the time it only reported a deficit of 3.7 per cent to Eurostat, the EU's statistics body.[40]

To repay their creditors, governments generally take out new debt. Unlike personal loans, bonds are paid back in a single instalment at the end: a government that borrows £100 at a rate of 5 per cent for ten years has to pay £5 in interest for nine years and then £105 of both the interest and the principal in the final year. This allows finance ministries to 'roll it over': new creditors, or even the existing bondholders, can replace the maturing debt with new bonds. As long as this process goes without a hitch, the only cost for governments to borrow is the interest rate.[41] Unlike people, nations can live forever, so it is possible that they can just roll over the debt eternally, repaying their creditors by borrowing from new ones. You or I cannot get away with this, but governments often can.

Greece could not. Following the revelations that the country had been borrowing much, much more than it had declared, investors started to demand ever higher interest payments to lend to the country. By March 2010, Greece could not afford to raise any new debt to repay its existing lenders[42] – interest would absorb so much of the country's tax revenue there would be nothing left over for the rest of the government's commitments, like pensions or teachers' salaries. Greece was effectively bankrupt[43] and turned to its eurozone partners for the first of three bailouts.[44]

Economic theory has it that government debt is sustainable so long as the interest payments remain an affordable portion of tax revenue.[45] Some part of the state's cash has to go to bondholders every year to service the debt, and without taxing more, borrowing more or printing more money, this leaves less for all those other things the government wants to do, whether waging war or building hospitals.

This, in the final analysis, means that defaulting on the debt is political:[46] at a certain point the public are not going to be satisfied with handing vast amounts of their hard-earned income to usually wealthy investors, even if there are sufficient national resources to pay them. It may be theoretically possible for a government to tax 60 to 70 per cent of national income, but most would struggle to maintain popular support at that level, especially if it was mostly going to bondholders rather than funding public services. These investors, whether domestic or international, have the power to make life difficult for governments, as we saw with Argentina in chapter 5, and so repaying can still be the best option.[47]

In the 1980s the Romanian socialist dictator Nicolae Ceauşescu tested this principle[48] to destruction. In a bid to repay the country's massive foreign debt, he imposed strict austerity measures: raising the price of food and other essentials in the country's central planning system, rationing them and imprisoning anyone caught hoarding. For months at a time the government would ban car driving in order to save petrol, which it would then export to the Western capitalist economies to get the dollars necessary to repay its debt.[49]

Few governments would be able to command popular support in such circumstances and Ceauşescu was no exception. No longer able to build legitimacy by demonstrating that his socialist policies could raise living standards, the dictator relied ever more heavily on his secret police.[50] This was not enough – he was overthrown in a 1989 revolution shortly after the country repaid its debt in full. It is these kind of fears of popular protest that mean many governments make the calculation that the cost of default – including the damage to political and social harmony from the economic fallout – is lower than the alternatives,[51] even if a nation cannot go bankrupt in the same way as a person or company.

While default is always a political calculation, there is a very simple set of mathematical rules, known as debt dynamics, that determine whether the national debt will snowball and become unfeasibly expensive.[52] Crucially, it depends on the interest rate. Every year the government not only has to pay the cost of servicing its existing stock of debt but also of the new borrowing that took place the previous year. This means that if the interest is too high the pace of borrowing will ratchet up, increasing exponentially.[53]

Economic growth on the other hand makes debt much easier to deal with.[54] A nation's productive capacity usually grows over time as the population increases, new technologies are discovered and people, on average, become healthier and better educated, increasing the resources available to the government for the same level of taxation. Debt is normally not linked to inflation, so increases in overall prices raise tax revenue but leave the interest on existing borrowing unchanged.[55]

A government does not need to run a surplus or a balanced budget in order to be solvent in the long term. It just has to run a sufficiently small deficit that inflation and economic growth do most of the work in managing the debt over a very long period of time.

For instance, in 2015 Britain finally paid off its historic debts dating back to 1752.[56] During the eighteenth century most of the country's debts were consols, bonds which never had to be repaid. Investors would lend the government a certain amount of money in exchange for receiving 3 per cent of their investment as income forever; they could even leave the right to receive this guaranteed income to their children. The government, for its part, could pay back the face value of the bonds whenever they wished.

This is one reason why when fortunes are discussed in Jane Austen's *Pride and Prejudice* they are measured in annual amounts.[57] Mr Darcy, a possible suitor for the heroine Elizabeth Bennet, is reputed to enjoy £10,000 a year – a considerable sum and a significant part of his attractiveness. If Lizzie could not find an eligible bachelor, her share of the inheritance from her father would be only £40 a year.[58] Wealth was measured like this because the aristocracy would typically invest their non-property wealth in these consols, receiving a fixed income for life.

These debts – used to finance everything from the Napoleonic Wars to famine relief for Ireland during the 1840s and payments to slave owners following the abolition of slavery in the British

Empire in 1833 – were restructured in 1888 and consolidated into a single debt issue with a 2.5 per cent return by George Goschen, the Anglo-German chancellor of the exchequer.[59]

By 2015, however, the £218m value of this consolidated debt was trivial to the UK government, which collected around half a trillion pounds in total tax revenue that year. With interest rates at a record low after the financial crisis – far below the 2.5 per cent rate it was paying on the debt – it made sense for the government to replace the bonds with new, lower-yielding ones.[60] At the same time, the UK paid off £1.9bn of debt that related to the First World War and £4m of debt that dated back to the infamous South Sea bubble of 1720 – all huge amounts of borrowing at the time but minuscule relative to the overall government budget by 2015, thanks to inflation and economic growth.

This shows how a government does not have to consistently run a balanced budget for its debt to be sustainable. Between 1700 and 2015, the British government ran an average deficit of 2.6 per cent, according to Bank of England data. In only 119 years out of the 315 did it run either a balanced budget or a surplus.[61] So long as a government only borrows a small amount each year, interest rates are low and income growth is high enough, this will be sufficient to keep the debt manageable – growth and inflation do most of the work for us.

The problem for Greece in 2010 was the increase in interest rates. With such steep borrowing costs there was no way that growth or inflation alone could do the work. The writing was on the wall. Greece was bankrupt[62] and had to go to its eurozone partners for a bailout. Whether the Greek government could have avoided that fate or not depends on whether they could have somehow reduced the interest rate they had to pay to private investors.

The widowmaker

Greece is not the most indebted country in the world: that honour belongs to Japan.[63] But while the Japanese government's debt is worth more than twice its national income – 256 per cent in 2020, compared to the 175 per cent that Greece had when it needed a bailout[64] – it has never faced any of the same problems. In fact, predictions of impending doom have come to naught so many times since the early 1990s that financial traders have nicknamed betting against Japanese government bonds the 'widowmaker' trade,[65] because of the number of victims it has claimed.

Japan's debt is so high relative to its national income because the country has had neither economic growth nor inflation for several decades.[66] Ever since a real estate bubble burst in the early 1990s the economy has stagnated. Income per person has risen,[67] partly thanks to a shrinking population, but the overall economy has stayed around the same size, raising the ratio of debt to income. In 1997 Japan's economy was worth ¥534tn, and by 2019 it was worth only ¥554tn – that is total growth, not annual growth, of 3 per cent in two decades, including inflation.[68]

Japan has also run a deficit. The country spends more than it taxes and has done for decades.[69] However, this pattern is not too dissimilar to the US, the UK or France. The key reason why the debt level has surged in Japan, from similar levels in all three countries in the early 1990s,[70] is that after the country's real estate bubble burst Japan has not been able to generate significant growth or inflation.

Despite all of this, Japan's borrowing costs are very low. For the nation to borrow for ten years cost just 0.03 per cent in 2020 – only marginally above zero.[71] Such cheap borrowing means that the country does not struggle to keep servicing its debts

– very little of the tax revenue levied from Japanese citizens has to go to bondholders and instead most goes to paying for public services.[72]

Partly these low rates can be explained by the fact that Japan is an ageing society;[73] its birth rates are among the lowest in the world,[74] and for decades so was its immigration.[75] Its population is shrinking, and older citizens need to make provision for a future when they cannot or do not want to work.

Government debt provides a valuable service for these savers – pension funds, banks and others like having somewhere safe to put their money. You can think of lending to a government like putting your money into a bank account; you do not receive much in interest but you can be relatively certain about getting your money back eventually. As new generations begin to save they will replace the older ones who have stopped saving and started living off their pensions and other assets.[76]

If savers are worried they will not get their money back, however, they can demand a 'risk premium' for lending to the government.[77] It stops being a safe, reliable place to put your money and instead becomes a form of speculation: you are taking risks and, for that reason, you demand a higher reward.

In late 2010, the Greek ten-year bond yield was 15 per cent – meaning they paid around a 9 percentage point premium compared to Germany,[78] widely considered the safest government in the eurozone. In all other respects these two bonds were identical; the premium was solely a measure of the additional risk of lending to the Hellenic republic – the market's view about the probability that the country would be unable to repay.[79]

This can become a self-fulfilling prophecy. Higher risk premiums make it harder for a government to finance itself and the debt dynamics turn from benign to explosive.[80] A credible commitment to repay can then restore a sustainable path by lowering the market's views of the probability of default.[81] This is part of the logic behind the International Monetary Fund – the backing of an institution with sufficient financial firepower should be able to reassure markets that the country will not default and therefore they can safely lend to it at lower interest rates.

This feedback between investors' belief in the likelihood of default and the actual prospect of it coming to pass is why the most acute phase of the eurozone crisis that was brought on by Greece's default was ended with just three words.[82] In a speech in London in 2012, Mario Draghi, the president of the European Central Bank, said he would do 'whatever it takes'[83] to keep the eurozone together. This commitment, backed up with monetary firepower, helped ease market pressure on the most fragile members by restoring trust in their debt.[84] It was eventually followed up with a eurozone quantitative easing programme;[85] but really the promise by Draghi was enough to solve the problem, in the same way as the belief that Greece was in trouble meant that it was.

The support of the central bank is a big reason why Japan has had no similar problem with its government debt. Roughly 45 per cent of the country's outstanding bonds[86] are owned by the Bank of Japan.[87] Through its various programmes the central bank has bought up the vast quantities of the national debt. Really the government owes the money to itself, paying tax receipts to the BoJ, which then sends them right back to the Ministry of Finance.[88]

The Japanese central bank keeps the government's interest rate costs low by means of a policy known as 'yield curve control'.[89] In 2016 the central bank announced that it would peg the interest rate on ten-year Japanese government bonds at zero per cent.[90] This means it has an unlimited commitment to buy and sell the government debt at this level, creating new money when it does – the scale of this commitment means there is never any need to worry about the Japanese finance ministry having insufficient yen to repay its debts.[91]

Effectively this means the Bank of Japan is following a very similar policy as the People's Bank under Lenin. The central bank has committed to provide the government with new money at zero cost; the crucial difference is that this is the central bank's choice and not the government's. In fact, despite having access to free money, reducing spending has often been one of the Japanese government's priorities since the early 1990s real estate bubble burst.[92]

When Greece went bankrupt, the European Central Bank had no similar scheme;[93] it may even have exacerbated the problem. During the early stages of the Greek crisis the ECB made it more expensive for banks to use lower-rated bonds as collateral to borrow reserves.[94] This meant that Greek debt, recently downgraded by the credit rating agencies,[95] was no longer as attractive as an asset for banks and investors. This contributed to raising Greece's borrowing costs.

The ECB waived its requirements for Greece in 2012 as part of the attempt to stabilize the country's financial sector.[96] This would, eventually, help facilitate the return of Greece to the bond markets and allow the country to borrow from investors at affordable rates.[97]

Central banks are meant to be independent from the government. The Bank of Japan's yield curve control policy, according to the central bank, is not designed to keep government borrowing cheap[98] – this is just a side effect of its attempts to raise inflation and economic growth. Instead, according to mainstream economic theory, its interest rate policy should be based on its view of the 'natural rate'.[99] The reason why the Bank of Japan has a policy of yield curve control is because there is no inflation in Japan.

The tricky question is what would happen if inflation ever returned.[100] In those circumstances the Bank of Japan ought to start raising interest rates, easing off the accelerator and increasing the cost of the Japanese government servicing its debt. But with debt-to-national-income ratios of more than 200 per cent, even a small increase in interest rate costs could become problematic for the government – the country could find itself looking more like Greece.

Suppose the BoJ kept rates low instead. In these circumstances Japan could face the same problem. Inflation is a concern for all those savers who rely on government bonds to fund their old age – it reduces the value of the money they have squirrelled away. Default – not getting their money back – is not the only risk facing savers, but also the possibility that the money they receive will not be worth as much as it used to be. What matters, for bondholders, is not the 'nominal' interest rate but the 'real' rate, that is how much they earn after accounting for inflation. Higher inflation expectations could likewise start raising the premium the government is charged[101] and so its interest costs.

Economists sometimes refer to the 'inflation tax'. Because the government borrows in a nominal amount – in yen for Japan and euros for Greece – inflation reduces the real value of the government's debt. It does, however, also reduce the value of other assets denominated in cash terms: a mortgage, a car loan or just cash shoved under a mattress. Higher inflation, then, transfers money from the owners of these assets to the government.

Often governments have relied on something called 'financial repression' to repay their debts. This is when, through various means, a government prevents interest rates from rising higher than inflation. That could mean directly capping the rate on bonds – the government could pass a law saying it was illegal to charge it too much in interest – or it could mandate that banks and pension funds have to own a certain amount of bonds and prevent investors, through capital controls which we will look at in the next chapter, from taking their money abroad. This is effectively a wealth tax and you would be entirely justified in asking whether it really merits being called repression.

The separation of powers between government finance ministries and central banks – one has control over spending and the other has control over money – is intended to protect the public from the government abusing its power to print money:[102] taxing away the value of the public's savings through inflation, just as Europe's kings once reduced the metal content of their currencies to fund their military adventures. Just like a political constitution is intended to protect the public from overweening state power by limiting the power of the sovereign, so too is the monetary constitution designed to keep money safe from our own governments.[103]

The monetary constitution

'We have gold because we cannot trust governments,' said US president Herbert Hoover in 1933,[104] and in its time the gold standard was seen as yet another means to constrain the power of the sovereign over money.[105] Gold is gone, but today central bank independence performs a similar role: reassuring investors and providing a stable framework for the management of money. Money is no longer anchored to precious metal but to the institutional independence of technocrats.[106]

By maintaining this operational independence central banks are supposed to have the necessary power to fight inflation[107] rather than being roped into supporting other agendas – the logic is that in the long run, this should better allow the economy to grow and flourish by providing an environment more conducive to economic activity than if politicians were allowed full control. It guarantees a stable and clear monetary regime, allowing people to plan for the future, whether that means launching a new business, buying a house or saving for a pension.

When the central bank treats debt sustainability as its overriding objective, rather than keeping the value of money stable, it is referred to as fiscal dominance.[108] This is an institutional risk as much as a financial one – we know that Stalin could have overridden the independence of Gosbank and forced it to simply hand more roubles to the People's Commissariat for Finance if he had really wanted to. Our governments could do this too, and at times of war central banks are often made to finance the war effort – during the coronavirus pandemic the British government made the Bank of England activate its overdraft facility in case it was needed.[109]

Perceptions of the independence of the central bank are important too. If you are a wealthy investor lending to a government you might be concerned that the government will take a significant amount of your money through the 'inflation tax'. For that reason you are likely to think about how truly independent the central bank is from political pressure when you decide to lend to a government – many times throughout history central bankers have found that in practice they have little ability to actually resist political pressure.[110]

Hyperinflations do not come about because central banks get economic theory wrong. Instead, the trigger is when some other objective is seen by the political system as much more important than low inflation. The civil war that faced the Soviet Union after the Bolshevik revolution was an existential threat so printing money helped it survive. In Weimar Germany, high rates of inflation turned into hyperinflation after the French occupation of the Ruhr valley: financing the non-violent resistance to this occupation was a higher priority for central bankers and politicians alike than keeping a lid on prices.

Central bank independence, just like the idea of the separation of powers in the US constitution, is contingent on how political operators, including the central bankers themselves, operate.[111] Nixon has not been the only US president to try to pressure the Federal Reserve into doing what he wanted.[112] Donald Trump, for example, frequently used his Twitter feed as a pulpit to encourage the Fed to try a negative interest rate policy, saying on one occasion the US should 'accept the GIFT' of negative interest rates.[113] The current accommodation between the Fed and the Treasury dates from the failed attempts[114] by President Harry Truman to pressure the central bank into keeping money cheap throughout the Korean War.

In early 2021, Turkey's president Recep Tayyip Erdoğan, who has long railed against what he calls the 'interest rate lobby', whom he believes want to see the country weakened through higher rates, fired the central bank president.[115] Only recently appointed, the central bank boss had been trying to tame Turkey's persistent inflation problem. The response of investors was to pull their money from the country, with the lira falling sharply and borrowing costs for the government increasing.[116] Violating the independence of the central bank, in this instance, made borrowing costs more, not less, expensive.

On the other hand, in the same way as a political constitution can be too inflexible and should not be treated as sacred and inviolable but open to change, so too should the monetary constitution. The credibility of central banks has been helpful in some circumstances – like Japan – but in other cases it has been paid for at a high price. The straitjacket of the gold standard helped contribute to the Great Depression and the ECB's determination not to engage in money printing hamstrung much of the currency bloc's response to the financial crisis – a price that ordinary Europeans paid for in job redundancies and wage cuts.

So we should not think that these particular institutional arrangements – hangovers from a different age – are the last word on how we should structure our economies. For instance, some economists – among them a group who advocate what they call Modern Monetary Theory[117] – suggest replacing the central bank's control over the money supply with a 'jobs guarantee'.[118]

MMT, as it is known, calls particular attention to the artificial separation between government spending and money creation, as well as to the fact that the 'inflation tax' is not automatic but mediated, as we saw in chapter 4 with the Phillips curve, by the overall capacity of the economy. Limiting this inflation is the true constraint on a government's ability to spend, rather than running out of the money that they can print themselves.

Under the job guarantee scheme, all workers would qualify for government employment and their wages would be paid for with newly created money.[119] When the economy was doing well, demand for workers in the private sector would increase and so fewer people would take up the guaranteed job and less new money would be created. In this way inflationary pressures would be mitigated without using the threat of unemployment. The economy could be kept at something close to full employment all the time – it would be the composition of jobs, between those on the guarantee and those off it, and not their amount that would change.

In many ways the innovation here is a matter of political economy – who controls money – rather than whether or not governments can fund themselves by printing it.[120] The debate is about where the limits to this process are drawn and whether the power to control money should be taken away from central bankers.

The monetary constitution was largely created in Europe in response to the rising power of the moneyed classes,[121] who had made their money from commerce and were demanding a say in how societies were run. Governments that provided re-assurance that they would pay their debts and not devalue their currency could borrow much more cheaply, giving them an advantage in the continent's wars.

The first central bank was created from the remnants of Stockholms Banco.[122] Sweden's first bank was reconstituted into the Bank of the Estates of the Realm, under the control of the Riksdag of the Estates and, deliberately, not the king[123] so he could not abuse the power to print money. The Riksdag was the Swedish parliament where representatives of the four 'estates' that made up Swedish society – the nobility, the clergy, the burghers and the peasants – would meet in a legislative assembly.[124] The peasants, however, were not given a seat on the bank's board.

The Bank of England, Europe's second central bank, was set up as a private company six years after England's Glorious Revolution in 1688, when the conservative king was replaced with his Dutch brother-in-law William of Orange, who signed the proto-constitution known as the Bill of Rights. The Bank of England fit with the politics of the time, and was, one historian said, a counterbalance on the side of the more liberal Whigs, against the Church which stood behind the conservative Tories.[125] It also helped the new king finance his wars more cheaply.

The origin of these central banks, the monetary constitution, then, emerged from the kind of class conflicts that fuelled Lenin's Bolshevik party's rise to power.[126] But rather than being the workers against the capitalists, in Britain and Sweden the rising middle classes wanted to constrain arbitrary, absolutist monarchies. That included their power over money as well as the other rights – parliamentary representation, habeas corpus and property rights – the bourgeois wanted to secure through written constitutions. And as constitutions limited political power, central banks would limit seignorage, the traditional ability of kings to finance themselves by devaluing the currency, helping provide the stability for a more commercial society. It was no accident that both Sweden and England's central banks came about through the exchange of ideas with the Dutch republic, where the burghers already held sway.

Central banks, today, are independent of governments: presidents and prime ministers are not supposed to tell them what to do beyond their mandates to stabilize the economy and control inflation. This is meant to insulate expert decision-making from political pressure, but it comes at the cost of accountability and democratic control. For critics, particularly those on the left, the result is an institution that while nominally 'politically neutral' actually represents a sort-of technocratic liberalism, protecting the wealthy from the inflation tax and financial repression but indifferent to the suffering that unemployment causes to workers. Not only that, but it is an institution that promotes a certain vision of society while lacking the legitimacy of being elected.

In practice many left-wing governments have stood steadfast behind independent central banks. A robust monetary constitution helped to limit conflict with bondholders – few radical governments preferred a distracting and time-consuming confrontation with investors when they had more pressing priorities for immediate reform.

Much of the attraction of Modern Monetary Theory today is its attempt to shift the balance in economic policymaking towards workers. At present, central bankers use the threat of unemployment to control inflation. Their goal is to stop workers from asking for too much by slowing down the economy when demands for higher wages start to grow louder. Central banks would argue this spares pain in the long run and, as Milton Friedman argued, there is no permanent trade-off between employment and inflation. This, in their view, prevents workers experiencing a repeat of the disinflationary pain of the 1980s.

MMT proponents counter that maintaining permanent unemployment is a political choice, and in the words of one advocate, the economist Stephanie Kelton, central banks assume they have 'the ability to move the economy to its sweet spot, where just the "right" number of people are kept on the sidelines, wanting to work but trapped in unemployment for the sake of keeping prices in check'.[127]

A job guarantee, however, is not necessarily an instrument of working class emancipation[128] either. Guaranteed government jobs do not have a particularly good record on this front and an element of coercion could easily creep into the system. The threat of workhouses and mandatory job placements have often been used by governments to push the unemployed to accept jobs they otherwise would not. Many of the austerity policies that governments launched after the financial crisis were motivated as much by the desire to get what were seen as overly generous social programmes under control as to prevent government default.[129]

A great deal of fiscal policy – tax and spend – is about deciding who has to foot the bill. To many, printing money offers a route out, a means of sidestepping social conflict by creating new, previously unclaimed resources. To some extent that is true: properly run monetary policy can make borrowing cheaper and reduce some of the costs of government spending. But it cannot, as we have seen in this chapter, replace it altogether: central banks and the way they are run are yet another front line in the constant conflict over who gets what and who pays for it.

But for many countries, particularly poorer ones, it is not these internal class conflicts that really matter in terms of who gets what. Instead it is an external conflict – one with foreign countries and foreign investors – that really determines what happens within their economies.

7. Why do countries use different money?

The US dollar has humble origins. Like so many Americans it can trace its roots back to a small town in the old country – in this case, the Czech Republic.[1]

Silver was first mined in the town of Jáchymov over half a millennium ago. Close to the border with Germany, Jáchymov was also known as St Joachimsthal or, in English, St Joachim's Valley, after Jesus's grandfather.[2] This would give the silver coins minted from the town's metal the name *thaler* or, as it would become in English, dollar.

At the start of the sixteenth century Jáchymov was part of the Habsburg Empire. Through skilful marriages the Habsburg dynasty, from their original home in the mountains of Switzerland, had become not only kings of Bohemia, which included the modern-day Czech Republic, but also by the middle of the century emperors of Spain and its possessions in the Americas, as well as the Holy Roman Empire, covering much of central Europe.[3] They had a strong claim to control the first ever empire on which the sun never set.

This chapter is about international economics, how countries relate to one another. It is important to remember that the only real difference between trading with someone in your own country and someone in a foreign country is that you cross a border: you move from one region of political control to another. Often, but not always, that means a different currency will be used.

This is a more recent phenomenon than you might expect. In the heyday of imperialism, precious metal currencies circulated without much concern for borders. Long before the US became a nation, the Habsburg dollars were the first international money,[4] facilitating the spread of trade and bringing most of the world into a single economic system underpinned by silver.

This was partly because the coins were universally seen as high quality and reliable. Previous European coins were hammered, that is they were made by striking a piece of metal held between two dies. This would imprint whatever was on the dies but would also flatten them into an irregular shape, allowing unscrupulous merchants or moneylenders to 'clip' or 'sweat' them, taking small amounts of precious metal off the edges. Over time the value of the coins would then fall.

New minting techniques meant the Habsburg dollars came with a serrated edge, making it easy to check if they had been tampered with. This simple way of providing trust was essential for international trade: whether you were in Mexico, Malaysia or Mali you could be sure the coin had kept its value so long as it had the distinctive edge.

A common currency helps to reduce 'transaction costs'. When businesses trade internationally, they not only have to pay for goods to physically move from one place to another, but also have to negotiate different legal codes, languages and social norms. Using the same money helps get rid of at least one of these costs. Some suggest this was one of the purposes of imperialism: establishing trading posts, client governments and colonies reduced transaction costs for the new trading ventures being created in Europe – they could be assured that the same rules applied abroad as at home.

Why do countries use different money?

So the dollars helped connect the Americas, Africa and Eurasia into a single global economy. Dollars were no longer produced using silver only from Jáchymov, but from any mine, especially the highly productive Mexican and Peruvian mines in Spain's American colonies.[5] The standard unit of Spanish money was a real, meaning 'royal'; the silver dollar had a value of eight reals, also giving them the English name 'pieces of eight',[6] familiar today thanks to the pirates who would steal this treasure from Spanish galleons.

From the port of Acapulco on Mexico's Pacific coast, the silver dollars were exported to the Philippines, and from there Filipino and Chinese traders carried them all around the Pacific rim, especially to China, in exchange for tea, spices and porcelain – all in heavy demand in Europe.[7]

Many Asian and American currencies still in use today trace their lineage back to these pieces of eight:[8] some, like the Singaporean or Hong Kong dollar, wear their heritage for all to see. The Chinese yuan, meanwhile, gets its name from a Mandarin word meaning 'round' after the shape of the dollars that Europeans brought for trade, which were imitated domestically[9] – the Japanese yen has a similar etymology and was created in 1871 as a native version of the Mexican dollar.[10]

When the newly independent United States was looking for a currency it turned to the dominant international money of the time, creating its own 'eagle dollar' modelled after the silver Mexican dollar,[11] which itself remained legal tender in the US until 1857.[12] The eagle dollar became a symbol of the infant republic's self-determination, carrying an image of the goddess of liberty.

While the Mexican version of the silver dollar ruled in the Pacific, in the Mediterranean it was another that dominated and became what is probably the most famous coin ever: the Maria Theresa dollar.[13]

The Habsburg princess Maria Theresa ascended to the Austrian throne aged twenty-three in 1740 – the Spanish and Austrian branches of the family having been divided[14] in the sixteenth century. The silver coins which bore her image were first minted a year later and have been coined ever since; on one side is an image of the empress in a low-cut gown and on the other the doubled-headed Austrian eagle with the Habsburg coat of arms[15] – a symbol of imperial power. That the empress had sixteen children, ten of whom survived to adulthood, helped their spread: the coins were reputed to help with fertility and were incorporated into wedding jewellery as well as dowries.

Partly these dollars owed their popularity to Vienna's café culture.[16] The Habsburg Empire imported vast quantities of coffee from Yemen, which, in the middle of the eighteenth century, had a monopoly on the bean. Coffee was bought with the dollars through dealers in the Ottoman Empire, and from Yemen's ports the coins would make their way into Ethiopia and Sudan, often as payment for slaves, and on through the rest of Africa's trading networks.[17]

The coins were so popular and so important for trade that the empire continued to mint them after the empress herself had died. For the next two centuries every single one of the silver coins would bear the date 1780, the year of Maria Theresa's death. These dollars, bearing the image of a long dead queen of an empire that no longer existed – the invasion of Napoleon brought the Holy Roman Empire to an end in 1806[18] – remained in circulation for centuries, used from Albania to Zanzibar. Other European countries would even coin copies of the Maria Theresa thaler for their own trade with Africa and Arabia, minting them in Birmingham, Brussels, London, Paris, Rome, Utrecht and, while India was part of the British Empire, even Mumbai.[19]

The Maria Theresa thaler eventually suffered the same fate

as the empire that birthed it: brought down by nationalism.[20] In the nineteenth century Europeans were increasingly thinking of themselves as belonging to individual nations, usually circumscribed by language barriers: Italians spoke Italian, Czechs spoke Czech, Hungarians spoke Hungarian and Romanians spoke Romanian. Each of these linguistic groups, at least partly, were part of the multicultural, multinational and multifaith Austro-Hungarian empire.[21]

These nations began to demand self-determination and rise up against their imperial rulers. As each of the countries where nationalism took hold began to free themselves, alongside a flag and a national anthem they would adopt their own currency as a symbol of self-government,[22] like the American eagle dollar. This process was helped along by new technologies – the development of steam powered mints allowed for the creation of huge quantities of copper coins for the lower classes that could likewise carry nationalist symbols.[23] Previously, poorer groups had been neglected; they could not use precious metal coins like silver dollars for everyday transactions.[24]

After its War of Independence in 1821, Mexico, like the US, began to mint its own silver dollars, displaying the Mexican eagle instead of the Pillars of Hercules that represented Spain's dominance of the Americas[25] – a ribbon snaking its way between these pillars is said, by some, to give the $ sign its shape. The Maria Theresa thalers disappeared first from Europe: they ceased to be legal tender in Austria in 1858, although the Viennese mint would continue to strike the coins for trade.[26]

In Arabia and Africa the dollars remained popular for longer. They were withdrawn in Ethiopia in 1945, with the country's stock sent to the US to be melted down into new coins, although their influence has not disappeared: Ethiopia's money is still known as the birr, meaning 'silver' in Amharic. The Maria

Theresa thaler similarly would give its name to several currencies on the Arabian peninsula (the Suadi riyal descends from the Spanish real), remaining one of the most important currencies in the region until it was finally replaced by a national currency in Oman in the 1970s.[27]

Today there are roughly 160 currencies worldwide,[28] according to the database of currency codes maintained by the International Standards Organization,[29] only slightly fewer than the 193 countries recognized by the United Nations.[30] As well as the transnational currencies of the euro and the CFA franc (the currency of several former French colonies in Africa), there is the East Caribbean dollar, and several smaller countries use the same currency as their larger neighbours – the microstate of Liechtenstein uses the Swiss franc, for example, while Vatican City uses the euro.

These are the exceptions. Money nowadays follows national boundaries. Coins like the Maria Theresa thalers or the pieces of eight, which were accepted anywhere without any heed for borders, are mostly a thing of the past.[31]

Even Europe's currencies show this shift from imperial to national money. Much of the continent's historic currencies, like the Italian and Turkish lira, comes from a coin of the Roman Empire, the *libra*. The £ sign for British money is a stylized L for lira. Similarly, the Spanish word for money, *dinero*, comes from the Roman *denarius*, another Roman coin that the contemporary Iraqi and Tunisian dinar descend from. More modern currencies, however, such as the Latvian lats or Lithuanian litas, both adopted after the Baltic states were briefly independent in the early twentieth century, are more likely to get their name directly from the nation they represent. The euro is not named for a unit of weight or a kind of precious metal, but after the community that uses it.

A common currency may make it easier to trade but this is not the only factor to consider. Countries also want to run their own affairs. Having your own money lets you decide how you want to manage it for yourself: you can conduct your own monetary policy as you see fit. No one other than the Austrian mint was meant to print the Maria Theresa thalers, while any country could print more of its own currency.

Ultimately it is not for economic reasons that money now follows borders so closely. It is an expression of a collective identity and the desire for national sovereignty. Modern money is a representation of the 'imagined community' of an individual nation.[32] Its value and power comes not from its metal content, like the silver imperial dollars that underpinned the first age of globalization, but belief in the durability and power of this community.

And as a vehicle for national identity it attracts all the controversy you might expect. For instance, in Northern Ireland the conflict between the mostly Catholic Republicans who identify as Irish and the generally Protestant Unionists who see themselves as British ended up being reflected on money: names of Republican paramilitary organizations were stamped by their supporters onto British pounds, while those of Unionist paramilitaries were stamped over Irish currency[33] – as well as sectarian slurs.

Money's value, nowadays, is based on the economic, legal and political order of an individual nation. Exchange rates – the relative price of currencies in terms of each other – reflect the strength of a particular economy and, for this reason, the sovereignty that countries hoped to gain with their own currencies has often been illusory. Instead of negotiating with transnational empires, it is international investors and their willingness to deploy their capital in a particular country that influences how sovereign a nation truly is.

The balance of payments

In 1993, the South Korean government noticed that the Steven Spielberg-directed dinosaur film *Jurassic Park* had earned as much foreign currency for the US as the east Asian country had earned selling 1.5 million Hyundai cars. This fact, noted in a presidential paper on science and technology, would, via an IMF bailout, lead to Korean pop, food and cinema taking over the world.[34]

To simplify massively, there are two ways of getting another country's currency: earning it by exporting, or borrowing it. In the 1990s South Korea did the latter and borrowed very heavily. Along with many other east Asian countries, which gained the nickname Asian Tigers because of their rapid growth, Korea was running a deficit on what is called the current account.[35] The country was importing more than it was exporting and foreign capital flowed in to finance the difference.

This is why Korea was so keen to find alternative export industries. Instead of borrowing from abroad, making it reliant on the good opinion of international investors, it wanted more autonomy and that meant promoting exports. Backing the arts and entertainment industry had the added advantage for Korea of protecting its cultural, as well as political, independence.

In the previous chapter we looked at how governments fund themselves by borrowing. This creates a potential class conflict between bondholders, taxpayers and users of government services, all with different interests in maintaining spending, raising taxes or defaulting. Borrowing from abroad is different: the country's creditors are no longer a domestic political constituency.[36] Nevertheless, defaulting on 'external debt', as it is known, can still cause all sorts of trouble, especially if the domestic private sector is similarly relying on foreign investors.

Statisticians and economists summarize transactions between

a particular country and the rest of the world in something called the 'balance of payments'.[37] It primarily consists of two parts: the current account, which includes trade, and the financial account, for money. The sum of the two must balance – a current account surplus must be accompanied by a deficit on the financial account and vice versa. The goods a country buys from the rest of the world must be paid for and that means either exporting, borrowing or attracting foreign investment to get hold of foreign currency.

With a big current account deficit, South Korea had to run a financial account surplus. The country had been getting more and more in debt to the rest of the world. Much of this was interbank debt that had to be repaid at short notice, the government had removed restrictions on banks borrowing from abroad in the early 1990s.[38] By 1996 South Korea was borrowing an amount equivalent to 4 per cent of its national income a year. Its foreign currency debts roughly doubled from around $90bn in 1994 to $173bn in 1997.[39]

Both sides of this balance of payments influence the value of a country's currency. If its exports are heavily in demand then the currency ought to rise compared to others, known as appreciation. Similarly, a greater desire to invest in a given country means its exchange rate will be pushed upwards. But when people are keen to sell these financial assets the value of the currency falls, which is known as depreciation. The US dollar, for example, tends to appreciate at times of economic stress as investors move their money to what is perceived as a safe haven[40] – US government bonds are considered to be the least risky asset in the world. If modern money is based on nothing more than the power of a country, then the most powerful country's currency is pretty attractive.

In this way, the demand to invest in Korea's growing economy during the early 1990s helped raise the value of the won.[41] The country was getting richer and investors wanted to share in that growth. This, in turn, made all that foreign currency borrowing cheaper and the cost of living for ordinary Koreans much lower. An appreciating currency raised the value of Koreans' incomes by lowering the cost of imports while leaving interest rates, initially at least, unchanged. Depreciation, however, would bring trouble: companies would struggle to repay international investors with their won, now worth much less.

This is exactly what happened. The trigger for what became known as the Asian financial crisis came when the Thai government was forced to break the baht's peg against the dollar.[42] The Federal Reserve had been raising interest rates throughout the late 1990s, concerned that rising wages in the US would pass through to higher consumer prices. The increase in interest rates tempted those investors who had been lending dollars to the Asian Tigers to bring them back to the US.

Fixing a currency is one way to reduce transaction costs. Investors who want to build a factory in Thailand, for example, do not want the profitability of that investment to depend on shifts in the baht's value. A carmaker or textile producer does not want to inadvertently become a currency trader, having their annual profit determined wholly by foreign exchange markets. To get rid of much of this risk, a company can buy what is called a 'currency swap' from a bank, but they have to pay the bank a fee to do so. It is much cheaper when there are investment flows going both ways. For poorer countries like Thailand, however, the capital usually flows one way.

A fixed currency means that the final item in the balance of payments – changes in the central bank's foreign currency reserves – becomes much more important. To keep the exchange rate stable the central bank has to lean against any moves in the current account or financial account, buying its own currency back if international investors sell. Its ability to do this depends on the stock of foreign currency it has accumulated.

While the Thai central bank could always create more baht, it could not create more dollars. It needed to have a pre-existing store.[43] The outflow of capital from Thailand to the US made the peg much more expensive to maintain.[44] The Thai central bank's reserve of dollars was quickly exhausted and it was forced to break the peg, allowing the baht to fall in value.

A fixed exchange rate is usually incompatible with an inflation target. The exchange rate becomes the new 'nominal anchor' for the currency and the central bank must direct its policy to preserving it. Interest rates can no longer be used as a tool for macroeconomic management: they cannot be cut to stimulate growth during a recession or raised to prevent inflation; instead they are subservient to maintaining the value of the currency. Neither can the central bank work as a lender of last resort by creating more money to help out banks that get in trouble.

A great deal of international economics – how countries interact through trade and finance – is about sovereignty. Countries have to make different choices about how they run their economies and there are inevitable trade-offs. A fixed exchange rate offers stability but it means the country loses the power to choose its own monetary policy, effectively becoming subordinate to the choices made elsewhere. For Thailand it meant the central bank was forced to respond to decisions made by the Federal Reserve in Washington, DC.

International investors have a say too. Much of the money that had arrived in South Korea, and the rest of east Asia, was in the form of so-called 'hot money' flows[45] – speculative funds that travel around the world looking for the best short-term interest rate. There are other ways of funding a current account deficit. Direct investment, when foreign investors take a stake in a company, is thought to be the safest. It tends to stick around, even in a crisis, and brings with it new ideas, technology and management techniques that can help make a country rich.[46]

The 'hot money' did not stick around. After the Thai baht started to fall, investors panicked and capital fled out of Korea too. The value of the won plummeted, making all that foreign currency debt much harder to repay. Higher interest payments meant the country was functionally broke and in 1997 had to go to the IMF, for what was at the time the largest loan the fund had ever made.[47]

Economists have labelled a country's inability to borrow in its own currency 'original sin' – the name comes from the fact it is not due to anything the country itself has done.[48] Many countries – those outside a select group including the US, the UK, the euro area, Switzerland, Japan, Canada and so on – cannot attract enough funding in their own currency and instead must turn to international markets.[49] Without a sufficient quantity of domestic savers – the 'sin' is deeper for smaller countries – or with a government that is not trusted to manage money – weak protections mean investors do not trust the government not to inflate away or otherwise expropriate their savings – they can only borrow cost effectively in a currency they do not control, usually the US dollar.

This creates a currency mismatch, where the government collects taxes in its own currency but needs to pay its creditors in a foreign one. Businesses and banks, for their part, earn revenues in one but have to pay investors in another.[50]

These mismatches are a source of financial instability. They can turn a balance of payments crisis into a financial crisis. When the currency depreciates, borrowers now need to earn more in their own currency to pay their creditors in another country – a drop in the value of the currency can make businesses and other institutions insolvent.[51]

Avoiding this fate was what was at stake in Korea developing a culture industry.[52] The government launched a Cultural Industry Bureau in the early 1990s after the presidential report that looked at *Jurassic Park*. The new South Korean president, Kim Dae-jung, who had taken over after the previous president resigned in disgrace over the IMF loan, not only noted how much the Americans made from Hollywood films but also how much the UK gained from the musicals of London's West End. In fact, during the 1960s, the dollar earnings of *The Beatles* and other 'British invasion' bands helped the UK avoid its own balance of payments crises.[53]

Funding for Korea's Cultural Industry Bureau was increased after the IMF loan, partly to earn more of that all-important foreign currency, but also to protect Korean culture by projecting it outwards in the face of globalization.[54] As part of the conditions for the IMF bailout Korea had to open its economy to the world, facing new cultural pressures as well as economic ones. Up until 1999 Japanese films were banned in Korea, and even after that only those that had won an award at an international film festival could be screened.[55] Animated films remained banned until 2006.

Policies to promote Korean culture have continued under subsequent governments[56] as part of a state-led strategy of development to find new exports. The industries it has spawned, and the Korean cultural wave – known as hallyu[57] – that started with soap operas before moving onto K-pop and Korean cinema, have also helped stimulate demand for Korean food and fashion. Countries that watch Korean TV buy more of the country's other products.

South Korea ended up paying off the IMF loan three years early[58] – this was by no means due only to the efforts to promote the culture industry but also to deep austerity policies. The president, following the announcement of the IMF bailout, told Koreans to prepare for 'bone-carving pain'. The government even encouraged ordinary Koreans to hand over their gold jewellery to be melted down to help repay the loan. The IMF bailout was referred to as Korea's 'second day of shame', the first being the date of Japanese colonization.[59]

Today, however, South Korea is not only regarded as a cultural powerhouse – in 2020 the anti-inequality film *Parasite* won the Oscar for best picture, ironically an example both of the success of the push into alternative export industries[60] and the costs of the accompanying transformation of Korean society the IMF rescue plan provoked – but also as an economic success story, growing its way out of crisis and perhaps, eventually, pushing its way into the small club of rich countries that can avoid 'original sin'. Many, however, wonder if perhaps there was an alternative route into this club, one that depended not on persuading foreigners to buy your goods but taming the forces of international capital.

Controlling capital

'All these countries have spent 40 years trying to build up their economies,' Prime Minister Mahathir Mohamad of Malaysia said in a 1997 speech, but then a 'moron . . . comes along with a lot of money'. Currency trading, he added, should be illegal.

Much of the debate about the Asian financial crisis, at the time at least, was whether it was because of some fundamental problem of the Asian Tigers or an overreaction by financial markets. To some, especially in the US, the financial crisis was caused by the failure of the 'Asian model' of capitalism. Close ties between financial institutions and the government, whether because of out-and-out corruption in some countries, or the state-directed lending that underpinned Korea's developmental model, had led to too many bad credit decisions. The collapse, when it came, just exposed the inefficient and bad lending that had taken place in the boom times.

For others, however, it was the global financial markets that were at fault. Whatever problems the Tigers had, they were not so bad that such a deep crash was inevitable. Instead it was a kind of bank run – the problem was the panic of international investors who pulled their money at the first sign of trouble. The rush for the exit destabilized the system and it would be preventing this, instead of the structural reform packages of the IMF, that would be essential to ending the crisis.

A year after his speech at the World Bank Conference Malaysia's prime minister had the policy to back up his attacks on financial speculators. While South Korea took an orthodox path following the Asian crisis – an IMF loan, austerity and, eventually, growing its way out of the crisis – Malaysia, after initially trying the same, would embark on a different route. In 1998 the country instituted what are known as 'capital controls', erecting a border to keep money out of, or inside, an economy.[61]

Like other borders – to trade or to people – the stated purpose is often to keep those inside safe.[62] Stopping companies borrowing from abroad prevents external vulnerabilities from building up in the first place. Or capital controls can be used – like Malaysia did – as a crisis-fighting measure, making it harder for international investors to take their money out of a country when things get bad.[63]

Sharp reversals in capital flows are known by economists as 'sudden stops',[64] following the joke that it is not speed that kills a dangerous driver or a parachutist whose chute fails but the sudden stop[65] at the end. When capital flows reverse and a country can no longer borrow, it needs to immediately adjust – that means a sharp fall in the exchange rate, and consumers, governments and others are suddenly forced to stop spending, leading to an even deeper recession.[66]

Using capital controls, like Malaysia did, aims to provide a softer landing. Malaysia pegged the value of its currency the ringgit – meaning 'jagged' after the serrated edges of the Mexican silver dollar[67] – at RM3.8 to \$1, and prohibited its export to insulate itself from the financial pressure that would force it to devalue. To prevent capital flows from undermining this peg, Malaysians were unable to take more than RM1,000 out of the country – enforced by random searches at the borders – while foreign investors could not take more than RM10,000 ringgit into or out of the country.[68] Non-Malaysian bank transactions in ringgit needed approval from the central bank. Instead of flowing so easily, now capital needed to find its way through a dam.

Malaysia did not have to turn to the IMF[69] but managed to protect its economy on its own. While South Korea was forced into austerity measures to repay the loan, Malaysia's government managed to spend more to support the recovery and the central bank could cut interest rates. Despite this very different approach Malaysia did about as well as the other Asian Tigers in its recovery from the financial crisis, and predictions of impending doom from many economists – some warned that the controls would only exacerbate capital flight by sending a damaging signal to investors – came to naught.[70]

Historically many economists have argued against capital controls.[71] In theory, capital is meant to flow to where it is the most useful. Countries with abundant savings can send them to countries going through economic transformation in a mutually beneficial transfer, earning a higher return for themselves but also funding the development of poorer regions.[72] The Asian Tigers were poor countries that were growing, and the influx of foreign capital helped create jobs, finance new factories and lift millions out of poverty. Stopping it would have left many workers mired in much worse conditions.

Since the Asian financial crisis, attitudes to capital controls among economists are more ambivalent:[73] in 2012 the IMF even suggested that they could play a part in managing balance of payments crises. The theory[74] goes that if footloose international capital can be constrained then there will be less potential for the kind of sudden destabilizing outflow that South Korea and Malaysia experienced.

The capital flight from Korea in 1997 forced the value of the won down, raising the cost of servicing the country's external debt and pushing its banking sector into bankruptcy. This did unnecessary damage.[75] Like during a bank run or a fire sale of assets – the sudden rush out the door amplifies the damage as everyone tries to be the first out. If everyone could just calmly make their way to the exit, it would benefit everyone, or at least so the argument goes.[76]

The empirical evidence on the overall effectiveness of capital controls, however, is mixed.[77] They can tilt borrowing towards more long-term forms and reduce the probability of a crisis, but they also raise financing costs, especially for smaller companies.[78] It is not clear if this trade-off is completely worth while, but it is obvious that capital controls do not carry such high costs as many economists predicted when Malaysia introduced them.[79]

Part of the problem may be that a country's decision to use these policies is not independent of the overall economic context,[80] muddying the data used to assess their effectiveness. Countries, like people, are often not aware of their vulnerabilities while they are riding high: we only get a clear view of the danger with hindsight. Similarly, it is often only after a crisis that countries are able to see the risks they were taking.[81]

Capital controls are therefore lifted when the economy is bubbling along nicely.[82] Politicians convince themselves that the trade winds they are enjoying will be here forever, the current boom is due to the wisdom of their policies, and the world is finally realizing the unique genius of their country. In those circumstances it is often hard for people to fight back against further liberalization – warning about risks while everyone else is making money can make you sound bitter and resentful.

At times of crisis, on the other hand, a backlash can build against international investors. Borders are put up when people feel scared and can come with a side order of xenophobia and conspiracism. This is the flip side of nations being 'imagined communities': those who are not part of the community can be aggressively excluded. In May 1998 the economic devastation caused by the Asian financial crisis contributed to riots in Indonesia. The main targets of the mob were the ethnic Chinese minority, an estimated 1,200 of whom died in riots.[83]

For many, the purpose of capital controls is not economic but political. The point of establishing a border is to allow those within it to choose their own destiny. The European Union's regulatory border, for example, keeps out US food that is produced to different standards. This allows the EU some independence in allowing its values to influence the shape of its economy; without a border it would simply have to accept whatever food standards the US chose.[84] Capital controls may similarly allow a country to manage the macroeconomy as it wishes: choosing its own interest and exchange rates, instead of having to rely on the good opinion of international investors,[85] and perhaps even raising taxes and nationalizing companies without risking investors pulling their money out of the country.

Countries, according to economic theory, can pick two out of the following three items: the free flow of capital, an independent monetary policy and a fixed exchange rate.[86] This is known by economists as the impossible trinity.[87] With a fixed exchange rate and no capital controls, the central bank must subordinate its monetary policy to defending the currency peg from speculative attack – when international investors bet they can exhaust the central bank's reserves of foreign currency and the peg will have to be broken. Restricting capital flows provides some protection. By controlling the movement of money into and out of the country with capital controls, interest rates can then be used to fight inflation or combat unemployment[88] instead, while maintaining a currency peg.

During the Bretton Woods era, this is exactly what the member countries chose.[89] Exchange rates were fixed against one another and central banks used their monetary policy to combat downturns in the domestic economy.[90] Capital controls were used to ensure that the system of fixed currencies could be maintained even as central banks focused on decreasing unemployment.

On the other hand, capital controls can not only stop potentially fruitful investment into a country – the more valuable foreign direct investment as well as the speculative hot money flows – but they also require restrictions on people's freedom. In the Bretton Woods period, for example, Britons could only take £100 out of the country a year and emigrants could only bring £5,000 of assets out the country with them.[91]

Many of those who were most concerned to tear down these barriers wanted to do so because they believed it was vital that owners of private property could take their money out of the reaches of a grasping government. In the words of one writer on the subject, they believed in a 'human right to capital flight', allowing them to escape from so-called 'financial repression'.[92]

Nevertheless, this freedom should not be easily dismissed. It is not only tax dodgers, financial speculators and tourists who want to take money out of the country, but also those fleeing genuine persecution and repression – borders can keep people trapped in, as well keeping others out. For example, Nazi Germany used capital controls as means of discriminating against the Jewish minority: would-be emigrants wanting to flee religious persecution had to pay a 'flight tax' allowing the government to seize their assets.[93] Internationally isolated and desperate for cash to pay for rearmament, Germany used every means it could to get foreign currency.

Other countries, meanwhile, would not accept the refugees. Partly because of their own anti-Semitic prejudices, but also because of financial concerns – how would the incomers support themselves in economies still devastated by the Great Depression if Germany was unwilling to allow refugees to take money with them? In 1938 Hjalmar Schacht, president of the Reichsbank, the Nazi central bank, attempted to use the assets of Germany and Austria's Jewish population as backing to secure a foreign currency loan to pay for their forced repatriation. The loan failed: it was supposed to be borrowed from a global network of Jewish bankers who only ever existed in the racist imagination of the regime.[94]

Capital controls today may not even work very well, only capturing those unable to get around them[95] by moving their money offshore. This is why, according to some writers,[96] it was the development of the eurodollar market in London that ultimately helped bring down the Bretton Woods era of capital controls. Offshore financial markets had become so large that governments could not have the autonomy they wished either way – there was ultimately more sovereignty to be had in a flexible exchange rate or allying with others in a single currency like the euro.

Using the same currency as other countries makes international trade much easier, but it also stops the 'imagined community' of a nation from controlling monetary policy for itself. Different nations use different currencies because they want to have this control over their own destinies; even this, however, is never absolute, and in doing so they must constantly negotiate with the forces of international capital. Poorer countries feel these trade-offs the most intensely: without much in the way of domestic finance they must borrow from elsewhere. Perhaps the best way for a country to use its own money to enhance its sovereignty, then, may be to try to get richer.

8. Can more money make us rich?

'What is the wealth of nations?' asked Adam Smith in the book that became the founding text of modern economics. His answer was that it was not gold, silver or any other kind of treasure, but the ability of the nation to produce the things that it wants.[1] Today we call this gross domestic product – the sum total of everything a country produces in a year, equivalent to national income.[2]

Smith was born in the Scottish port town of Kirkcaldy in 1723. Ironically, for a man who is most famous for his arguments that there should not be any barriers to international trade, he was the son of a customs officer. Smith's father, however, died shortly before he was born, leaving his mother to raise him alone. We do not know many details of Smith's personal life. He was intensely private and tried to avoid any attention from journalists – he had his papers burned after his death. He never married and died six years after his mother, with whom he lived for much of his life. He said of her that she 'certainly loved me more than any other person ever did or ever will love me'.[3]

At the time of Smith's birth Scotland was a poor and religiously conservative country. It had just entered into a union with its southern neighbour, England, in 1707 after what was a tumultuous century of civil and religious war in the two countries, as well as their neighbour Ireland. The next century, however, would be a golden age for Scotland: Smith was a key figure in the country's enlightenment, alongside his close friend and fellow philosopher David Hume. As well as *The Wealth of Nations*, Smith wrote the philosophical work *The Theory of Moral Sentiments*, arguing ethics emerges naturally from humans, thanks to our empathy and desire to be well-regarded.

He would, after resigning from a position as professor at the University of Glasgow and touring Europe as a private tutor instead, become known as the premier chronicler of the new kind of commercial society emerging in his time. As well as the intellectual effervescence of the Scottish enlightenment, Britain would soon start the most important event in economic history: the industrial revolution.

The industrial revolution was the fundamental transformation in how economies operated. It is no exaggeration to say that before the revolution, which has no definitive start or end date, the world was poor and after it started to become rich. It was the first sustained rise in incomes and would, eventually, lead to a dramatic increase in living standards as societies learned how to produce more and more kinds of goods at lower cost.

It transformed everything: what we ate, how we lived and how we worked. Rather than the predominantly home-based production of European peasant life – Scots, say, might farm sheep themselves, shear their coats and then spin their wool into cloth at home – textile workers would now be gathered into factories and operate newly-invented mechanical looms. What's more, the revolution was all powered not only by human muscle but fossil fuel: Britain, at the time, was rich in coal that could be used to power the looms or provide the raw material for steel furnaces.

The ongoing debate about what caused this sudden rise in productivity is complex, controversial and nuanced.

Economic historians have often split into different camps, stressing different factors. Some focus on the political and institutional changes in Britain, or how the enlightenment led to a different intellectual climate and attitude towards research, allowing for improvements in technology.

Others look at European imperialism and whether the expansion of the British Empire created new export markets for the output of the factories or financed the investment within them.

Smith, for his part, was clear: imperialism was a waste as well as a crime. Not only did it require those in Britain to pay for the defence of the colonies through higher taxes, but it diverted investment from where it could be most productive – colonial monopolies for companies like the East India Company were an act of theft, forcing consumers to pay more solely to enrich their few shareholders. The investments could be better used at home, funding industrialization. 'Under the present system of management, therefore, Great Britain derives nothing but loss from the dominion which she assumes over her colonies,' he wrote.

Smith's focus on productivity as the foundation of national wealth was a relatively new idea. At the time he was writing – *The Wealth of Nations* was published in 1776, the same year as the US Declaration of Independence – a group nowadays known as the mercantilists dominated economic thinking.[4] These theorists believed that a country should gather as much precious metal as it could by restricting imports and encouraging exports. Gold and silver, like the dollars from the previous chapter, would flow in to pay for these exports while little would flow out to pay for imports. The country would then, thanks to this trade surplus, gradually amass a hoard of treasure.

Stores of precious metal, the main money at the time, were meant to make a country stronger: they were essential for war. Equipment and soldiers needed to be paid for and that, ultimately, meant gold.[5] These ideas were the pre-Smithian economic logic supporting European imperialism. Indeed, the purpose of having colonies was to deliver as much precious metal to the metropole as possible,[6] increasing their power relative to potential rivals. Colonies were forced to buy exports from the motherland ensuring precious metal flowed out to their imperial master.

Three years before Smith's book was published, these ideas had led settlers in Britain's thirteen lower colonies in North America to tip crates of tea into Boston Harbour,[7] helping spark the American Revolution. Mercantilism had inspired a whole set of different restrictions on international trade, known as the Navigation Acts; these aimed to ensure that Britain benefited as much as possible from trade with its colonies, while its geo-political rivals – the Dutch, French and so on – were excluded.

To try to curtail smuggling and help out the financially strug-gling British East India Company – most of the tea in the North American colonies was smuggled in from its Dutch competitor – the company was given an exemption from the Navigation Acts. This threatened to ruin the colonial smugglers and tea importers who objected to the effective monopoly the exemption would grant to the East Indian Company.[8] Along with political objections to taxes, this persuaded the revolutionaries in Boston to destroy the shipments of tea arriving in the harbour in protest.

But these policies, according to Smith, were all misguided anyway. Gold and silver were just tokens that represented the real source of value, labour. He wrote: 'It was not by gold or by silver, but by labour, that all the wealth of the world was origin-ally purchased; and its value, to those who possess it, and who want to exchange it for some new productions, is precisely equal to the quantity of labour which it can enable them to purchase or command.'[9]

When a shoemaker buys a coat, they are really exchanging

the work they did to make shoes for the work a coat maker did to make coats, according to Adam Smith. Money solely works to facilitate this exchange. Improvements in the productivity of our labour then allow more to be exchanged – more coats can be made if the tailor invests in new machines, for example, or maybe takes evening classes to learn some new techniques. This investment in coat-making productivity then allows them to get more shoes. Differences of this kind are ultimately why some nations are richer than others, not accumulating treasure.[10]

Importing, rather than making a country poorer, can make it richer: it increases the amount it can get from what it produces.[11] As an example, Smith compared his native Scotland with France. Scotland could produce wine with sufficient quantities of greenhouses, but this would use resources that could be better employed elsewhere. He estimated that around thirty times as much labour and capital would be needed to produce one decent bottle of wine in Scotland than in Burgundy.[12] Instead Scotland should focus on what it is good at – whisky, say – then just swap the Scotch for the Burgundian wine, allowing it to get more wine than if it had tried to grow and ferment the grapes for itself.

Countries, for this reason, should not raise barriers to trade. The division of labour – separating production into many different smaller tasks, as was happening in Britain's factories – enhanced the productivity of all involved. Imagine if you had to make everything you rely on for yourself – building your own house, making your own clothes – it would take you much longer and you would end up with a lot less than by exchanging the work you are good at for the work others are good at. For Smith, the same logic worked between countries: trade could make two countries richer by allowing them to swap some of their productive power.

This productivity, too, rather than gold and silver, is what allowed countries to win wars. 'Fleets and armies are maintained, not with gold and silver, but with consumable goods,' Smith wrote. In other words, an army marches on its stomach. If a country wants to fund an army it needs either to produce the food and munitions itself or trade with some other country for them – and that means swapping the things it produces for them. Ultimately, the more productive a country is, not the more gold in its coffers, the stronger its military should be.

In correcting the error of the mercantilists, however, Adam Smith introduced a new one into the annals of economic thought: that money does not matter. The idea, shared by many modern economists, is that money is merely a 'veil' over barter.[13] When we buy or sell things, we are really swapping goods for goods and money is just the medium by which this happens – money cannot affect prosperity, which ultimately depends on the productivity with which we can create new things to exchange with one another.

In the jargon of economics this is called the 'neutrality' of money, and nowadays is usually thought by mainstream economists to be true only in the long run.[14] This is one of the most controversial ideas in economics; the interaction between finance, money and production is at the heart of debates about what makes industrial society so unstable – why it seems so prone to self-generating crises. Pre-industrial agrarian societies had their recessions too, but these could be explained by outside factors: a drought, a crop blight and so on, but with the industrial revolution came a 'business cycle'.

Today, economists who work within the mainstream neoclassical tradition tend to think money matters in the short term when it can influence the fluctuations of the economy and produce this cycle, with consequences for the immediate prosperity of various groups.[15] In the longer term productivity – in the largest possible sense – is thought to determine how wealthy we are. This depends on things like technology, preferences and institutions – the equipment available to a country, how well educated the populace is, and how efficiently trade and production are carried out.[16] These deep, fundamental features of a society, the factors that were changing during the industrial revolution, determine how rich it is, and money is irrelevant – just an arbitrary symbol. More money, according to this argument, cannot truly make us rich.

The price of information

Without a competitive market, money does not work very well. This was obvious in the centrally planned economy of the Soviet Union.[17] Lenin had nationalized all the banks almost immediately after coming to power. They were the capitalist equivalent of a planning ministry, he thought, assigning funding to different economic activities. 'The big banks are the state apparatus which we need to bring about socialism and which we take ready made from capitalism,' he wrote on the eve of the October Revolution.

As the single bank for the Soviet Union,[18] Gosbank took over this role. Every organization and citizen was meant to have an account with Gosbank.[19] If a branch of the state-owned steel company needed to buy something from the state-owned coal company, funds would be transferred between their accounts at Gosbank – the bank's balance sheet was meant to be a single ledger recording all the transactions in the Soviet Union, a monetary mirror of the plans made by Gosplan. This was known as 'control by the rouble':[20] companies had to follow the plan in order to get the money they needed.

But the plans were often incoherent,[21] so companies had no way of actually completing them as they were instructed. Some resorted to barter to get the goods they needed, unable to unlock the money required but fearful of telling officials. The car-making company, not able to pay for enough steel, might trade some of its excess rubber with another company to get the steel it needed.[22] Or it might trade rubber for knives and then melt them down to get the steel – actually destroying whatever value had been created by the workers who had made the knives.

A disordered monetary system made the citizens of the Soviet Union poorer, and this was poorer in the sense that Adam Smith meant: less productive. Money did not work as a medium of account. In this centrally planned economy, it failed to do this job properly: prices did not reflect either the work put into producing something, or how much it was desired by consumers. It was as if it was cheaper to produce wine in Scotland than France, misdirecting labour and capital away from where it was best utilized.

A cartoon in the Soviet satirical magazine *Krokodil*[23] summed up the problem: a single giant nail hangs suspended by a crane above two workers. One asks, 'Who needs a nail that big?'; the other, possibly his boss, replies, 'That's besides the point. The main thing is we've immediately fulfilled the entire plan for nails . . .' The joke was based on a real problem: the value of a factory's output was often determined not by price but by weight. Some factories avoided adopting a more efficient production process precisely because it would make a lighter product.[24] Money could not provide any information about what sort of things should happen in an economy.

It was exactly this kind of failure of central planning that made the Austria-born economist Friedrich Hayek believe that while money could not make us richer, it very much could, and often did, make us poorer.[25] Hayek was a political philosopher as well as an economist and one of the chief critics of Keynes during his lifetime,[26] although the two men would become personal friends, at one point serving together as air raid wardens in Cambridge during the Second World War. The debates between Keynes and Hayek – while often obscure and arcane – still resonate today. In 2010 a YouTube video made by fans of Hayek turned their arguments over the origins of the business cycle into a rap battle. The video went viral – at least by the standards of economics.

It was at the instigation of Lionel Robbins, head of the economics department at the London School of Economics and a long-time opponent of Keynes, that Hayek moved to London in the 1930s. Hayek's brilliance was partly intended to take Keynes down a peg or two,[27] raising the profile of the LSE against the University of Cambridge, where Keynes held sway. Hayek had been an admirer of the British economist as a young man; Hayek had worked with the Austrian government on some of the details of the Treaty of Saint-Germain, negotiating their surrender at the end of the First World War. Keynes' stock was high in the German-speaking world because of his warning to the victorious Allies about the vindictiveness of reparations claims.[28] The two men, however, disagreed intensely about economics.

Like Keynes, Hayek was interested in money and why recessions happen, but he saw them as coming not from the failure of the market economy but the policymakers who tried to control it.[29] In his typically combative 1974 Nobel Prize victory speech he blamed economists for the 1970s stagflation, saying the profession had 'made a mess of things'.[30] Margaret Thatcher, the right-wing British prime minister, is reported to have once slammed one of his philosophical works on the table, exclaiming 'this is what we believe'.[31]

Hayek used the term 'the neutrality of money' in a different way to the economists who came after him. For Hayek, 'neutrality' was not a description of how an economy worked but an ideal to aspire to.[32] The best outcome would be for money not to influence the kind of activity that would take place, instead letting competition and prices do their work. He was not, primarily, worried about the effect of money on the general level of prices – inflation – but on relative prices, the way in which goods were valued against one another. This was the method by which the market, unlike central planning, could work out what needed to be produced.

Hayek spent much of his career arguing against state management of the economy.[33] His objection was not only economic but also political: he believed this was the first step on a road that would lead to totalitarianism. Born in 1899,[34] he had started his career in 'Red' Vienna, the nickname for the Austrian capital at the time, because of the dominance of the democratic socialist party who had won the city's first elections after the dissolution of the Habsburg monarchy.[35]

The von Hayek family lost the honorific 'von' with the declaration of the republic that followed, and much of their wealth too in Austria's post-war hyperinflation.[36] Hayek was a socialist as a young man, but gradually grew more liberal, particularly after becoming a disciple of Ludwig von Mises, the leading Austrian economist of the time and a robust defender of the free market.

Hayek became a British subject after Nazi Germany invaded Austria in 1938[37] – regaining the 'von' on his British passport in the process. The British administrators handling the naturalization process were presumably unaware of Austrian honorifics and must have believed, after they read it on his birth certificate, that it was part of his surname.

The fascism occupying his original homeland and threatening his adopted one, Hayek believed, shared a common ancestor with the socialism[38] of the Soviet Union. Both these ideologies placed the individual under the subservience of the state and, he thought, the socialist ideas popular with his academic contemporaries in Britain – insulated from the totalitarianism on the continent – would inevitably lead to oppression. This was the subject of his classic *Road to Serfdom*, published in 1944, a bestseller in the US[39] both in its own time and again after the bank bailouts that followed the 2008 financial crisis.

Instead Hayek was an advocate of classical liberal political philosophy and the free market in particular. He believed that economic competition guaranteed that prices contained information about the world and this was information that no central planner – whether fascist or socialist – was able to access. The fisherman knew more about how to get fish than any bureaucrat and the fishmonger knew more about public demand for them. All this 'local information'[40] that individuals had was then incorporated in the prices they charged others.

The free market was a vast and impossibly sophisticated information-synthesizing machine.[41] Each person only had to know about themselves – what they wanted and how much they were willing to give up to get it would ensure that goods and services would get to the people who valued them the most, and similarly those who were most willing and able to do various kinds of work would end up doing it.[42]

A practical example shows how this works. In 2005 the US food bank charity Feeding America recruited some economists to reform its system of getting food to where it was most needed. Some branches in Alaska faced a shortage – the charity, which used a centralized system to distribute food, assumed the cost of transporting fresh produce there would be too high. This left

Alaska with a lot of pickles but not much else. Idaho, meanwhile, was flooded with home-grown potatoes.[43] Other local food banks similarly had ties to their own regional producers. The food bank managers on the ground with their 'local knowledge' were frustrated by the centralized planning system.

The economists had an idea: creating an internal market. The scheme met with some resistance from the staff. John Arnold, a director of a Western Michigan food bank, was typical, saying, 'I am a socialist. That's why I run a food bank. I don't believe in markets. I'm not saying I won't listen, but I am against this.'[44] This was understandable. America's food banks rely not on the principle of self-interest, which is meant to govern the market, but mutual aid. They would not function at all if people did not voluntarily try to help each other. Many of those working in the food banks had consciously rejected the ethics of a system that leaves the poorest with nothing.

Feeding America's internal market relied on a system of fake money, with a name to reflect the principles of cooperation: shares. The local managers could use these shares to bid in auctions – sealed bids, meaning they could not see each other's offers. The managers could even bid negative amounts: meaning they would be paid to take some donated food that was expensive to store off the system's hands. For the food banks, goods had prices very different from those outside the system: peanut butter was incredibly expensive – it lasted forever and was a good source of protein. Milk, like all dairy, was very cheap because it was so hard to store.

Money offered a way for the individuals working in the system to communicate their 'local knowledge' to the network at large: the prices could then reflect this information and communicate it to others. This did better than centralized planning at getting the food to the right place. Canice Prendergast, one of the economists involved, estimated that the reforms effectively doubled the quantity of food available to the charities[45] – partly by removing some of the storage issues that stopped banks from accepting donations and partly due to the local operations getting food they thought was more valuable. This is one reason why Hayek valued the market and rejected attempts to interfere with its operation: there were big gains on offer when the market could deliver efficiency.

The big monetary problem, for Hayek,[46] was that central banks' manipulation of interest rates would misdirect capital. He concluded, following Wicksell, that there was some neutral (or 'natural') interest rate based on the supply and demand for saving; an interest rate that would match the desired amount of investment and saving. This relative price – an inter-temporal price, meaning the price for money today in terms of money tomorrow – would direct money to those who could use it best, in the same way as the internal market let Feeding America ensure food got to the place where it was most valued.

The world of barter, where money was irrelevant, was not a description of how the economy behaved – central bankers saw to that – but it was the goal. In this world prices would reflect not the desire of the central planner, nor of the central banker, but the genuine preferences of a society. The relative price of present and future consumption would emerge from the choices of millions of individuals – their time preference – rather than being manipulated by the technocrats who really had neither the information nor the expertise to be able to fine-tune an economy.

When central banks lowered the rate of interest compared to this neutral interest rate it no longer fulfilled this role, no more than the prices charged in the Soviet Union actually represented the value that Soviet citizens placed on the goods and services in the shops. The consequence was that too much would be invested in longer production processes – recall Böhm-Bawerk's views on the role of time in investment.

In previous chapters we have discussed consumption goods – the things that people actually want; and capital goods – which are used to make those things. Now we can introduce a third category: intermediate goods. These are produced in the process of making consumer goods: bread is a consumer good, an oven is a capital good, but flour is an intermediate good. To make bread, first you need flour, and someone has to mill that flour from wheat. It sits in the middle of the production process.

Think about manufacturing a car. To make a car you need all the machines that fit out a factory, but you also need lots of intermediate goods: rubber tyres, steel frames, leather seats and so on. These all need to be made before you can actually make the car: they are the intermediate goods. Some of them will need to be produced earlier or later in the process. To make the electronics for the in-car systems you will need copper wiring; to make the wiring you will need copper; and to get that copper you will need all sorts of mining and smelting equipment. Production requires these long processes with earlier and later stages.

A fall in the money rate of interest, according to Hayek, will mean more is invested in these first stages: mining projects with a decades-long payout will become profitable, for example. But as this shift is provoked by a manipulation of the interest rate by the central bank, rather than a change in consumers' desire to save, the previous level of spending on consumer goods will continue.

Because more has been invested in the longer processes, there will now be fewer consumer goods available. Businesses are building mines rather than new cars. This scarcity raises consumer prices. At first this increase will tempt the banks to lend even more: there are bigger profits on offer. For a year or two, the economy is booming. Investment is high, consumer spending is high and inflation is steadily rising. All fuelled by money that has been manipulated to be cheaper than it would be in the absence of government intervention.

Then comes the inevitable bust. The rise in consumer prices will make the longer processes less profitable relative to producing things for immediate sale. Investment will shift from projects with a distant payout, like a mine, to those with a quicker return, such as car manufacturing. This will leave some investors with a lot of unfinished, no longer valuable projects. These will come to a sudden stop; and the workers employed in producing them will be thrown out of work.

With the scale of the misdirected investment becoming clear a correction would ensue, meaning a recession that would liquidate the bad investments. Only once this had been done could the economy recover – the Keynesian policy prescription of fiscal stimulus would merely delay the job losses and company failures that were necessary to clear out the bad investments.

Hayek wrote in his book *Prices and Production*, which set out his view on the origin of recessions, that 'we arrive at results which only confirm the old truth that we may perhaps prevent a crisis by checking expansion in time, but that we can do nothing to get out of it before its natural end, once it has come.'[47] More money could only make us richer temporarily. The hangover would inevitably follow.

Money and long-run growth

On the cause of recessions, although not the wider philosophical arguments, Hayek ultimately lost the battle to Keynes. Outside of the Austrian school, a much-diminished part of the field nowadays, most economists believe his explanation of the business cycle simply does not work. Partly that was due to fierce, and often obscure, controversies among academic economists about the nature of capital – was it a length of time, an amount of 'intermediate goods' or a kind of fund? Mainstream economics, as we saw, ultimately rejected Böhm-Bawerk's theory of 'roundaboutness' as part of the explanation of the origin of interest and only focused on the differences in subjective time preferences we looked at in chapter 3. The Austrian theory of the business cycle that Hayek and others built on top of this theory of capital was one casualty.[48]

The idea that booms contain the seeds of their own destruction still lives on but nowadays the most popular version is that a long economic expansion breeds complacency. Banks and investors gradually take more risks when they lend. The bust follows, not because the length of production has got too long, but because of some sudden reversal in sentiment, and lenders stop extending credit to borrowers who rely on taking out more debt to repay their existing creditors. Recessions are still, in this theory, a necessary corrective, weeding out bad investments until only the good, sustainable, ones remain.

Research by Milton Friedman in the 1960s[49] – followed up in the 1990s[50] – found that the evidence did not support this idea; there was no correlation between the size of an economic expansion and the recession that followed it. In other words, it did not appear as if busts were necessary to correct the poorly directed investment that took place during a boom.[51] Sometimes a deep recession could follow a period of only slow growth, or a shallow one could follow a rapid expansion.

Friedman proposed, based on this data, what he called the 'plucking model' instead. He compared the economy to a string tightly stretched underneath a plank of wood: when the string was plucked downwards it would bounce back, but it could never go above the wooden plank. There was some ceiling above which economic output could not rise – sharp contractions in the money supply could produce recessions, Friedman argued, but increases would not lead to growth, or even a boom, only inflation.

The biggest reason why the Austrian theory of recessions fell out of favour was not the theoretical arguments between economists but the experience of the Great Depression. In the 1930s the politicians who ran much of the world thought, like Hayek,[52] that allowing businesses to fail was the only way to get out of a recession – the free market would do its job weeding out the weak and allowing the strong to survive.[53] Only once this purging was complete would the economy recover.[54]

In his memoirs Herbert Hoover, US president from 1929 to 1933, quoted his Treasury secretary Andrew Mellon, whose advice on dealing with the Depression was: 'Liquidate labor, liquidate stocks, liquidate the farmers, liquidate real estate. It will purge the rottenness out of the system. High costs of living and high living will come down. People will work harder, live a more moral life. Values will be adjusted, and enterprising people will pick up the wrecks from less competent people.'[55]

Hoover disagreed with this cold-hearted analysis but his attempt to stabilize the economy still consisted of trying to keep the government's budget balanced[56] – his argument was that this would restore confidence in the financial system. While he increased government spending on relief programmes, he also raised taxes, which offset the effectiveness of the stimulus efforts.

More damaging, however, were the actions of the Federal Reserve. The US central bank, keen to defend the value of the dollar in terms of gold, raised interest rates – other central banks elsewhere did the same. Predictably this led to further bank failures and the quantity of money circulating in the US economy shrank as savers withdrew their funds: bank runs were a frequent occurrence. While the amount of physical cash in the economy increased, the volume of bank deposits shrank[57] as depositors pulled their money out of the institutions.

Milton Friedman and his co-author Anna Schwartz's opus *A Monetary History of the United States* laid responsibility for the Great Depression firmly at the feet of the Federal Reserve.[58] The contractionary policies that the central bank used to try to keep the value of the dollar stable relative to gold choked off economic growth. Less money had ultimately made America poorer. Friedman was an admirer of Hayek's political philosophies but not of his work as an economist[59] – his view of Keynes was the reverse.[60]

Over seventy years later during the 2008 financial crisis, very much the sequel to the Great Depression, policymakers in the US tried a different approach. Ben Bernanke, the Fed chair at the time, had written extensively about the history of the Great Depression – in a 2002 ceremony honouring Friedman, Bernanke said of the Great Depression that 'you're right, we did it. We're very sorry. But thanks to you, we won't do it again.'[61] Unlike during the 1930s, the central bank opened the monetary floodgates.[62]

The aftermath of the 2008 financial crisis was not a success for economics but it was not as bad as the Great Depression. The economists had failed to see the crash coming – partly because they subscribed to Smith's idea that money did not matter and they followed Hayek's belief that those with local knowledge,[63] in this case the bankers, were better placed than the regulators and governments in assessing risk.[64] Neglecting money – many of the dominant economic models mostly ignored banking[65] – may have made us poorer.

However, they had learned something from the Great

Depression, and so the central banks made more money available, cutting interest rates and launching quantitative easing programmes,[66] their priority was stabilizing the economy and the financial system rather than trying to protect the value of their currency in terms of gold. Politicians too, at least at first, did not try to balance their budgets but tried to stimulate economies by borrowing more, cutting taxes and announcing new spending programmes.[67] In this way a repeat of the Great Depression was avoided.

In the models that dominate economics today, there is some grit in the wheels of Hayek's information-synthesizing machine: prices are sticky.[68] What this means is that they do not adjust very quickly. Workers and consumers expect the businesses they deal with to keep prices relatively stable. Businesses similarly want to maintain market share and prevent their competitors from gaining an advantage, so they do not want to be the first to raise prices and thereby lose customers to their competitors.[69]

This all means that prices adjust slowly to new information; and so quantities, like the volume of production or the number of workers employed, adjust instead. When prices do adjust, however, the economy should bounce back to its long-term capacity, as determined by productivity. (Remember from chapter 3 that Keynes dissented from this view, thinking this might not happen and falling wages could, instead, just prolong the slump.)

A fierce ongoing debate among economists as I write is whether booms and busts can affect this supposed ceiling. The least controversial hypothesis is that periods of high unemployment can lead to a permanently higher natural rate of unemployment.[70] The argument is that recessions cause 'scarring': long periods of unemployment mean workers become discouraged, lose skills and find it much harder to find jobs.[71] The main way that money can make us richer is by ensuring recessions are as short and shallow as possible.

Perhaps the secret to Britain's industrial revolution in the eighteenth century was not some ingredient that led to a rapid acceleration in growth but something that stopped its economy from shrinking as much. Indeed, the data suggests that growth was not especially fast in the period.[72] Instead what distinguished the country from its peers in the rest of Europe was that their recessions became less frequent and less bad.[73] It is not completely clear why – it could be the end of centuries of religious war, and the relative domestic peace when Smith was writing.

More controversial, however, is the idea that booms can lead to permanently lower unemployment. Some contemporary economists advocate running the economy 'hot',[74] meaning central banks should allow inflationary pressures to build and encourage the kind of boom that Hayek saw as nothing but a distortion and a potential disaster.[75] The idea is that in the same way as recessions cause scarring – permanent damage to an economy – booms can cause permanent improvements.

This argument too has a counterpart for Adam Smith's time. One of the most popular modern explanations for the surge in innovation and technical invention in Britain during the industrial revolution is that wages were high in the country compared to elsewhere in Europe, especially relative to the price of fuel. It therefore made sense for businessmen to work out ways of substituting capital for labour, replacing expensive muscle with cheaper coal to increase their profits.[76]

This could then be repeated today by encouraging the economy to operate at full capacity. If interest rates are held low then businesses, consumers and governments will all keep spending. As this persists, a shortage of workers and rising wages will encourage companies to innovate and adopt more productive techniques, to try to save on labour costs. Companies are forced by the shortage of workers to try to attract those from disadvantaged groups, drawing them into the labour market and providing experience and training.[77] It is only because demand is high – and expected to remain high – that companies invest in the machinery or the training that ultimately raises productivity.[78] Money can then make us permanently richer.

Both of these two theories – that keeping recessions short can stop scarring and running the economy 'hot' can create new jobs – strike at Friedman's view that central banks cannot permanently increase employment.[79] The natural rate of unemployment is not 'natural' at all and cannot be taken as given by central bankers.

These theories are currently being put into practice in the US. To aid the recovery from the coronavirus pandemic the relatively new administration of President Joe Biden will, in its own words, 'go big' on fiscal stimulus. In a speech in mid-2021, President Biden said, 'When it comes to the economy we're building, rising wages aren't a bug; they're a feature. We want to get something economists call "full employment". Instead of workers competing with each other for jobs that are scarce, we want employees to compete with each other to attract work. We want the companies to compete to attract workers.'[80]

Many traditionally minded economists hit back, arguing that the attempt to run the economy 'hot' would merely lead to 'overheating'. Instead of creating new jobs or encouraging productivity to grow it would just lead to higher inflation and, eventually, the Federal Reserve would have to raise interest rates to try to bring it back under control again. It would end up just being a repeat of the inflationary 1970s, followed by the painful unemployment of the early 1980s. Money will not make us richer and a lot of people will be hurt along the way.

Reading between the lines in this chapter, you might have

figured out that while economists can point to some helpful factors for increasing productivity – competition, education, peace, investment – they do not know what fundamentally drives it. There is a lot at stake between who is right and who is wrong. Many of the previous chapters have looked at how money lies at the heart of social conflicts, how the way it is managed can influence the prosperity of different groups. Economic growth promises a route out of conflict – if the size of the pie grows then everyone can get a bigger slice without it coming at the expense of someone else.

9. How do we save money?

In 2019 protests rocked Chile.[1] The causes were diffuse: originally sparked by a 30-peso rise in the price of rush hour metro tickets in the capital, Santiago, the set of grievances quickly broadened out. An estimated million people took to the streets demanding a wholesale change in how the country operated. Some adopted the slogan 'It's not about 30 pesos, it's about 30 years'.[2]

The protests marked three decades since the transition to democracy following the military dictatorship of General Pinochet.[3] Optimism had since faded. Economic growth had slowed, inequality was high and the expectations of the country's growing middle class had been routinely frustrated.[4] Towards the top of the list of grievances, however, was something that rarely provokes such intense feelings: pensions.[5] The Pinochet-era system, now in its fourth decade, had failed to ensure Chileans saved as much for their retirement as anticipated, leaving thousands trapped in old age poverty.

The problems with Chile's pension system were a reflection of a common challenge facing all of us: how do we save for the future? How do we make sure that we will have enough to survive when or if we can no longer work? How can you transfer money you get today to when you will really need it and be sure it will still be there?

In the early 1980s Chile had introduced a system of individual pension saving accounts that earned plaudits from the World Bank and became the model for similar reforms[6] across poorer countries. Previously Chile had only used a pay-as-you-go system: workers were meant to contribute throughout their lives, and these funds were immediately transferred to the retired. When the currently contributing workers reached their retirement age, the next generation would bear the responsibility for funding their pensions.[7] With little connection between the amount workers paid in and the amount they received, most would pay only the minimum – or avoid it altogether. It became more and more expensive for the few who could not avoid contributing to support the rest.

José Piñera, the Minister of Labour under Pinochet, oversaw the privatization of this system. He was part of a group that became known as the 'Chicago Boys'[8] – Chilean students who had studied economics at the University of Chicago under Milton Friedman and brought back ideas for reforming the country's economy. Piñera said that reading Friedman's classic *Capitalism and Freedom* as a student had changed his life. That experience would, in turn, change his country and become an experiment, closely watched by the rest of the world, into whether financial markets and a purely private pension system could be enough to save for the future.[9]

Pinochet's brutal regime turned to the Chicago Boys to provide his anti-communist military coup with an economic vision, restoring the nation after the hyperinflation during the prior democratically elected socialist government.[10] For their part, while sympathetic to anti-communism, the Chicago Boys also saw in the regime a chance to transform the economy along 'scientific' and 'technical' grounds absent political pressure.[11] And, they told themselves at least, the torture and disappearance of activists were isolated events unrelated to economic policy.

Under the privatized pension system each Chilean worker would put money into their individual savings pot and it would be used, on their behalf, by money managers to buy financial assets – government bonds, corporate shares and so on. Eventually the pot was meant to grow so large that the income it generated would be enough for when they could no longer work.[12] At its core, the system is the most basic way of saving for the future: you accumulate promises from other people.[13]

This does not have to mean using financial markets. Worldwide, one of the most popular means of saving is known as a susu in West Africa and the Caribbean,[14] from a Yoruba term *esusu*. They are popular right across the developing world and in diaspora communities in rich countries: known as chit funds in India, hui in China, ekub in Ethiopia, stokvel in South Africa, arisan in Indonesia and tanda in Mexico.[15] These are all just different names for the same thing: a rotating savings club.

Every month the members of the club all put a fixed amount of money into a kitty – the English term kitty for a common fund descends from the Hindi *chit* – and one person gets the whole thing, rotating at subsequent meetings.[16] Some who need the money right now get a loan: they get their turn early and spend the rest of the time paying into the pot for the rest of the club. Others, who want help saving, get their turn at the end, having paid in the rest of the time. Some people need to save and others need to borrow. The club matches the two groups together, to their mutual benefit.

These rotating saving clubs rely on trust.[17] Ideally the members are people that can be relied on – neighbours, friends, relatives, coworkers and so on – and it is enforced by social convention and the threat of ostracization.[18] In bigger communities something more impersonal is usually needed. For instance, residents of the mega city of Delhi, who were persuaded by a group of economists to keep 'money diaries', reported that it was hard to find trusted neighbours to take part in such a club.[19]

When we invest our money with pension funds, banks or investment companies they gather promises on our behalf and ensure people we have never met will meet their obligations to us. These promises are financial assets. Government debt, which we looked at in chapter 6, is a promise by the government to pay investors a regular interest payment and, eventually, the amount they borrowed. Businesses similarly sell debt to investors – or get loans from banks – but they can also sell corporate equity, shares in the company usually entitle investors to a portion of any dividends that are paid out of the profits.[20] Investing brings with it risks: promises can be broken or not fulfilled in the way you expect. Much of finance is concerned with how to measure, price and tame these risks, letting us save money, hopefully safely, for the future.

Playing risk

Finance and probability grew up together. In the seventeenth century a set of French mathematicians started to think, more formally, about chance.[21] They had started with games and gambling but the statisticians that followed would find a more practical application: calculating life expectancies. This was helpful because for many in eighteenth-century France saving for the future meant hoping that thirty young women in Geneva would live long lives.[22]

Later, economists would draw a distinction between risk and uncertainty. Risk is calculable – a coin when flipped will show heads half the time; the probability of a dice showing a particular number when rolled is one in six. Uncertainty, however, is when you have no basis whatsoever to calculate a probability – you may not even know all of the potential outcomes: the chance of a revolution in France, for instance.[23]

The difference is so important because if you know the probability of a bet coming good it can be reflected in the price: you can have a good idea what the fair value for an investment or gamble would be.[24] One of the first problems the mathematicians had looked at was how to fairly divide a stake after two gamblers had been interrupted. They came up with an early version of what is now known as 'expected value'.[25] If each player would win half the time and the winner takes the whole pot, you would simply divide it in two; whereas if one would win a third of the time, they would get a third of the pot and the other would get two-thirds – the 'expected value' of a gamble would be the amount you would win weighted by the likelihood.

Being able to estimate how long someone would live could help you work out the fair value of an income for their whole life. This was critical because the French monarchy in the eighteenth century funded itself using *rentes viagères*, life annuities, which it sold to wealthy investors.[26] At the time, the French state did not sell debt – the Catholic Church prohibited lending at interest. Investing in a life annuity meant the investors would never receive their money back – getting around the Church's prohibition – but would get a stream of regular income payments; after their death a portion of the national debt would disappear.[27]

Saving for the future usually means collecting promises. The investors who relied on these *rentes* were relying on a promise from the French state to continue to pay them.[28] That promise turned out to be untrue: the French government was functionally bankrupt and would never have been able to repay the debts – the debts were restructured after several cycles of the French

Revolution in 1794. That uncertainty might have given the investors trouble in the end but, for the time being, probability promised a way of pricing risk: using life expectancies they could work out what the fair value would be for these assets.

Following the Seven Years War and the American Revolution, France was virtually bankrupt.[29] The expense of the two military conflicts had left the country deep in debt. The sclerotic state of the country, on the eve of the French Revolution, had made gathering taxes harder than ever. Nobles were exempt from many state levies, leaving the common people to mostly fund the government, including through the *gabelle*, a hated salt tax that would vary massively across the different regions of France, encouraging smuggling.[30]

So to attract the funding it needed, the French state began offering 10 per cent interest on these *rentes* irrespective of the age of the participant.[31] Originally, contracts on younger people would receive a lower payment and older ones higher, but the expense of France's wars had made the government desperate for cash.[32] While its main rival England had managed to solve its own problem of how to fund wars through the constitutional innovations of a central bank and parliamentary supremacy, providing legitimacy for taxation and reassurance for investors, France was still struggling with the problem.[33]

Crucially, the person named in the annuity contract – known as 'the head' – did not have to be the same as the one who bought it – anyone could be nominated. So in the 1770s a set of wily Genevan bankers – there were no similar restrictions on lending in the Protestant city – pooled their money and spread it across thirty young women. The Genevan bankers repackaged the contracts they had taken out into new securities and sold these on to others – German army officers, French doctors and Swiss priests all bought into the scheme, even one of the French queen Marie Antoinette's advisors.[34] So long as the thirty young women were alive, those who invested in the scheme would get a portion of the income.

Women were chosen because of the new, and spreading, science of statistics.[35] Detailed life expectancy figures were starting to become available for the first time. The British astronomer Edmond Halley, who calculated the orbit of the comet that now bears his name, was among the first to demonstrate the significance of life expectancy for finance.[36] In 1694 he published work showing that the English government was selling annuities – bonds that paid out every year for the life of the owners – to young people for far too little.[37] Halley had obtained data on mortality for the Silesian city of Breslau, modern-day Wrocław in Poland, and extrapolated from this to his home country.

The Genevan doctor Louis Odier, an advocate of smallpox vaccination, published his own estimates based on an investigation of the Swiss city's mortuaries, allowing the bankers to work out who would be the best to nominate for the contracts. As it turned out, seven-year-old girls were the people on whom the *rentes* were the most mispriced – in other words, the government lost the most money to anyone who took out a contract on the head of a seven-year-old girl. In the same way as the mathematicians could work out the expected value of each player's position in an interrupted card game, so too could the bankers work out the fair price of a contract on a given individual.

The thirty young women – many of them may have had no idea they were being used in a financial contract in this way – mostly came from upper middle class and aristocratic families. They were cousins, daughters and nieces of the bankers who arranged the scheme,[38] including Louis Odier's own daughter. The bankers also knew that, on average, the young women would live longer than their male peers; some boys who were a nominated head in other contracts were paid not to take up careers in the military. Similarly, they knew that those over seven were more likely to have developed an immunity to smallpox – later, the discovery of a vaccine would mean the bankers thought it prudent to take out contracts on four-year-olds.

Today the financial industry still promises to tame and manage risk on our behalf. Statistics like the life expectancy tables compiled by Edmund Halley were the forerunner to the gigabytes of data nowadays used by so-called quant funds that run complicated statistical models to try to identify mispriced assets.[39] Ones, like the *rentes*, that will earn a higher return for the buyers than their sellers anticipate.

When probabilities of some eventuality can be calculated, prices can represent information, as Friedrich Hayek suggested, not only in terms of what the world is currently like but also what it could be. Expectations about the future are embedded in the price we pay for different goods – if our houses disappeared after thirty years then we would not take out such big mortgages to buy them; when art is sold for millions it partly reflects its potential resale value and not only the buyers' opinions of its artistic quality.

The expense of these annuity contracts has been blamed for the French Revolution – the meeting of the Estates General that led to the political crisis was called because the government needed some way of raising funds to repay the national debt, and that meant getting rid of the nobility's privileges.[40] On the other hand it was likely France had to resort to such expensive measures because it was already functionally bankrupt.[41] Like Greece two centuries later, France had to pay high interest rates because its lenders were sceptical they would ever get their money back.[42]

Early finance of this sort was almost entirely about funding government[43] and today private pensions still rely on public sector debt as a safe promise.[44] Gradually, however, private chartered companies stared offering 'shares' for sale too.

Shares are a different kind of promise from debt. Debt usually involves someone promising to pay you the full value of what you lent to them – the principal – as well as the interest, a periodic sum depending on how much they borrowed. Shares, however, are less explicit. Owning a share in an enterprise does not involve the company guaranteeing that you will get your money back at any point – the money now permanently belongs to the company – instead you buy a portion of the company and receive a share of any dividends that management decide to pay from the profits.

If the venture is unprofitable, however, you can lose everything. The company's creditors, on the other hand, get to take it over and sell its assets to recover their investment. The fair value of a share ought to depend on how profitable you expect the company to be. Even if the company does not pay any dividends, then the value of the company still ought to reflect how profitable it is – remember from chapter 2 that if a business fails shareholders are entitled to everything that is left over after debtors are repaid, and that means any profit that has been reinvested in the business.

If Jane Austen's *Pride and Prejudice* can be said to be a novel about government debt, then Herman Melville's *Moby-Dick* is one about corporate shares.[45] When the novel's narrator Ishmael joins Captain Ahab's quest for vengeance against the white whale who took his leg, he is not paid any wages; instead he takes what was called a 'lay'.[46] The whaling ships of Nantucket were partly funded by their workers, who took a proportion of the profits depending on the size of lay they got – not getting their pay until after the journey was done.

Ishmael complains because he only receives a 300th lay as a

general sailor, meaning that he will only receive 0.3 per cent of the voyage's profits. Any of Melville's readers familiar with whaling would know this was a comically low amount. Meanwhile Queequeg, the harpooner, earned a 90th lay, roughly 1.1 per cent of the profits – his skills were in much higher demand.[47]

While government debt promises safety and reliable repayment, shares in whaling companies promised the opposite. Bonds entitle their owners to a regular interest payment while shares do no such thing. Only if the company returns a share of the profit will an investor earn an income. In exchange, corporate equity has a greater upside: if a company earns huge profits then the investor gets a bigger payout. New England's whaling companies earned for their investors an average return of 14 per cent.[48]

Failure, too, was common – as readers of *Moby-Dick* are well aware – and those who backed the ships would frequently lose all their invested capital. The investors knew this and, like the Genevan bankers, would take steps to mitigate this risk. Instead of investing all their money in a single whaling venture they would spread it across multiple different ships. If one went down they could still collect on the others.

Diversification was the key to keeping your money safe – the same technique used by the Genevan bankers of spreading and managing risk by taking out thirty contracts on different people. If one of the young girls had an unexpected accident it would only reduce the value of the investment by one-thirtieth and not the whole amount.

The lay system of compensation, too, shared the risk of failure between the owners of the vessels and their workers. If the venture made nothing – it failed to catch any whales – then the owners would not have to pay any wages; if it did well, however, the crew would share in any profits. Much of finance, in this way, is about determining who bears risk, on whose shoulders is it carried, and who loses if the world does not work out the way we hope.

These early innovations used exactly the same tools we use today to save for the future. Risk sharing, diversification and gathering accurate information all remain basic building blocks of the financial industry. Indeed, before the 2008 financial crisis the banks packaged mortgages up and sold them on to other investors in a similar way the Genevan bankers did for the *rentes*. Finance, however, is not only about a set of techniques for managing risk but also about institutions, and there is still one very important innovation missing from our picture of the industry: the investment fund.

Managing money

Chileans, when they saved for their pensions, did not usually buy government debt or corporate shares directly. Instead it was left to someone else to manage their savings: a fund manager.[49]

An investment fund works on the same principle as the thirty heads from Geneva. The fund buys multiple different securities – bonds and shares – to offer diversification to its investors:[50] just as if something happened to one of the thirty Genevan girls you would lose only one-thirtieth of your debt, if something happens to one of the assets in a fund, then the others may be able to compensate. Not all your eggs will be in one basket.

There are other advantages too. Instead of having to buy and worry about the value of, say, a hundred companies' shares, you only need to buy a share in the fund once and worry about the price of that. This means the fund can offer more liquidity – the ease of buying and selling – to its investors.[51] Having to transact in a hundred different shares would be very expensive, while selling a single share in a fund which owns a hundred is much easier.[52]

For all these services and more – like research into companies or trying to ensure you get the best price when they trade assets on your behalf – the fund management company charges fees. These can have a significant impact on how much you end up saving; one reason why the Chilean pension funds did not provide as big an income as anticipated was because a large proportion of the return the assets generated went to paying the companies who managed the pension plans.[53]

When you save you should pay close attention to how much you will be charged. An old joke has it that when a visitor to New York's Financial District was shown the grand yachts of all the bankers, he asked, 'Where are the customers' yachts?',[54] naively believing that the goal of the financial sector was to increase their clients' wealth rather than their own.

There is plenty of risk involved in investing, and uncertainty too, but you can be relatively sure – with enough investigation into the terms and conditions – of how much you will have to pay a fund management company for its services.[55] This will have a big impact on how much you actually save, probably more so than making sure you select exactly the right investments.

A lot of finance is about 'information economics': about who knows what and how it affects how they behave. That includes what is called the 'principal-agent problem'[56] – when someone, the principal, delegates a decision to someone else, the agent. In such cases the principal cannot always be sure the agent will act in their interests. A principal-agent problem could mean ensuring the chief executive of a company acts in the way its shareholders want, or making sure a fund actually works for its investors and not for those who run it.

Often though, information is about prices.[57] Financial markets try to incorporate information about the world into the values of different assets, like the life expectancy tables allowed the Genevan bankers to work out how much the *rentes viagères* were truly worth. Nowadays, the presence of thousands of financial traders all trying to get an edge should mean that any new information about the potential profitability of a company is quickly reflected in the price of its shares; and the potential solvency of a government should end up being mirrored in the interest rates it pays on its debt.

This means that the second thing to do when investing – after you have fully investigated the fees – is to be sceptical about how much you truly know about the world.[58] The efficient markets hypothesis, a view of financial markets first fully articulated in 1970 by the Chicago school economist Eugene Fama,[59] suggests that all the publicly available information about the value of a security is already reflected in its price. As soon as new information comes to light that would influence the potential return from an investment, it will be either bought or sold by traders[60] until the price changes enough so that it returns to fair value.[61]

If this is true it means it is virtually impossible to 'beat the market'[62] – earning more than most by being able to predict the movements in prices. To do so must mean either having some information which has not yet been made public or getting very lucky. Instead your returns should reflect the risk you are taking: a German government bond that pays a negative interest rate will be relatively safe, a corporate junk bond will pay you more but there's a higher chance the company will default. Market prices would then represent a trade-off between risk and reward – you can do better, but only if you take more risk. And remember there is uncertainty as well – the events that traders are not capable of incorporating into prices at all.

As well as being sceptical about your own ability to systematically beat the market, so too should you be wary of any superstar fund manager who claims they are willing to give you the benefit of their skills in exchange for paying them a big fee.[63] Very few actively managed funds consistently outperform the market as a whole – in other words you would normally have done better by indiscriminately buying all the biggest stocks rather than relying on a professional to pick and choose some for you.[64] Instead you may find yourself paying a lot for someone to lose you money.

Some, rarely, do manage to beat the market.[65] And to do this they take advantage of the gaps in the efficient markets hypothesis – those features of financial markets that economists sometimes refer to as 'frictions'.[66] These are the things that prevent financial capital from flowing easily and simply towards those assets that seem to promise the best return. A truly efficient market is impossible; otherwise there would be no reason for all those who trade assets and ensure information is reflected in prices to get involved in the first place.

Many of those best placed to take advantage of these inefficiencies work in what are known as hedge funds.[67] Originally called a hedged fund because the first version bet on stocks going down as well as up – a hedge – the 'd' was soon dropped. There is no definitive definition of a hedge fund nowadays and the industry has tried to rebrand itself as 'alternative asset managers'.[68] Generally they are open only to particularly rich investors or to other investment institutions, like pension funds, because the risky strategies they can adopt are not suitable for everyone.[69]

Perhaps the closest thing to a defining feature of a hedge fund, however, is its fee structure. Instead of only taking a flat management fee – a percentage of the assets under management – the hedge funds combine it with a performance fee. This used to be 'two and twenty' – the hedge fund would take 2 per cent of the value of the fund for its management services and 20 per cent of the total returns the fund made. This is very expensive – many of the richest people in the world run hedge funds.[70]

In exchange, they try to beat the market. This is difficult but not impossible. The efficient markets hypothesis (EMH) relies on several different assumptions, none of which always hold in practice, and these offer the opportunity for those outside the normal constraints to take advantage. The EMH needs completely rational investors with publicly available information: the real world falls far short of such exacting standards.

Providing an exhaustive list of all the ways in which hedge funds may be able to profit from the gaps in the EMH would be a book in itself.[71] But for an example we can take a look at the opportunities that come from the fact that investors are not rational. Some of these are behavioural biases – economists have identified countless ways in which people do not always resemble the efficient calculators of formal models. In finance this includes being 'loss averse', not wanting to sell your losing bets and holding on to bad investments in case things turn around.

Others are institutional. Hedge funds can take advantage of the fact that regular funds receive strict instructions from their investors. If you invest in a bond fund because you want safety and stability you would be pretty annoyed if it started taking punts on start-ups. Because of this attempt to solve a 'principal-agent problem' there can emerge pricing discrepancies between securities that, mathematically, ought to behave very similarly – based on whether they fall on one side or another of an arbitrary definition.

The more flexible hedge funds can then profit from arbitraging the two securities[72] – buying one and selling the other to take advantage of any discrepancy in their prices. This might involve making only tiny returns but the hedge funds, which are less regulated, can use leverage to boost it into something more significant.

Recently, however, hedge funds have not been doing so well,[73] particularly since the 2008 financial crisis.[74] The 'two and twenty' fee structure is in retreat:[75] instead they have had to cut the amount they charge to investors. While there are still a handful of hedge funds that are heavily in demand and consequently charge high fees to their clients, the industry has, in general, lost a lot of its lustre.[76] Big institutional investment managers like public sector pensions schemes and university endowments have been cutting their allocations to hedge funds or getting out of the sector altogether.

Perhaps the most successful innovation in the fund management industry in recent years is the polar opposite of a hedge fund.[77] Index or passive funds that do not promise they will beat the market in exchange for high fees, instead offering rock-bottom fees and to simply do as well as the market.

Because beating the market is very hard and most actively managed funds do not manage it, more and more investors have stopped buying into the idea of superstars who justify high fees and instead go for the cheapest option available, a low-cost, diversified fund that does something like buy all the biggest 500 companies in the US or the biggest 600 in Europe. There is no clever technique or strategy, they simply try to capture the whole stock, or bond, market.

These index funds – sometimes known as tracking funds – have become more and more popular. In 2020, about $15tn was invested in passive funds.[78] Investors concluded that if it was so hard to beat the market then there was simply no point in trying. Right or wrong, the efficient markets hypothesis may have saved a lot of people a lot of money, just not fund managers.

Blowing bubbles

In 2010, Eugene Fama, the Nobel prizewinning economist who had done the most of anyone to popularize the view of financial markets as informationally efficient, revealed he had cancelled his subscription to *The Economist*, the magazine that pitches itself as the bible of free marketeers. The problem, he said, was that its writers were using the word 'bubble' far too much. It seemed that anytime asset prices went up or down they would call it a bubble.[79]

Bubble is a colloquial term for when a market seems to get away from itself:[80] optimism and exuberance lead investors to overvalue particular investments, believing they are much more valuable than they really are. They have a tendency to pop, leaving those who failed to time the market properly without their savings and destabilizing the economy for the rest of us.

History is replete with periods today seen as bubbles.[81] That includes the famous tulip mania in the Netherlands[82] – where bulbs of the flower would sell for a fortune – or the dotcom bubble in the early 2000s, in which the stocks of internet businesses without anything approaching a real business model would command a high price. A personal favourite of mine, for sheer absurdity, is the late 1990s bubble in Beanie Babies – a collectible stuffed animal toy.[83] Rather more seriously, Albania descended into civil war in 1997 after a set of pyramid schemes that gripped much of the country collapsed.[84]

Yet despite how common they seem, in his Nobel Prize lecture, delivered in 2013,[85] Fama said there was really no such thing. By this he meant that you could not, by looking at any particular asset, predict that the bubble would pop. The candidates that people put forward – stock markets in the 1920s, technology companies in the early 2000s and US housing in the later part of that decade – could not have been forecast. That some claimed to have done so was just down to selection: we only hear about the people who get it right and not the countless failed predictions.

What's more, he pointed out, US stock markets had recovered after these 'bubbles' had popped. So which part were we meant to believe was irrational – the initial rise in share prices or their swiftly reversed collapse? Allegations of irrationality, he said, were mostly just sniping, based on trawling the data for pricing anomalies that disappeared the moment anyone tried to trade on them. The efficient markets hypothesis was testable and, partly by prompting the shift from active investment management to passive index tracker funds, had changed the world.

Fama's prickly defensiveness in this lecture is understandable. He had to share his Nobel Prize – the highest accolade in academic economics – with another two economists, including one with a very different view of what drives markets:[86] Robert Shiller. While Fama had spent his career arguing that markets synthesized information and did so efficiently, Shiller spent his doing the opposite, arguing that their movements reflected shifts in collective sentiment and our innate human capacity for story-telling.

One of Shiller's most famous findings was that stock markets were 'excessively volatile'[87] – they moved around far too much than could be justified by the underlying information that they were meant to reflect.[88] Shiller compared stock prices to the actual dividends of companies. The dividends were far more stable than the share prices. Changes in corporate profits would have had to be many times larger than during the Great Depression in order to justify such movement. It looked more like the market was overreacting than rationally incorporating new information.

Shiller is a key figure in the development of behavioural finance,[89] an approach that tries to look for systematic ways in which people deviate from the rationality assumed by the efficient markets model. This includes, for example, the fact that people herd.[90] We can get carried away by other people's greed and fear. When we see a limited edition $5 Beanie Baby reselling for thousands, we think 'that could have been me' and get involved ourselves. When we see people rushing for the exits in a market panic, we get swept away and hurriedly sell.

Perhaps at the heart of the debate is the somewhat hazy concept of 'rationality'. Getting information from other people's behaviour is not stupid. Most of us have to deal with situations where we do not have all the information and have to rely on rules of thumb: that people we trust are telling us to buy something could be an important and useful signal. In the animal kingdom, following the herd can often be the best strategy for staying alive.

On the other hand, the most robust version of the efficient markets hypothesis never relied on the idea that investors were rational or even particularly smart.[91] The argument instead was that just a few investors would be able to exploit any systematic deviation from fair value and profit by pushing prices back to efficiency – like in the example of a hedge fund arbitraging two very similar securities. Another argument was that any irrationality was essentially just random, and people who were irrationally optimistic would be counterbalanced by people who were too pessimistic.

The first problem is that arbitrage is often quite risky and can be costly itself. If I think the stock market is too high and bet against it, I might turn out to be right eventually, but if the market keeps going up I could still lose a lot of money in the process. A popular adage in finance, which gets trotted out whenever investors lament with a shake of their head that everyone seems to have gone mad, is that 'the market can remain irrational longer than you can remain solvent'. People may herd, but those who try to stand in their way often get trampled by the stampede.

Behavioural finance, too, has found that people are systematically irrational, contrary to the efficient markets hypothesis, and in ways that you can make money from. Two of the most popular are known as 'momentum' and 'value'.[92] Momentum refers to the principle that stocks that have gone up recently are likely to keep going up for a bit longer, while ones that have fallen keep falling. This is not what the efficient markets hypothesis predicts: prices should adjust to new information and then stop. However, because of the herd tendency, there is something that seems like a bandwagon effect for rising stocks.

Value[93] is the tendency for cheap stocks to outperform in the long run. One of the most successful findings of those who criticized the efficient markets hypothesis was that the book value of a company – the accounting price of its assets – was a decent predictor of long-term market returns. Companies that had a market price that was low relative to their book value would outperform; this meant that contrary to the efficient markets hypothesis there was some publicly available information that could predict higher returns.[94]

Value investing and momentum investing are somewhat opposed: momentum traders need to follow the herd, while value traders go against them, buying unloved stocks and selling popular ones. Both, though, are thought to be rooted in behavioural finance research: people tend to underreact in the short term but overreact in the long term.

There is a big difference in world view between followers of Shiller and devotees of Fama – that the two academics shared a

Nobel Prize for diametrically opposed theories provoked quips about the lamentable state of economic knowledge. And the debate has not been comprehensively settled. For example, Fama[95] has pointed out that the finding about 'book value' may reflect that these are in some way fundamentally riskier companies. Earning more by investing in them just reflects that the investors are taking bigger gambles. Money managers, too, have struggled to consistently beat the market by following Shiller's theories.[96]

For those of us worried about saving for the future, however, working out which side is right might not be that helpful. Both agree that beating the market is very hard. Even those who point out that there are systematic biases that investors can take advantage of would admit that we can never really be sure whether or not we are, in fact, the ones being taken advantage of.

Lifetime savings

Asset management companies[97] were some of the big winners from Chile's reforms, but so too was the Chilean government. Encouraging domestic savings funds meant that, unlike many of its peers, notably Argentina, the government did not need to rely on international investors to finance its borrowing but could sell its debt to Chileans who wanted to accumulate promises in pesos. Wealthy Argentinians, on the other hand, often wanted to save in dollars, having lived through hyperinflations and devaluations.

Chile had a particularly strict version of the monetary constitution, too[98] – the Pinochet regime spent its final years aiming to bind its democratic successor into following its policies.[99] The central bank has been independent since 1980 and in the 2000s the government followed fiscal rules[100] to prevent them from using high copper prices – Chile exports a lot of the metal – to fund short-term giveaways; any windfalls were put into a sovereign wealth fund. Even the 30-peso rise in metro fares that sparked the 2019 protests was the decision of a technocratic committee.[101]

Not only did this mean Chile avoided the problems of its neighbour over the Andes but it helped the economy to grow rapidly, becoming the star performer of Latin America. In 2009, Chile was invited to join the OECD group of rich countries. Alongside South Korea, Chile is one of the few recently poor countries to gain admission to this club. This aggregate economic performance, however, masked considerable inequality,[102] particularly access to social protection like pensions and healthcare.

The human life cycle has a universal rhythm.[103] When we are children, we need someone else to take care of us. Likewise in old age, when we cannot work. In the middle part of our lives we must take responsibility for the other generations.[104] In effect, society is just a bigger version of a susu. When we are young we are like those who get paid out first: we take from the club and then pay back as we get older. The old, meanwhile, are like those who get paid at the end: they have contributed to the others who must now give to them in turn.[105]

There are many institutional ways of arranging this. We can put all the emphasis on family obligation: parents must pay for their children and grown-up children must pay for their elderly parents. Instead of having a pension system it is all kept within the family. This is how it works in many poorer economies.[106] There is a gendered element here too: the duty of taking care of young children and infirm parents has often been placed, by tradition, on women.

Or we can say that the collective has a common responsibility.

In the welfare state, working-age adults pay taxes and this is then transferred to pay for childcare, education and old age pensions.[107] It can also include social insurance for the sick and disabled, state-provided childcare or payments to families based on the number of children they have. Taxation and government spending then do the work of the susu, transferring resources between the generations. Some of these collective schemes are organized at the level of employers or industries, with all the workers in a particular business or sector contributing to a common pension scheme.

The last option is to put the emphasis on the individual and use financial means to transfer resources.[108] Few would seriously suggest that young children should take out loans to pay for their own childcare or education, but this is how many societies make sure young adults who do not work can get by: outstanding US student debt, for example, is estimated to be in the trillions of dollars. Instead of paying high taxes, working-age adults repay these student loans and, hopefully, begin to invest some of their pay in financial assets. To save for your old age in a market-based system you accumulate promises through the financial markets, instead of government entitlements.

This is just another version of the susu, though.[109] Imagine you buy government bonds. The interest on those bonds will be paid for by the taxes on the working-age population. If you invest in corporate bonds it will be paid for through the resources that the working-age population create by going to work at the company. In all circumstances a portion of society's production is transferred between the generations; it just happens through different institutional setups, whether traditional families, welfare states or markets. Unless you try to hoard physical goods – storing tinned food and fuel around your house, that you also own – you will need some way of laying claim to a portion of what the working-age population produce.[110]

Societies make different choices about which institutional setup they want to use to achieve this – although really all are hybrids of varying degree. A young Dane who receives free university education and free healthcare from the government will pay higher taxes during his working life.[111] A young American who has to rely on student loans and health insurance will pay insurance premiums and interest on his student debt instead. If they do similar jobs, however, their disposable income is likely to end up quite similar[112] – at least if they are middle-income earners.

But these choices have other effects, particularly in terms of who bears the risk if things do not work out as planned. A collective system of health insurance like the one in Denmark protects everyone from the risk of poor health;[113] an individual system can mean you are on your own – as many Americans have found to their cost. The big differences emerge when you are either at the top of the income distribution – in America you contribute less – or at the bottom – in Denmark you get a bit more social protection.

The Chilean pension reforms shifted the country from a collectivist system to an individualist one.[114] The problem with the pensions, and the factor that brought many Chileans out onto the streets, was that they did not accumulate valuable enough promises. Piñera's reforms were predicated on a number of assumptions: Chileans would remain in stable jobs, earn at least a 5 per cent return on their investment and experience no change in life expectancy. This would guarantee a pension worth 70 per cent of their final salary. All three turned out to be wrong.

With falling interest rates and rising life expectancy, Chileans had to save a bigger proportion of their wages to guarantee they would get a satisfactory income when they retired. A casual and precarious labour market, too, meant that many did not spend enough time in work to accumulate the promises they needed.

Women, in particular, were disadvantaged – taking time off work to take care of children or elderly relatives meant less time to save. Throughout many societies the gender pay gap in our working lives is reflected in old age by a gender pensions gap.[115]

Saving for the future is about coping with uncertainty. If we rely on other people's promises then there is always a chance that things can go wrong. The particular design of Chile's pension system meant that these risks were borne by individuals, particularly poorer ones. Rather than relying, for example, on a government system of social security or the sort of personal relationships behind a susu, ordinary Chileans bore the risks that there would not be enough for them to live on in old age.

Reforms in 2008 supplemented the system of private pensions with a state-guaranteed minimum, a so-called solidarity pillar. This meant that the risk would be shared a bit more between individuals and the state. During the coronavirus pandemic,[116] the government allowed Chileans struggling with the economic fallout to dip into their pots and spend now. Further reforms were proposed, too, that would make employers contribute and extend the solidarity pillar.[117]

The hope was that this would ameliorate some of the disadvantages of Chile's system and guarantee a decent standard of living for all, reducing the inequality that has frustrated the hopes for higher living standards in a democratic Chile. Critics, however, have warned that the reforms would also imperil the advantages the 1981 privatization had brought, the pool of domestic savings that helped fuel the country's rapid growth and the hard-won fiscal and monetary credibility that allowed it to borrow so cheaply. This credibility let it provide other forms of social protection in moments of economic crisis; the government borrowing at a lower rate to stimulate the economy during a crisis and the central bank launching a quantitative easing program.

As I write, Chileans have just elected the delegates to a constitutional assembly[118] that will rewrite much of the political constitution, potentially abolishing the remaining Pinochet-era limitations on democratic government. A referendum on constitutional change was one of the government's responses to the 2019 protests. Perhaps Chile will, finally, make good on its promises.

10. What is the future of money?

One November evening in 2016, Narendra Modi, the prime minister of India, announced in a live unscheduled television broadcast that in just four hours' time the two largest notes in circulation, worth 500 rupees and 1,000 rupees, would be invalid.[1] Overnight,[2] 86 per cent of the total value of money in circulation in the world's most populous country would simply evaporate.

In the rest of the world cash is disappearing too, albeit much more slowly. Paper and metal money, the physical tokens that have represented monetary value ever since they were first used in ancient Anatolia, have started to be replaced by something even more abstract: purely digital money.

Digital money faces few of the limitations of cash. But in deciding how it works, and the principles behind that design, those who create the future of money are engaged in a fierce debate about what the future of the rest of society looks like too. Money, over the next few decades, will take a central role in debates about privacy, censorship and identity, as well as the age-old conflict between the state and private business.

To some the eradication of cash promises to strike a vicious blow against criminality. Cash is anonymous and hard to track, beloved of drug dealers and tax avoiders alike. Prime Minister Modi's goal in abolishing India's largest banknotes was to destroy stockpiles of illegal wealth, so-called 'black money' that gangsters and criminals used to store the proceeds of their crimes.[3] Law-abiding Indians had two weeks to exchange their 500- and 1,000-rupee banknotes at banks or state-run enterprises like India's nationalized petrol companies and railway operators.

On the surface Modi's demonetization policy appeared a disaster.[4] Not only did it fail to flush out the criminals' ill-gotten gains – 99 per cent of the banknotes were either deposited or exchanged for new ones,[5] suggesting the gangsters found some means of laundering their cash – but it quashed growth in the Indian economy, reducing the rate of expansion by an estimated 2 percentage points, according to one study.[6]

Crucially there was not enough of the new cash to replace the old notes and Indians had to spend their days queuing up at banks to exchange their now worthless notes for the new money.[7] The cash shortage hit the poorest Indians hardest, many of whom lacked bank accounts and worked in the informal cash-based economy.[8] Those living in remote villages, without access to banks, and the army of domestic workers were often the most dependent on having access to cash.

Some, however, have since attempted to recast the policy as a success,[9] pointing out that the chaos helped to usher in the new, and bright, future of money. In order to exchange their now redundant notes into still valuable ones, millions of Indians had to open bank accounts for the first time. Demonetization, too, provided rocket boosters for the spread of new payment technologies.[10] This all shifted India from one of the world's most financially underdeveloped countries, with only 35 per cent of the population having any kind of bank account in 2011, to the technological frontier and a place where the future of money was being decided.

Following demonetization, India's financial technology

companies,[11] which provide digital banking and payment services, reported a surge in interest. Paytm, one of the largest of these 'fintech' companies, took out ads in newspapers thanking Modi for his decision[12] to abolish the old notes. By 2018, rickshaw drivers and market traders – professions not normally seen as cutting edge – were allowing their clients to pay using QR codes or fingerprints.

Critically, much of the public infrastructure for this digital transformation was already in place: the same year as Mr Modi banned the Rs500 and Rs1000 notes, the Indian central bank, along with a consortium of thirty-six private banks, unveiled the 'unified payments interface' or UPI. This innovation aimed to provide a single framework for digital money in India. Payment companies, like the Facebook-owned WhatsApp Pay or the domestic giant Paytm, could use the UPI to communicate with the state-regulated banking sector, providing instructions to transfer money[13] between accounts. This was frictionless, instantaneous and open all hours.

Essentially the UPI worked like email: users had a single address from which they could send or receive money. This meant that it was completely interoperable: the same address would work whether you used WhatsApp, PayPal, Google Pay, Amazon Pay or Paytm to actually make your payments. But to do this, the system needed a means of verifying identities: a big problem in the financial sector where fraud is common and anti-money laundering 'know your client' regulations – the authorities' attempt to clamp down on digital black money – can be onerous and costly.

Cash can easily be transferred person to person, but you need to be physically next to each other to do so. When money is transferred at distance, through the banking system or otherwise, you need some means of verifying who it is being sent to. That could just mean an anonymous account number – as in private Swiss banks[14] – but normally governments try to tie bank accounts to specific individuals. As anyone who has tried to open a bank account in a foreign country knows, this costs: it can be time-consuming and irritating to try to prove you are who you say you are. Even once the account is open we have to remember passwords or answers to security questions to prove our identities. Indeed, nowadays, most attempts to steal from a bank do not involve the traditional balaclavas, guns and get-away drivers but pretending to be someone else.

India's UPI built on a pre-existing scheme for identity verification, known as Aadhaar. This, the name coming from a Hindi word meaning 'foundation' or 'base', was the largest identification programme in human history. For much of the previous decade, the Indian government had sent officials to trawl the length and breadth of the country, scanning eyeballs and recording fingerprints, taking photographs in city slums and isolated villages.

Aadhaar built a biometric database of India's 1.25 billion people to improve bureaucracy, one of its first uses was to ensure that everyone received the correct amount of subsidized rice.[15] But the mass identification programme also enabled a whole new suite of technologies and government services, including a brand-new form of money. Indians can, depending on the bank they use, now shop and transfer money solely using their fingerprints and twelve-digit Aadhar number – their unique identifier for dealing with both the state bureaucracy and also the public-private partnership of the unified payments interface.

There are many benefits to these innovations. Those who cannot read have access to a unique form of identification. It speeds up India's notoriously sclerotic bureaucracy and allows millions to access more formal credit markets and financial services rather than relying on loan sharks.

Yet there are challenges here too: these new ways of paying mean the future of money could ending up looking a lot like its past.[16] In the pre-monetary gift economies we discussed in the very first chapter of this book, you relied on your reputation and the good opinion of your neighbours to get goods and services.[17] In these small communities everyone would know you and what you had given to the community and could therefore estimate your worth.

The key benefit of currency was that it created a way of impersonally transferring trust; no longer was it necessary to know the person with whom you were dealing. Instead, currency – whether metal, paper or cowrie shells – could retain its value independent of the individual. Money was fungible; in other words, one piece was as good as any other – it came with no distinguishing features to mark where it had been or to whom it had previously been attached.

This meant that payment was now detached from an individual's identity. All it required was to verify that a gold coin, a banknote or anything else was the genuine article. This brought with it freedom: we no longer had to rely on the group but could strike out on our own. While community may bring all sorts of benefits it can also bring with it the pressure to conform and harsh sanctions for those who stand out. Anonymity, on the other hand, can mean independence, privacy and more freedom to define who you are for yourself.

Electronic money risks tying the ability to pay to an individual's identity and reputation once again,[18] with drastic consequences for privacy. The dangers come not only from authoritarian governments but also from the technology companies who wish to monetize and sell it on to advertisers.

Money accompanies us through everything we do, down to our medical problems and our relationships. Our greatest fears and desires are all expressed in what we buy and sell. Giving an electronic record of every transaction we have made to companies and governments means giving over this intimate information to them. It also potentially means giving them the power to decide which transactions are legitimate and which are not – some online services have cut off payments and locked the accounts of sex workers,[19] far-right activists[20] and publishers selling 'obscene' books.[21] WikiLeaks, a whistle-blower website, said it was subject to a 'financial blockade' from banks and payment services after it published US national security secrets.[22]

Aadhaar has been labelled the 'world's biggest surveillance system'[23] by critics, an attempt to create an Indian Big Brother, after the system of total surveillance in George Orwell's anti-authoritarian novel *Nineteen Eighty-Four*. Activists campaigning against Mr Modi's policies, many of which are perceived as targeting India's Muslim minority, have warned that they feel under constant surveillance. A whole set of cases against the Aadhaar system have been brought to the Supreme Court, which in 2018 ruled in response that Indian citizens have a right to privacy.[24]

These same battles – preventing digital communications technology from becoming a tool of surveillance – are at stake in the battle over the future of money. As money moves online it becomes another form of data; our spending patterns and habits risk becoming both a means for the government to keep track of us and a commodity for private companies to trade with one another.

Cryptocurrencies

Preserving privacy is, for many, the attraction of crypto-currencies.[25] These decentralized electronic tokens are designed to be completely private and unrelated to governments. Guaranteeing pseudonymity, they hold the promise of allowing their users to carry out proscribed economic activities and be free from any state control over commerce.[26] Their inventors have put forward a potential future of money, one that reflects very different ideas of how society could be organized from those behind India's UPI.

Cryptocurrencies' origins go back to the depths of the financial crisis in 2008. A figure calling himself Satoshi Nakamoto – his true identity is still a mystery today – struck a blow for the rebellion in the battle over the future of money. He published a paper detailing the mathematics that could provide the foundation for an alternative vision: bitcoin, a kind of digital money that could be kept out of the hands of governments and corporations alike.[27]

The first block of the bitcoin blockchain, the technology that underpins the digital currency, was 'mined' by Nakamoto in early 2009. Within was a reference to a newspaper headline, a string of text saying 'The Times 03/Jan/2009 Chancellor on brink of second bailout for banks'. This worked as both a record of the date when it was first created and, at the foundation of the new project, an implicit criticism of the relationship between the state and a demonstrably unstable banking sector.[28]

Avoiding banks and governments does not mean crypto users can sidestep the need for trust, however.[29] Bitcoins do not exist as physical entities, so at each point in time there must be some digital means of verifying how many there are and who owns them. Compare it with a bar tab, for example, nothing more than a centralized ledger to record transactions and who owes what; it is under the control of a central authority – the barman – who enforces claims and takes responsibility for the record's accuracy. Central and private banks do this same job in the wider modern monetary system, keeping record books of who is owed what.

Cryptocurrencies are decentralized by design and deliberately wish to avoid any authority that can keep track of the transactions.[30] Neither do the users wish to have their identity and reputation tied to the service, as we have to – for anti-money-laundering law and other purposes – with banks.

So the network uses mathematics as a substitute for authority and reputation.[31] Thanks to a nifty bit of programming, anyone can create a completely trustworthy version of the ledger that records who owns the electronic tokens.[32] The ledger contains a record of every single transaction that has taken place – a chain going back to the beginning.[33] This is then supplemented by adding additional 'blocks', which record only the latest transfers of ownership.

The promise of cryptocurrencies is the chance to create a digital equivalent to cash or gold: anonymous, private and with a relatively stable value. Other kinds of digital money are plentiful but they only really exist on a bank's balance sheet – your deposit with a bank is an entry on their centralized ledger. Bitcoin and other cryptocurrencies can be owned independent of the banks or the central banks, just like you can keep cash in your wallet or under your mattress – or hoard gold in a vault.

For this reason bitcoin, and similar cryptocurrencies, often come with a side order of libertarianism.[34] In the same way as many advocates for these principles hark back to the days of the gold standard – constraining big government and providing a foundation for money beyond social constructivism – others see bitcoin as a solution to the problem caused by the end of Bretton Woods in the early 1970s,[35] when money became unmoored from anything real and was instead solely backed by government fiat – power that ultimately rests, as they see it, on the state's capacity for violence, as expressed through courts, police and prisons.[36]

The mathematics behind the cryptocurrencies provides an alternative.[37] The code ensures they are artificially scarce and bakes in deflationary pressure: it becomes harder and harder to 'mine' new bitcoins as time goes on, aping the idealized properties of precious metal.

This is why, for many, cryptocurrencies promise to make good on a 1974 call by Hayek to denationalize money,[38] taking it out of government control and allowing different private providers to compete and offer the most stable currency. The only way to protect money, and therefore freedom, was to remove it from political influence, Hayek argued, suggesting banks should compete to offer the best 'currency' to their clients.[39]

Many cryptocurrency advocates were inspired by these ideals,[40] although the 2008 crisis had made it clear that the banks and governments were in league with one another. If modern money is a public–private partnership between these two, then cryptocurrencies promised to make it purely private, getting rid of the role of the state entirely. What was needed was a coin that no authority could control, neither big governments nor big banks.

Cryptocurrencies also offer to their advocates fulfilment of the early idea of the internet as a free, unregulated and open space – one that governments cannot control or censor. Unlike other payment systems, each member of the bitcoin network can be pseudonymous. The cryptography replaces the need for a good reputation; you do not need to verify the identity of the person making the transaction, only the maths behind it – it works as the cryptographic equivalent of biting a gold coin to test its softness or raising a paper note to the light to check its watermark.[41]

Users have a pseudonymous 'public key', a string of letters and numbers that works as their identity within the network, like the clients of private Swiss banks just had a string of numbers identifying their account. To send some crypto to an individual means sending it to this public key – it is not automatically tied to an individual's offline identity like India's Aadhaar system, and you could, if you wanted, have multiple public keys. The system is by no means immune to the security services – if you can establish a link between an individual and their public key then you can see all their transactions – but it is, in the words of its advocates, censorship resistant.

This makes the tokens – like anonymous cash – an attractive proposition to drug dealers, sex workers, criminals, political activists and anyone else who wants to avoid the attention of the authorities. The Silk Road online drug marketplace, where bitcoin was used to keep the transactions secure, was one of the most high-profile examples of a cryptocurrency being used as an actual medium of exchange.[42]

So far, however, these cryptocurrencies have generally not worked very well as currency.[43] They fail to fulfil any of its traditional three functions. Their price has been extremely volatile: using them as a means of account would mean changing the price of goods and services daily according to the views of speculators.[44] It also makes them an inadequate store of value: while their price has often rocketed upwards – helping some of the first to mine them or bet on their value to become millionaires – there is little guarantee you will be able to preserve this purchasing power for the future.

As a means of exchange, too, they have struggled. The

algorithms make them secure but the volume of computing power needed to provide the proof of security has made small transactions prohibitively expensive.[45] The bitcoin protocol is designed to release a new coin every ten minutes or so, but as more and more miners compete, the amount of computing power in the network increases.[46] In response the protocol makes it much harder to successfully complete new blocks and so more computing power is needed – this verification is extremely expensive. In 2021 the total energy used by the bitcoin payments system was estimated to be roughly equal to the amount used by Argentina[47] – that is a lot of damage to the environment for not much benefit.

The size of the potential market for transactions is limited too. The majority of people are, for better or worse, unconcerned about their online privacy: outside of illegal drugs and sex work, there has been only limited demand for anonymous currency.[48] For most of the public the values of the cryptocurrencies' creators – freedom, secrecy and privacy – are a much lower priority compared to the convenience and reliability of state monies.

Perhaps the most promising use case for the technology is among activists and protestors facing oppressive governments – those who risk persecution for their activity but need some way of being able to buy and sell the services they need.[49]

Money is another front in protest movements. Activists need resources for paying legal fees or buying the tools necessary to fight the security services on something approaching equal terms. But this exposes them to the state's power to regulate finance. Hence why protestors in Lebanon, Hong Kong and Iran have all tried to use bitcoin to dodge government attempts at censorship and get funds to those on the ground.[50]

It is in Nigeria, however, where bitcoin has really caught on. In 2021, the West African country was the third biggest user of the cryptocurrency after the US and Russia.[51] Some of this was an attempt to get involved in a chance to get rich quick – with bitcoin's price surging, if you managed to buy at the right time there were big profits to be made.[52] But with the End SARS mass protests against police brutality, bitcoin provided a much needed alternative currency after the government froze the accounts of the leaders of the movement and others found that payments from their organization's accounts had mysteriously slowed down.[53]

Generally, however, activists have found that cryptocurrencies are not particularly useful, though they may often be better than the alternatives. Internet connections can be shut off by the government and financial transactions need to be accompanied by more traditional messages, using a service that the government can monitor or ban – being able to transfer money secretly is useless if you cannot contact your financial backers securely.[54] The transactions themselves may be pseudonymous but the people on either side need to know they are sending the money to the right place and that needs some way of verifying identities.

So far, its drawbacks mean bitcoin has mostly been of interest to futurists, libertarians, hobbyists and criminals, as well as speculators and the sort of low-level fraudsters and chancers who accompany every new financial technology. Their price often spikes upwards for no discernible reason, attracting those who want a means to get rich quick like a kind of high-tech lottery ticket or Beanie Baby. Plenty of hedge funds, too, have tried to sell their clients on the idea that both will profit if the fund trades bitcoin on their behalf.[55]

Whatever their merits, cryptocurrencies helped inspire social media giant Facebook to make its own stab at setting a direction for the future of money.[56] After a number of scandals focusing on the company's treatment of user data and spreading misinformation during the US presidential election in 2016 prompted public anger, Facebook was looking for a means to rehabilitate its reputation and worked with other companies to create what it called the Libra Association. Whatever disadvantages such a controversial company had as the creator of a cryptocurrency, it had one big advantage: billions of users.

The company's pitch for Libra, as they called their digital money, was as a means to serve the unbanked and provide a cheap way of transferring money across borders.[57] Among other reasons, 'know your customer' regulations that force banks to check whether or not they are unwittingly facilitating the illegal drugs trade or terrorist financing, means that international money transfers are enormously expensive[58] – the costs of obeying these laws are multiplied as money hops through each stage of the corresponding banking network that lets us transfer bank deposits across borders.

Cryptocurrencies, as pseudonymous electronic tokens, can step around these regulations. A user in Boston can send a bitcoin as cheaply to Baghdad as they can to Birmingham. That's great but only so long as you want to stay within the bitcoin ecosystem; the problem for many speculators comes when they try to use their gains to buy other assets. In 2018 Britain's young bitcoin millionaires found that they were unable to use their profits as a deposit to buy a house:[59] the banks and mortgage brokers could not verify exactly where the money came from.

Libra presented itself as a more grown-up version of bitcoin.[60] The company said it would obey the law and ensure it met anti-money laundering regulations.[61] It would allow cheap money transfers but would not be pseudonymous, instead being based upon some online identity verification – a global version of Aadhaar, presumably related to Facebook's social media offering, although it was not spelled out precisely how this would work.[62]

Facebook left a lot to be desired as the manager of a currency. The company had a notoriously lax attitude to protecting its users' data and was aggressive in using their personal information to get advertising contracts – although the design of Libra denied Facebook access to its users' transaction history. The biggest threat to Libra, however, came not from a consumer backlash but from a regulatory one. While governments may have initially tolerated Facebook's 'move fast and break things' attitude when it came to misinformation and consumer privacy, its attempt to rival the state's control over money was swiftly quashed.

Congresspeople on the Finance Committee of the US House of Representatives called for Facebook to immediately halt all work on its cryptocurrencies after a hearing with the company's chief executive Mark Zuckerberg.[63] The concerns were numerous – demand for the social media company's currency could unsettle trading in traditional currencies; the proposal contained little detail on how Libra's managers would stop money laundering or terrorist financing. Others were worried about what a private currency with the size and power of Libra might mean for their attempts to keep their own currencies under control.

Bruno Le Maire,[64] the French minister of finance, was typical in his attitude to the proposal, though unusually forthright. 'We cannot authorise the development of Libra on European soil,' he said, adding that the 'monetary sovereignty of states is at stake' thanks to the 'possible privatisation of a currency . . . held by a single actor that has more than two billion users'.[65] Bitcoin and other cryptocurrencies were tolerated as the province of eccentrics and gamblers. Facebook's money was seen as a more serious rival to the state.

Libra was meant to be a stablecoin. These aim to avoid the pitfalls that bitcoin fell into. To guarantee a stable value they use the same techniques that central banks have historically tried to fix the value of currencies: keeping reserves of other assets to exchange for the currency at a fixed ratio.[66] Stablecoins were pegged to either an ordinary currency, importing stability from the actions of the central banks who managed it, or to precious metals like gold and silver.

As central banks rely on a stock of reserves to manage a fixed currency, so too would the Libra Association. The stablecoin would be backed by a portfolio of different money or money-like financial instruments – short-term government debt, bank deposits and so on – that would be exchangeable for Libra.[67] For central bankers this was a concern: it could end up being similar to the shadow banking funds that offered money-like assets and whose failure had made the 2008 financial crisis worse. If the coin became as popular as Facebook's social media offering, the management of Libra would have significant implications for financial stability and the operation of the monetary system. Central bankers were barely more comfortable with the proposed idea than the politicians.[68]

The project was watered down.[69] Today the mooted currency is called Diem and will solely be backed by the dollar. In fact, while the company is, at the time of writing, preparing to launch its digital wallet software, it is unclear whether the stablecoin will ever exist. Facebook's attempt to stake out a role in deciding the future of money may not be much different from any other payments company.[70]

The challenge from Libra did, however, prompt central banks[71] to redouble their own efforts at creating digital currencies.[72] Control over money is closely guarded by the central banks and the possibility of an entity the size of Facebook rivalling them spurred their attempts to stake out first their own vision of the future of money.

Central bank digital money

At the end of 2020, Jack Ma, one of the richest people in China, disappeared.[73] Ma, a tech billionaire like Facebook's Mark Zuckerberg, was the creator of Alibaba, an e-commerce outfit, and Ant Group, formerly known as Alipay, a payments company.[74] Ma had spun off Alipay from Alibaba in controversial circumstances, keeping it under his personal control while the rest of the e-commerce company he founded was controlled by shareholders.

Ma disappeared in November.[75] It ought to have been a fantastic month for the tech billionaire: he had planned to sell shares in Ant Group, the world's largest payments company, to the public for the first time, allowing them to trade on stock exchanges.[76] This would lead to a big payout for the entrepreneur and his staff. It would be yet another highlight to Ma's career as a symbol of the new, entrepreneurial and bold China, often leading global innovation.[77]

To many, Ma's downfall had the ring of a Greek tragedy: he flew too close to the sun. In October he had given a speech[78] railing against how China's financial system was regulated, saying the authorities prioritized stability over innovation. If he thought his wealth and fame – he was the world's 25th richest person at the end of 2020[79] (he started the year even higher in the rankings) – would give him the leeway to offer a public challenge to the Chinese authorities, he was wrong. The share sale was cancelled and a government inquiry was launched into whether Ant Group was too large and should be broken up.[80]

For unknown reasons, Ma stopped making public appearances for three months.[81] While he did eventually resurface unharmed, his disappearance showed what was at stake in the battle over the future of money.

Ant Group is a payments company but it is also a data company, although in the internet age they are fundamentally the same thing. The company has a system called Sesame Credit[82] that aims to synthesize 'big data' – the record of transactions in its system – into a single measure of an individual's creditworthiness, taking in everything from their purchases on Alibaba's marketplace to metro tickets. From this, customers get rewards and tailored recommendations, while Ant can,[83] supposedly, use the data to work out who it is most profitable to lend to.

The People's Bank of China would like this data,[84] partly in order to share it with the country's state-owned banks – companies that have long been the target of Mr Ma's criticism.[85] The worry is that defaults could start to rise after China's long economic boom and spread to the rest of the financial system, imperilling its stability.[86] Ant's data offers a chance for the government to work out which loans are likely to be repaid and which should just be written off.

As with many new technologies we should be sceptical about how useful big data is in actually solving these problems. Is there much information that can help us assess creditworthiness beyond someone having a high income relative to their debts and a record of having paid their creditors back in the past? Credit scoring in other countries works reasonably well and does not need to use such granular or intrusive data gathering.[87]

But even if it does not offer much in terms of assessing creditworthiness, this big data does offer something else the government values: control.[88] Much of the fear about Sesame Credit in the west – a lot of it inflected with anti-Chinese prejudice and misinformation[89] – is that it could be the building block of a system of 'social credit'. Information on payments could be used as a form of surveillance in which the government was able to monitor everything you do and give you a ranking – the equivalent of a credit score – to reflect how good a citizen you are. Get too low a score, buy the wrong things and you might soon find you had less freedom.

This may be why China, which first brought paper money to the world, is now in the vanguard of creating new state-backed digital money.[90] The People's Bank of China has one of the most advanced plans to launch a digital currency of any central bank.[91] For the 2021 lunar new year, celebrating the Year of the Ox, the Chinese government handed out traditional red envelopes to some lucky lottery winners containing RMB200 worth of digital renminbi. If this electronic currency can be widely adopted as the main method of making mobile payments, it would mean regaining control from the private companies, like Ant Financial and its rival Tencent, that have become the biggest providers of payments in China.

Digital currency offers governments much more control than cash. Think about the potential for capital controls with a digital currency – how a government could, by pressing a button, suddenly cut off attempts to transfer money out of a country, freezing the accounts of dissidents who are trying to flee. In the words of Mu Changchun, the deputy director of payments at the People's Bank of China, the development of digital yuan is 'to protect our monetary sovereignty and legal currency status. We need to plan ahead for a rainy day.'[92]

In this contest between Ant Group and the Chinese authorities, many of the concerns that inspired the crypto movement are on full display: the close links between governments and banks; the ability of governments to use money as a method of control; and the way in which political concerns can distort the role of money as a neutral medium of exchange. Crypto promises to create apolitical money. Remember how Herbert Hoover said that 'we have gold because we can not trust governments'? Now we have bitcoin too.

Others, however, see it very differently: money really ought to be controlled.[93] A community is entitled to run its affairs in the way it sees fit, and cryptocurrencies, whether the decentralized network of bitcoin or the brainchild of big tech like Libra, are a way of removing yourself from that community. You might be okay with people using cryptocurrencies to fund protests, pay for sex work or get high, depending on your values, but they can also be used to pay for child pornography[94] or pay ransoms[95] to hackers.

Economic management, as well as enforcing the law, depends on governments exercising some degree of control over money. Cryptocurrencies can be used as a means of avoiding tax or to undermine welfare states and other government programmes. The development of the eurodollar market and offshore finance helped undermine the Bretton Woods system by allowing the rich to hide their money away from the authorities. If you are a libertarian concerned with government expropriation that might seem a very good thing, but it looks very different to social democrats.

No one elected Jack Ma or Mark Zuckerberg and gave them the right to pick and choose which rules to follow. Cutting the ties between currency and gold may have opened up the ability for governments to 'debase' it, but it also allowed for the possibility of managing money in the interests of the community, for example aiming to reduce unemployment in recessions. A purely private money may sound to some like a freedom-filled utopia but to others it sounds more like a return to a pre-welfare-state era of exploitation but with new big-tech robber barons, or just a high-tech version of those Swiss bank accounts, letting the rich avoid taxes. Orwell may have warned in *Nineteen Eighty-Four* about the dangers of a totalitarian surveillance state, but when he reviewed Hayek's *Road to Serfdom* he wrote that 'a return to "free" competition means for the great mass of people a tyranny probably worse, because more irresponsible, than that of the State. The trouble with competitions is that somebody wins them.'[96]

Of course no one elected the Chinese government either, and our attitudes to government control over money are likely to reflect our attitudes towards state power generally. For example, Sweden and Germany are, in a lot of ways, very similar. They are both rich, highly educated European democracies. When it comes to the future of money, however, they are in different worlds. In Sweden, the country that brought paper money to Europe, cash is now disappearing the fastest;[97] Germany, however, is a laggard. Hard currency remains incredibly popular.[98]

The difference may come down to attitudes to privacy and government power. The taboo on government surveillance in Germany is strong; the experience of the secret police of both the Nazi regime and the Stasi in East Germany has made Germans value deeply their privacy with regard to the state.[99]

Swedes, with their comparatively peaceful recent history and efficient state, are far more trusting of government institutions. The most remarkable thing about BankID,[100] a universal banking identity in Swedish – the equivalent of India's UPI though entirely run by a group of banks rather than the government – is how uncontroversial it is. Sweden, like China, is in the vanguard of creating a digital money, known as the e-krona.[101]

The European Central Bank is also working on its own central bank digital currency. A 'digital euro' serves a number of purposes but one of the main ones appears to be a means for the EU to retain its sovereignty[102] – if another bloc develops digital money first, then the ECB is worried it may find that there is a currency it cannot control circulating within its territory.[103] The ECB does not want to lose the 'first mover advantage' to someone else, whether China, the US or even Facebook.

The other, stated goal of the project is to create a digital equivalent to cash. Banknotes, like reserves, are a liability of the central bank. But these bits of paper and plastic are the only central bank money – the ultimate means of settlement – the public have access to; otherwise they have to rely entirely on private banks.[104] Reserves are nothing but entries on a balance sheet – they only exist as an accounting concept and only banks with a licence can own them directly. If cash disappears for good, so does the only form of government money you can own.

Digital central bank currencies offer the chance to create a brand-new form of public money[105] that would let the public own something close to central bank reserves themselves – perhaps in state-owned digital wallet apps. This would allow us to have a completely safe form of money, backed by the central bank.[106] We could own the money at the top of the hierarchy – the ultimate means of settlement.

When depositors run on a bank, it is because they are worried the money of that private institution will no longer keep its value relative to the state's money – their bank deposits will not be worth their face value. Central bank digital currencies, however, could do away with the need for private banks altogether, making the monetary system purely public instead.[107] Central bank digital currencies could inadvertently fulfil a Great Depression-era scheme to take banks' power to create money away from them,[108] turning the fractional reserve banking system into a much more regulated 'narrow banking system',[109] in which every deposit would have to be backed 100 per cent by reserves. This, its advocates argue, would not only be safer for individuals but prevent the kind of destabilizing lending booms that can devastate a whole economy.[110]

The other service that cash offers – alongside safety – is privacy. Central banks are working on ways to make their new digital currencies anonymous.[111] One option would be for any transactions under a certain limit to be kept hidden from the central bank, while those over it would be visible. One IMF staffer who wrote an explainer on the subject aimed at his mother suggested that her transactions in the marketplace would not leave a trace but maybe they would if she bought something as expensive as a car.[112]

The problem is that whistle-blowers like Edward Snowden and Chelsea Manning have undermined any trust that these will be genuinely anonymous services. Security services have demanded technology companies insert back doors that can violate the privacy of communication tools.[113] Surveillance has extended to international payment systems. In 2013 the German magazine *Der Spiegel* revealed that the US National Security Agency had been spying on the Belgium-based Society for Worldwide Interbank Financial Telecommunication (SWIFT) that administers the inter-country bank messaging system.[114] Would we really trust their assurances they would not do the same for central bank digital currencies?

In chapter 6 we talked about the 'monetary constitution': the settlements that were reached between the rising commercial classes and the old feudal order over how to keep money safe from governments. The institution of an independent central bank, taking away the power to create new money, was meant to protect these wealthy burghers from having the value of their cash inflated away.

Now we are at the start of a new conflict, one where the fear is not that governments will abuse their control over money to erode its value but that they will extend their authority to places where it does not rightly belong. And here the future is still unwritten: there is as yet no settlement over what the future of money will be like. Similar protections for our digital identities and privacy are, at the moment, being decided – such as in the decision of the Indian Supreme Court that the country's constitution includes a right to privacy.

Although, perhaps, discussions of all these possible futures are just a sideshow – and a damaging one at that, given the enormous energy requirements of bitcoin – to the real monetary question about the future. What can we do to stop the future from being far, far too hot?

11. Can money save the world?

Climate change is, as well as everything else, a financial problem. Money, as we know by now, is intimately connected with time, risk, uncertainty and therefore the future of our planet.

Preventing further global warming means planning, and much of the social machinery for doing so is in the hands of the financial sector. Banks and investment funds provide the backing for wind farms or oil rigs. Start-ups that hope to bring new green technology to market may begin in university research departments but, at a certain point, will come to venture capital funds or bankers for the funds necessary to turn them into viable companies.

It would be hard, however, to find a bigger example of markets failing than climate change. Prices have not worked to disseminate the right information across the economy: too much of some things have been produced, like coal, and too little of other things, like renewable energy, with the consequence that the world is getting inexorably hotter. The problem is that we need not just the local knowledge described by Hayek, but a kind of global knowledge too about how our actions can affect others, even those thousands of miles away. Self-interest alone cannot stop global warming.

In many ways financial and environmental problems are similar: both are about how systems are interdependent. Finance suffers from the same sort of feedback loops and tipping points as ecosystems where one small change can spiral into something much more profound. Millions of people doing what appears to be in their best interest can lead to instability – one person defaulting on their debts can be easily absorbed by banks' capital buffers but millions all doing so at the same time could bring down the financial system.

For this reason, central banks are joining the fight against climate change.[1] Christine Lagarde, the president of the European Central Bank, pledged in 2020 to use the central bank's quantitative easing programme to tackle global warming.[2] She said that the central bank 'has to look at all the business lines and the operations in which we are engaged in order to tackle climate change, because at the end of the day, money talks'.[3]

This might seem an unusual mission for a central bank. The economists, accountants and regulators at these institutions normally shy away from politically sensitive topics. Environmentalism, with all its attendant hot-button topics about individual lifestyles like meat-eating and car driving, is the sort of thing that a central bank would usually avoid at all costs. Much of the public do not know what a central bank is and many of those who helm them would not enjoy the full glare of media attention.

The values of the public at large and the kind of society they want to live in are a topic for politicians who have the legitimacy of being elected.[4] Central bankers are appointed for their expertise, not because they can articulate and advocate certain political philosophies, interests or values – those are the jobs of politicians. While the mandates from which central banks derive their legitimacy – set by elected governments – usually contain words to the effect of 'the central bank should support the government's economic policies',[5] these technocrats are appointed to keep inflation and the financial sector stable and not to tell us how to live our lives.[6]

Climate change, the central bankers argue, is a threat to both inflation and financial stability, and therefore firmly within their wheelhouse.[7] As private banks invest in companies reliant on fossil fuels and we use bank debts as money, a sudden collapse in the value of their loans could damage our monetary system, just as a fall in US house prices led to a financial crisis. Insurance companies, meanwhile, are liable for houses that sit on the coast or on flood plains;[8] and private pensions are invested in companies whose activities emit carbon dioxide.[9] When we come to rely on the income from those pensions, we might find that these businesses are no longer viable.

Volatile weather patterns – extreme events like flooding and forest fires – can feed through into consumer prices and economic growth.[10] Central bankers try to 'look through' such transitory price rises – an increase in the cost of heating due to a cold snap is likely to fade as the weather warms up. Adjusting interest rates to offset every change in the weather patterns will not do much for the long-term strength of the economy – although in the nineteenth century the Bank of England installed a weather vane to keep track of the trade winds: when the winds allowed more ships to dock in London's ports it could affect the amount of goods for sale or, if they carried gold, the money supply.[11]

Mostly, though, the central banks argue, the focus on climate change comes from the financial stability part of their mandate. In 2015, then Bank of England and former Bank of Canada governor Mark Carney warned of the possibility of a moment of financial reckoning[12] when asset values collapse suddenly because of the realization that the fossil fuel-linked assets owned by banks and pension funds will be made worthless by government efforts to tackle climate change. Acting now to ensure that the financial sector is properly pricing the risks they are taking is intended to forestall a future financial crisis.

Economists normally start thinking about climate change and other aspects of environmental economics using the lens of what they refer to as 'externalities'. These are when the actions of two consenting parties affect the well-being of a third, non-consenting party.[13] The classic example is a polluting factory: the business and its customers may both be perfectly fine with it, but a village or firm that lies further down the stream may suffer. These third parties do not have their preferences taken into account when the other two trade.

The goal is to get those who produce externalities to internalize them.[14] This means forcing them to incorporate all the costs they are incurring into their decision making, including those experienced by third parties. Probably the most popular way of doing this, among economists if not the rest of the world, is to use tax[15] – petrol taxes, for example, raise the cost of driving and make people consider the externalities of pollution and congestion when they do. That is the idea, at least.

Externalities are a kind of market failure, in other words when prices do not represent all the important information and therefore cannot efficiently allocate resources. The fisher may know more about the best fishing grounds than any bureaucrat but has little incentive to think of their actions' effects on third parties. If all the fishers take as much as they want and can manage – following the incentives of the market – then fish stocks will be depleted.

It is easy to see how this works for climate change too. The atmosphere and the environment are common resources, and individuals who only consider their own desires can take from them without worrying about harming these common resources. This is exactly what has happened with the world's oceans – overfishing has exhausted the world's stocks and upset the balance of their ecosystems[16] – as well as the amount of carbon in the atmosphere.

In finance externalities are usually a bit different. Often they are what might be called risk externalities;[17] there is no guarantee that they hurt others but the behaviour increases the chance that someone else suffers. A risk externality might be, for example, a driver speeding.[18] This does not always harm someone, but it increases the chance that they will hit a pedestrian: it places a third party at risk.[19] Speed limits, traffic calming measures and mandatory insurance help constrain drivers and force them to internalize, to some extent, the risks they are creating for the rest of the world.

Banks can similarly take big risks without having to pay the full cost if things go wrong. This is because banks' liabilities are the main kind of money within our economy and governments are reluctant to let them go bust – when they have, during the Great Depression and in 2008, the economic consequences have been devastating. The banks are interdependent too – customers of Boring Bank may have been prudent and careful in where they put their money, but a failure of Risky Bank can still see them lose out.[20] Workers who had nothing to do with either may lose their jobs as the wider economy suffers.[21]

When it comes to climate change the worry is that the financial sector is not only facilitating the creation of too much carbon through its lending activities but also neglecting to incorporate how fast the world needs to move to zero emissions in its lending decisions. When the catch-up comes, it will lead to a financial crisis – Mark Carney's moment of reckoning.

Turning finance green

For the central bankers and regulators who try to stop the financial sector from blowing up the rest of the economy, the challenge is working out ways to ensure that banks and fund managers properly take into account the effect of their actions on others.[22] Most of the victims of climate change, whether future generations or the residents of poorer countries most exposed to flooding and droughts, do not have a seat on banks' boards. While some individual bankers may be socially conscious and want to do their best to help the planet, they face all the same incentives and pressures as the rest of us (if not more so) to divorce ourselves from our personal opinions at work.

Generally central bankers want to keep the good parts of the financial system – the fact that we have institutions full of professionals whose job it is to assess and monitor borrowers and markets that share and disseminate this information.[23] They just want to adjust the incentives facing these institutions to better take into account their effect on others – including future generations.[24] The idea is to fix failing markets, not replace them.

By raising the cost of finance for the polluting parts of our economies and lowering it for the green parts, the hope is that over time the financial system becomes greener. Technologies like electric cars or wind farms become relatively more profitable while oil rigs and the internal combustion engine become less profitable[25] and the banks' balance sheets adjust as a consequence. This will hopefully make our economies less prone to emitting greenhouse gases over time while ensuring that markets still do their job by directing capital to its most productive uses.

One option for central bankers and regulators is to increase the capital charges that banks face on holding so-called brown assets,[26] as opposed to non-polluting green ones. Regulators set requirements for how much capital banks have as a proportion of assets: let's say 10 per cent to make the maths simple. If a bank lends out £100 for mortgages it has to make sure it has at least £10 of capital to backstop that lending in case of losses, if it lends £2,000 then it needs £200 and so on. This means the bank, or at least its shareholders, has to put up some of its own money when lending – banks cannot only finance their lending by borrowing, including from depositors.[27]

Not all kinds of lending are equal, however. Boring Bank may invest solely in government bonds, which tend not to default, while Risky Bank could focus on junk bonds – debts that pay much higher rates of interest. For this reason, regulators can demand that banks 'risk weight'[28] their assets, meaning that they need to have more capital if the regulators believe they are taking more risks with depositors' money. Because of the interconnected nature of the financial system, customers of Boring Bank and the rest of society are exposed to the lending decisions of Risky Bank too.[29]

At the moment the debts of major fossil fuel companies are among the most highly rated in the world. Big oil companies like Royal Dutch Shell[30] or Saudi Aramco[31] are treated as not too different from the US federal government[32] or France[33] in terms of safety; the debts of large car companies like Volkswagen, which rely on sales of internal combustion engines, are similarly highly rated.[34] Historically these companies have always been able to repay their debts because of the large cash flows they generate.

Climate change, however, is fundamentally about how the future will be different from the past.[35] There are all kinds of risk that we do not fully understand yet. From how policy could change to try to reduce our dependence on fossil fuels – perhaps making ExxonMobil less profitable if it does not switch its business lines – to how the climate itself reacts to changes in the volume of carbon emissions. Judgements of risk based on the way we used to do things will, we know for sure, turn out to be wrong.

Regulators could raise the capital charges on so-called brown assets by changing their risk weighting,[36] making them reflect the ways in which the world will likely change. If banks want to lend more to fossil fuel companies, car manufacturers or airlines, then they would have to raise more capital – reducing the returns to their existing shareholders and forcing them to internalize, to some extent at least, the costs of their actions. That will hopefully reduce the chance of a sudden reversal in market sentiment towards fossil fuels from spiralling out into a wider crisis.

It could also, at the margin, change how much investment is channelled towards such polluting sectors of the economy.[37] If Risky Bank wanted to lend more to a new coal mining project, for example, it would not only have to increase its capital by the ordinary 10 per cent requirement in our example, but some higher amount to reflect the risk the bank is placing on society. As capital is a more expensive form of funding than debt[38] – shareholders generally demand a higher return than bondholders to compensate them for the risk they are taking – this would increase the cost of making these decisions relative to investing in less polluting assets. Over time this could transform the way our economies look.

Another alternative is to make existing quantitative easing programmes green.[39] The European Central Bank and the Bank of England, two of the central banks which are looking most closely at incorporating climate change into their policy decisions, both have corporate bond purchase programmes.[40] Not only do they create reserves and use them to buy government debt, they also buy up debt from the private sector. Excluding environmentally unfriendly companies from these policies may have the same effect as increasing the capital charges on banks lending to them.[41]

But there are problems here. The first is deciding what counts as brown and what counts as green. If the central bankers come up with their own definitions then the technocrats will be wading into debates about how and how fast to make our economies less reliant on fossil fuels – definitively not their job. In fact, many critics argue they should not be discussing climate change at all. Plenty of other things could affect banks' balance sheets and do not generate so many speeches from central bankers.

Even if they do try to tackle climate change, however, these policies are likely to only have marginal effects. According to research done by the European Central Bank,[42] the cost of borrowing for companies eligible for the quantitative easing programme fell by 0.25 per cent while the cost for similar companies that were ineligible fell by 0.20 per cent. As money is fungible – one dollar is as good as any other – private investors who sell green bonds to the central bank for newly created reserves can reinvest into the brown bonds, reducing the difference between the two assets. That 0.05 per cent interest rate cost on its own is definitely not enough for the kind of shift the world needs for the energy transition.

Some call for more radical policies: instead of green quantitative easing making the existing set of central bank policies greener, they argue that the central banks should finance the climate transition directly. Central bank reserves could be created to fund green projects, perhaps via institutions like the European Investment Bank.[43] Governments have often thrown away the traditional rulebook on public spending when it comes to emergencies – funding themselves in wartime by printing money, and at least considering it during the coronavirus pandemic – and what could be a bigger emergency than climate change?

In this case, however, the problem is not that governments, or at least those of rich countries, cannot afford to invest in the green transition – the potential outlays are not that high relative to the benefits they would bring,[44] especially because the expenditure would, ideally, be balanced by carbon taxes. Instead the difficulty is that reducing emissions will necessarily mean changing how people live their lives, making them drive less, eat less meat or take fewer hot showers. It will mean shuttering coal mines and finding those who work at them new jobs.[45] Imposing such costs will make it more difficult for governments to remain in power.

As technocratic institutions central bankers do not need to worry about re-election – unlike the politicians, who could raise the cost of meat or petrol through taxation but risk losing votes from some carnivores and drivers.[46] Central bankers can move faster too, and the obscurity of regulations like 'risk weighting' or the operation of quantitative easing can give them some cover over political controversies.

They have less power, however. Fiddling with the mechanics of the financial system might make a difference at the margin – and there is no reason why central banks should not be as green as possible when going about their normal business – but would mobilize nowhere near enough resources for the scale of the challenge presented by global heating. The only organization that has the power to heavily tax the activities of carbon-emitting companies and channel public money to infrastructure and research for the green transition is the state – and, for that, you need elected governments.

Ethical investing

Perhaps, then, those of us frustrated with the pace of political change should take matters into our own hands instead of relying on the regulators and the central banks. The growing demand for environmentally and socially 'good' investment funds has fundamentally the same idea behind it as the central banks' tinkering: by investing our savings and pensions into sectors that help towards the green transition the cost of capital for environmentally friendly projects will be lower than for polluting ones.[47]

One of the fastest growing trends in the world of finance is so-called environmental, social and governance investing, or ESG for short. Instead of relying solely on financial metrics – profit and loss, revenue, cashflow – ESG investors try to pay attention to how well companies are meeting their social responsibilities.[48] That does not solely mean how they deal with the environment, but also with people: checking that their suppliers are not engaging in slavery and exploitation, for example, or ensuring their board of directors is diverse[49] and represents the societies the companies are working in.

Companies who can show they can meet these standards are included in dedicated funds.[50] Once again, this means that ESG funds and the whole ethical investment arena is a problem of trust. We need to make sure not only that our money is genuinely going to the areas we want, but also that the companies are doing what they say they will. The market may be an information-gathering system but, at the same time, it provides massive incentives to mislead. Such opportunities to trick others and make off with their money are one reason why markets so often fail.

The Nobel prizewinning American economist Joseph Stiglitz once described banks as 'social accountants': they have the job, similar to the banker in a game of Monopoly, of keeping score.[51] They measure an individual's contributions to the economy and their entitlement to goods and services in exchange. They put potential borrowers into different categories, screening them based on risk, and monitor them to ensure they keep up with their obligations. We can broaden this out to the entire financial system – fund managers do much the same job.

You can still get quite far by lying. History is littered with countless examples of financial fraud, such as the audacious Gregor MacGregor, a nineteenth-century Scotsman who invented a fake country and then sold its government bonds, or the fraudster Charles Ponzi.[52] Ponzi promised to earn his investors huge returns through an arbitrage scheme on postal reply coupons, and his early investors made a fortune. He was, however, just using the money of the later investors to pay off those who got in first. Others are more prosaic, like the accounting frauds of the California electric company Enron or the German electronic payments system Wirecard;[53] these companies simply faked their accounts. And, remember, these are the ones we have heard about: no one other than those who got away with them knows about the truly successful frauds.

Accountants, rating agencies, auditors and even corporate lawyers are as integral a part of the financial system as banks. Their job is to make sure that people are telling the truth and that the picture we have of their financial activities is accurate. We need to know that people are doing what they say they are doing: that the profits they claim to be earning are really being earned. You can imagine how fiercely definitions of profit are contested between investors and the companies they are investing[54] in, and how much companies urge financial journalists reporting on corporate results to focus on a particular, more flattering but non-standard metric.[55]

The growth of ESG investing, then, calls for its own set of information monitors: not so much to assure investors that the cash flows are the size the company says, but to make sure they are genuinely doing good. The problem, however, is that making ethical judgements is a very different kind of challenge from working out if someone is going to pay you back – if 'profitable' is a contested idea, then 'good' is even trickier to pin down.

In 2020, the electric carmaker Tesla was rated as among the most environmentally friendly by one ratings agency, because its cars do not emit any greenhouse gases while they are being driven. Others ranked it far lower, because they focused on the emissions coming from the car-maker's factories.[56] ESG ratings are opinions, perhaps particularly well-informed ones, given the data the ratings companies gather, but still, at the end of the day, judgements. Ordinary rating companies have a more straightforward question to answer – whether the company will default or not. It might be hard but at least in principle there will be a reliable answer.

Take the case of green bonds[57] – these are debts from which the company must use the proceeds it raises to reduce the impact of climate change.[58] There is a fierce debate over what should count as green. Many who invest their savings in them might think that buying a green bond means you are investing in a green company, but that is not quite right. It is just that the proceeds are used in ways that lower emissions.

Amsterdam's Schiphol airport,[59] for instance, has sold green bonds despite how bad flying is for the environment. But as the proceeds were used to improve the energy efficiency of the airport's buildings and to buy electric vehicles for transporting passengers it still counted as green.

Critics accuse companies like this of 'greenwashing',[60] but others take a more consequentialist standpoint: if the company is reducing the damage it does then perhaps that is still good on balance. Philosophers have been debating these ethical dilemmas for centuries, if not millennia, and different people take different approaches:[61] some want to invest with integrity and refuse to make money off environmentally unfriendly companies; others just want to accelerate the shift away from fossil fuels and are willing to get their hands dirty in the process.

Among the biggest issuers of green bonds are banks and governments.[62] Both of these fund hundreds of different green initiatives – high-speed rail links, environmentally friendly housing, electric car projects and so on – but they inevitably fund hundreds of damaging projects too. Banks and governments are huge organizations that finance all sorts of things.

This gets to the biggest problem with ESG investing: money is fungible.[63] If an organization can fund its green activities through a lower cost of capital, then this frees up other resources for the brown activities – a bank with lower costs can do more of everything.[64] Even if ethical investing works perfectly it allows others to get a better deal: anyone happy to invest in polluting companies, or gun manufacturers, tobacco companies or anything else you might object to, can pick them up much more cheaply and consequently enjoy a much higher return.[65]

Still, there are other ethical arguments. Consequentialists may dismiss the idea that profiting from an unethical activity is bad if it would happen anyway. But for others it is a question of personal integrity:[66] they do not want to participate in activities they believe should not happen. Profiting from something you object to would be hypocritical at the very least, but then on the other hand nothing is ever completely 'pure'. How you answer these ethical questions may change how you make financial decisions, but not many of them are traditionally seen as the province of finance.

Ultimately, this is why much of the policy debate about ESG investing is about setting out new standards and policing them properly, whether that is a classification system for different kinds of green bonds or more transparent reporting standards for companies' activities. Forcing companies to disclose more information would allow people to make these decisions for themselves and act as their own social accountants.[67] Or perhaps it could be a new role for money managers – rather than deciding exactly how your pension fund should be managed to meet ethical standards, you could delegate to a trusted individual, paying them a fee to do the job for you of sorting the dark green assets from the merely greenish brown.

So far, ESG investing has not had a particularly significant impact on the climate transition. As of yet there is very little improvement in the cost of capital for companies and banks that sell green bonds or rely on ESG investment – in fact, monitoring and conforming with their strict standards means it can actually be more expensive than raising normal funding.[68] There is a risk of government failure too, to match market failure – many of the bloc's member states threatened to veto the original version of the EU's green taxonomy unless it included natural gas as an environmentally friendly technology.[69]

There are good reasons to care about where your money is going and what it is funding. It is not, however, going to do much to save the world. The financial system ultimately rewards companies that are profitable – ESG investors may not care so much about financial returns but they will never be the only ones – and as long as big oil companies, or any other set of companies that is doing something you object to, can make a profit they will find someone willing to fund them. The key to stopping climate change is to make damaging the environment an unprofitable way of doing business.

Pricing carbon

Money is, as we have seen countless times in this book, a stand-in for value. It is an abstraction that allows us to put a price on all sorts of different things – it can even stand in for other concepts like time and risk. This allows us to make trade-offs: how much do I value a bigger house compared to everything else I could spend the money on? What sort of risk versus return am I happy to take with my pension savings? Do I want that new car right now and to pay interest on a loan or would I rather wait and save up instead?

It also allows a society as a whole to make trade-offs – prices provide signals to assign time and resources to produce certain things. If something is particularly valuable then we want companies to invest in producing it – or researching how to economize on it. For decades the relatively high price of oil compared to the costs of acquiring it incentivized companies to explore, carry out geological surveys and drill for it – the profits were the reward for providing these services. Those prices can go wrong – thanks to different kinds of market failure – but they can also simply be missing.

The concept of economic growth is based on national income, also known as gross domestic product[70] – the sum total of everything produced within the country. To compare the very different things a society produces – from childcare to jet engines – statisticians use their market price. This provides a common scale for weighting different goods and services, all dependent on the relative value that society – as expressed through its willingness to pay – places upon them.

This concept, while useful, is rightly criticized for what it misses out. All sorts of important things do not have a price, from a free state-provided education to the biodiversity of the Amazon rainforest.[71] Statisticians use substitutes, for example spending on teachers' salaries for the value of an education or the cost of renting as a proxy for the benefits of owning your own home.[72] But, inevitably, these comparisons are imperfect and much is missed or excluded by the internationally agreed standards.

That includes the damage that burning fossil fuels does to the planet. In the absence of such a price, excavating more and using them to produce electricity or power cars will be profitable: the companies that do so will find consumers, earn revenues and attract investors. Governments could do that through regulation – outright banning of certain activities – or by putting a price on greenhouse gases so that individuals have to fully reflect on how much damage they are doing to the world and decide if the benefit they get from flying, driving or eating meat is really worth the true cost.

The most popular idea among economists is a so-called cap and trade scheme.[73] Governments set a limit to how much carbon companies can emit – the cap – and companies have to buy the permits in an auction. Then, if they ended up using fewer than they had bid for they can sell them on to other companies who used more – in this way carbon emissions would be priced and only the environmentally unfriendly activities that we value the most would take place. At the moment the EU's emissions trading scheme puts the price of a tonne of carbon dioxide equivalent at around €60 a tonne.[74]

Some want to put a price on the priceless directly. Some economists advocate an idea known as 'natural capital'[75] to reflect that our economies depend not only on stores of money – financial capital – and productive materials – physical capital – but also a healthy planet. Economies would not have got very far without clean water and fertile soil.

Including this natural capital in accounting would put a monetary amount on the other side of the ledger when we consider whether some types of economic activity are truly worthwhile. The environment provides us with all kinds of services – forests sequester carbon as well as delighting hikers. Putting a monetary value on these 'ecosystem services' and from that a price on the natural capital means that we can put these resources on the same scale as all the other things that are valued using money. And then we can decide whether the damage we are doing to the natural world is worth it.

For instance, in Gabon in central Africa, one company is attempting to sell a bond not backed by a government tax or corporate sales revenue but by a forest.[76] The idea is that companies elsewhere who are eager to reduce their own carbon footprint will pay for the trees in the Congolese basin not to be cut down. Those companies can then use this investment to offset their own emissions because the forest sequesters carbon as it grows, reducing their bill on the EU's emissions trading system. Putting a price on the forest allows the Gabonese people to get an economic benefit from leaving the forest as it is rather than cutting it down and farming cattle, for example.

These market-based solutions are not without controversy, partly because they have not been fully implemented. The EU's emissions trading scheme, for example, excludes large parts of the trade bloc's economy, partly thanks to the lobbying of some carbon-intensive industries. Externalities may mean that markets fail, but that does not mean that the governments that attempt to correct them do not fail in their own way too. At present, the trading scheme does nothing about the 'embedded carbon' in imports either – without some form of tariff at the border, companies will just move production to areas with less stringent environmental regulations.[77]

Critics argue that all these market-based policies are simply too timid. They try to adapt a broken economic system rather than rebuilding it totally. There is, they say, a deeper conceptual problem with trying to use money to help the environment. Aiming to put a price on everything moves us from a 'market economy' to a 'market society', and in doing so we lose sight of what is really important.[78] Climate change itself was caused by just such a shift, as the relentless pursuit of money and economic growth that followed the industrial revolution alienated us from the natural world and more sustainable forms of living. The real problem is not that the planet sits too far down on our hierarchy of value but that we rely on money to place things in such hierarchies at all.

12. Has money made us unequal?

In 2020, as the coronavirus pandemic was raging, hospitals were filled with the sick and millions were losing their jobs, plunging into poverty and destitution, the world's billionaires still, somehow, managed to get even richer.[1]

That year, the investment bank UBS estimated that the 2,189 billionaires it could identify had increased their wealth to $10.2tn, beating the previous record of $8.9tn in 2017.[2] No doubt with one eye on drumming up business for its wealth management outfit, the Swiss bank attributed this to the savviness of the billionaires: they had successfully timed the shifts in market prices, buying when everyone else had panicked, and so profited as the stock market recovered.

There was a far less flattering reason why the billionaires had become richer: it was a relatively automatic result of the policies that central banks had pursued to prevent the recession from being deeper than necessary. The Federal Reserve, along with its peers elsewhere, hosed the financial system with new reserves through a quantitative easing programme that was intended partly to calm the panic that was engulfing markets, lowering interest rates, especially long-term ones, even further. This has the effect of mechanically raising the value of financial assets, and so the fortunes of those who already had the most.[3]

A billionaire is someone with at least a billion dollars of wealth.

This may seem obvious but it is worth thinking about exactly what that means. Wealth is a stock measure; in other words, you can think of it as the financial equivalent of a reservoir, a store that stays there year after year. The amount of wealth is, effectively, the water level, how much is in the reservoir at one particular point in time.

It is not an amount of money – none of these billionaires had a billion dollars of cash kept Scrooge McDuck-like in some underground vault – but the estimated resale value of all the assets they own, including property wealth, financial and pension wealth.[4] To add up all the disparate assets owned by a billionaire – farm land, beach houses, rockets to Mars, corporate shares – statisticians use their market price, how much someone else would be willing to pay for them. Money, as a unit of account, provides a common scale to measure someone's wealth.

Income, the amount someone earns, is a flow, more like a stream or river. It, too, is measured in money even if it includes some non-monetary benefits, but has to be defined in terms of time: an hourly wage, a monthly pay packet or an annual salary.

As we know from chapter 3, wealth generally produces an income – the interest on capital. If you own a house you can rent it out; if you own a herd of cattle they give you milk. The more wealth you have, the more income you can earn from it: own two houses and you can, perhaps, earn twice as much rent.

But the converse is true as well. If your cows are particularly productive and give more milk than others then they should be worth more. If your houses rent out for a higher amount then they should command a higher resale value. In an at the least somewhat competitive market there ought to be a link between the income an asset can earn for its owner and its price, in the same way there should be a link between the level of a reservoir and the amount of water it can supply to a community for a year or a decade – the value of the store and the size of the flows should be connected.

Traditionally economists believe that financial markets work out the value of assets – the price of the store – using a method known as 'discounting'. This works out the 'present value' of a right to an income that will last for years, estimating how much it would be reasonable to pay for the billionaire's stock of assets. To do this you discount the flows of income by how long you have to wait for them, adding up the total of these amounts into a single lump sum.

For the discounts, markets are supposed to use the value of time that Böhm-Bawerk identified: the interest rate. Money in twenty years' time is worth a lot less than money today, and money in a hundred years' time even less than that – money tomorrow, though, is barely different from money today. So the further in the future you receive some payment, the less its 'present value' to reflect that you have to wait longer for it.

Suppose you put £100 in your bank account. If the interest rate was 10 per cent, that would turn into £110 in a year's time: in other words, at current market prices, £110 next year is worth £100 today. Therefore £110 in one year's time has a 'present value' of £100. Thanks to the magic of compound interest, the longer you left the money, the more it would grow: that £100 deposited in an account today would become £672 in twenty years' time at a 10 per cent interest rate. So the 'present value' of receiving £672 in twenty years is also £100.

Discounting flips these kinds of calculation around: £100 in twenty years is equivalent to about £15 today at a 10 per cent rate of interest. So £15 is the present value of £100 in two decades. To value an asset like a share in a company or a government bond, you can apply this discount rate to all the income it is expected to generate, discounting distant payments by more and the closer ones less. The total resale value of the asset should then be equivalent to the sum of all the discounted flows it generates, at least in a rational financial market.

When long-term interest rates fall, as they did during the coronavirus pandemic, it should also raise asset values. This is one of the ways in which monetary policy is meant to boost economic growth by making investment more attractive. Those assets which last a very long time or with a more distant payoff ought to be the most sensitive to interest rates.

That included shares in tech companies. Some of these investments are not expected to pay off for decades, as the companies mature and more people start to use their tech. This is one of the chief reasons why the super rich, especially tech billionaires, got even richer during the coronavirus pandemic. While they also profited from people staying at home and using their companies' services – increasing the income the assets generated – the cut in interest rates lowered the rate of discount, increasing the market value of their wealth.[5]

This kind of loose monetary policy is intended to help workers. It is meant to stimulate economic growth so more people stay employed and wages do not fall as far in a recession.[6] But the way this medicine works means it comes with a side effect. The goal is to make investing more attractive, but the effect of this change in the time value of money means it also raises asset prices and boost wealth inequality. Money, then, makes us unequal in this sense – those who have assets get even richer, those without do not.

The wealth of nations

In late 2020, the New Zealand government told its central bank that it must do something about these side effects of monetary policy: the nation had seen house prices increase by 20 per cent during the coronavirus pandemic,[7] pricing young people out of the housing market and the economic security that homeownership can bring.[8]

Partly this had something to do with the government's (at the time) successful attempt to keep the virus out of the country. Plenty of those under lockdowns and confined to their homes elsewhere were no doubt jealous, not only of the country's beautiful scenery but also of the relative freedom it enjoyed.[9] The super rich had already seen the isolated and peaceful New Zealand as a potential bolthole[10] – from terrorism, nuclear war or a civilizational collapse. Successfully quarantining from a pandemic only reinforced this impression.

But it also reflected those factors that had propelled the billionaires' fortunes higher elsewhere: cheap money and low interest rates.[11] The New Zealand Reserve Bank, as its central bank is known, had cut interest rates to 0.25 per cent from 1.5 per cent in its bid to keep the economy stabilized during the pandemic.[12] This helps support house prices, partly by making mortgages more affordable – at least for those who can find the deposit – but also by lowering the 'discount rates' for asset values.

Houses are a bit more complicated than the financial assets we have looked at in previous chapters. No one buys a particular bond or corporate share because it is in a safe neighbourhood, has a beautiful garden or they can imagine their children growing up there. Houses are not only used as a vehicle for saving or speculating but they also provide a necessity: somewhere to live.

Economists have nevertheless suggested that homeowners can think of the flow of income produced by their own house as 'housing services' rather than monetary income.[13] Every year someone lives there they get access to shelter, comfort and so on. If they rent the house to someone else, they are effectively selling these services and so their market price, the return produced by homeownership, is rent.[14]

So houses, even ones that are not rented out by landlords, can be valued using the discounting method,[15] the same as other assets: more distant flows of housing services can be discounted by more, and nearer flows by less. When interest rates fall, without a change in market rents, the price of houses should rise along with other assets. This is exactly what has happened in many countries over the past four decades as interest rates have fallen[16] since their peak in the early 1980s at the time of the 'Volcker shock'.

Think about this in terms of what we saw in chapter 3 about how cutting interest rates stimulates investment. Say you can borrow money at 1 per cent, but you can rent out a house for 5 per cent of its value per year. It would make sense to take out a mortgage and buy a house, earning the difference in profit. Now, of course, you would probably not earn the full 4 per cent – there would be some extra costs, like fixing anything that breaks, and some additional risks, like the chance that you cannot find a tenant and the house is empty. However, with a higher return on the physical capital, the house, compared to the cost of financial capital, it would make sense to keep buying houses until the price of houses rose to equalize the risk-adjusted return.

Ideally house builders would make the same calculation and respond to the cut in interest rates by building more and therefore spending more on investment and employing more people. But with lots of restrictions on where and what you can build, the supply of houses does not respond as much to low interest rates as we might wish. Partly for that reason, it is higher prices rather than lower rents that usually ensures the rate of return between the two kinds of capital is equalized.

Rising house prices have increased the gap between the haves and the have-nots. Those who own see the value of their assets increase, while those who rent see no change in their wealth. The effect, all else being equal, is to move property ownership further out of the reach of renters – the cost of a mortgage might fall with interest rates but first-time buyers need a bigger deposit thanks to higher prices.[17] Housing, simultaneously being the most widespread form of wealth and an essential service, makes this one of the most damaging ways that money can make us unequal, introducing greater divisions within our societies. Some desperate young New Zealanders even resorted to pushing flyers through letterboxes to find someone willing to help them buy a house.[18]

So, in 2021, the New Zealand government changed the Reserve Bank's remit.[19] The country's finance minister told the central bank that it must now consider the impact of its decisions on house prices. This did not amount to a change in the central bank's objectives, which remained keeping inflation low, supporting employment and ensuring financial stability, but the bank was told to 'take into account government policy relating to more sustainable house prices, while working towards its objectives'. It would now have to regularly explain how it was doing so[20] and justify its policies to the government in light of their impact on house prices.

New Zealand already has a reputation as an innovator when it came to central banking.[21] The country's Reserve Bank was the first to embrace inflation targeting in 1989, becoming the example for other countries.[22] The modern central bank is, in essence, a New Zealand invention: in addition to its inflation target, the Reserve Bank was made operationally independent and told to provide the public with regular updates on its decision making – the rest of the world followed.

The latest innovation is unlikely to catch on. Using monetary policy as a tool to control house prices leaves a lot to be desired.[23] Central banks struggle enough to hit their inflation targets and trying to use interest rates to lower house prices would mean running a very different policy from the one that would be justified by the rest of the economic data, especially unemployment.

Making money more expensive in the midst of the coronavirus pandemic would have meant deliberately allowing more businesses to fail and workers lose their jobs in order to reduce the market price of a house.[24] This could have, if anything, reduced slightly the number of actual houses available by making it less attractive for property developers to build them and more expensive for banks to grant house buyers credit.[25] Falling wages, too, could have put houses further out of the reach of workers even if the price of a house fell.

When asked about the impact of their policies on inequality, central bankers will often concede that lower interest rates have boosted asset prices.[26] But this, they say, is not their fault. When they make policy they choose their policy rates with reference to their view of the 'natural interest rate', and it is the fall in this over the past three decades – thanks to declining productivity, ageing societies and potentially many other factors – that has lowered 'discount rates'. If the central bankers had tried to resist this change in economic reality it would have meant deflation, mass unemployment and a repeat of something close to the Great Depression.[27]

Perhaps the problem is that we rely on the central banks too much. There are two broad categories of how governments can respond to a downturn: the monetary policy of central banks and the fiscal policy of government spending. In very general terms, the economic orthodoxy for the past few decades has been that governments should focus on keeping the national debt a sustainable proportion of national income and leave the job of macroeconomic stabilization to the technocrats who control interest rates.[28]

More fiscal stimulus, however, could raise market interest rates without increasing unemployment. In the mainstream paradigm of economics, it would raise the 'natural interest rate' by increasing the demand for capital. For instance, in late 2020 and early 2021 interest rates rose after the US Democratic Party won fifty seats in the Senate, as investors anticipated that higher government spending following the centre-left party's victory would alleviate deflationary pressures and central banks would lift their policy rates.[29] The news that the president was trying to pass the largest programme of fiscal stimulus in US history, relative to the size of the economy, then led to a sell-off in technology stocks.[30]

There are other options too. Perhaps governments could look at wealth taxes, directly redistributing the unearned windfall the super-rich get from lower interest rates. Or perhaps stricter regulatory restrictions on house purchases are needed – the New Zealand central bank introduced limits on how much house buyers could use debt.[31] House prices may be sensitive to interest rates but this process is mediated by banks and the availability of mortgage finance. Other countries rely less on homeownership to supply housing services and instead use tightly regulated, long-term rental contracts or government-owned housing. This offers housing security without having to own your own home.[32]

In this way, it is worth thinking about the whole suite of things a government does, not just how it responds to recessions. Wealth inequality is just one kind of inequality, and possibly not even the most important kind.[33] Economists have generally focused more on the disparity in incomes, the difference in what people earn. Alternatively we might be concerned that everyone has equal access to a certain set of basic services like housing, healthcare or childcare.[34] Equality is multidimensional.

Take two countries with very different approaches: Sweden and the United States. Measuring wealth inequality is hard, but according to some estimates social democratic Sweden, with free healthcare, university education, high rates of union membership and a generous welfare state, is actually more unequal[35] than the US, with its more individualist and market-based approach to public services. *The Economist* magazine once wrote that only tax havens and kleptocracies had more wealth inequality than Sweden.[36] Despite this, many American socialists hold up the Nordic model's approach to inequality as something to emulate.[37]

For good reason. Collectively owned assets or entitlements to state services often do not show up in personal wealth statistics.[38] If statisticians valued free lifetime access to Sweden's system of state-provided healthcare in the same way as markets value financial assets – discounting the right to this service for life by the interest rate – then poorer groups in the Nordic country would look a lot richer.[39] State pensions, too, often do not show up in measures of personal wealth, unlike private pensions – if the poor do not need to accumulate savings in Sweden because they can be assured of support through their retirement, then do they really need to worry about wealth as much as Americans?

The problem with wealth inequality is that the value of capital increases relative to the cost of labour and wages. The rich have a greater ability to pay others to do things for them – they can sell some of their shares and use the money it generates to pay others to, for example, help them fly to space or to lobby for policies they favour. A rising concentration of wealth is concerning because it allows just a handful of people to command what thousands of others do as the value of their assets has got higher relative to the wages that others depend on for survival. In the words of the philosopher Jean-Jacques Rousseau, 'by equality, we should understand, not that the degrees of power and riches are to be absolutely identical for everybody; but that . . . in respect of riches, no citizen shall ever be wealthy enough to buy another, and none poor enough to be forced to sell himself'.[40]

Rather than trying to equalize wealth, a society could try to diminish its importance in people's lives: New Zealand could make renting a better, more stable option, for example. That might prevent young New Zealanders from feeling as if they have to beg others to help them buy a house. Perhaps the biggest reason why wealth inequality is less controversial in Sweden than in the US is that it does not lead to such unequal access to status, power and security.

Sweden, however, has started to become more unequal in recent decades. Since the 1990s income inequality has been rising much faster than in most of the OECD group of rich countries.[41] Many commentators blame this on a change in the ideology of the governing parties since the 1980s, inspired by the same turn to the free market that was happening in the US under Ronald Reagan or with the Chicago Boys in Chile.[42]

One of the forms this turn took in Sweden was the introduction of vouchers for education[43] – trying to use money's role as a way of disseminating information to improve efficiency, as it did for the American food banks we looked at in chapter 8. But bringing market thinking into education, critics allege, has led to both a more unequal society and a worse school system – access to education is very different from distributing food more efficiently.[44]

This gets to the heart of what might be one of the most controversial ways that money can make us unequal: it gets inside our heads. And perhaps the best way to keep this at bay is to keep money only where we are sure it really belongs.

It's a rich man's world

Money changes the way we think. That includes how we think about each other: for whatever reason, when cash is involved it provides some measure of psychological distance that allows us to have less empathy with the people we are dealing with. When money is involved it's not personal, it's just business.

People treat monetary incentives differently from non-monetary ones.[45] Countless studies have shown if you pay people to do something they think of it differently than if they do it for free. One famous example comes from the world of childminding: a nursery fed up with parents turning up late to collect their children began to fine them if they did not arrive at the scheduled time. This had the opposite effect. Parents would no longer arrive on time, interpreting the fine as a payment for additional services. The monetary cost of giving up a little bit of cash was less painful than the psychological cost of feeling guilty about not being there on time for your child.[46]

Prices and the market are one way societies have of organizing production – what gets made – and distribution – who gets it – but so are social norms, the unwritten codes that guide our behaviour.[47] Many of these norms are about when it is and when it is not appropriate to use money; where the principles of market exchange fit and where they do not. When money intrudes into areas we do not expect – a parent bribing their child's way into a good university, for example – we can react with shock and disgust.[48]

Many of the strongest taboos about money are related to our bodies. Selling organs is prohibited, as is selling blood in many parts of the world – although not in the United States. Sex work, for example, has been ubiquitous as long as there has been money, and it has similarly been condemned and prohibited.[49] Commercial surrogacy, paying a woman to become pregnant with another family's child, is illegal in many countries[50] and deeply controversial in those where it is not.[51]

Perhaps relatedly, there are also a set of taboos about the role of money and what might be called 'care work'. Within a family, money is not supposed to play any role in the provision of care for one another – at least for parents towards their children. On his twenty-first birthday Ernest Thompson Seton, one of the founders of the Boy Scouts of America, was presented with a bill from his father.[52] The invoice was for the cost of raising him, including the charge for his delivery at the hospital.

Families are meant to remain islands of gift economies in a sea of market relations. Adam Smith famously said that we did not rely on the 'munificence of the baker'[53] for our evening meal but appealed to his self-interest; later writers have pointed out that Smith may have got his beef and bread thanks to the market, but he still relied on his mother to cook for him. We do not know why his mother, Margaret Douglas, did this – history is mostly silent about her – but Smith appeared to rely on her munificence at least.[54]

Just because they work in a different way from calculations about interest rates does not mean that these norms are irrational. Many of the worries about bringing money into these transactions are legitimate concerns about exploitation.[55] You cannot sell yourself into slavery any more, for example. In Victor Hugo's nineteenth-century novel *Les Misérables* the tragic Fantine is forced to sell her teeth and hair and to prostitute herself to care for her infant daughter – her desperation drives her to exchange her body for money, and the abuse she receives when she does eventually kills her.[56]

If our concern about inequality is, like Rousseau, that it allows the rich to be able to, effectively, buy and sell the poor, then these taboos set out a limit on the extent of the market society: what the rich should not be able to pay the poor to do. Slavery is rightly banned, but the limits of what people should morally be allowed to be paid for are far murkier. For example, in Germany, commercial surrogacy is banned as violating the dignity of women. Meanwhile, in the US, a group of women sued an industry body of fertility doctors to secure the right to be allowed to set their own prices for their eggs, alleging the guidelines over pay rates amounted to illegal price fixing.[57] What some see as exploitative market relations others see as autonomy over their own bodies.

It should be obvious that many of these taboos about the role of money are entwined with gender. Care work and sex work are both disproportionately done by women. Often the same woman: a single mother like Fantine relying on sex work to pay the bills is by no means unusual.[58] Men, on the other hand, predominate in those areas of life where money rules – the stereotype is that money and commerce are masculine, or at least not very feminine.

Historically most finance ministers, bankers and central bankers have been male. Janet Yellen became the first female head of the Federal Reserve in 2010;[59] Christine Lagarde became the first female head of the IMF in 2011 and then the first woman to helm the European Central Bank in 2019.[60] Since the eurozone central bank was set up in 1998 there has only been one female head of a European national central bank – the Central Bank of Cyprus. While the UK has had two female prime ministers it has still never had a female Chancellor of the Exchequer, as the country's finance minister is known.[61]

The world of money seems to be even more stubbornly resistant to gender equality than other areas of life: the gender imbalance among doctoral students studying economics is worse than in science and technology.[62] Meanwhile women are over-represented in sociology, psychology and anthropology, social scientific disciplines[63] that similarly look at how people make decisions, just not usually about money. In economics itself there is a pattern of gender segregation, with men more likely to publish papers in macroeconomics and finance and women in areas like labour and development economics.[64] It suggests that academic economics reflects wider stereotypes about how rationality, calculation and commerce are coded as male, while care and emotions are seen as feminine, and money, many wrongly think, solely belongs to the former.[65]

Emotions come into monetary matters all the time. Gender norms might be particularly strong and influential, but these are by no means the only controversies where the values of the market – price, exchange and efficiency – confront what are not supposed to be financial matters. Often the concern is not exploitation but corruption: money changes the character of the thing that is traded.[66] You should not be able to buy your way to the front of a race or purchase some honour. Many academics have complained that since the UK introduced tuition fees for university education, students act like consumers and feel entitled to a good grade because of the money they have paid.[67]

Yet excluding certain things from the logic of the market can mean they are not valued highly.[68] We esteem caring professions but pay them badly; we condemn the greed of hedge fund managers but our society rewards them well. Nurses are held up as exemplars of goodness but many of them would prefer more

monetary rewards as well. Numerous feminist economists[69] –
Margaret Reid in her 1934 book *The Economics of Household
Production*,[70] for instance – have pointed out that much of the
production at offices and factories that is remunerated by the
market depends upon unpaid work done at home, mostly by
women. The difference between something being priceless and
it being treated as worthless is often smaller than we think.

Today some suggest the barriers between the spheres where
money dominates and where other rules hold sway are falling
down. Moral values are gradually being displaced by financial
values as the logic of the market is extended to areas where it
previously did not belong,[71] like Sweden's education reforms.
Personally, I am not sure about that. It is hard to tell over the
great sweep of human history whether morality is really
changing: buying and selling human beings used to be much
more commonplace, for example. Marriage was once regarded
as something close to a market transaction, with dowries or
bride prices, whereas now in many societies it is meant to be
solely for love, and the gold digger, the woman who marries
for money instead, is condemned. Social norms do not only go
in one direction.

Money is emotionally messy.[72] It can provoke strong, sometimes contradictory reactions. Discussing money can fill us with
anxiety and dread – in many countries the taboo against telling
people how much you earn remains incredibly strong. Perhaps
it is because there is no way of coming well out of these conversations: earn too much and you can provoke envy and resentment
among your friends; earn too little and they could see you as
failing to meet a particular standard of success.

Ultimately, our attitudes to money are best described as
ambivalent:[73] our societies may desire money but they are simultaneously slightly disgusted by it and by those who pursue it to

the exclusion of all else. Money is chiefly associated with in-authenticity, individualism and selfishness – despite its deeply social nature, it is regarded as antisocial. Part of the problem seems to be that while we all know what money is worth, we do not always quite know what it means.

The value of everything

'You never say thank you,' Peggy Olson, a young advertising creative, yells at her boss and sometime mentor Don Draper during one episode of the TV series *Mad Men*, furious that he has not given her enough credit for his award-winning ad idea. Don yells back, equally angrily, 'That's what the money is for!'[74]

One of the themes of this book is that money is a symbol. We have seen that it can stand in for social trust, provide re-assurance against an uncertain future and represent national sovereignty or the lack of it. Prices, meanwhile, as we have seen, can carry information – a means of communicating with strangers what you want them to do – or risk – the chance that the world will turn out in a way we would rather it did not.

But symbols can sustain many different interpretations. Two people can look at the same money and see very different things in it: is it a token of esteem, a representation of how much you value what someone has done for you; or an indication of just how little you value their contribution, not respecting them as a friend and a peer but seeing your relationship as purely transactional?

Money allows us to put a value on anything – it allows us to rank very different things by how much they are worth and to exchange them for one another. This is useful, as we have seen many times. But worth cannot be exclusively captured by money either – it may fail to reflect the value we place on things like privacy, the natural world or the unpaid care work done mostly by women. A single symbol cannot stand in for everything. Neither should we necessarily want it to.[75]

To many people the problem is that money is corrupting.[76] It breaks down boundaries between the areas where money is meant to be banished and those where it is tolerated as useful. Taboos keep some things sacred and free from the grasping ethos of the market[77] – whether that is family life or our love lives. For those on the right of politics, money undermines traditional values, and for the left, it displaces solidarity and empathy. Those across the political spectrum would agree that it can be flattening, reducing the diversity of human experience to a single metric.

Now, if you would permit me, after twelve chapters, a moment of self-indulgence, I would like to speak in defence of my subject.

Throughout this book I have told you stories of revolution, conflict and social transformation all featuring money. In many of them money has been quirky, unusual and deeply reflective of the societies that use it – take the Maria Theresa thalers, which spread not only due to their reliable value but also because they were regarded as helpful in promoting fertility. More recent shifts like the rise of ESG investing or cryptocurrencies have demonstrated how we see the world.

Nowadays, the images on our money are probably the most reproduced artworks in human history, telling the story of who we are, what we care about and who we would like to be. For example, in 2017 Britain put a portrait of the novelist Jane Austen on its £10 note.[78] In a way the novelist might have appreciated, this exposed the particular insecurities and social niceties of the modern UK. This started from its inception – as part of a social media campaign by the activist Caroline Criado Perez, who sought to ensure that at least one of the country's banknotes featured a woman other than the queen, and received plenty of abuse in recompense – and continued right through to its launch: that the newly plastic money used animal fat in its production spurred a debate about whether it was suitable for vegans.

It is not just physical money that reveals something about our societies, of course; so does the way we behave towards money. For instance, the sociologist Viviana Zelizer has investigated how we invest particular bits of money with meaning.[79] Money is meant to be fungible, all exchangeable for one another and all identical. But really particular money is tied to particular ideas and stories. She examined how money was treated in turn-of-the-century American marriages, with the money that working husbands paid to their stay-at-home wives. She separated it into three categories: payment, entitlement and gift.

Money as payment, she wrote, came with the associations that we have referred to as the principles of the market: emotional distance, efficiency and bargaining. But as a gift, there were ideas of subordination from those who can give to those who depend on charity, and it was arbitrary – husbands could withdraw it at any time. As an entitlement, however, the money embodied a woman's power and autonomy in the domestic sphere. The same amount of money may have changed hands, for the exact same purposes, but the meaning placed upon it changed how the relationship worked.

While money is often used antisocially, it always remains deeply social. It can only really exist as a relationship between people, money fundamentally is us. In other words, money does not corrode our values but expresses them; it is another symbolic medium, like language or art, for demonstrating precisely who we are.

Perhaps you are reading this book in a cafe. If you look around, you can see all the many ways money reflects society. From the till where you paid for your coffee and the waiting staff working for their daily wage, or out the door to the street, where a busker is performing for change, a commuter hurries to work to pay their mortgage, or even, more unhappily, someone gets mugged. Behind closed doors a divorcing couple rows over how to divide their assets; a gambler yells happily at the football match on television; a drug dealer sells his client some product, for cash of course.

Money accompanies us through everything we do, the good and the bad. All human life is there. We might not like what we see in the mirror but we cannot really blame the mirror for that. Ultimately, if money has made us unequal it is because we have let it.

13. What happened next?

For the most part, I wrote this book during the plague year of 2020, often locked down and stuck at home. It was an odd experience, sitting at a makeshift desk in me and my girlfriend's bedroom, trying to write my first book while, every day, the numbers of infected were being read out on the news and health experts were urging everyone to remain at home to avoid spreading the virus. Despite being an act of communication with your readers, writing a book can be a lonely and difficult experience. Writing it while isolated due to a pandemic, doubly so.

However, my own struggles were a luxury compared to those faced by the scientists and medics on the frontline, racing to find a cure or fighting to keep patients healthy. The pandemic also became an economic emergency. Central bankers and finance ministers fretted that the economies they managed were heading for deflation, or that the whole financial system could topple over, potentially leading to a repeat of the deep recessionary pit of the Great Depression. The puzzle that policy-focused economists were trying to figure out was how to keep economies growing through lockdowns and people employed, rather than how to bring surging prices to heel.

In the world of money, a lot has changed in the nine months since the first UK edition of this book was published in January 2022. The Russian invasion of Ukraine the following month and the consequent jump in energy prices has rippled throughout the world. The invasion brought with it the risk of a re-run of the Great Inflation of the 1970s, when an oil price shock – that time provoked by war in the Middle East – combined with pre-existing inflationary pressure to push rich countries towards stagflation: a lethal combination of low growth and high inflation. After a slow start, central banks reacted: the world of cheap money, such as the negative interest rates we discussed in chapter 3, has gone into retreat. The long boom in financial markets that such loose monetary policy encouraged has consequently come to an end or, at least, a temporary pause.

The twists and turns of 2022 provide us with opportunities to put into practice many of the lessons in this book. For instance, understanding how banks work, the subject of chapter 2, helps us make sense of the sanctions applied to Russia by Europe and the US; in particular how they function and why those countries rely on money being not coin but a promise. The theories expounded in chapter 4 provide a lens to understand the recent return of inflation, and the examination of interest rates in chapter 3 can help us understand how central banks view their job of taming it.

Let's start with the sanctions. The use of money as a tool for the powerful to get what they want is a topic that we touched on in chapter 5 when we looked at the unique position of the US in the world economy. That the dollar is the most important currency in the world allows the country to project power far beyond its borders. In 2022, that advantage became a means for Ukraine's allies to support the country's continued existence against its larger, aggressive neighbour.

For Ukraine, the return of open war to Europe was an economic tragedy as well as human one. Data is scarce – collecting statistics can be hard when you are fighting for your life – but the country's national income likely fell by around half in the first few months after the invasion. Such a drop makes sense. An estimated six million refugees fled the invading forces to neighbouring countries. The physical capital of the economy was literally destroyed. Buildings, factories, railways, roads, schools and colleges were all bombed by Russia into rubble. Ukraine depended on support from its allies to fund its resistance, and even then it has continued to remain on the verge of a financial crisis.

Russia has not been immune to the economic devastation unleashed by its war either. This is partly because Ukraine's allies in the West – in Europe and North America – responded to the invasion by launching the most comprehensive package of sanctions the world had ever seen. In doing so they took a step that no one, including Russia itself, had expected: they placed the Russian central bank itself under sanctions. This has only been done a handful of times before, to countries like Venezuela and North Korea, which were already isolated from much of the world economy.

The pre-eminent role of the dollar in the global economy gives the US a very powerful weapon and means it can, essentially, cut other nations off from the world's financial system. Most money is a kind of promise, usually a bank deposit, so if the US bans its banks from dealing with certain countries it makes those promises worthless. Banks have to choose between stopping doing business with those on the sanctions list or facing the wrath of the US government. For most, the choice is easy.

Russia knew this was a possibility and, before it invaded Ukraine, it ran an economic strategy that has become known as 'Fortress Russia'. Ever since the country annexed the Crimean Peninsula in 2014, the Russian government avoided borrowing from abroad and ran a big fiscal surplus, meaning the government taxed much more than it spent. This, along with exporting oil and gas, allowed the country to gather more and more foreign exchange reserves. As we saw in chapter 7, which looks at why countries use different currencies, having to rely on borrowing from abroad, in a foreign currency, undermines a country's sovereignty: it requires keeping international investors sweet so they will continue to lend to the country.

Russia's goal through the 'Fortress Russia' strategy had been to avoid that financial dependence. The Russian central bank's foreign exchange reserves had climbed 70 per cent by the time of the 2022 invasion of Ukraine. The total stockpile amounted to $635bn, roughly equivalent to about a third of Russia's national income.

It is easy to imagine these foreign exchange reserves as vast piles of US dollars or gold bars kept in vaults but, as we know, that is not what most money is: it is a promise. Foreign exchange reserves are usually promises from other countries, either their governments or private companies. A dollar on the Russian central bank's balance sheet, for example, could be a record of a promise from an American bank or even some US government debt. The idea is to keep the reserves in safe, liquid assets – ones that are easily exchangeable for actual goods and services.

In building its fortress, however, Russia mostly avoided using dollars, which are usually the most popular reserves thanks to the liquidity, abundance and relative safety of dollar-denominated assets. Instead, the country kept its foreign exchange reserves mostly in gold, euros and the Chinese renminbi. The idea was that even if the US imposed sanctions on Russia the country would still be able to buy the goods and services it needed on the international markets by using these other currencies.

Even so, the fortress held out for only a matter of weeks. The response from the EU in particular was stronger than predicted.

Russia's autocratic president Vladimir Putin had expected sanctions from the US but calculated that a divided Europe, dependent on Russia's natural gas, would be reluctant to anger its neighbour and imperil its domestic economies solely for the sake of Ukraine. That was not an unreasonable assumption on Putin's part: the 2014 annexation had been met by a fairly meek response from the EU. For example, Germany had continued to support the construction of the Nord Stream 2 pipeline which, if it had ever been completed, would have allowed Russia to bypass Ukraine and not pay its neighbour royalties when sending natural gas to Germany.

The key policy was to sanction the Russian central bank directly. Any foreign bank acting with the Russian banking system or the central bank – a necessary condition for using its foreign exchange reserves – risked being cut off from the much more valuable dollar trading system. It was just one part of the sanctions package, however. Russian banks were also thrown out of the SWIFT messaging system for international transactions. Yachts owned by Russian oligarchs were seized. Even the Nord Stream 2 pipeline project was cancelled.

The goal behind these sanctions was to prevent Russia from accessing the foreign currency necessary to continue fighting the war. War requires material: assembling a tank requires components, planes need chips for onboard computers, and so on. Russia is a big country with plenty of natural resources but it is not self-sufficient and needs to buy things from abroad to continue its war, especially more advanced western technology. By imposing such wide-ranging sanctions, the goal was to deprive the Russian government of this equipment without risking a direct confrontation between two nuclear superpowers.

Perhaps the most potent sanctions have been among the least discussed. Financial sanctions and seizing oligarch's yachts may have captured the headlines but industrial measures were more effective. Measures to ban companies from exporting components to Russia – including the restriction of any product made using American software, tools or other goods – made it much harder for the country to continue to manufacture and use weapons.

Russia was forced to direct its industrial production into keeping its war going rather than providing its citizens with the goods that would actually make their lives better. The production of fridges, for instance, was 40.3 per cent lower in the first six months of 2022 than during the same period in 2021, while output of passenger cars fell 61.8 per cent. Russia may have plenty of national resources but it lacks the technology of the EU and US. Components normally directed to the civilian economy had to be diverted to the military. A new 'sanctions-proof' Lada, a Russian-made car, came without any airbags, for example.

However, there was a gaping hole in the economic blockade that had been placed around Russia. Oil and gas trade was initially given an exemption from the sanctions. European and American businesses were permitted to continue trading energy products. The rest of Europe's dependence on Russia for fuel meant that governments were unwilling to cut the country off altogether. However aggressive the sanctions were, they remained limited: hydrocarbons were overwhelmingly Russia's main and most lucrative export.

Russia's trade balance – the difference between what a country earns from selling its exports and pays for buying imports – improved dramatically. The country stopped publishing its own trade statistics, but aggregating data from its export partners showed Russia was on track to hit a record surplus during the first half of 2022. This was not necessarily good news for Russia but a reflection of the fact that it could not buy anything from abroad. Imports cratered. Russia managed to sell its oil, often at a deep discount, but the money other countries paid was just a promise and one they would, generally, be unwilling to keep.

The sanctions did not stop the war. The so-called 'economic weapon' is not all powerful, and autocrats are often willing to make their citizens poor to achieve their goals and will rally around the flag as the country's enemies try to impoverish it. US sanctions on Iran have not stopped the country from working towards developing nuclear weapons, neither have they brought down Venezuela's dictatorial and corrupt regime. Cuba's communist government has continued under a US trade blockade for decades.

Sanctions can often be counterproductive if the goal is to encourage citizens to rise up and change a foreign government. It is possible that, by completely isolating Russia, the West will undermine the growth of the foreign-oriented middle class that is the most opposed to Vladimir Putin and will reinforce the siege mentality of the country, which sees itself as uniquely victimized on the international stage. Money might be a powerful geopolitical force but nationalism can often be far stronger. Russia inflicted far more damage on Ukraine's economy through its invasion but the Ukrainians have no intention of giving up in response either. Neither, for that matter, did European solidarity with Ukraine wane as the war provoked a spike in energy costs and a squeeze on living standards.

Inflation returns

Even before Russian tanks and troops crossed Ukraine's borders, there were warnings that inflation was returning. As the world emerged from lockdowns, and vaccines made the pandemic manageable, price pressures returned from their long slumber. In January 2022, Eurozone inflation was at 5.1 per cent, the fastest rate since the single currency had been created in 1999 (just the previous year the currency bloc had been flirting with deflation). In the US, things were even worse. The consumer price index was 7.5 per cent, higher that January than it had been the previous year. That was the fastest rate of inflation in forty years, since the disinflationary 'Volcker shock' of the early 1980s that features in chapter 4.

Some of this price surge can be traced back to the disruption caused by the pandemic. Take one category of goods that have become vital to the modern economy: computers chips. Semi-conductors are used in everything, from video game consoles to cars. The pandemic subjected the market to constantly shifting supply and demand dynamics, leading to shortages and sky-rocketing prices.

The move to home-working, for example, raised demand for electronics. Employees needed new laptops or PCs to continue working smoothly, and others thought it was a great time to invest in a new TV. Spending patterns moved all at once in the same way across the world. Consequently, prices for the components that went into consumer electronics rose sharply.

Rapid whipsaws in consumer demand as economies locked down, reopened, locked down and reopened again, led to a phenomenon known as the 'bullwhip effect' on supply chains. Car manufacturers believed that the pandemic would cause a deep and prolonged global recession. Thinking that would mean fretful consumers would avoid buying new cars, they reduced production. That decision rippled out through their supply chains – fewer cars being made meant less demand for engines, and so on – and their suppliers also cut back on production.

With the discovery of vaccines, heavy levels of government

spending to maintain jobs and incomes, and the return of consumer confidence, demand did not drop as much as antici-pated. So supply chains whipped back the other way. Used car prices rocketed as the pandemic shutdowns and scarcity of semiconductors contributed to a shortage of new cars at the exact time more people were shunning public transport to avoid contracting the virus. Just as a small flick by someone holding the handle of a whip can lead to a huge movement at the other end, small changes in demand led to huge shifts in prices.

Before the Russian invasion, fuel prices had already spiked. Some of this was due to the same sort of rapid shifts in supply and demand affecting chip supplies and car manufacturers. Oil producing countries, such as Saudi Arabia, had cut back produc-tion and investment during the pandemic. They anticipated that the shutdowns would quash demand for fuel: no planes were flying, for instance. With the end of lockdowns, demand surged back much faster than supply could be switched on and prices for oil skyrocketed. The cost of Brent crude, the main interna-tional benchmark, reached around $85 per barrel by the end of January 2022, up from around $47 per barrel the year before.

In Europe, the fuel shortages were particularly bad. In hind-sight it is clear that Russia was preparing for its invasion of Ukraine by reducing natural gas shipments to the EU, so flows from Russia to Europe were down by a quarter compared to the same time in 2021. That put the squeeze on European buyers, and the cost of natural gas reached a record in December 2021, hitting about eight times the level seen the previous winter. Gas storage too was running far below its usual volumes. The Russian plan had clearly been to ensure that Europe would have little gas stored so it wouldn't support Ukraine and thereby risk Russia switching the gas off.

Chips, fuel and cars were not the only bottlenecks. Some

countries found that instead of the anticipated mass unemployment following the pandemic-induced recession, they actually had a shortage of workers. Truck drivers, for instance, were in short supply. The job has often been quite grim: pay is low, the hours are bad and the days can be lonely. Many drivers gave up altogether during the pandemic. These departures might have been OK if more drivers could have been recruited to replace those who left but the pandemic made that harder. Not least because border restrictions made immigration more complicated. Trucking companies were forced to raise wages to keep hold of the drivers they had and to attract new workers to the industry.

These kind of 'labour supply' problems were not limited to just a handful of occupations but were widespread across Europe and America. Something seemed to have been knocked loose in the relationship between workers and bosses. Whatever it was, it became known as The Great Resignation or the Big Quit as workers went looking for something new. In the US, where the phenomenon was the most acute, the proportion of workers switching jobs reached the highest rate in November 2021 since the Bureau of Labour Statistics started measuring in December 2000.

There are economic explanations for what was happening in the jobs market. Vacancies were at a record high and workers were responding, rationally, to the situation in front of them: their skills were in demand, why not look for something better? It also felt as if something more profound was happening. The brush with mortality, in the form of the coronavirus, made people ask whether they really wanted to spend their brief lives in jobs they did not truly like. Working from home eroded the bonds of friendship and the feelings of obligation that can keep people tied to jobs. Perhaps, too, there was a desire to regain control after a period in which we were restricted by forces beyond our control.

Either way, the trend definitively had economic implications. In chapter 4, we looked at where inflation comes from. As we saw, the starting point for most modern economists is the Philips curve, which describes a hypothetical relationship between unemployment and inflation. The lower unemployment gets, the more inflationary pressure there is meant to be: when unemployment is low, workers are meant to have more power to demand higher wages and companies, in need of staff, have to accede. As labour is the most important cost for most businesses, changes in the price of labour right across the economy can quickly feed through into prices.

For the decade after the 2008 financial crisis, it seemed as if this relationship had broken down. Unemployment kept falling but inflation remained, for the most part, quiescent. Possibly the Philips curve had gone away or its slope had flattened. Even record high employment rates in many countries were not accompanied by growing wages or much in the way of price pressure.

Post-pandemic, however, it looked as if the Phillips curve had returned, and with a vengeance. The Great Resignation demonstrated that workers had got their confidence back and were quite willing to tell their bosses that they had plenty of other options and would not stick with low pay and poor conditions. Indeed, wage growth returned. From a post-financial crisis norm of around 2 to 3 per cent a year, the annual pace of US wage growth rose to about 4 per cent by the start of 2022 and kept rising to around 6 per cent by the middle of the year. The growth was also bigger for those on the very lowest salaries, who saw annual increases of around 6 per cent by January 2022.

In the US, some of this was due to the economic policies of President Joe Biden. In chapter 8, we talked about how some economists argue that 'running the economy hot' could stimulate productivity improvements. The theory is that if overall demand is very high and labour is expensive then companies will make labour-saving investments to meet that demand. This idea appeared to have some currency in the US when it came to actual practical policy. On taking office in 2021, the president had said that the goal of his administration was to engineer full employment so that businesses would have to invest, hopefully raising productivity for the long-term, making the US richer and providing workers with better jobs.

To make good on this goal, the administration pursued a grand programme of fiscal stimulus. It was meant to come in two parts. The first, the American Rescue Plan Act, focused on short-term measures to help the economy bounce back from the coronavirus pandemic. A second part, known as Build Back Better, would include long-term spending that aimed to alter the structure of the US economy, including measures to tackle climate change and expand childcare to help parents get back to work. However, the second part became bogged down in congressional wrangling and would eventually re-emerge as the Inflation Reduction Act in July 2022, focused on measures to reduce bottlenecks that were contributing to higher inflation and encourage investment in technologies to fight climate change.

The first part of the programme, however, was significant enough in its own right to make a big impact on the US economy and, therefore, the rest of the world. Encompassing $1.9tn of government spending, the package included expanding unemployment benefits, extra tax credits for those with children and direct payments of $1,400 to individuals earning below a threshold. In total, it was the largest package of fiscal stimulus launched by the American government since the Second World War. Many in Biden's Democratic Party believed the government had been too timid after the 2008 financial crisis and did not want to repeat the mistake that led to a decade of weak growth. Better to do too much, they thought, than too little.

The Federal Reserve, the US central bank, had similarly sought to learn from its mistakes in 2008 and wanted to do more this time to help the recovery from the coronavirus pandemic. As we saw in chapter 8, it explicitly shifted its policy mandate to put more weight on getting to full employment rather than fighting inflation. In 2020 it had said it would even allow inflation to overshoot its 2 per cent target to make up for periods when inflation was below target. What this meant, in practice, was extremely vague, but the general indication was that the central bank would be much more tolerant of inflation than it had been in the past.

It can, and will continue to, be debated how much these changes in policy contributed to the inflation that followed. It is clear, with hindsight, that the Federal Reserve and the US government were too relaxed about the rising inflationary pressure. In the UK, the government did not pursue any strategy aiming at full employment: coronavirus support programmes ended almost completely in winter 2021 and a set of tax rises were planned for the following year. Similarly, the Bank of England did not change its mandate, and its focus, in law at least, was supposed to be the same 2 per cent goal it had maintained for fifteen years. Despite this different policy, mix inflation accelerated, reaching 10.1 per cent in July 2022.

On the other hand, some argue that Britain's relatively high level of inflation was due to its own idiosyncrasies. In particular, the trade-related bottlenecks brought on by its departure from the EU's single market and customs union, known as Brexit. Perhaps the country's central bank and government had done as much to stimulate demand as their equivalents across the Atlantic, but they had done more to restrict economic supply by setting up barriers with their closest trade partner and putting tougher restrictions on immigration from the trade bloc.

Either way, the general pattern right across the rich world – with the notable exception of Japan – was that there was much more demand than anticipated and supply was not adjusting to meet it. Even if the theory behind 'running the economy hot' was correct, the supply side of the economy clearly would not expand at the speed required to bring inflation down swiftly. The wage gains for workers were being eroded by higher prices – 6 per cent wage growth might sound like a lot if inflation had not been 9 per cent. Waiting for the supply side of the economy to expand in response to high spending seemed like a far too slow solution opposed to using higher interest rates to tamp down demand.

For central banks, the key question was how much of this spike in inflation was transitory and how much was permanent. Pandemic-related shortages ought to fade. Higher-than-usual spending on consumer electronics would stop as lockdowns ended and consumers could go out and spend on restaurants, tourism and so on. Natural gas prices might stay high but they would not keep rising year after year. Government spending pro-grammes would, eventually, have come to an end.

The Great Resignation, too, may have been a temporary phenomenon. It could have been a one-off shift in the kind of jobs people wanted to do, and the value of low-paid work in particular relative to other jobs, rather than permanently higher wage growth. Think of it like the moment in a folk dance when people change partners – ideally it all happens smoothly but often there may be some confusion and bumps along the way as people search for someone new to dance with. The equiva-lent may have happened in the jobs market as the end of lockdowns prompted millions to try and find new positions all at the same time.

Acting too fast to quash temporarily high inflation could have caused a recession while doing very little to actually prevent prices from rising; the Federal Reserve has no direct power to get more oil out of the ground, it can only try to reduce how much people can spend on driving or heating homes by making their mortgages and other loans more expensive. Even so, the worry for central bankers was that if they stood by and did nothing then these temporary price pressures could have had a permanent effect on inflation long after the pandemic retreated into history.

The chief concern was that higher inflation expectations could become a self-fulfilling prophecy, following the theories of Milton Friedman explained in chapter 4. The idea is that workers will try to prevent the loss of real income in the face of inflation by trying to keep wages high and negotiating higher salary settlements. Businesses, keen to preserve their profit margins, will then raise prices. If everyone expects inflation to continue, and acts to keep their incomes the same, then that will fuel even higher inflation. The best thing the central banks could do for everyone, workers and bosses alike, was to take the heat out of the economy as soon as possible. Waiting might mean more drastic action is required.

Indeed, it soon become clear that inflation had broadened out from the pandemic-related disruptions. While natural gas prices, car prices and so on stayed high, the price of other things started to join them. It was not just that a handful of goods were temporarily unavailable because of the pandemic but a widespread increase in the price of goods and services. In other words, the change in prices was a decline in the purchasing power of money and, therefore, something that central bankers should really worry about.

With inflation getting out of hand, they began to increase interest rates. At its December 2021 meeting the Federal Reserve, indisputably the world's most important central bank, delivered a surprise to markets. While it did not raise interest rates from the near-zero level of 0.25 per cent it had cut them to during the most acute phase of the coronavirus pandemic, the minutes of the meeting revealed that the policymakers who sit on its board had changed their minds: next year they predicted they would raise rates at least three time. The era of zero interest rates was coming to an end, and a new monetary age was set to begin.

The end of cheap money

Over the past decade, since emergency measures were first adopted in the wake of the devastation of the 2008 financial crisis, the world has grown accustomed to cheap money. The interest rate rises pursued by central banks were initially modest – at the December meeting the Fed's open market committee predicted that interest rates would rise to just 0.75 per cent – but this was still enough to send stock markets plummeting in the first six months of 2022. In fact, the half-year period went down as one of the most dramatic drops in the value of the US stock market in history.

The first tremors in the financial markets came in the shares of technology companies. That might be unsurprising. Tech shares had rocketed over the past decade. A potent mix of cheap interest rates, a little bit of hype and the shift to online during the pandemic had helped propel the value of the world's biggest tech companies to new highs. That made the industry ripe for a fall. When it came it was seen most vividly in the parts of the stock market that are the most speculative: so-called pre-revenue tech companies. These are businesses that earn no profits and whose value is based on the idea that one day they might. If investors are right they can earn a packet, if they are wrong the investment is likely to be utterly worthless.

These companies' share prices are, therefore, particularly sensitive to interest rates. In chapter 3 we looked at where interest comes from – one theory is that it represents the cost of time. When interest rates go up, it makes waiting relatively more expensive. Investors in companies that are not earning anything are required to be patient: profits will come in the future. Chapter 12 showed how, because of this, when interest rates are cut, it can fuel wealth inequality as the value of long-term assets rise, delivering a windfall to their existing owners. When interest rates start to rise, however, this process goes into reverse.

A lot of investors had banked on interest rates staying low for a long time. Companies' shares were trading at big multiples of their underlying profits, indicating that investors were discounting the future very heavily. When the inevitable readjustment came it resulted in a big fall. About a fifth of the value of the S&P 500 – the main US index of stock prices and a good bellwether for financial sentiment more generally – was wiped off in the first half of 2022.

It was by no means just tech companies that were hit badly, however. Cryptocurrency similarly went into retreat. The world's most prominent crypto asset Bitcoin lost 60 per cent of its value during the first half of 2022. Overall, around half of the so-called market capitalization of cryptocurrencies, a measure of the total value of all the assets, was lost in the same time span. Rather than acting as a kind of 'digital gold', resistant to inflation, the world of cryptocurrency appeared to be even more exposed to it than more traditional financial assets.

Panic about what is going on in the rich world's financial

markets can be overdone. Even with such a drop in asset values over the first six months of 2022, the S&P 500 was still about 8 per cent higher than before the pandemic. Irrational exuberance was quashed and (I'm touching wood as I write this) there appears to have been little spillover of the carnage in stock markets into the debt markets, which play more of a role in financing companies, nor into the banking system that we rely on for providing the foundations of the monetary system. There will, hopefully, be no repeat of the 2008 financial crisis.

That is not to say all was well. The worst effects of higher interest rates – the most concerning ones – were seen in poorer countries. As we saw in chapter 7, 'original sin' means that in many countries the government and businesses have to finance themselves from abroad, borrowing in a foreign currency. When the Federal Reserve started raising interest rates, the dollar appreciated dramatically – in April 2022 it reached its highest rate in comparison to other currencies for two decades. In combination with higher interest rates, this made financing foreign currency debts harder. This is what precipitated the Asian financial crisis in the late 1990s that was the focus of chapter 7.

Indeed, during the Volcker shock – the last time central banks had tried to quash inflation through high rates – the Fed's monetary tightening provoked a wave of defaults in poorer countries. Latin America was, in the 1980s, at the centre of the storm: a higher US dollar helped push much of the region into default, creating a lost decade of anaemic economic growth and fraught negotiations with the International Monetary Fund and other creditors. Such are the effects of 'original sin'.

This time, the increase in interest rates was made even worse by the Russian invasion of Ukraine. Ukraine is a major grain exporter, providing wheat to the Middle East and North Africa in particular. Russia's invasion reduced the country's capacity to provide this grain. Poor countries not only faced higher financing costs on their dollar-denominated debt but also had to spend more of their valuable foreign currency earnings on food and fuel. This was a toxic combination: poorer countries saw their currencies drop in value while their export bills rose.

Sri Lanka was one of the first to fall into difficulty. The South Asian island nation fell into default on its over $50bn external debt pile in May 2022. As well as a falling currency and higher import costs, the pandemic had deprived the country of its all-important tourist revenue. The former president, who fled the country in July 2022 amid protests in the capital, had spent heavily on vanity infrastructure projects in his home state, often funded by borrowing from China, and had exacerbated the food crisis by banning all fertilizer imports at very short notice in order to make the country's agricultural sector completely organic.

Sri Lanka was by no means alone in struggling with these problems: many other countries were already in default on their debts. Many were seeing markets charge them high interest rates in anticipation of financial stress. A wave of poorer countries defaulting following the Fed's monetary tightening had an added element this time as well: China became a major creditor, lending to many of the countries that got into difficulty. Going forward, it will not just be the IMF and US Treasury discussing with poorer countries how to restructure their debts but also the Chinese government.

Meanwhile, in Europe, the old problems of the Eurozone – a monetary union without a political union – rose to the surface once again. Italy, rather than Greece, was the flashpoint this time. Remember in chapter 6 how we talked about debt dynamics? If a country's deficit is sufficiently small and interest rates are low enough, then economic growth and inflation can do most of the hard work in shrinking the debt relative to national income. Italy's economy has been virtually stagnant for three decades and, consequently, its debt burden is high relative to national income – the country's total public debt was worth more than 150 per cent of its gross domestic product by summer 2022.

That inflation helps to make debts easier to pay is a simplification. There is a difference between inflation that is generated domestically, leading to higher nominal wages and profits, and inflation from higher import prices, which lowers real domestic incomes. Governments can only tax their own citizens, so higher prices in the domestic economy increase tax revenues while leaving debt levels unchanged. Higher import prices, however, make the country as a whole poorer and the government has potentially less economic activity to tax. With Italy having to contend with the end of a loose monetary policy and an energy shock, it was forced to pay more to borrow.

In July 2022, the European Central Bank announced a new policy to keep a lid on Italy's borrowing costs (although that was not how the central bank justified it). It argued that its new 'Transmission Protection Instrument', which allowed the central bank to buy more government bonds from countries with higher borrowing costs, would ensure that its monetary policy worked as intended. Whatever the merits or truth of that argument, the policy did manage to keep a lid on Italian borrowing costs and stop investors speculating as to whether the country would be the next domino to fall. Trust was, for the time being, restored.

Nevertheless, by the middle of 2022, the conversation had switched from the inflationary risks of running the economy too hot to the possibility of a global recession just two years after the previous one. The energy shock had, by itself, taken some of the heat out of economies: consumers simply had less discretionary spending power. Adding to the dismal picture for the global economy was China, by some measures the world's largest economy, which was still trying to keep coronavirus at bay and locking down whole cities to prevent its spread.

Had the Federal Reserve made the mistake of raising interest rates too far and too fast? The downturn was unlikely to have been prompted by the shift in monetary policy. Interest rates only reached 2.5 per cent by July 2022 – the same level they reached before the coronavirus pandemic – although investors predicted there would be at least another 2 percentage points. It was also likely too soon for this rate increase to have had a particularly large impact on economic activity. It takes a while for the movements in financial markets to feed through into the wider economy. Instead of monetary policy, higher energy costs did most of the work in pushing the economy towards recession.

The impact of the higher rates still remains to be seen but it appears as if, after dragging their feet in switching from loose to tight monetary policy, central bankers are now happier to overshoot the other way and slow down growth to lower inflation. It may not be until 2023 that we see the full impact of this tighter monetary policy on the world and whether it leads to a dramatic slowdown in employment growth, manages to bring inflation back under control or even provokes a wider financial crisis if companies and banks start to get in trouble, or families cannot pay their mortgages. In Europe, however, the worst had already arrived: stagflation. Whatever monetary policy did, higher energy prices would push the region towards recession and a long, cold, difficult winter.

How do we get out of this mess?

It is likely that the central banks will be successful, at least when it comes to bringing prices down. Writing this in the autumn of 2022, market-based expectations of long-term inflation, derived from the premium that investors will pay for certain kinds of inflation-protected assets, have returned to 2 per cent and central banks have made it clear that they will keep raising interest rates until inflation is brought under control. This disinflation is likely to be less painful and monetary policy less tight than during the 1980s. Worker bargaining power is weaker than in the heavily unionised 1970s and this episode of inflation has, so far, become less embedded in the world economy.

The events of the past year, however, have revealed many of the limits of the conventional way of running monetary policy. The shortages – which were not limited to energy, cars and chips and even included such commodities as lumber or services like container ships – have demonstrated that the rich world has not been investing enough in the supply side of the economy for a long time. Capital spending, as a proportion of national income, has been falling in most of the rich world. Out of the G7 nations, only Canada has continued to invest as much as it did in the 1970s. The US, Japan, Germany, the UK, France and Italy have all cut back compared to the past. This left the world with little spare capacity to ramp up as it emerged from the coronavirus-induced slowdown.

This came at the end of a period in which interest rates were at rock-bottom lows and inflation was scarcely a worry. According to the economic theories discussed in this book, those factors ought to have encouraged capital spending. As we saw in chapter 3, Knut Wicksell hypothesized that if interest rates on financial assets were below the potential profits on real assets –

such as gas pipelines or chip-making factories – then there should be more capital spending. Low inflation should protect creditors from having the value of their investments gradually eroded. The decade of low interest rates and low inflation did not spur an investment boom even as it boosted the prices of financial assets, such as shares in tech companies or cryptocurrencies.

Perhaps that should make the world reconsider the work of John Maynard Keynes, who argued that interest rates alone would not guarantee sufficient investment in a market society. The animal spirits of investors – their fears and hopes for the future – matter too. The uncertainty inherent to investing would normally lead the private sector to invest far too little, even outside of recessions. Keynes argued that the state should take over and, by investing enough, ensure that there would eventually become a world of abundance.

Public sector investment, however, has fallen even faster than private sector investment over the past few decades, particularly following the financial crisis. Much of that was due to the fear that states were over indebted and too constrained by such borrowing piles to spend heavily. Infrastructure spending, which often involves the disruption and noise of building sites, was an easier type of spending to cut than the services that the public experiences directly, such as healthcare, education and policing.

Restarting public investment will be difficult. Government debt piles have grown even higher thanks to coronavirus support programmes. In Europe, the state is spending heavily to protect the public from the effects of higher energy prices, often through capping retail prices for energy. While consumers will be protected from higher costs in the short term, the bill will eventually come due either through higher taxes or lower future spending. Real interest rates may fall again after the current bout of inflation – long term trends, that we discussed in chapter 3, ought to put pressure on the 'natural rate' of interest rates – but they are unlikely to fall quite as low as they were immediately after the financial crisis.

The potential rewards to spending more, however, are still large. Fighting climate change – without dramatically lowering living standards in the rich world – involves deploying vast amount of capital. Fossil fuel power stations will need to be replaced by renewables, homes will need to be insulated and electric cars will need charging infrastructure. Many of these investments could even pay for themselves by lowering the amount that society spends on fossil fuels, leaving more resources to dedicate to the kind of goods and services that actually make life better. Ultimately these kind of investments are how the world will get out of this mess and, possibly, avoid some future ones as well.

Such a possibility might seem remote today but if there is one lesson that we can very comfortably take from the last three years it is that the most extraordinary changes can happen in a very short space of time. When I started writing this book, all that time ago, the challenge was how to explain to readers the topsy-turvy world of quantitative easing, negative interest rates and booming stock markets that had followed the 2008 financial crisis. Now, on the other side of the coronavirus pandemic, it is to explain a world of scarcity, inflation and higher interest rates. This period, too, will eventually come to an end. The lessons we have learned about money, however, will remain just as useful in explaining what comes next.

Acknowledgements

This book would not have happened without Robin Harvie at Pan Macmillan, who is owed credit for coming up with the idea and approaching me to write it. Thank you for allowing me to turn your inspiration into something concrete, and for taking a chance on the voice of an unpublished young journalist. Kate Berens provided an invaluable copy-edit and Trevor Horwood and Natalie Young were the proofreaders. Readers should give them extra thanks for wading through my originally comma, en-dash- and semi-colon-strewn sentences on their behalf. Charlotte Merritt, my agent at Andrew Nurmberg Associates, as well as Charlotte Seymour, have been able guides and advocates through the publishing process. Thanks for telling me, so often, that yes, this is perfectly normal.

My colleagues at the *Financial Times* Thomas Hale, Claire Jones and Martin Sandbu have all provided excellent feedback as well as being the source of many fascinating conversations and intense arguments about the intricacies of money as well as much else. I am very grateful, too, for many such conversations with Jo Michell, who took the time to look over and help improve an early draft. James Vincent, one of my oldest friends, not only provided many excellent comments on exactly how to lift the book to the next level, but also made the whole process easier by sharing the experience as he wrote his first book, *Beyond*

Measure, at the same time. Duncan Robinson, at *The Economist*, very kindly subjected an early draft to his unerring eye for the best turn of phrase.

Thank you to Roula Khalaf, editor at the *Financial Times*, and Neil Buckley, the chief leader writer, for giving me the time to write the book. Neil also provided some help with Russian translation. To my friends: David Bass, helped with some French and Italian translation, Harald Weiler with some German and Tara Oakes and Edmund Lewis with some Latin translation. Fred Isaac and Josh Treacy provided a vital sounding board for the first chapter and an indication that I was on the right track. While not directly contributing to the book, Martin Wolf and Chris Giles at the *Financial Times* and Beata Javorcik at the University of Oxford have all been instrumental in developing my ability and confidence to write entertainingly and boldly about macroeconomics.

This book owes so much to so many more people too but probably most of all my fiancée Gabriele Pumeryte. Thanks so much for all your patience and support over the past two years. Writing a book is hard and often annoying: you made it much easier. Thank you to my parents, Martin Jackson and Anne Dawson, who always encouraged me to read widely and think for myself. This book, and so much else in my life, would not have happened without all your encouragement.

Notes

Introduction

1. King-Miller, L. (2019) The Tooth Fairy economy, explained. *Vox*. https://www.vox.com/the-highlight/2019/5/31/18644508/tooth-fairy-rate-kids-traditions
2. Arrow, K. J. (1994) 'Methodological individualism and social knowledge'. *American Economic Review*, vol. 84, no. 2, pp.1–9. https://www.jstor.org/stable/2117792
3. *The Onion* (2010) 'US economy grinds to halt as nation realizes money just a symbolic, mutually shared illusion'. *The Onion* [online]. https://www.theonion.com/u-s-economy-grinds-to-halt-as-nation-realizes-money-ju-18 19571322
4. Spang, R. (2015) *Stuff and Money in the Time of the French Revolution*. Harvard University Press, Cambridge, MA.
5. Mill, J. S. (1867) *Principles of Political Economy*. Longmans, Green, Reader, and Dyer, London.
6. Hazlitt, H. (1946) *Economics in One Lesson* [online]. Kindle edition.

1. What is money?

1. Felix, M. (2014) *Money: The Unauthorised Biography*. Vintage, London.
2. Murphy, A. E. (1978) 'Money in an economy without banks: The case of Ireland'. *The Manchester School*, vol. 46, no. 1, pp.41–50.
3. Bowles, S., Carlin, W. and Stevens, M. (2017) 'Banks, money, housing and financial assets, Unit 10 in The CORE Team'. *The Economy*. http://www.core-econ.org.
4. Buckley, D. (1999) 'How six month banking strike rocked the nation'. *Irish Independent* [online]. https://www.independent.ie/business/how-six-month-bank-strike-rocked-the-nation-26130249.html

5. Alsop, B. and Shore, A. (2017) 'Change is good! A history of money'. Curator's Corner [British Museum blog], March. https://blog.british museum.org/change-is-good-a-history-of-money

6. Smith, A. (1776) *An Inquiry into the Nature and Causes of the Wealth of Nations*. Oxford University Press, Oxford.

7. Graeber, D. (2011) *Debt: The First 5,000 Years*. Melville House, Brooklyn, NY.

8. Mauss, M. (1966) *The Gift: Forms and Functions of Exchange in Archaic Societies*. Cohen & West, London.

9. Mitchell-Innes, A. (1913) 'What is money?'. *Banking Law Journal*, pp.377–408.

10. Panoff, M. (1970) 'Marcel Mauss's "The Gift" revisited'. Man, vol. 5, no. 1, pp.60–70. https://www.jstor.org/stable/2798804

11. Nairn, C., and Granada Television International (1976) *Ongka's Big Moka: The Kawelka*. Granada Television International, London.

12. Goetzmann, W. N. (2016) *Money Changes Everything: How Finance Made Civilization Possible*. Princeton University Press, Princeton, NJ.

13. Van der Spek, R. J. and Leeuwen, B. (2018) *Money, Currency and Crisis. In Search of Trust, 2000 BC to AD 2000*. Routledge, London.

14. Graeber, D. (2011)

15. Weatherford, J. (1997) *The History of Money*. Three Rivers Press, New York, NY.

16. Schumpeter, J. A. (2014) *A Treatise on Money* [online]. Kindle edition. WordBridge publishing, Aalten. Original work published 1970.

17. Patinkin, D. (1956) *Money, Interest and Prices*. Harper & Row, New York, NY.

18. McIndoe-Calder, T., Bedi, T. and Mercado, R. (2019) *Hyperinflation in Zimbabwe: Background, Impact and Policy*. Palgrave, London.

19. *The Economist* (2008) 'A worthless currency'. *The Economist* [online]. https://www.economist.com/middle-east-and-africa/2008/07/17/a-worthless-currency

20. McGee, P., Ndzamela, P. and England, A. (2015) 'Zimbabwe ditches "worthless" currency for the US dollar'. *Financial Times* [online]. https://www.ft.com/content/34d75e42-10e8-11e5-8413-00144feabdc0

21. Radford, R. A. (1945) 'Economic organisation of a prisoner of war camp'. *Economics*, vol. 12, no. 48, pp.198–201.

22. Wall & Broadcast (2017) The Secret Prison Economy. youtube.com/watch?v=2du_M8zSe3U

23. Goodhart, C. (1998, March) 'The two concepts of money: Implications for the analysis of optimal currency areas'. *European Journal of Political Economy*,

vol. 14, no. 3, pp.407–432. https://modernmoneynetwork.org/sites/default/files/biblio/goodhart_-_two_concepts_of_money.pdf

24. Woll, A. (1981) 'How Hollywood has portrayed hispanics'. *New York Times* [online]. https://www.nytimes.com/1981/03/01/movies/how-hollywood-has-portrayed-hispanics.html

25. Katz, F. (1998) *The Life and Times of Pancho Villa*. Stanford University Press, Stanford, CA.

26. McLynn, F. (2000) *Villa and Zapata: A Biography of the Mexican Revolution*. Jonathan Cape, London.

27. Felix, M. (2014)

28. Scheck, J. (2008) 'Mackerel economics in prison leads to appreciation for oily fillets'. *Wall Street Journal* [online]. https://www.wsj.com/articles/SB122290720439096481

29. Helleiner, E. (2002) *The Making of National Money: Territorial Currencies in Historical Perspective*. Cornell University Press, Ithaca, NY, and London.

30. Şaul, M. (2004) 'Money in colonial transition: Cowries and francs in West Africa'. *American Anthropologist*, vol. 106, no. 1, pp.71–84. https://www.jstor.org/stable/3567443

31. Ofonagoro, W. I. (1979) 'From traditional to British currency in southern Nigeria: Analysis of a currency revolution, 1880–1948'. *Journal of Economic History*, vol. 39, no. 3, pp.623–654. https://www.jstor.org/stable/2119685

32. Naanen, B. (1993) 'Economy within an economy: The manilla currency, exchange rate instability and social conditions in south-eastern Nigeria, 1900–48'. *Journal of African History*, vol. 34, no. 3, pp.425–446. https://www.jstor.org/stable/183101

33. The Federal Reserve (2021) Money stock measures - H.6 Release. https://www.federalreserve.gov/releases/h6/current/default.htm

34. McLeay, M., Radia, A. and Thomas, R. (2014) 'Money creation in the modern economy'. *Bank of England quarterly bulletin* Q4.

35. Keynes, J. M. (2018) *Treatise on Money* [online]. Kindle edition. Endeavour Media, Aalten. Originally published 1930.

36. McLeay, M., Radia, A. and Thomas, R. (2014)

2. How do banks work?

1. Knowles, D. (2020) 'Hawala traders are being squeezed by regulators and covid-19'. *The Economist* [online]. https://www.economist.com/finance-and-economics/2020/11/28/hawala-traders-are-being-squeezed-by-regulators-and-covid-19hawala-traders-are-being-squeezed-by-regulators-and-covid-19

2. Gaines, T. C. (1960) 'Money supply and liquidity'. Note to the Federal Open Market Committee, Federal Reserve. https://www.federalreserve.gov/monetarypolicy/files/FOMC19600620memo01.pdf

3. Nikolaou, K. (2009) 'Liquidity (risk) concepts, definitions and interactions'. European Central Bank working paper series, no. 1008. https://www.ecb.europa.eu/pub/pdf/scpwps/ecbwp1008.pdf

4. Keynes, J. M. (2018) *Treatise on Money* [online]. Kindle edition. Endeavour Media, Aalten. Originally published 1930.

5. Fifield, A. (2008) 'How Iranians are avoiding sanctions'. *Financial Times* [online]. https://www.ft.com/content/6ca69788-0a48-11dd-b5b1-0000779fd2ac

6. Thompson, E. A. (2008) 'An introduction to the concept and origins of hawala'. *Journal of the History of International Law*, vol. 10, no. 1.

7. Knowles, D. (2015) 'The Economist explains: How hawala money transfer is changing'. *The Economist* [online]. https://www.economist.com/the-economist-explains/2015/10/15/how-hawala-money-transfer-schemes-are-changing

8. Thompson, E. A. (2011) *Trust is the Coin of the Realm: Lessons from the Money Men in Afghanistan*. Oxford University Press, Oxford.

9. Munzele Maimbo, S. (2003) 'The money exchange dealers of Kabul: A study of the hawala system in Afghanistan'. The World Bank. http://documents1.worldbank.org/curated/en/335241467990983523/pdf/269720PAPER0Money0exchange0dealers.pdf

10. El-Qorchi, M. (2002) 'Hawala'. *Finance and Development*, vol. 39, no. 4. https://www.imf.org/external/pubs/ft/fandd/2002/12/elqorchi.htm

11. Zhou, R. (2000) 'Understanding intraday credit in large-value payment systems'. *Economic Perspectives*, Federal Reserve Bank of Chicago. https://www.chicagofed.org/publications/economic-perspectives/2000/3qepart3

12. Committee on Payment and Settlement Systems (2003) 'The role of central bank money in payment systems'. Bank for International Settlements. https://www.bis.org/cpmi/publ/d55.pdf

13. Bologna, P. (2018) 'Banks' maturity transformation: Risk, reward and policy'. IMF working paper no. 18/45. https://www.imf.org/en/Publications/WP/Issues/2018/03/09/Banks-Maturity-Transformation-Risk-Reward-and-Policy-45683

14. Ho, T. S. Y. and Saunders, A. (1981) 'The determinants of bank interest margins: Theory and empirical evidence'. *Journal of Financial and Quantitative Analysis*, vol. 16, no. 4, pp.581–600. https://www.jstor.org/stable/2330377

15. Felix, M. (2014). *Money: The Unauthorised Biography*. Vintage, London.

16. Wetterberg, G. (2009) *Money and Power: From Stockholms Banco 1656 to Sveriges Riksbank Today*. Atlantis, Stockholm. https://www.riksbank.se/en-gb/about-the-riksbank/history/money-and-power--the-history-of-sveriges-riksbank

17. Shiells, R. (1897) 'Swedish copper plate money'. *American Journal of Numismatics*, vol. 32, no. 2. https://www.jstor.org/stable/43582838

18. Wetterberg, G. (2009)

19. McLeay, M., Radia, A. and Thomas, R. (2014) 'Money creation in the modern economy'. *Bank of England quarterly bulletin* Q4.

20. Handa, J. (2009) *Monetary Economics*, 2nd ed. Routledge, London and New York, NY.

21. Admati, A. and Hellwig, M. (2013) *The Bankers' New Clothes*. Princeton University Press, Princeton, NJ.

22. Edvinsson, R. (2009) 'The multiple currencies of Sweden-Finland 1534–1803'. *Stockholm Papers in Economic History* no. 7. https://www.riksbank.se/globalassets/media/forskning/monetar-statistik/volym1/4.pdf

23. Högberg, S. (1961) 'Sweden's first bank notes'. *Scandinavian Economic History Review*, vol. 9, no. 1, pp.206–208. https://www.tandfonline.com/doi/pdf/10.1080/03585522.1961.10411442

24. Diamond, D. W. and Dybvig, P. H. (1983) 'Bank runs, deposit insurance and liquidity'. *Journal of Political Economy*, vol. 91, no. 3, pp.401–419. https://www.jstor.org/stable/1837095

25. Högberg, S. (1961)

26. Postlewaite, A. and Vives, X. (1987) 'Bank runs as an equilibrium phenomenon'. *Journal of Political Economy*, vol. 95, no. 3, pp.485–491. https://www.jstor.org/stable/1831974

27. Heckscher, E. F. (1934) 'The Bank of Sweden in its connection with the bank of Amsterdam', in J. G. van Dillen (ed.), *History of the Principal Public Banks*, pp.161–200. Frank Cass & Co, London.

28. Admati, A. and Hellwig, M. (2013)

29. European Central Bank (2019) 'Why do banks need to hold capital?' https://www.bankingsupervision.europa.eu/about/ssmexplained/html/hold_capital.en.html

30. McLeay, M., Radia, A. and Thomas, R. (2014)

31. Farag, M., Harland, D. and Nixon, D. (2013) 'Bank capital and liquidity'. *Bank of England quarterly bulletin* Q3. https://www.bankofengland.co.uk/-/media/boe/files/quarterly-bulletin/2013/bank-capital-and-liquidity.pdf

32. Lehman Brothers balance sheet 2007. SEC. https://www.sec.gov/Archives/edgar/data/806085/000110465908005476/a08-3530_110k.htm

33. Kalemli-Ozcan, S., Sorensen, B. and Yesiltas, S. (2011) 'Leverage across firms, banks, and countries'. NBER working paper no. 17354. https://www.nber.org/papers/w17354

34. Adrian, T. and Song Shin, H. (2010) 'The changing nature of financial intermediation and the financial crisis of 2007–2009'. *Annual Review of Economics*, vol. 2, pp.603–618.

35. *Uncut Gems* (2019) [digital] Directed by Safdie, B. and Safdie, J. UK: Netflix.

36. Tooze, A. (2018) *Crashed: How a Decade of Financial Crises Changed the World*. Penguin Random House, London.

37. Shleifer, A. and Vishny, R. W. (2010) 'Fire sales in finance and macroeconomics'. NBER working paper no. 16642. https://www.nber.org/papers/w16642

38. Wolf, M. (2007) 'From a bank run to nationalising deposits'. *Financial Times* [online]. https://www.ft.com/content/02658970-65ec-11dc-9fbb-0000779fd2ac

39. Farag, M., Harland, D. and Nixon, D. (2013)

40. Goel, T., Lewrick, U. and Tarashev, N. (2017) 'Bank capital allocation under multiple constraints'. BIS working paper no. 666. https://www.bis.org/publ/work666.pdf

41. Smith, R. (2017) 'Bank recapitalisations spur rights issue surge'. *Financial Times* [online]. https://www.ft.com/content/f57e5f5e-31b8-11e7-9555-23ef563ecf9a

42. Adrian, T. and Song Shin, H. (2011) 'Financial intermediary balance sheet management'. *Annual Review of Financial Economics* no. 3, pp.289–307. https://www.newyorkfed.org/research/staff_reports/sr532.html

43. Norman, B., Shaw, R. and Speight, G. (2011) 'The history of interbank settlement arrangements: Exploring central banks' role in the payment system'. Bank of England. https://www.ecb.europa.eu/home/pdf/research/Working_Paper_412.pdf

44. Rule, G. (2015) 'Understanding the central bank balance sheet'. Centre for Central Banking Studies, Bank of England. https://www.bankofengland.co.uk/ccbs/understanding-the-central-bank-balance-sheet

45. Committee on Payment and Settlement Systems (2003)

46. Norman, B., Shaw, R. and Speight, G. (2011)

47. Capie, F., Goodhart, C. and Schnadt, N. (1994) 'The development of central banking', in *The Future of Central Banking*, Capie, F., Fischer, S., Goodhart, C. and Schnadt, N. (eds). Cambridge University Press, Cambridge. http://eprints.lse.ac.uk/39606/1/The_development_of_central_banking_%28LSERO%29.pdf

48. Wetterberg, G. (2009)

49. Kynaston, D. (2017) *Till Time's Last Sand: A History of the Bank of England*. Bloomsbury, London.

50. Committee on Payment and Settlement Systems (2003)

51. DeLong, J. B. (2012) 'This time, it is not different: The persistent concerns of financial macroeconomics', in *Rethinking the Financial Crisis*, Blinder, A. S., Lo, A. W. and Solow, R. M. (eds). Russell Sage Foundation, New York, NY. https://www.jstor.org/stable/10.7758/9781610448154

52. Goodhart, C. (2008) 'Liquidity risk management'. *Financial Stability Review*, issue 11, pp.39–44. https://core.ac.uk/download/pdf/6612148.pdf

53. Bagehot, W. (1878) *Lombard Street: A Description of the Money Market*. Paul, London.

54. Money and Banking blog (2016) 'The lender of last resort and the Lehman bankruptcy'. https://www.moneyandbanking.com/commentary/2016/7/25/the-lender-of-last-resort-and-the-lehman-bankruptcy

55. Bernanke, B. (2013) 'A century of US central banking: Goals, frameworks, accountability'. *Journal of Economic Perspectives*, vol. 27, no. 4, pp.3–16. https://pubs.aeaweb.org/doi/pdfplus/10.1257/jep.27.4.3

56. Federal Reserve (2020) 'Recent balance sheet trends'. https://www.federalreserve.gov/monetarypolicy/bst_recenttrends.htm

3. Why do we pay interest?

1. Anagol, S., Etang, A., Karlan, D. (2013) 'Continued existence of cows disproves central tenets of capitalism?' NBER working paper no. 19437. https://www.nber.org/papers/w19437

2. *The Economist* (2013) 'Udder people's money'. *The Economist* [online]. https://www.economist.com/news/finance-and-economics/21587226-cattle-may-be-terrible-investment-decent-savings-vehicle-udder-peoples

3. Goetzmann, W. N. (2016) *Money Changes Everything: How Finance Made Civilization Possible*. Princeton University Press, Princeton, NJ.

4. Hodgson, G. M. (2014) 'What is capital? Economists and sociologists have changed its meaning: Should it be changed back?' *Cambridge Journal of Economics*, vol. 38, no. 5, pp.1063–1086. https://academic.oup.com/cje/article-abstract/38/5/1063/2875364

5. Wicksell, K. (1898) 'Interest and prices'. (trans. Khan, R. F.). Sentry Press, New York, NY. 1962. https://cdn.mises.org/Interest%20and%20Prices_2.pdf

6. Gårdlund, T. (1958) *The Life of Knut Wicksell*. Edward Elgar, Cheltenham.

7. Wetterberg, C. C. (2021) 'Anna Kristine Margrete Bugge Wicksell'. Svenskt kvinnobiografiskt lexikon. www.skbl.se/sv/artikel/AnnaBuggeWicksell

8. Gårdlund, T. (1978) 'The life of Knut Wicksell and some characteristics of his work'. *Scandinavian Journal of Economics*, vol. 80, no. 2, The Arne Ryde Symposium on the theoretical contributions of Knut Wicksell, pp.129–134. https://www.jstor.org/stable/3439877

9. Turner, A. (2013) 'Credit, money and leverage: What Wicksell, Hayek and Fisher knew and modern macroeconomics forgot'. Speech at Stockholm School of Economics. https://cdn.evbuc.com/eventlogos/67785745/turner.pdf

10. Wicksell, K. (1907) 'The influence of the rate of interest on prices'. *Economic Journal*, vol. 17, no. 66, pp.213–220. https://www.econlib.org/library/Essays/wcksInt.html

11. Wicksell, K. (1898)

12. Woodford, M. (2003) *Interest and Prices: Foundations of a Theory of Monetary Policy*. Princeton University Press, Princeton, NJ, and Oxford.

13. Greenspan, A. (1993) 'Semiannual monetary policy report to the Congress: Testimony before the Committee on banking, housing and urban affairs', United States Senate. https://fraser.stlouisfed.org/title/statements-speeches-alan-greenspan-452/semiannual-monetary-policy-report-congress-8490/fulltext

14. Federal Reserve Board of San Francisco. (2005) 'What is neutral economic policy?' https://www.frbsf.org/education/publications/doctor-econ/2005/april/neutral-monetary-policy

15. Artistotle 'Politics', in McKeon, R. (ed.) (1941) *Basic Works of Aristotle*. Random House, New York, NY.

16. Marx, K. (1867) *Capital: Volume 1*. (trans. Fowkes, B.). London, Penguin Books. 1990.

17. Ibid.

18. Hennings, K. H. (1997) *The Austrian Theory of Value and Capital: Studies in the Life and Work of Eugen von Böhm-Bawerk*. Edward Elgar, Cheltenham.

19. Böhm-Bawerk, E. von (1890) *Capital and Interest: A Critical History of Economic Theory* (trans. Smart, W. A.). Macmillan, London.

20. Böhm-Bawerk, E. von (1891) *The Positive Theory of Capital* (trans. Smart, W. A.). Macmillan, London.

21. Veblen, T. (1906) 'Fisher's rate of interest'. *Political Science Quarterly*, vol. 24, no. 3, pp.296–303. https://www.jstor.org/stable/2140821

22. Kurlansky, M. (2003) *Salt: A World History*. Walker and Company, New York, NY.

23. Moloney, E., Tsoukalas, G. and Trichakis, N. (2015) Credem: banking on cheese. Harvard Business School case study. https://www.hbs.edu/faculty/Pages/item.aspx?num=48733

24. Fisher, I. (1930) *The Theory of Interest*. Macmillan, New York, NY.

25. Yueh, L. (2018) *The Great Economists*. Viking, New York, NY.

26. Skidelsky, R. (2003) *John Maynard Keynes: 1883–1946: Economist, Philosopher, Statesman*. Pan Macmillan, London.

27. Harford, T. (2021) 'Lessons in investing from John Maynard Keynes'. *Financial Times* [online]. https://www.ft.com/content/5aef7730-a311-470e-9ed3-3f246f0d3eab

28. Skidelsky, R. (2003)

29. Keynes, J. M. (1919) *The Economic Consequences of the Peace*. Macmillan, London.

30. Chanandavarkar, A. (1989) *Keynes and India: A Study in Economics and Biography*. Macmillan, Basingstoke.

31. Rupee in Oxford Dictionary. https://www.lexico.com/definition/rupee

32. Littlefield, H. M. (1964) 'The Wizard of Oz: A parable on populism'. *American Quarterly*, vol. 16, no. 1, pp.47–58. https://www.jstor.org/stable/2710826

33. Rockoff, H. (1990). 'The "Wizard of Oz" as a monetary allegory'. *Journal of Political Economy*, vol. 98, pp.739–760.

34. Hansen, B. A. (2002) 'The fable of the allegory: The Wizard of Oz in economics'. *Journal of Economic Education*, vol. 33, no. 3, pp.254–264. https://www.jstor.org/stable/1183440

35. Fisher, I. (1933) 'The debt-deflation theory of great depressions'. *Econometrica*, vol. 1, no. 4, pp.337–357. https://www.jstor.org/stable/1907327

36. Keynes, J. M. (1913) *Indian Currency and Finance*. Macmillan, London.

37. Weldon, D. (2021) *Two Hundred Years of Muddling Through*. London, Little, Brown.

38. Keynes, J. M. (1936) *The General Theory of Employment, Interest and Money*. Wordsworth Editions, Hertfordshire.

39. Samuleson, P. A. (1958) *Economics*, 5th ed. McGraw-Hill, London.

40. Keynes, J. M. (1937) 'The general theory of employment'. *Quarterly Journal of Economics*, vol. 51, no. 2, pp.209–223. https://macroeconomiauca.files.wordpress.com/2012/05/keynes_general_theory_of_employment_qje_1937.pdf

41. Tily, G. (2012) 'Keynes' monetary theory of interest'. Bank for International Settlements, vol. 65, pp.51–81. https://www.bis.org/publ/bppdf/bispap65c_rh.pdf

42. Wigglesworth, R. and Martin, K. (2019) 'Negative yields: Sweden leads the world below zero'. *Financial Times* [online]. https://www.ft.com/content/385b06cc-ba80-11e9-8a88-aa6628ac896c

43. Schnabel, I. (2020) 'Going negative: The ECB's experience'. Speech at the 25th Congress of the European Economic Association. Frankfurt am Main,

26 January. https://www.ecb.europa.eu/press/key/date/2020/html/ecb.sp200 826~77ce66626c.en.html

44. Harding, R. (2016) 'Japan joins negative rates club'. *Financial Times* [online]. https://www.ft.com/content/23ff8798-c63c-11e5-b3b1-7b2481276e45

45. German 10-year government bond yield. https://markets.ft.com/data/ bonds/tearsheet/summary?s=GM10YB

46. Siemens AG (2019) 'Strong demand for Siemens bonds despite negative yields'. https://press.siemens.com/global/en/pressrelease/strong-demand-siemens-bonds-despite-negative-yields

47. Hicks, J. (1937) 'Mr Keynes and the "classics": A suggested interpretation'. *Econometrica*, vol. 5, no. 2. pp.147–159. https://www.jstor.org/stable/1907242

48. Romer, D. (2000) 'Keynesian macroeconomics without the LM curve'. *Journal of Economic Perspectives*, vol. 14, no. 2, pp.149–169. https://pubs. aeaweb.org/doi/pdfplus/10.1257/jep.14.2.149

49. Buiter, W. H. and Panigirtzoglous N. (1999) 'Liquidity traps: How to avoid them and how to escape them'. NBER working paper no. 7245. https:// www.nber.org/papers/w7245

50. Dominguez, K. M., Rogoff, K. S. and Krugman, P. (1998) 'It's baaack: Japan's slump and the return of the liquidity trap'. *Brookings Papers on Economic Activity*, no. 2. https://www.brookings.edu/bpea-articles/its-baaack-japans-slump-and-the-return-of-the-liquidity-trap

51. Eggertsson, G. B. and Woodford, M. (2003) 'The zero bound on interest rates and optimal monetary policy'. *Brookings Papers on Economic Activity*, no. 1, pp.139–211. https://www.jstor.org/stable/1209148

52. *Reuters* (2016) 'Negative ECB rates fuel demand for safe deposit boxes, German banks say'. *Reuters* [online]. https://uk.reuters.com/article/germany-banks-savings/negative-ecb-rates-fuel-demand-for-safe-deposit-boxes-german-banks-say-idUSL5N16P45T

53. Lewis, L. and Harding, R. (2016) 'Japan: The dash to stash'. *Financial Times* [online]. https://www.ft.com/content/831ace74-3471-11e6-bda0-04585c31 b153

54. Woodford, M. and Xie, Y. (2020) 'Fiscal and monetary stabilisation policy at the zero lower bound: Consequences of limited foresight'. NBER working paper no. 27521. https://www.nber.org/papers/w27521

55. Lhuissier, L., Mojon, B. and Rubio-Ramirez, J. (2020) 'Does the liquidity trap exist?' BIS working paper no. 855. https://www.bis.org/publ/work855. pdf

56. Arnold, M. (2020) 'ECB rebuffs bank complaints about negative interest rates'. *Financial Times* [online]. https://www.ft.com/content/52de6e70-56bc-4da9-adf7-b228c8da79a0

57. Wigglesworth, R. (2019) 'Pension funds need to make the case against negative interest rates'. *Financial Times* [online]. https://www.ft.com/content/a730ce84-f95e-11e9-98fd-4d6c20050229

58. Rajan, A. (2020) 'Negative interest rates can be a doom loop for pension investors'. *Financial Times* [online]. https://www.ft.com/content/d54227c2-3ca9-4060-a0fe-b17fb011421d

59. Brand, C., Bielecki, M. and Penalver, A. (2018) 'The natural rate of interest: Estimates, drivers, and challenges to monetary policy'. ECB occasional paper series, no. 217. https://www.ecb.europa.eu/pub/pdf/scpops/ecb.op217.en.pdf

60. Giles, C. (2017) 'Central bankers face a crisis of confidence as models fail'. *Financial Times* [online]. https://www.ft.com/content/333b3406-acd5-11e7-beba-5521c713abf4

61. Godlin, I., Koutroumpis, P., Lafond, F. and Winkler, J. (2020) 'Why is productivity slowing down?' OMPTEC working paper no. 1. https://www.oxfordmartin.ox.ac.uk/downloads/academic/ProductivitySlowdown.pdf

62. Harding, R. (2020) 'The mysterious death of the market rentier'. *Financial Times* [online]. https://www.ft.com/content/7236fa60-0681-4c14-9758-f5be60379449

63. Brown-Collier, E. K. and Collier, B. E. (1995) 'What Keynes really said about deficit spending'. *Journal of Post Keynesian Economics*, vol. 17, no. 3, pp.341–355. https://www.jstor.org/stable/4538449

4. Where does inflation come from?

1. Nwani, A. O. (1975) 'The quantity theory in the early monetary system of West Africa with particular emphasis on Nigeria, 1850–1895'. *Journal of Political Economy*, vol. 83, no. 1, pp.185–194. https://www.jstor.org/stable/1833279

2. Fisher, S. and Modigliani, F. (1978) 'Towards an understanding of the real effects and costs of inflation'. NBER working paper no. 303. https://www.nber.org/papers/w0303

3. Akerlof, G. A., Dickens, W. T. and Perry, G. L. (1996) 'The macroeconomics of low inflation'. *Brookings Papers on Economic Activity*, no. 1. https://core.ac.uk/download/pdf/6340327.pdf

4. Doepke, M. and Schneider, M. (2006) 'Inflation and the redistribution of nominal wealth'. *Journal of Political Economy*, vol. 114, no. 6. https://faculty.wcas.northwestern.edu/~mdo738/research/Doepke_Schneider_JPE_06.pdf

5. Yang, B. (2018) *Cowries Shell and Cowrie Money: A Global History*. Routledge, Abingdon.

6. Hogendorn, J. and Johnson, M. (1986) *The Shell Money of the Slave Trade*. Cambridge University Press, Cambridge.

7. Ibid.

8. Ibid.

9. Law, R. (1992) 'Posthumous questions for Karl Polanyi: Price inflation in pre-colonial Dahomey'. *Journal of African History*, vol. 33, no. 3, pp.387–420. https://www.jstor.org/stable/183139

10. Hogendorn, J. and Johnson, M. (1986)

11. Ibid.

12. Johnson, M. (1970) 'The cowrie currencies of West Africa. Part I'. *Journal of African History*, vol. 11, no. 1, pp.17–49. https://www.jstor.org/stable/180215

13. Hogendorn, J. and Johnson, M. (1986)

14. Law, R. (1992)

15. Robertson, D. H. (1922) *Money*. Nisbet, London. https://archive.org/details/moneyrober00robeuoft/page/4/mode/2up

16. Fisher, I. (1911) *The Purchasing Power of Money*. Macmillan, New York, NY. https://oll.libertyfund.org/title/brown-the-purchasing-power-of-money

17. Ibid.

18. Hogendorn, J. and Johnson, M. (1986)

19. Green, T. (2019) *A Fistful of Shells: West Africa from the Rise of the Slave Trade to the Age of Revolution*. Penguin, London.

20. Law, R., Schwarz, S. and Strickroft, S., ed. (2013) *Commercial Agriculture, the Slave Trade & Slavery in Atlantic Africa*. James Currey, Woodbridge, Suffolk.

21. Tobin, J. (1956) 'The interest-elasticity of transactions demand for cash'. *Review of Economics and Statistics*, vol. 38, no. 3, pp.241–247. https://www.jstor.org/stable/1925776

22. Whalen, E. L. (1966) 'A rationalisation of the precautionary demand for cash'. *Quarterly Journal of Economics*, vol. 90, no. 2, pp.314–324. https://www.jstor.org/stable/1880695

23. Keynes, J. M. (1936) *The General Theory of Employment, Interest and Money*. Wordsworth Editions, Hertfordshire.

24. Bordo, M. D. and Rockoff, H. (2011) 'The influence of Irving Fisher on Milton Friedman's monetary economics'. NBER working paper no. 17267. https://www.nber.org/papers/w17267

25. Galbraith, J. K. (1955) *The Great Crash, 1929*. Penguin Books, London.

26. Yueh, L. (2018) *The Great Economists: How Their Ideas Can Help Us Today*. Penguin Random House, London.

27. Leeson, R. (1999) 'Keynes and the "Keynesian Phillips curve"'. *History of Political Economy*, vol. 31, no. 3, pp.493–509. https://read.dukeupress.edu/hope/article-pdf/31/3/493/426892/ddhope_31_3_493.pdf

28. Phillips, A. W. (1958) 'The relation between unemployment and the rate of change of money wage rates in the United Kingdom, 1861–1957'. *Economica*, vol. 25, no. 100. https://onlinelibrary.wiley.com/doi/full/10.1111/j.1468-0335.1958.tb00003.x

29. McIvor, A. (1984) 'Employers' organisation and strikebreaking in Britain, 1880–1914'. *International Review of Social History*, vol. 29, no. 1, pp.1–33. https://www.jstor.org/stable/44583736

30. Hetzel, R. L. (2013) 'The Monetarist-Keynesian debate and the Phillips curve: Lessons from the Great Inflation'. *FRB of Richmond Economic Quarterly*, vol. 99, no. 2, pp.83–116. https://www.richmondfed.org/~/media/richmondfedorg/publications/research/economic_quarterly/2013/q2/pdf/hetzel.pdf

31. Samuelson, P. A. and Solow, R. M. (1960) 'Analytical aspects of anti-inflation policy'. *American Economic Review*, vol. 50, no. 2, pp.177–194. https://www.jstor.org/stable/1815021

32. Stewart, M. (1967) *Keynes and After*. Penguin, London.

33. Skidelsky, R. (2018) *Money and Government*. Penguin Books, London.

34. Crafts, N. and Toniolo, G. (2012) '"Les Trente Glorieuses": From the Marshall Plan to the oil crisis', in *The Oxford Handbook of Postwar European History*, Stone, D. (ed.) Oxford University Press, Oxford.

35. FRB of St Louis (2020) 'Inflation, consumer prices for the United States'. Retrieved from FRED, Federal Reserve Bank of St Louis. https://fred.stlouisfed.org/series/FPCPITOTLZGUSA.

36. FRB of St Louis (2020) 'Consumer price inflation in the United Kingdom'. Retrieved from FRED, Federal Reserve Bank of St. Louis. https://fred.stlouisfed.org/series/CPIIUKA

37. DeLong, J. B. (1996) 'America's peacetime inflation', in *Reducing Inflation: Motivation and Strategy*, Romer, C. D. and Romer, D. H. (eds). University of Chicago Press, IL. https://www.nber.org/books-and-chapters/reducing-inflation-motivation-and-strategy

38. Hamilton, J. D. (1983) 'Oil and the macroeconomy since World War II'. *Journal of Political Economy*, vol. 91, no. 2, pp.228–248. https://www.jstor.org/stable/1832055

39. Friedman, M. (1977) Money and inflation. Lecture sponsored by the University of San Diego. https://miltonfriedman.hoover.org/objects/57219/money-and-inflation

40. Yueh, L. (2018)

41. McCracken, P. W. (1996) 'Economic policy in the Nixon years'. *Presidential Studies Quarterly*, vol. 26, no. 1, pp.165–177. https://www.jstor.org/stable/27551556

42. Abrams, B. A. (2006) 'How Richard Nixon pressured Arthur Burns: Evidence from the Nixon tapes'. *Journal of Economic Perspectives*, vol. 20, no. 4, pp.177–188. https://fraser.stlouisfed.org/files/docs/meltzer/jep_2006_abrams_how_richard_nixon.pdf

43. Ibid.

44. FRB of St Louis (2020)

45. Mankiw, N. G. (2018) 'Friedman's presidential address in the evolution of macroeconomic thought'. *Journal of Economic Perspectives*, vol. 32, no. 1, pp.81–96. https://www.aeaweb.org/articles?id=10.1257/jep.32.1.81

46. Friedman, M. (1968) 'The role of monetary policy'. *American Economic Review*, vol. 58, no. 1, pp. 1–17. http://www.jstor.org/stable/1831652

47. Ibid.

48. Ball, L. and Mankiw, N. G. (2002) 'The NAIRU in theory and practice'. *Journal of Economic Perspectives*, vol. 16, no. 4, pp.115–136. https://www.jstor.org/stable/3216917

49. Vincent, J. (2018) 'The kilogram is dead; long live the kilogram'. *The Verge* [online]. https://www.theverge.com/2018/11/13/18087002/kilogram-new-definition-kg-metric-unit-ipk-measurement

50. Woodford, M. (2009) 'Convergence in macroeconomics: Elements of the new synthesis'. *American Economic Journal: Macroeconomics*, vol. 1, no. 1, pp.267–279. http://www.columbia.edu/~mw2230/Convergence_AEJ.pdf

51. ECB (2020) Measuring inflation – the harmonised index of consumer prices (HICP). The ECB [online]. https://www.ecb.europa.eu/stats/macroeconomic_and_sectoral/hicp/html/index.en.html

52. Friedman, M. (1970) 'The counter revolution in monetary theory'. IEA occasional paper no. 33. https://miltonfriedman.hoover.org/objects/56983/the-counterrevolution-in-monetary-theory

53. Friedman, M. (1956) *The Quantity Theory of Money: A Restatement, in the Optimum Quantity of Money* (Friedman, ed.). Routledge, Abingdon.

54. Ibid.

55. Friedman, M. (1999) 'Mr Market'. *Hoover Digest*. https://www.hoover.org/research/mr-market

56. Hetzel, R. L. (1986) 'Monetary policy in the early 1980s'. *FRB of Richmond Economic Review*. https://core.ac.uk/download/pdf/6917477.pdf

57. *The Times* (2019) 'Paul Volcker obituary'. *The Times* [online]. https://www.thetimes.co.uk/article/paul-volcker-obituary-2lbr8q7gg

58. Goodfriend, M. (2007) 'How the world achieved consensus on monetary policy'. NBER working paper no. 13580. http://www.nber.org/papers/w13580

59. Hamilton, J. D. (2013) 'Historical oil shocks', in *Routledge Handbook of Major Events in Economic History*, Parker, R. E. and Whaples, R. M. (eds), pp.239–65. Routledge, New York, NY.

60. Friedman, M. (1965) *A Program for Monetary Stability*. Fordham University Press, New York, NY.

61. FRB of St. Louis (2021) Inflation, consumer prices for the United States. https://fred.stlouisfed.org/series/FPCPITOTLZGUSA

62. FRB of St. Louis (2021) Unemployment rate. https://fred.stlouisfed.org/series/UNRATE

63. Applebaum, B. and Hersey Jr., R. D. (2019) 'Paul A. Volcker, Fed chairman who waged war on inflation, is dead at 92'. *New York Times* [online]. https://www.nytimes.com/2019/12/09/business/paul-a-volcker-dead.html

64. Beyer, A., Gaspar, V., Gerbeding, C. and Issing, O. (2009) 'Opting out of the Great Inflation: German monetary policy after the breakdown of Bretton Woods'. ECB working paper series, no. 1020. https://www.ecb.europa.eu/pub/pdf/scpwps/ecbwp1020.pdf

65. Tooze, A. and Eich, S. (2015) 'The Great Inflation', in *Vorgeschichte der Gegenwart*, eds. Manteuffel, A. D., Lutz Raphael, L. and Schlemmer, T. Vandenhoeck & Ruprecht, Göttingen.

66. Issing, O. (2005) 'Why did the Great Inflation not happen in Germany?' *FRB of St. Louis Economic Review*. https://files.stlouisfed.org/files/htdocs/publications/review/05/03/part2/Issing.pdf

67. Goodhart, C. (1989) 'The conduct of monetary policy'. *Economic Journal*, vol. 99, no. 396, pp.293–346. https://www.jstor.org/stable/2234028

68. Skidelsky, R. (2018)

69. Hetzel, R. L. (2008) 'What is the monetary standard, or, how did the Volcker-Greenspan FOMCs tame inflation?' *Economic Quarterly*, vol. 94, no. 2, pp.147–171. https://core.ac.uk/download/pdf/6755398.pdf

70. *The Economist* (2020) 'A surge in inflation looks unlikely'. *The Economist* [online]. https://www.economist.com/briefing/2020/12/12/a-surge-in-inflation-looks-unlikely

71. Goodhart, C. (1989)

72. Carlson, J. B. and McElravey, J. N. (1989) 'Money and velocity in the 1980s'. Federal Reserve Bank of Cleveland, Economic Commentary. https://www.clevelandfed.org/en/newsroom-and-events/publications/economic-commentary/economic-commentary-archives/1989-economic-commentaries/ec-19890115-money-and-velocity-in-the-1980s.aspx

73. Jahan, S. and Papageorgiu, C. (2014) 'What is monetarism?' *Finance and Development*, vol. 51, no. 1. https://www.imf.org/external/pubs/ft/fandd/2014/03/basics.htm

74. Friedman, M. (1984) 'Lessons from the 1979–82 monetary policy experiment'. *American Economic Review*, no. 74. https://www.jstor.org/stable/1816392

75. Market, T. (2019) 'Other people's blood'. *N+1 Magazine*. https://nplusonemag.com/issue-34/reviews/other-peoples-blood-2/

5. What is the power of money?

1. Weatherford, J. (1997) *The History of Money*. Three Rivers Press, New York, NY.

2. Jones, D. (2013) 'Election 2013: reforming the City of London corporation.' *OpenDemocracy* [online]. https://www.opendemocracy.net/en/opendemocracyuk/election-2013-reforming-city-of-london-corporation/

3. Glasman, M. (2014) 'The City of London's strange history'. *Financial Times* [online]. https://www.ft.com/content/7c8f24fa-3aa5-11e4-bd08-00144fe-abdc0

4. Origins of the Lord Mayor's show. https://lordmayorsshow.london/history/origins

5. Goetzmann, W. N. (2016) *Money Changes Everything: How Finance Made Civilization Possible*. Princeton University Press, Princeton, NJ.

6. Velde, F. (2013) On the Origin of Specie. http://people.bu.edu/chamley/HSFref/Velde-originmoney.pdf

7. Horsefield, J. K. (1982) 'The stop of the Exchequer revisited'. *The Economic History Review new series*, vol. 35, no. 4, pp.511-528. https://www.jstor.org/stable/2595405

8. Ingham, G. (2020) *Money*. Polity Press, Cambridge.

9. Federal Reserve Sunshine Act (2009) S.604, 111th Congress. https://www.congress.gov/bill/111th-congress/senate-bill/604

10. Federal Reserve Transparency Act (2009) H.R.1207, 111th Congress. https://www.congress.gov/bill/111th-congress/house-bill/1207

11. Edelstein, M. (1994) 'Foreign investment and accumulation, 1860–1914', in Floud, R. and McCloskey, D. N. (eds) *The Economic History of Britain since 1700* (vol. 2). Cambridge University Press, Cambridge.

12. Kynaston, D. (2012) *City of London: The History*. Vintage, London.

13. Weldon, D. (2021) *Two Hundred Years of Muddling Through*. Little, Brown, London.

14. Smith, A. (1981) *Paper Money*. Summit Books, New York, NY.

15. Schenk, C. R. (1998) 'The origins of the eurodollar market in London: 1955–1963'. *Explorations in Economic History*, vol. 35, no. 2, pp. 221–238, April.

16. Burn, G. (1999) 'The state, the City and the euromarkets'. *Review of International Political Economy*, vol. 6, no. 2, pp.225–261. https://www.jstor.org/stable/4177309

17. Gibson, H. D. (1989) *The Eurocurrency Markets, Domestic Financial Policy and International Instability*. Macmillan, London.

18. Friedman, M. (1971) 'The euro-dollar market: Some first principles'. *Federal Reserve Bank of St Louis Review*, vol. 53. https://files.stlouisfed.org/files/htdocs/publications/review/71/07/Principles_Jul1971.pdf

19. Kynaston, D. (2012)

20. Schenk, C. R. (1998)

21. Eichengreen, B. (2011) *Exorbitant Privilege: The Rise and Fall of the Dollar and the Future of the International Monetary System*. Oxford University Press, Oxford.

22. Boz, E., Casas, C., Georgiadis, G., Gopinath, G., Le Mezo, H., Mehl, A. and Nguyen, T. (2020) 'Patterns in invoicing currency in global trade'. IMF working paper no. 20/126. https://www.imf.org/en/Publications/WP/Issues/2020/07/17/Patterns-in-Invoicing-Currency-in-Global-Trade-49574

23. Smith, A. (1981)

24. Committee on the Global Financial System (2020) 'US dollar funding: An international perspective'. Bank for International Settlement. https://www.bis.org/publ/cgfs65.pdf

25. Bullough, O. (2018) *Moneyland*. Profile Books, London.

26. Szalay, E. and Smith, C. (2020) 'Global funding squeeze forces dollar higher'. *Financial Times* [online]. https://www.ft.com/content/3ee752c6-684e-11ea-800d-da70cff6e4d3

27. Ibid.

28. Eren, E., Schrimpf, A. and Sushko, V. (2020) 'US dollar funding markets during the Covid-19 crisis – The international dimension'. *BIS Bulletin*, no. 15. https://www.bis.org/publ/bisbull15.htm

29. Wheatley, J. (2020) 'Global investors dump $42bn of EM assets since start of outbreak'. *Financial Times* [online]. https://www.ft.com/content/8562417c-63c4-11ea-b3f3-fe4680ea68b5

30. Bahaj, S. and Reis, R. (2020) 'Central bank swap lines during the Covid-19 pandemic'. *Covid Economics*, issue 2. http://personal.lse.ac.uk/reisr/papers/20-covicbswaps.pdf

31. Tooze, A. (2018) *Crashed: How a Decade of Financial Crises Changed the World*. Penguin Books, London.

32. Fleming, M. J. and Klagge, N. J. (2010) 'The Federal Reserve's foreign exchange swap lines'. *Current Issues in Economics and Finance*, vol. 16, no. 4. https://www.newyorkfed.org/medialibrary/media/research/current_issues/ci16-4.pdf

33. Eichengreen, B. (2011)

34. CIA (1982) 'Economic sanctions and the Iran experience'. CIA. https://www.cia.gov/readingroom/document/cia-rdp83m00914r00280004 0051-6

35. Fleming, S. (2019) 'Currency warrior: Why Trump is weaponising the dollar'. *Financial Times* [online]. https://www.ft.com/content/5694b0dc-91e7-11e9-aea1-2b1d33ac3271

36. Beattie, A. (2020) 'Trump weaponises the dollar in drive to put America first'. *Financial Times* [online]. https://www.ft.com/content/acc48fc6-169a-11ea-b869-0971bffac109

37. Schanzer, J. (2018) 'The biggest sanctions-evasion scheme in recent history'. *The Atlantic* [online]. https://www.theatlantic.com/international/archive/2018/01/iran-turkey-gold-sanctions-nuclear-zarrab-atilla/549665

38. Riordan, P. and Liu, N. (2020) 'Hong Kong's leader has "piles of cash" at home after US sanctions'. *Financial Times* [online]. https://www.ft.com/content/0f9f0e98-faac-4ecd-8896-8cda3746a920

39. Eichengreen, B. (2011)

40. Steil, B. (2013) *The Battle of Bretton Woods: John Maynard Keynes, Harry Dexter White, and the Making of a New World Order*. Princeton University Press, Princeton, NJ.

41. Eichengreen, B. (2008, ed. 2019) *Globalising Capital: A History of the International Monetary System*, 3rd ed. Princeton University Press, Princeton, NJ.

42. Steil, B. (2013)

43. Boughton, J. M. (2002) 'Why White, not Keynes? Inventing the postwar international monetary system'. IMF working paper no. 02/52. https://www.imf.org/en/Publications/WP/Issues/2016/12/30/Why-White-Not-Keynes-Inventing-the-Post-War-International-Monetary-System-15718

44. Steil, B. (2013)

45. Boughton, J. M. (2000) 'The case against Harry Dexter White: Still not proven'. IMF working paper no. 00/149. https://www.imf.org/en/Publications/WP/Issues/2016/12/30/The-Case-Against-Harry-Dexter-White-Still-Not-Proven-3727

46. Boughton, J. M. (1998) 'Harry Dexter White and the International Monetary Fund'. *Finance and Development*, vol. 35, no. 3. https://www.imf.org/external/pubs/ft/fandd/1998/09/boughton.htm

47. Bordo, M. D. (1993) 'The Bretton Woods international monetary system: A historical overview', in *A Retrospective on the Bretton Woods System: Lessons for International Monetary Reform*, Bordo, M. D. and Eichengreen, B. (eds) University of Chicago Press, Chicago, IL. https://www.nber.org/books-and-chapters/retrospective-bretton-woods-system-lessons-international-monetary-reform/bretton-woods-international-monetary-system-historical-overview

48. Khan, M. (2019) 'Kristalina Georgieva selected by EU for IMF top job'. *Financial Times* [online]. https://www.ft.com/content/7b89aa12-b543-11e9-8cb2-799a3a8cf37b

49. Steil, B. (2013)

50. Bordo, M., Monnet, E. and Naef, A. (2017) 'The gold pool (1961–1968) and the fall of the Bretton Woods system: Lessons for central bank cooperation'. NBER working paper no. 24016. https://economics.ucdavis.edu/events/papers/copy2_of_417Bordo.pdf

51. Simard, D., Bordo, M. and White, E. N. (1994) 'France and the breakdown of the Bretton Woods international monetary system'. IMF working paper no. 94/128. https://www.imf.org/en/Publications/WP/Issues/2016/12/30/France-and-the-Breakdown-of-the-Bretton-Woods-International-Monetary-System-1314

52. Bordo, M. (2017) 'The operation and demise of the Bretton Woods system: 1958 to 1971'. *VoxEU*. https://voxeu.org/article/operation-and-demise-bretton-woods-system

53. O'Rourke, K. H. (2017) 'Two great trade collapses: The interwar period and great recession compared'. NBER working paper no. 23825. http://www.nber.org./papers/w23825.

54. Dreher, A. and Jensen, N. M. (2007) 'Independent actor or agent? An empirical analysis of the impact of US interests on International Monetary Fund conditions'. *Journal of Law and Economics*, vol. 50, no. 1, pp.105–124. https://www.jstor.org/stable/10.1086/508311

55. Rogoff, K. (2003) 'The IMF strikes back'. *Foreign Policy Magazine*. https://scholar.harvard.edu/files/rogoff/files/imf_strikes_back.pdf

56. Phillips, S. T. and Lane, T. D. (2000) 'Does IMF financing result in moral hazard?' IMF working paper no. 00/168. https://www.imf.org/en/Publications/WP/Issues/2016/12/30/Does-IMF-Financing-Result-in-Moral-Hazard-3824

57. Appiah, K. A. (2007) 'A slow emancipation'. *New York Times* [online]. https://www.nytimes.com/2007/03/18/magazine/18WWLNlede.t.html

58. Testart, A. (2001) 'Slaves that are not slaves, yet really are'. http://www.alaintestart.com/UK/documents/engslaves2011.pdf

59. Testart, A. (2002) 'The extent and significance of debt slavery'. *Revue française de sociologie*, vol. 43, Supplement: An annual English selection, pp.173–204. https://www.jstor.org/stable/3322762

60. Coleman, P. J. (1999) *Debtors and Creditors in America: Insolvency, Imprisonment for Debt, and Bankruptcy, 1607–1900*. State Historical Society of Wisconsin, Madison, WI.

61. Efrat, R. (2006) 'Bankruptcy stigma: Plausible causes for shifting norms'. *Emory Bankruptcy Developments Journal*, vol. 22, no. 2. http://dspace.calstate.edu/bitstream/handle/10211.2/1800/EfratRafi2006.pdf?sequence=1

62. Lee, M. (2016) 'Fact check: Has Trump declared bankruptcy four or six times?' *Washington Post* [online]. https://www.washingtonpost.com/politics/2016/live-updates/general-election/real-time-fact-checking-and-analysis-of-the-first-presidential-debate/fact-check-has-trump-declared-bankruptcy-four-or-six-times/

63. Davies, D. (2018) *Lying for Money*. Profile Books, London.

64. Coleman, P. J. (1999)

65. Reinhart, C. and Rogoff, K. (2009) *This Time is Different*. Princeton University Press, Princeton, NJ.

66. Lowenthal, A. F. (1970) 'The United States and the Dominican Republic to 1965: Background to invention'. *Caribbean Studies*, vol. 10, no. 2, pp.30–55. https://www.jstor.org/stable/25612211

67. Rippy, J. F. (1937) 'The inititiation of the customs receivership in the Dominican Republic'. *Hispanic American Historical Review*, vol. 17, no. 4, pp.419–457. https://www.jstor.org/stable/2507126

68. Topik, S. C. (2000) 'When Mexico had the blues: A transatlantic tale of bonds, bankers and nationalists, 1862–1910'. *American Historical Review*, vol. 105, no. 3, pp.714–738. https://www.jstor.org/stable/2651807

69. De la Torre, A., Yeyati, E. L., Schmukler, S. L., Ades, A. and Kaminsky, G. (2003) 'Living and dying with hard pegs: The rise and fall of Argentina's currency board'. *Economía*, vol. 3, no. 2, pp.43–107. https://www.jstor.org/stable/20065441

70. Beattie, A. (2009) *False Economy: A Surprising Economic History of the World*. Penguin Books, London.

71. Blustein, P. (2006) *And the Money Kept Rolling In (and Out)*. Public Affairs, New York, NY.

72. Ibid.

73. Mussa, M. (2002) 'Argentina and the Fund: From triumph to tragedy'. Institute for International Economics, Washington, DC.

74. *The Economist* (2002) 'A decline without parallel'. *The Economist* [online]. https://www.economist.com/special-report/2002/02/28/a-decline-without-parallel

75. Independent Evaluation Office of the IMF (2003) The role of the IMF in Argentina, 1991–2002. https://www.imf.org/External/NP/ieo/2003/arg/index.htm

76. IMF (2020) 'Argentina: Transactions with the Fund from May 01, 1984 to November 30, 2020'. https://www.imf.org/external/np/fin/tad/extrans1.aspx?memberKey1=30&endDate=2099-12-31&finposition_flag=YES

77. National Public Radio (2011) 'Planet Money: The price of default'. https://www.npr.org/transcripts/141365144?t=1609180226226

78. National Public Radio (2013) 'All things considered: Argentine leader's plane grounded by credit holders'. https://www.npr.org/2013/01/10/169077531/argentine-leaders-plane-grounded-by-credit-holders

79. Foley, S. (2014) 'Paul Singer: Argentina's nemesis is a tenacious tactician'. *Financial Times* [online]. https://www.ft.com/content/97f9e168-f62f-11e3-83d3-00144feabdc0

80. Schumacher, J., Trebesch, C. and Enderlein, H. (2018) 'The legal cost of default: How creditor lawsuits are reshaping sovereign debt markets'. *VoxEU*. https://voxeu.org/article/how-creditor-lawsuits-are-reshaping-sovereign-debt-markets

81. Eavis, P., Stevenson, A., Romero, S. and Alden, W. (2014) 'In hedge fund, Argentina finds a relentless foe'. *New York Times*. https://dealbook.nytimes.com/2014/07/30/in-hedge-fund-argentina-finds-relentless-foe/

82. Alloway, T. and Cotterill, J. (2014) 'Tough judge Thomas Griesa weighs Argentina's fate'. *Financial Times* [online]. https://www.ft.com/content/d8d895ec-18b4-11e4-a51a-00144feabdc0

83. *The Economist* (2016) 'At last'. *The Economist* [online]. https://www.economist.com/the-americas/2016/03/05/at-last

84. Hébert, B. and Schreger, J. (2017) 'The costs of sovereign default: Evidence from Argentina'. *American Economic Review*, vol. 107, no. 10. https://www.aeaweb.org/articles?id=10.1257/aer.20151667

85. Roos, J. E. (2021) *Why Not Default? The Political Economy of Sovereign Debt.* Princeton University Press, Princeton, NJ.

86. Mander, B. and Moore, E. (2016) 'Argentina puts an end to long holdouts saga'. *Financial Times* [online]. https://www.ft.com/content/516ab98a-08a1-11e6-876d-b823056b209b

87. Stott, M. and Mander, B. (2019) 'Argentina: How IMF's biggest ever bailout crumbled under Macri'. *Financial Times* [online]. https://www.ft.com/content/5cfe7c34-ca48-11e9-a1f4-3669401ba76f

88. *The Economist* (2020) 'Argentina defaults yet again, but hopes to get off lightly'. *The Economist* [online]. https://www.economist.com/the-americas/2020/05/23/argentina-defaults-yet-again-but-hopes-to-get-off-lightly

89. Eichengreen, B., Mehl, A. and Chivu, L. (2017) *How Global Currencies Work: Past, Present and Future*. Princeton University Press, Princeton, NJ.

90. Sandbu, M. (2019) 'Europe first: Taking on the dominance of the US dollar'. *Financial Times* [online]. https://www.ft.com/content/3165c19c-0ba0-11ea-bb52-34c8d9dc6d84

91. Company, R. (2015) 'What's the difference between the renminbi and the yuan? The answer to this and other questions in "Renminbi internationalisation"'. Brookings Institution Press. https://www.brookings.edu/blog/brookings-now/2015/08/19/whats-the-difference-between-the-renminbi-and-the-yuan-the-answer-to-this-and-other-questions-in-renminbi-internationalization

92. Wildau, G. and Mitchell, T. (2016) 'China: Renminbi stalls on road to being a global currency'. *Financial Times* [online]. https://www.ft.com/content/e480fd92-bc6a-11e6-8b45-b8b81dd5d080

93. Lockett, H. and Szalay, E. (2019) 'Why the renminbi's challenge to the dollar has faded'. *Financial Times* [online]. https://www.ft.com/content/ba410544-ecba-11e9-ad1e-4367d8281195

94. Choyleva, D. (2020) 'Investors need to position for a US-China clash of civilisations'. *Financial Times* [online]. https://www.ft.com/content/59febbd8-46d6-11ea-aeb3-955839e06441

95. Prasad, E. S. (2014) *The Dollar Trap: How the US Dollar Tightened its Grip on Global Finance*. Princeton University Press, Princeton, NJ.

96. Gopinath, G. and Stein, J. C. (2018) 'Banking, trade and the making of a dominant currency'. NBER working paper no. 24485. https://www.nber.org/papers/w24485

97. Ilzetzki, E., Reinhart, C. M. and Rogoff, K. S. (2019) 'Why is the euro punching below its weight?' NBER working paper no. 26760. https://www.nber.org/papers/w26760

98. Cœuré, B. (2016) 'Sovereign debt in the euro area: Too safe or too risky?' Keynote address at Harvard University's Minda de Gunzburg Centre for European Studies. https://www.ecb.europa.eu/press/key/date/2016/html/sp161103.en.html

99. Feldstein, M. S. (2011) 'The euro and European economic conditions'. NBER working paper no. 17617. https://www.nber.org/papers/w17617

100. Bordo, M. and James, H. (2008) 'A long term perspective on the euro'. NBER working paper no. 13815. https://www.nber.org/papers/w13815

101. Van Middelaar, L. (2019) *Alarums and Excusions: Improvising Politics on the European Stage*. Agenda Publishing, Newcastle upon Tyne.

102. Kaplan, J. J. and Schleiminger, G. (1989) *The European Payments Union: Financial Diplomacy in the 1950s*. Clarendon Press, Oxford.

103. James, H. (2012) *Making the European Monetary Union*. Harvard University Press, Harvard, MA.

104. Marsh, D. (2009) *The Euro: The Politics of the New Global Currency*. Yale University Press, New Haven, CT.

105. Hung, J. (2011) 'German aversion to the ECB printing money isn't about the "national psyche"'. *Guardian* [online]. https://www.theguardian.com/commentisfree/2011/dec/22/germany-ecb-national-psyche-hyperinflation

106. Hetzel, R. L. (2012) 'German monetary history in the first half of the twentieth century'. *FRB Richmond Economic Quarterly*, vol. 88, no. 1, pp.1–35. https://core.ac.uk/download/pdf/6993605.pdf

107. Guin, B. (2017) 'Culture and household saving'. ECB working paper series, no. 2069. https://www.ecb.europa.eu/pub/pdf/scpwps/ecb.wp2069.en.pdf

108. Buck, T. (2018) 'Why are Germans so obsessed with saving money?' *Financial Times* [online]. https://www.ft.com/content/c8772236-2b93-11e8-a34a-7e7563b0b0f4

109. Zatlin, J. R. (2000) Review: 'Making money: The Bundesbank and the German political economy'. *German Politics & Society*, vol. 18, no. 1, pp.135–151. https://www.jstor.org/stable/23737435

110. Bundesbank (2012) Different views on the Deutsche Bundesbank – Academic and political voices. https://www.bundesbank.de/en/tasks/topics/different-views-on-the-deutsche-bundesbank-academic-and-political-voices-626924

111. Bordo, M. and Redish, A. (2013) 'Putting the "system" in the international monetary system'. National Bureau of Economic Research working paper no. 19026. https://voxeu.org/article/putting-system-international-monetary-system

112. Boughton, J. M. (2002)

113. Webb, M. C. (1995) *The Political Economy of Policy Coordination: International Adjustment since 1945*. Cornell University Press, Ithaca, NY, and London.

114. McKinnon, R. I. (1996) *The Rules of the Game: International Money and Exchange Rates*. MIT Press, Cambridge, MA.

115. Eichengreen, B. (2008)

116. James, H. (2012)

117. Sauga, M., Simons, S. and Wiegrefe, K. (2010) 'Was the Deutsche Mark sacrificed for reunification?' https://www.spiegel.de/international/germany/the-price-of-unity-was-the-deutsche-mark-sacrificed-for-reunification-a-719940.html

118. Marsh, D. (2009)

119. Marsh, D. (2009)

120. Sauga, M., Simons, S. and Wiegrefe, K. (2010)

121. Jones, C. (2018) 'Jens Weidmann on Draghi and the ECB'. *Financial Times* [online]. https://www.ft.com/content/92b476e4-16f3-11e8-9e9c-25c814761640

122. Tooze, A. (2018)

123. Bordo, M. and James, H. (2008)

124. Henkel, I. (2015) 'German public opinion is caught between scapegoating Greeks and love-bombing them'. LSE European Politics and Policy blog. https://blogs.lse.ac.uk/europpblog/2015/07/21/german-public-opinion-is-caught-between-scapegoating-greeks-and-love-bombing-them/

125. Brundsden, J., Fleming, S. and Khan, M. (2020) 'EU recovery fund: How the plan will work'. *Financial Time*s [online]. https://www.ft.com/content/2b69c9c4-2ea4-4635-9d8a-1b67852c0322

126. Isenson, N. (2012) 'Merkel: No eurobonds "as long as I live"'. *Deutsche Welle* [online]. https://www.dw.com/en/merkel-no-eurobonds-as-long-as-i-live/a-16052083

127. Sandbu, M. (2020) 'EU crosses the Rubicon with its emergency recovery fund'. *Financial Times* [online]. https://www.ft.com/content/bd570dde-3095-4074-bd37-18003f2bd3c2

128. Hall, B., Fleming, S. and Chazan, G. (2020) 'Is the Franco-German plan Europe's "Hamiltonian moment?"' *Financial Times* [online]. https://www.ft.com/content/2735a3f1-bc58-477c-9315-c98129d12852

6. Why don't governments just print money?

1. Moore, L. and Kaluzny, J. (2005). 'Regime change and debt default: The case of Russia, Austro-Hungary, and the Ottoman Empire following World War One'. *Explorations in Economic History*, vol. 42, no. 2, pp.237–258.

2. Malik, H. (2018*) Bankers and Bolsheviks: International Finance and the Russian Revolution*. Princeton University Press, Princeton, NJ.

3. Ibid.

4. O'Donnell, A. (2017) 'The Bolsheviks versus the deep state'. *New York Times* [online]. https://www.nytimes.com/2017/03/27/opinion/the-bolsheviks-versus-the-deep-state.html

5. Reed, J. (1919) *Ten Days that Shook the World*. Penguin, London.

6. Sargent, T. J. (1982) 'The ends of four big inflations', in *Inflations Causes and Effects*, Hall, R. E. (ed.) University of Chicago Press, Chicago, IL. https://www.nber.org/books-and-chapters/inflation-causes-and-effects/ends-four-big-inflations

7. Figes, O. (1996) *A People's Tragedy: The Russian Revolution, 1891–1924.* Vintage, London.

8. Arnold, A. Z. (1937) *Banks, Credit and Money in Soviet Russia.* Columbia University Press, New York, NY. https://www.degruyter.com/columbia/view/book/9780231878791/10.7312/arno90448-007.xml

9. Efremov, S. M. (2012) 'The role of inflation in Soviet history: Prices, living standards, and political change'. Electronic Theses and Dissertations. Paper 1474. https://dc.etsu.edu/etd/1474

10. Ferguson, N. (2002). *The Cash Nexus: Money and Politics in Modern History, 1700–2000.* Penguin, London.

11. Nove, A. (1992) *An Economic History of the USSR.* Penguin Books, London.

12. Pickersgill, J. E. (1968) 'Hyperinflation and monetary reform in the Soviet Union, 1921–26'. *Journal of Political Economy*, vol. 76, no. 5, pp.1037–1048. https://www.jstor.org/stable/1830035

13. He, L. (2018) *Hyperinflation: A World History.* Routledge, Abingdon.

14. Shmelev, K. (1931) 'Public finances during the civil war', in Sokolnikov, G. Y. et al. (1931), *Soviet Policy in Public Finance, 1917–1928.* Stanford University Press, Stanford, CA.

15. Arnold, A. Z. (1937)

16. Nove, A. (1992)

17. Ibid.

18. North, D. C. and Weingast, B. R. (1989) 'Constitutions and commitment: The evolution of institutions governing public choice in seventeenth-century England'. *Journal of Economic History*, vol. 49, no. 4, pp.803–832. https://www.jstor.org/stable/2122739

19. Figes, O. (1996)

20. Tomz, M. (2007) *Reputation and International Cooperation: Sovereign Debt across Three Centuries.* Princeton University Press, Princeton, NJ.

21. Kelton, S. (2020) *The Deficit Myth.* John Murray, London.

22. US Department of the Treasury (2015) 'Remarks by acting assistant secretary for financial markets Daleep Singh.' Evolving Structure of the US Treasury Market: Second Annual Conference. https://www.treasury.gov/press-center/press-releases/Pages/jl0592.aspx

23. Skidelsky, R. (2018) *Money and Government.* Penguin Books, London.

24. Reis, R. (2016) 'Can the central bank alleviate fiscal burdens?' NBER working paper no. 23014. https://www.nber.org/papers/w23014

25. Breedon, F. and Turner, P. (2016) 'On the transactions cost of quantitative easing'. BIS working paper no 571. https://www.bis.org/publ/work571.pdf

26. Mackenzie, M. and Oakley, D. (2009) 'Boom time for bond traders'. *Financial Times* [online]. https://www.ft.com/content/f829b344-d422-11de-990c-00144feabdc0

27. Bernanke, B. S. (2013) 'Long term interest rates'. Annual Monetary/Macroeconomics Conference: The Past and Future of Monetary Policy, sponsored by Federal Reserve Bank of San Francisco, San Francisco, 1 March. https://www.federalreserve.gov/newsevents/speech/bernanke2013 0301a.htm

28. Bernanke, B. S. (2009) 'The crisis and the policy response'. Stamp Lecture, London School of Economics, London, 13 January. https://www.federal-reserve.gov/newsevents/speech/bernanke20090113a.htm

29. Blinder, A. S. (2010) 'Quantitative easing: Entrance and exit strategies'. *Federal Reserve Bank of St. Louis Review*, vol. 92, no. 6, pp.465–479. https://files.stlouisfed.org/files/htdocs/publications/review/10/11/Blinder.pdf

30. Bank of England (1995) Bank of England report and amounts 1995. https://www.bankofengland.co.uk/-/media/boe/files/annual-report/1995/boe-1995.pdf?la=en&hash=1C1A063C3BEEEFEFD25BE7C584C DFDB483711213

31. He, L. (2018) *Hyperinflation: A World History*. Routledge, Abingdon.

32. Wen, Y. and Arias, M. A. (2014) 'What does money velocity tell us about low inflation in the US?' Federal Reserve Bank of St. Louis. On the Economy Blog. https://www.stlouisfed.org/on-the-economy/2014/september/what-does-money-velocity-tell-us-about-low-inflation-in-the-us

33. Blyth, M. (2013) *Austerity: The History of a Dangerous Idea*. Oxford University Press, Oxford.

34. Horton, M., Jumar, M. and Mauro, P. (2009) 'The state of public finances: A cross-country fiscal monitor'. IMF Staff Position Note. https://www.imf.org/en/Publications/FM?page=3

35. Wren-Lewis, S. (2015) 'The Austerity Con'. London Review of Books [online]. https://www.lrb.co.uk/the-paper/v37/n04/simon-wren-lewis/the-austerity-con

36. Ferguson, N. (2010) 'A Greek crisis is coming to America'. *Financial Times* [online]. https://www.ft.com/content/f90bca10-1679-11df-bf44-00144feab49a

37. Osborne, G. (2009) 'The threat of rising interest rates is a Greek tragedy we must avoid'. *Telegraph* [online]. https://www.telegraph.co.uk/finance/recession/6855499/The-threat-of-rising-interest-rates-is-a-Greek-tragedy-we-must-avoid.html

38. Eur-Lex (2020) 'Excessive debt procedure'. https://eur-lex.europa.eu/summary/glossary/excessive_deficit_procedure.html

Notes

39. Barber, T. (2010) 'Greece vows action to cut budget deficit'. *Financial Times* [online]. https://www.ft.com/content/3e7e0e46-bd47-11de-9f6a-00144 feab49a

40. Papaconstantinou, G. (2016) *Game Over: The Inside Story of the Greek Crisis*. CreateSpace [online].

41. Ball, L., Elmendorf, D. W. and Mankiw, N. G. (1995) 'The deficit gamble'. NBER working paper no. 5015. https://www.nber.org/papers/w5015

42. Hope, K. (2010) 'Greece agrees €24bn austerity package'. *Financial Times* [online]. https://www.ft.com/content/c036a694-53b2-11df-aba0-00144 feab49a

43. Roubini, N. (2010) 'Greece's best option is an orderly default'. *Financial Times* [online]. https://www.ft.com/content/a3874e80-82e8-11df-8b15-001 44feabdc0

44. Tooze, A. (2018) *Crashed: How a Decade of Financial Crises Changed the World*. Penguin Random House, London.

45. Blanchard, O. (2019) 'Public debt and low interest rates'. *American Economic Review*, vol. 109, no. 4, pp.1197–1229. https://www.aeaweb.org/articles?id= 10.1257/aer.109.4.1197

46. Reinhart, C. M. and Rogoff, K. (2011) *This Time is Different: Eight Centuries of Financial Folly*. Princeton University Press, Princeton, NJ.

47. Roos, J. E. (2021) *Why Not Default? The Political Economy of Sovereign Debt*. Princeton University Press, Princeton, NJ.

48. Ban, C. (2012) 'Sovereign debt, austerity and regime change: The case of Nicolae Ceauşescu's Romania'. *East European Politics and Societies*, vol. 26, no. 4, pp.743–776. https://journals.sagepub.com/doi/abs/10.1177/088832 5412465513

49. *Associated Press* (1989) 'Romania pays off its debts but problems linger'. *Associated Press* [online]. https://apnews.com/article/aaf1d94fbd52c0b708 928703625baa36

50. Ban, C. (2012)

51. Roos, J. E. (2021)

52. Mehrotra, N. R. (2017) 'Debt sustainability in a low interest rate world'. Hutchins Centre working paper no. 32. https://www.brookings.edu/ wp-content/uploads/2017/06/wp32_mehrotra_debtsustainability.pdf

53. Ball, L., Elmendorf, D. W. and Mankiw, N. G. (1995)

54. Barrett, P. (2018) 'Interest-growth differentials and debt limits in advanced economies'. IMF working paper no. 18/82. https://www.imf.org/en/ Publications/WP/Issues/2018/04/11/Interest-Growth-Differentials-and-Debt-Limits-in-Advanced-Economies-45794

55. Reinhart, M. C. and Sbrancia, C. M. (2011) 'The liquidation of government debt'. NBER working paper no. 16893. https://www.nber.org/papers/w16893

56. Castle, S. (2014) 'That debt from 1720? Britain's payment is coming'. *New York Times* [online]. https://www.nytimes.com/2014/12/28/world/that-debt-from-1720-britains-payment-is-coming.html

57. *The Economist* (2005) 'Percents and sensibility'. *The Economist* [online]. https://www.economist.com/special-report/2005/12/20/percents-and-sensibility

58. Austen, J. (1813) *Pride and Prejudice*. Penguin Classics, London.

59. Kolleew, J. (2014) 'Paying the price of war: Britain makes good on historic debts'. *Guardian* [online]. https://www.theguardian.com/business/blog/2014/oct/31/paying-the-price-of-war-britain-makes-good-on-historic-debts

60. Moore, E. (2014) 'UK to repay tranche of perpetual war loans'. *Financial Times* [online]. https://www.ft.com/content/94653f60-60e8-11e4-894b-00144feabdc0

61. Bank of England (2020) 'A Millennium of Macroeconomic Data. The Bank of England'. https://www.bankofengland.co.uk/statistics/research-datasets

62. Wolf, M. (2010) 'A bail-out for Greece is just the beginning'. *Financial Times* [online]. https://www.ft.com/content/de21becc-57af-11df-855b-00144feab49a

63. IMF (2020) *World Economic Outlook*. https://www.imf.org/en/Publications/WEO/weo-database/2020/October

64. Ibid.

65. Harding, R. (2017) 'The fears about Japan's debt are overblown'. *Financial Times* [online]. https://www.ft.com/content/e26d36e6-918b-11e7-a9e6-11d2f0ebb7f0

66. Guillemette, Y. and Stráský, J. (2014) 'Japan's challenging debt dynamics'. *OECD Journal: Economic Studies*. https://www.oecd.org/economy/growth/Japan-s-challenging-debt-dynamics-OECD-Journal-Economic-Studies-2014.pdf

67. Pilling, D. (2014) *Bending Adversity: Japan and the Art of Survival*. Penguin, London.

68. IMF (2020)

69. Ibid.

70. Guillemette, Y. and Stráský, J. (2014)

71. FT markets data (2021) 'Japan 10 year GB'. *Financial Times* [online]. https://markets.ft.com/data/bonds/tearsheet/summary?s=JP10YB

72. Ministry of Finance, Japan (2020) Highlights of the FY 2021 budget. https://www.mof.go.jp/english/budget/budget/fy2021/01.pdf

73. Carvalho, C., Ferrero, A. and Nechio, F. (2016) 'Demographics and real interest rates: Inspecting the mechanism'. *European Economic Review*, vol. 88, pp.208–226. https://www.sciencedirect.com/science/article/abs/pii/S001 4292116300678

74. Han, F. (2019) 'Demographics and the natural rate of interest in Japan'. IMF working paper no. 19/31. https://www.imf.org/en/Publications/ WP/Issues/2019/02/15/Demographics-and-the-Natural-Rate-of-Interest-in-Japan-46550

75. Harding, R. (2018) 'Japan demand for labour sparks immigration debate'. *Financial Times* [online]. https://www.ft.com/content/6f47f576-de8c-11e8-9f04-38d397e6661c

76. Aiyagari, S. R. and McGrattan, E. R. (1998) 'The optimum quantity of debt'. *Journal of Monetary Economics*, vol. 42, no. 3, pp.447–469. https://www. sciencedirect.com/science/article/abs/pii/S0304393298000312

77. Blanchard, O. (2019)

78. Gibson, H. D., Hall, S. G. and Tavlas, G. S. (2011) 'The Greek financial crisis: Growing imbalances and sovereign spreads'. Bank of Greece working paper no. 124. https://www.bankofgreece.gr/Publications/Paper2011124.pdf

79. Segoviano, M. A., Caceres, C. and Guzzo, V. (2010) 'Sovereign spreads: Global risk aversion, contagion or fundamentals?' IMF working paper no. 10/120. www.imf.org/en/Publications/WP/Issues/2016/12/31/Sovereign-Spreads-Global-Risk-Aversion-Contagion-or-Fundamentals-23829

80. Calvo, G. A. (1988) 'Servicing the public debt: The role of expectations'. *American Economic Review*, vol. 78, no. 4. pp.647–661. https://www.jstor.org/ stable/1811165

81. Lorenzoni, G. and Werning, I. (2019). 'Slow moving debt crises'. *American Economic Review*, vol. 109, no. 9, pp.3229–63. https://www.aeaweb.org/ articles?id=10.1257/aer.20141766

82. Tooze, A. (2018)

83. Draghi, M. (2012) Speech by Mario Draghi, President of the European Central Bank at the Global Investment Conference in London, 26 July 2012. https://www.ecb.europa.eu/press/key/date/2012/html/sp120726. en.html

84. Barber, L. and Steen, M. (2012) 'FT Person of the Year: Mario Draghi'. *Financial Times* [online]. https://www.ft.com/content/8fca75b8-4535-11e2-838f-00144feabdc0

85. Jones, C. (2015) 'European Central Bank unleashes quantitative easing'. *Financial Times* [online]. https://www.ft.com/content/aedf6a66-a231-11e4-bbb8-00144feab7de

86. Ministry of Finance, Japan (2021) 'Central government debt'. https://www.mof.go.jp/english/jgbs/reference/gbb/e202103.html

87. Bank of Japan (2021) 'Japanese government bonds held by the Bank of Japan'. Bank of Japan. https://www.boj.or.jp/en/statistics/boj/other/mei/index.htm/

88. Bank of Japan (2020) 'Annual accounts'. https://www.boj.or.jp/en/about/account/zai2005a.pdf

89. Lewis, L. (2018) 'Bank of Japan bond buying leaves traders twiddling their thumbs'. *Financial Times* [online]. https://www.ft.com/content/d2793ddc-b1d0-11e8-99ca-68cf89602132

90. Bank of Japan (2020) 'Price stability target' and 'Quantitative and qualitative monetary easing with yield curve control.' https://www.boj.or.jp/en/mopo/outline/qqe.htm/

91. Akram, T. (2019) 'The impact of the Bank of Japan's monetary policy on Japanese government bonds' low nominal yields'. Levy Economics Institute working paper no. 938. http://www.levyinstitute.org/pubs/wp_938.pdf

92. Blanchard, O. and Tashiro, T. (2019) Fiscal policy options for Japan. Peterson Institite of International Economics policy brief. https://www.piie.com/system/files/documents/pb19-7.pdf

93. Mody, A. and Nedeljkovic, M. (2019) 'The ECB's performance during the crisis: Lessons learned'. *VoxEU*. https://voxeu.org/article/ecb-s-performance-during-crisis

94. Gabor, D. and Ban, C. (2015) 'Banking on bonds: The new links between states and markets'. https://onlinelibrary.wiley.com/doi/abs/10.1111/jcms.12309

95. Shellock, D. (2010) 'Eurozone debt crisis prompts flight to quality'. *Financial Times* [online]. https://www.ft.com/content/a7a4c0ee-5230-11df-8b09-00144feab49a

96. ECB (2012) ECB announces change in eligibility of debt instruments issued or guaranteed by the Greek government. https://www.ecb.europa.eu/press/pr/date/2012/html/pr121219.en.html

97. Moore, E. and Hope, K. (2014) 'Greece launches sale of five-year bond'. *Financial Times* [online]. https://www.ft.com/content/404ef5ba-bf17-11e3-8683-00144feabdc0

98. Bank of Japan (2021) 'Assessment for further effective and sustainable monetary easing'. https://www.boj.or.jp/en/announcements/release_2021/k210319c.pdf

99. Blanchard, O. and Pisani-Ferry, J. (2020) 'Monetisation: Do not panic'. *VoxEU*. https://voxeu.org/article/monetisation-do-not-panic

100. Kihara, L. (2021) 'Analysis: Global bond rout puts BOJ's yield curve control in spotlight'. *Reuters* [online]. https://www.reuters.com/article/us-japan-economy-boj-ycc-analysis-idUSKBN2AV2U9

101. Fisher, I. (1930) *The Theory of Interest*. Macmillan, New York, NY.

102. Barro, R. J. and Gordon, D. B. (1981) A positive theory of monetary policy in a natural-rate model. NBER working paper no. 807. https://www.nber.org/papers/w0807

103. Debelle, G., Masson, P., Savastano, M. and Sharma, S. (1998) 'Inflation targeting as a framework for monetary policy'. *IMF Economic Issues* no. 15. https://www.imf.org/external/pubs/ft/issues/issues15

104. Skidelsky, R. (2018)

105. Bordo, M. D. and Rockoff, H. (1996) 'The gold standard as a "good housekeeping seal of approval"'. *Journal of Economic History*, vol. 56, no. 2, pp.389–428. https://www.jstor.org/stable/2123971

106. Tucker, P. (2018) *Unelected Power: The Quest for Legitimacy in Central Banking and the Regulatory State*. Princeton University Press, Princeton, NJ.

107. Rogoff, K. (1985) 'The optimal degree of commitment to an intermediate monetary target'. *Quarterly Journal of Economics*, vol. 100, no. 4, pp.1169–1189. https://www.jstor.org/stable/1885679

108. Sargent, T. J. and Wallace, N. (1981) 'Some unpleasant monetarist arithmetic'. *Federal Reserve Bank of Minneapolis Quarterly Review*, no. 531. https://www.minneapolisfed.org/research/quarterly-review/some-unpleasant-monetarist-arithmetic

109. Bank of England (2020) HM Treasury and Bank of England announce temporary extension to Ways and Means facility. https://www.bankofengland.co.uk/news/2020/april/hmt-and-boe-announce-temporary-extension-to-ways-and-means-facility

110. Capie, F., Goodhart, C. and Schnadt, N. (1994) 'The development of central banking', in *The Future of Central Banking*, Capie, F., Fischer, S., Goodhart, C. and Schnadt, N. (eds), Cambridge University Press, Cambridge. http://eprints.lse.ac.uk/39606/1/The_development_of_central_banking_%28LSERO%29.pdf

111. Edvinsson, R., Jacobson, T. and Waldenström, D. (eds) (2018) *Sveriges Riksbank and the History of Central Banking*. Cambridge University Press, Cambridge.

112. Granville, K. (2017) 'A president at war with his Fed chief, five decades before Trump'. *New York Times*. https://www.nytimes.com/2017/06/13/business/economy/a-president-at-war-with-his-fed-chief-5-decades-before-trump.html

113. Wingrove, J. (2020) 'Trump hails "gift" of negative rates that Fed officials disdain'. Bloomberg news service. https://www.bloomberg.com/news/articles/2020-05-12/trump-says-u-s-deserves-gift-of-negative-interest-rates

114. Hetzel, R. L. and Leach, R. F. (2001) 'The Treasury-Federal Reserve accord: A new narrative account'. *Federal Reserve Bank of Richmond Economy Quarterly*, vol. 87, no. 1, pp.33–55. https://www.richmondfed.org/publications/research/economic_quarterly/2001/winter/leachhetzel

115. Szalay, E., Samson, A. and Yackley, A. J. (2021) 'Turkey's lira tumbles after Erdogan sacks central bank chief'. *Financial Times* [online]. https://www.ft.com/content/6be3efd1-a8e9-47a8-abac-966db2d3cf93

116. Martin, K., Wheatley, J., Samson, A. and Yackley, A. J. (2021) 'Investors left shocked after Erdogan upends Turkey's markets'. *Financial Times* [online]. https://www.ft.com/content/fb5f31e8-9189-494f-af39-466606fd00c1

117. Wray, L. R. (2019) 'Alternative paths to modern money theory', in *Modern Monetary Theory and its Critics* (Fulbrook, E. and Morgan, J., eds). WEA, Bristol.

118. Wray, L. R., Dantas, F., Fullwiler, S., Tcherneva, P. R. and Kelton, S. A. (2018) Public service employment: A path to full employment. Levy Economics Institute. http://www.levyinstitute.org/pubs/rpr_4_18.pdf?mod=article_inline

119. Kelton, S. (2020)

120. Wray, L. R. (2014) Central bank independence: Myth and misunderstanding. Working paper no. 791. Levy Economics Institute of Bard College. https://www.econstor.eu/bitstream/10419/110036/1/780085973.pdf

121. Ferguson, N. (2001)

122. Wetterberg, G. (2009) *Money and Power: From Stockholms Banco 1656 to Sveriges Riksbank Today*. Atlantis, Stockholm. https://www.riksbank.se/en-gb/about-the-riksbank/history/money-and-power--the-history-of-sveriges-riksbank

123. Ibid.

124. Edvinsson, R., Jacobson, T. and Waldenström, D. (2018)

125. Macaulay, T. B. (1848) 'The history of England from the accession of James II'. https://www.gutenberg.org/author/Thomas+Babington+Macaulay+Baron+Macaulay

126. North, D. C. and Weingast, B. R. (1989)

127. Kelton, S. (2020)

128. Bruenig, M. (2018) Randy Wray argues a job guarantee will suppress wages. People's Policy Project. https://www.peoplespolicyproject.org/2018/06/02/randy-wrays-argument-that-a-job-guarantee-will-suppress-wages/

129. Blyth, M. (2013)

7. Why do countries use different money?

1. Weatherford, J. (1997) *The History of Money*. Three Rivers Press, New York, NY.

2. Stein, E. (2020) 'Welcome to Jáchymov: The Czech town that invented the dollar'. BBC [online]. http://www.bbc.com/travel/story/20200107-welcome-to-jchymov-the-czech-town-that-invented-the-dollar

3. Rady, M. (2020) *The Habsburgs: The Rise and Fall of a World Power*. Penguin, London.

4. Goodwin, J. (2003) *Greenback: The Almighty Dollar and the Invention of America*. Hamish Hamilton, London.

5. Andrew, A. P. (1904) 'The end of the Mexican dollar'. *Quarterly Journal of Economics*, vol. 18, no. 3, pp.321–356. https://www.jstor.org/stable/1884074

6. MacGregor, N. (2012) *A History of the World in 100 Objects*. Penguin, London.

7. Gordon, P. and Morales, J. J. (2017) *The Silver Way: China, Spanish America and the birth of globalisation, 1565–1815*. Penguin Specials, London.

8. Heaver, S. (2018) 'How China and Hong Kong's currencies were shaped by Spanish, Mexican silver dollars'. *South China Morning Post* [online]. https://www.scmp.com/lifestyle/article/2132260/how-china-and-hong-kongs-currencies-were-shaped-spanish-mexican-silver

9. Xinwei, P. (1993) *A Monetary History of China, Volumes One and Two*. Center for East Asian Studies, Western Washington University, Bellingham, WA. https://cedar.wwu.edu/easpress/17/

10. Andrew, A. P. (1904)

11. Nussbaum, A. (1957) *A History of the Dollar*. Columbia University Press, New York, NY.

12. Andrew, A. P. (1904)

13. Tschoel, A. E. (2001) 'Maria Theresa's thaler: A case of international money'. *Eastern Economic Journal*, vol. 27, no. 3, pp.443–462. https://www.jstor.org/stable/40326061

14. Judson, P. (2016) *The Habsburg Empire: A New History*. Harvard University Press, London.

15. Semple, C. (2005) *A Silver Legend: The Story of the Maria Theresa Thaler*. Barzan Publishing Gloucester.

16. Harrigan, P. (2003) Tales of a thaler. Saudi Aramco World. https://archive.aramcoworld.com/issue/200301/tales.of.a.thaler.htm

17. Pond, S. (1941) 'The Maria Theresa thaler: A famous trade coin'. *Bulletin of the Business Historical Society*, vol. 15, no. 2, pp.26–31. https://www.jstor.org/stable/3110662

18. Rady, M. (2020)

19. Gotić, K. (2018) 'The thaler of Maria Theresa from 1780: Der Levantetaler'. *Povijesni prilozi*, vol. 37, no. 55, pp.333–343. https://hrcak.srce.hr/ojs/index.php/povijesni-prilozi/article/view/8364

20. Tschoel, A. E. (2001)

21. Judson, P. (2016)

22. Gilbert, E. and Helleiner, E. (eds) (1999) *Nation-states and Money: The Past, Present and Future of National Currencies*. Routledge, New York, NY, and London.

23. Helleiner, E. (2002) *The Making of National Money: Territorial Currencies in Historical Perspective*. Cornell University Press, Ithaca, NY, and London.

24. Selgin, G. (2008) *Good Money: Birmingham Button Makers, the Royal Mint, and the Beginnings of Modern Coinage, 1775—1821*. The Independent Institute, Oakland, CA.

25. Gordon, P. and Morales, J. J. (2017)

26. Tschoel, A. E. (2001)

27. Ibid.

28. Author's calculations

29. International Standards Organization (2021) ISO 4217. https://www.iso.org/iso-4217-currency-codes.html

30. United Nations (2021) Member States. https://www.un.org/en/about-us/member-states

31. Helleiner, E. (2002)

32. Anderson, B. (1983) *Imagined Communities*. Verso, London.

33. Cross, J. (2013) Coins of the Irish troubles. The Ipswich Numismatic Society. http://www.ipnumsoc.org.uk/articles/PST19-06-13Troubles.pdf

34. Hong, E. (2014) *The Birth of Korean Cool*. Simon & Schuster. Kindle edition.

35. Kihwan, K. (2006) The 1997–98 Korean financial crisis: Causes, policy response and lessons. International Monetary Fund. https://www.imf.org/external/np/seminars/eng/2006/cpem/pdf/kihwan.pdf

36. Roos, J. E. (2021) *Why Not Default? The Political Economy of Sovereign Debt*. Princeton University Press, Princeton, NJ. https://press.princeton.edu/books/paperback/9780691217437/why-not-default

37. International Monetary Fund (2012) *Balance of Payments and International Investment Position Manual*, 6. IMF. https://www.imf.org/external/pubs/ft/bop/2007/pdf/BPM6.pdf

38. Noland, M. (2005) 'South Korea's experience with international capital flows'. NBER working paper no. 11381. https://www.nber.org/system/files/working_papers/w11381

39. Kihwan, K. (2006)

40. Scholtes, S., Morajee, R. and Turner, D. (2007) 'Government bonds rise on safe haven buying'. *Financial Times* [online]. https://www.ft.com/content/83e50b20-d194-11db-b921-000b5df10621

41. Blustein, P. (2003) *The Chastening: Inside the Crisis that Rocked the Global Financial System and Humbled the IMF.* Public Affairs. Kindle edition.

42. Carson, M. and Clark, J. (2013) Asian financial crisis. Federal Reserve History blog. https://www.federalreservehistory.org/essays/asian-financial-crisis

43. Corsetti, G., Pesenti, P. and Roubini, N. (1998) What caused the Asian currency and financial crisis? Part II: The policy debate. NBER working paper no. 6834. https://www.nber.org/papers/w6834

44. Corsetti, G., Pesenti, P. and Roubini, N. (1998) What caused the Asian currency and financial crisis? Part I: A macroeconomic overview. NBER working paper no. 6833. https://www.nber.org/papers/w6833

45. Radelet, S. and Sachs, J. (2000) 'The onset of the East Asian financial crisis', NBER working paper no. 6680. https://www.nber.org/papers/w6680

46. Javorcik, B. S. (2004) 'Does foreign direct investment increase the productivity of domestic firms? In search of spillovers through backward linkages'. *American Economic Review*, vol. 94, no. 3, pp.605–627. https://www.jstor.org/stable/3592945

47. Blustein, P. (2003)

48. Eichengreen, B., Hausmann, R. and Panizza, U. (2002) 'Original sin: The pain, the mystery, and the road to redemption'. http://www.financialpolicy.org/financedev/hausmann2002.pdf

49. Hausmann, R. and Panizza, U. (2003) 'On the determinants of original sin: An empirical investigation'. *Journal of International Money and Finance*, vol. 22, no. 7, pp.957–990. https://www.sciencedirect.com/science/article/abs/pii/S0261560603000743

50. Eichengreen, B., Hausmann, R. and Panizza, U. (2003) Currency mismatches, debt intolerance and original sin: Why they are not the same and why it matters. NBER working paper no. 10036. https://www.nber.org/papers/w10036

51. Eichengreen, B. (2003) *Capital Flows and Crises.* The MIT Press, London.

52. Lee, H-K. (2019) *Cultural Policy in South Korea: Making a New Patron State.* Routledge, London.

53. Hong, E. (2014)

54. Ryoo, W. and Jin, D. Y. (2018) 'Cultural politics in the South Korean cultural industries: Confrontations between state-developmentalism and neoliberalism'. *International Journal of Cultural Policy*, vol. 26, no. 1, pp.31–14. https://www.tandfonline.com/doi/full/10.1080/10286632.2018.1429422

55. Hong, E. (2014)

56. Kwon, S-H. and Kim, J. (2014) 'The cultural industry policies of the Korean government and the Korean wave'. *International Journal of Cultural Policy*, vol. 20, no. 4, pp.422–439.

57. Yecies, B. (2015) *The Changing Face of Korean Cinema: Planet Hallyuwood*. Routledge, London.

58. Blustein, P. (2003)

59. Sharma, S. D. (2003) *The Asian Financial Crisis: Crisis, Reform and Recovery*. Manchester University Press, Manchester.

60. Chen, B. X. (2020) '"Parasite" and South Korea's income gap: Call it dirt spoon cinema'. *New York Times* [online]. https://www.nytimes.com/2019/10/18/movies/parasite-movie-south-korea.html

61. Khatri, Y., Lee, I., Liu, O., Meesook, K. and Tamirisa, N. (2001) Capital controls in response to the Asian financial crisis. https://www.elibrary.imf.org/view/IMF084/04463-9781589060470/04463-9781589060470/ch05.xml

62. Rebucci, A. and Ma, C. (2019) Capital controls: A survey of the new literature. NBER working paper no. 26558. https://www.nber.org/papers/w26558

63. Klein, M. W. (2012) Capital controls: Gates versus walls. NBER working paper no. 18526. https://www.nber.org/papers/w18526

64. Cecchetti, S. and Schoenholtz, K. (2018) 'Sudden stops: A primer on balance-of-payments crises'. *VoxEU*. https://voxeu.org/content/sudden-stops-primer-balance-payments-crises

65. Dornbusch, R., Golffan, I. and Valdés, R. O. (1995) 'Currency crises and collapses'. *Brookings Papers on Economic Activity*, no. 2. https://www.brookings.edu/wp-content/uploads/2016/07/1995b_bpea_dornbusch_goldfajn_valdes_edwards_bruno.pdf

66. Korinek, A. (2017) Regulating capital flows to emerging markets: An externality view. NBER working paper no. 24152. https://www.nber.org/papers/w24152

67. Eong, S. E. (1974) 'Ringgit'. *Journal of the Malaysian Branch of the Royal Asiatic Society*, vol. 47, no. 1, pp.58–65. https://www.jstor.org/stable/41511014?seq=1

68. Sharma, S. D. (2003) 'The Malaysian capital control regime of 1998: Implementation, effectiveness and lessons'. *Asian Perspective*, vol. 27, no. 1, pp.77–108. https://www.jstor.org/stable/42704398

69. Dornbusch, R. (2002) 'Malaysia's crisis: Was it different?', in *Preventing Currency Crises in Emerging Markets* (Edwards, S. and Frankel, J. A. eds). National Bureau of Economic Research. https://core.ac.uk/download/pdf/6483631.pdf

70. Kaplan, E. and Rodrik, D. (2002) 'Did the Malaysian capital controls work?', in *Preventing Currency Crises in Emerging Markets* (Edwards, S. and Frankel, J. A. eds). National Bureau of Economic Research. https://core.ac.uk/download/pdf/6778252.pdf

71. Dornbusch, R. (1998) 'Capital controls: An idea whose time is gone'. Massachusetts Institute of Technology. http://www.kleinteilige-loesungen.de/globalisierte_finanzmaerkte/texte_abc/d/dornbusch_capital_controls.pdf

72. Bhagwati, J. (1998) 'The capital myth: The difference between trade in widgets and trade in dollars'. *Foreign Affairs*, vol. 77, no. 3, pp.7–12. https://www.jstor.org/stable/20048871

73. International Monetary Fund (2012) The liberalisation and management of capital flows: An institutional view. https://www.imf.org/external/np/pp/eng/2012/111412.pdf

74. Rebucci, A. and Ma, C. (2019)

75. Radelet, S. and Sachs, J. (2000)

76. Korinek, A. (2017)

77. China, M. D. and Ito, H. (2005) What matters for financial development? Capital controls, institutions and interactions. NBER working paper no. 11370. https://www.nber.org/papers/w11370

78. Forbes, K. J. (2003) One cost of the Chilean capital controls: Increased financial constraints for smaller traded firms. NBER working paper no. 9777. https://www.nber.org/papers/w9777

79. Kaplan, E. and Rodrik, D. (2002)

80. Rodrik, D. (1998) Who needs capital account convertibility? https://drodrik.scholar.harvard.edu/files/dani-rodrik/files/who-needs-capital-account-convertibility.pdf

81. Herrera, H., Ordoñez, G. and Trebesch, C. (2014) Political booms, financial crisis. NBER working paper no. 20346. https://www.nber.org/papers/w20346

82. Prasad, E. S., Rogoff, K. S., Wei, S-J. and Kose, M. A. (2004) Financial globalisation, growth and volatility in developing countries. NBER working paper no. 10942. https://www.nber.org/papers/w10942

83. Damiana, J. (2018) 'Twenty years on, victims of 1998 Indonesia violence still seek justice'. Reuters [online]. https://www.reuters.com/article/us-indonesia-riots-anniversary-idUSKCN1IL04C

84. Rodrik, D. (2011) *The Globalisation Paradox: Why Global Markets, States and Democracy Can't Coexist*. Oxford University Press, Oxford.

85. Blakely, G. (2019) 'Why 70 per cent tax rates would require capital controls'. *New Statesman* [online]. https://www.newstatesman.com/politics/economy/2019/01/why-70-cent-tax-rates-would-require-capital-controls

86. Aizenman, J., China, M. and Ito, H. (2009) 'Assessing the emerging global financial architecture: Measuring the trilemma's configurations over time'. *VoxEU*. https://voxeu.org/article/empirical-evidence-monetary-policy-trilemma-1970

87. *The Economist* (2016) 'Two out of three ain't bad'. *The Economist* [online]. https://www.economist.com/schools-brief/2016/08/27/two-out-of-three-aint-bad

88. Klein, M. W. and Shambaugh, J. C. (2013) Rounding the corners of the policy trilemma: Sources of monetary policy autonomy. NBER working paper no. 19461. https://www.nber.org/papers/w19461

89. Monnet, E. (2018) 'Macroprudential tools, capital controls, and the trilemma: Insights from the Bretton Woods era'. *VoxEU*. https://voxeu.org/article/macroprudential-tools-capital-controls-and-trilemma

90. Eichengreen, B. (2008, ed. 2019) *Globalising Capital: A History of the International Monetary System*, 3rd ed. Princeton University Press, Princeton, NJ.

91. Bank of England (1967) 'The UK exchange control: A short history'. *Bank of England quarterly bulletin* Q3. https://www.bankofengland.co.uk/quarterly-bulletin/1967/q3/the-uk-exchange-control-a-short-history

92. Slobodian, Q. (2018) *Globalists: Neoliberalism and the End of Empire*. Harvard University Press, Cambridge, MA.

93. Tooze, A. (2007) *The Wages of Destruction*. Penguin, London.

94. Ibid.

95. Goodman, J. B. and Pauly, L. W. (1993) 'The obsolescence of capital controls? Economic management in an age of global markets'. *World Politics*, vol. 46, no. 1, pp.50–82. https://www.jstor.org/stable/2950666

96. Webb, M. C. (1995) *The Political Economy of Policy Coordination: International Adjustment since 1945*. Cornell University Press, Ithaca, NY, and London.

8. Can more money make us rich?

1. Norman, J. (2018) *Adam Smith: What He Thought and Why It Matters*. Penguin Books, London.

2. UN Statistics Division (2008) System of national accounts 2008. https://unstats.un.org/unsd/nationalaccount/sna2008.asp

3. Rasmussen, D. C. (2019) *The Infidel and the Professor: David Hume, Adam Smith and the Friendship that Shaped Modern Thought.* Princeton University Press, Princeton, NJ.

4. Viner, J. (1930) 'English theories of foreign trade before Adam Smith'. *Journal of Political Economy*, vol. 38, no. 3, pp.249–301. https://www.jstor.org/stable/1822244

5. Brezis, E. S. (2003) 'Mercantilism', in Mokyr, J. (ed.), *The Oxford Encyclopaedia of Economic History*. Oxford University Press, Oxford.

6. Mun, T. (1664) England's treasure by foreign trade. https://quod.lib.umich.edu/e/eebo/A51598.0001.001?view=toc

7. Du Rivage, J. (2017) *Revolution Against Empire: Taxes, Politics, and the Origins of American Independence*. Yale University Press, New Haven, CT, and London.

8. Taylor, A. (2016) *American Revolutions: A Continental History, 1750–1804*, New York, NY.

9. Smith, A. (1776) *An Inquiry into the Nature and Causes of the Wealth of Nations*. Oxford University Press, Oxford.

10. Spengler, J. J. (1959) 'Adam Smith's theory of economic growth – part 1'. *Southern Economic Journal*, vol. 25, no. 4, pp.397–415. https://www.jstor.org/stable/1055411

11. Spengler, J. J. (1959) 'Adam Smith's theory of economic growth – part 2'. *Southern Economic Journal*, vol. 26, no. 1, pp.1–12. https://www.jstor.org/stable/1055862

12. Smith, A. (1776)

13. Klausinger, H. (1990) 'The early use of the term "veil of money" in Schumpeter's monetary writings: A comment on Patinkin and Steiger'. *Scandinavian Journal of Economics*, vol. 92, no. 4, pp.617–621. https://www.jstor.org/stable/3440398

14. Lucas, R.E., Jr. (1996) 'Nobel lecture: Monetary neutrality'. *Journal of Political Economy*, vol. 104, no. 4, pp.661–82. https://www.jstor.org/stable/2138880

15. Handa, J. (2009) *Monetary Economics*, 2nd ed. Routledge, London and New York, NY.

16. Mankiw, G. (2018) *Macroeconomics*. Worth, New York, NY.

17. Lieberman, M. (1992) 'Banking in the former Soviet Union', in *The Road to Capitalism: Economic Transformation in Eastern Europe and the Former Soviet Union*, Kennet, D. and Lieberman, M. (eds). Dryden, London.

18. Gregor, P. R. (2003) *The Political Economy of Stalinism*. Cambridge University Press, Cambridge.

19. Garvy, G. (1977) Money, financial flows and credit in the Soviet Union. Ballinger Publishing Company, Cambridge, MA. https://www.nber.org/books-and-chapters/money-financial-flows-and-credit-soviet-union

20. Nove, A. (1992) *An Economic History of the USSR*. Penguin Books, London.

21. Gregory, P. and Harrison, M. (2005) 'Allocation under dictatorship: Research in Stalin's archives'. *Journal of Economic Literature*, vol. 43, no. 3, pp.721–761. https://www.jstor.org/stable/4129474

22. Ellman, M. (2018) 'Money, prices and payments in planned economies', in *Handbook of the History of Money and Currency*. https://link.springer.com/referenceworkentry/10.1007%2F978-981-10-0622-7_40-1

23. Shaffer, H. G. (1963) 'A new incentive for Soviet managers'. *The Russian Review*, vol. 22, no. 4, pp.410–416. https://www.jstor.org/stable/126674

24. Nove, A. (1992)

25. Caldwell, B. (2004) *Hayek's Challenge: An Intellectual Biography of F. A. Hayek*. Chicago University Press, Chicago.

26. Wapshott, N. (2012) *Keynes–Hayek: The Clash that Defined Modern Economics*, New York, NY.

27. Caldwell, B. (2004)

28. Wapshott, N. (2012)

29. Yueh, L. (2018) *The Great Economists*. Viking, New York, NY.

30. Hayek, F. A. (1974) The pretence of knowledge. Lecture to the memory of Alfred Nobel, December 11, 1974. https://www.nobelprize.org/prizes/economic-sciences/1974/hayek/lecture

31. Wapshott, N. (2012)

32. Patinkin, D. and Stieger, O. (1989) 'In search of the "veil of money" and the "neutrality of money": A note on the origin of terms'. *Scandinavian Journal of Economics*, vol. 91, no. 1, pp.131–146. https://www.jstor.org/stable/3440167

33. Caldwell, B. (2004)

34. Yueh, L. (2018)

35. Polanyi-Levitt, K. (2012) 'The power of ideas: Keynes, Hayek and Polanyi'. *International Journal of Political Economy*, vol. 41, no. 4. https://www.jstor.org/stable/23408607

36. Ebenstein, A. (2001) *Friedrich Hayek: A Biography*. St Martin's Press, New York, NY.

37. Ibid.

38. Hayek, F. A. (1944) *The Road to Serfdom*. Routledge, London.

39. Schuessler, J. (2010) 'Hayek: The back story'. *New York Times* [online]. https://www.nytimes.com/2010/07/11/books/review/Schuessler-t.html

40. Hayek, F. A. (1945) 'The use of knowledge in society'. *American Economic Review*, vol. 35, no. 4, pp.519–530. https://www.jstor.org/stable/1809376
41. Ibid.
42. Bowles, S., Kirman, A. and Sethi, R. (2017) 'Retrospectives: Friedrich Hayek and the market algorithm'. *Journal of Economic Perspectives*, vol. 31, no. 3, pp.215–30. https://www.aeaweb.org/articles?id=10.1257/jep.31.3.215
43. National Public Radio (2015) *Planet Money*. Episode 665: 'The pickle problem'. https://www.npr.org/sections/money/2015/11/25/457408717/episode-665-the-pickle-problem
44. Prendergast, C. (2017) 'How food banks use markets to feed the poor'. *Journal of Economic Perspectives*, vol. 31, no. 4, pp.145–62. https://www.aeaweb.org/articles?id=10.1257/jep.31.4.145
45. Prendergast, C. (2017) The allocation of food to food banks. https://www8.gsb.columbia.edu/faculty-research/sites/faculty-research/files/finance/Canice%20Prendergast%20-%20Fall%202016.pdf
46. Hayek, F. A. (1931) Prices and production and other works. Ludwig von Mises Institute, Auburn, AL. https://cdn.mises.org/prices_and_production_and_other_works.pdf
47. Cohen, A. J. (2003) 'The Hayek/Knight capital controversy: the irrelevance of roundaboutness, or purging process in time?' *History of Political Economy*, vol. 35, no. 3, pp.469–490. https://read.dukeupress.edu/hope/article-abstract/35/3/469/12131/The-Hayek-Knight-Capital-Controversy-The
48. Hayek, F. A. (1931)
49. Friedman, M. (1964) 'Monetary studies of the National Bureau', in *The Optimum Quantity of Money and Other Essays*. Routledge, London.
50. Friedman, M. (1993) 'The "plucking model" of business fluctuations revisited'. *Economic Inquiry*, vol. 31, no. 2, pp.171–177. https://onlinelibrary.wiley.com/doi/abs/10.1111/j.1465-7295.1993.tb00874.x
51. Kim, C-J. and Nelson, C. R. (1999) 'Friedman's plucking model of business fluctuations: Tests and estimates of permanent and transitory components'. *Journal of Money, Credit and Banking*, vol. 31, no. 3, part 1, pp.317–334. https://www.jstor.org/stable/2601114
52. DeLong, J. B. (1990) 'Liquidation' cycles: Old-fashioned real business cycle theory and the Great Depression. NBER working paper no. 3546. https://www.nber.org/system/files/working_papers/w3546/w3546.pdf
53. White, L. H. (2008) 'Did Hayek and Robbins deepen the Great Depression?' *Journal of Money, Credit and Banking*, vol. 40, no. 4, pp.751–768.
54. Bernanke, B. S. (2004) 'Money, gold and the Great Depression'. Parker Willis Lecture in Economic Policy, Washington and Lee University, Lexington, VA, 2 March. https://www.bis.org/review/r040305e.pdf

55. DeLong, J. B. (1990)

56. De Long, J. B. (1998) 'Fiscal policy in the shadow of the Great Depression', in Bordo, M. D., Goldin, C. and White, N. E. (eds), *The Defining Moment: The Great Depression and the American Economy in the Twentieth Century*. University of Chicago Press, Chicago. https://www.nber.org/system/files/chapters/c6888/c6888.pdf

57. Friedman, M. and Schwartz, A. J. (1971) *A Monetary History of the United States*. Princeton University Press, Princeton, NJ.

58. Ibid.

59. Garrison, R. W. (2007) Hayek and Friedman: Head to head. http://webhome.auburn.edu/~garriro/hayek%20and%20friedman.pdf

60. Friedman, M. (1986) 'Keynes' political legacy', in *Keynes's General Theory: Fifty Years On*, pp.45–55. Institute of Economic Affairs, London.

61. Bernanke, B. S. (2002) On Milton Friedman's ninetieth birthday. Remarks by Governor Ben S. Bernanke at the conference to honour Milton Friedman, University of Chicago, November 8. https://www.federalreserve.gov/boarddocs/speeches/2002/20021108/

62. Tooze, A. (2018) *Crashed: How a Decade of Financial Crises Changed the World*. Penguin Random House, London.

63. Krugman, P. (2009) 'How did economists get it so wrong?' *New York Times* [online]. https://www.nytimes.com/2009/09/06/magazine/06Economic-t.html

64. Belsey, T. and Hennessy, P. (2009) Letter to the Queen, 22 July. https://www.ma.imperial.ac.uk/~bin06/M3A22/queen-lse.pdf

65. Stiglitz, J. E. (2018) 'Where modern macroeconomics went wrong'. *Oxford Review of Economic Policy*, vol. 34, issue 102, pp.70–106. https://academic.oup.com/oxrep/article/34/1-2/70/4781816

66. Bernanke, B. S. (2009) The crisis and the policy response. Stamp lecture, London School of Economics, London, January 13. https://www.federalreserve.gov/newsevents/speech/bernanke20090113a.htm

67. Tooze, A. (2018)

68. Akerlof, G. A. and Yellen, J. L. (1985) 'Can small deviations from rationality make significant differences to economic equilibria?' *American Economic Review*, vol. 75, no. 4, pp.708–720. https://www.jstor.org/stable/1821349

69. Blinder, A. S. (1991) Why are prices sticky? Preliminary results from an interview study. NBER working paper no. 3646. https://www.nber.org/system/files/working_papers/w3646/w3646.pdf

70. Blanchard, O. J. and Summers, L. H. (1986) Hysteresis in unemployment. NBER working paper no. 2035. https://www.nber.org/papers/w2035

71. Pissarides, C. (1992) 'Loss of skill during unemployment and the persistence of employment shocks'. *Quarterly Journal of Economics*, vol. 107, no. 4, pp.1371–1391. https://www.jstor.org/stable/2118392

72. Crafts, N. (2018) *Forging Ahead, Falling Behind and Fighting Back*. Cambridge University Press, Cambridge.

73. Broadberry, S.and Wallis, J. J. (2017) Growing, shrinking and long run economic performance: historical perspectives on economic development. NBER working paper no. 23343. https://www.nber.org/papers/w23343

74. H. C. (2018) 'The economist explains: Running the economy hot'. *The Economist* [online]. https://www.economist.com/the-economist-explains/2018/02/23/running-the-economy-hot

75. Hilsenrath, J. and Harrison, D. (2016) 'Yellen cites benefits to running economy hot for some time'. *Wall Street Journal* [online] https://www.wsj.com/articles/yellen-cites-benefits-to-running-economy-hot-for-some-time-1476466215

76. Allen, R. C. (2015) 'The high wage economy and the industrial revolution: a restatement'. *Economic History Review*, vol. 68, no. 1, pp. 1-22. https://www.jstor.org/stable/43910008

77. Hotchkiss, J. L. and Moore, R. E. (2018) Some like it hot: Assessing longer-term labor market benefits from a high-pressure economy. Atlanta Fed working paper no. 2018-1c. https://www.atlantafed.org/research/publications/wp/2018/01c-assessing-longer-term-labor-market-benefits-from-a-high-pressure-economy-2020-12-03.aspx

78. Garcia, C. (2016) 'Janet Yellen to macroeconomists: That whole (aggregate) supply-demand thing might need a rethink'. FT Alphaville. https://www.ft.com/content/972dfdae-55a9-35eb-979c-8e5f22d7ae77

79. Blanchard, O. (2018) 'Should we reject the natural rate hypothesis?' *Journal of Economic Perspectives*, vol. 32, no. 1, pp.97–120. https://www.aeaweb.org/articles?id=10.1257/jep.32.1.97

80. Joe Biden (2021) Remarks by president Biden on the economy, Cuyahoga Community College, Cleveland, OH. The White House. https://www.whitehouse.gov/briefing-room/speeches-remarks/2021/05/27/remarks-by-president-biden-on-the-economy-2/

9. How do we save money?

1. Taub, A. (2019) '"Chile woke up": Dictatorship's legacy of inequality triggers mass protests'. *New York Times* [online]. https://www.nytimes.com/2019/11/03/world/americas/chile-protests.html

2.   *The Economist* (2020) 'Can Chile reinvent itself?' *The Economist* [online]. https://www.economist.com/the-americas/2020/03/12/can-chile-reinvent-itself

3.   Spooner, M. H. (2011) *The General's Slow Retreat: Chile After Pinochet.* University of California Press, London.

4.   Pribble, J. (2019) 'Chile's crisis was decades in the making'. *Financial Times* [online].   https://www.ft.com/content/81801886-f650-11e9-bbe1-4db3476c5ff0

5.   Mander, B. (2019) 'The death of Chile's pension promise'. *Financial Times* [online].   https://www.ft.com/content/4f8107f8-0fd4-11ea-a7e6-62bf4f9e548a

6.   Mander, B. (2016) 'Chile pension reform comes under world spotlight'. *Financial Times* [online]. https://www.ft.com/content/b9293586-7680-11e6-bf48-b372cdb1043a

7.   Ruiz-Tagle, J. V. and Castro, F. (1998) The Chilean pension system. OECD working paper AWP 5.6. http://www.oecd.org/pensions/public-pensions/2429310.pdf

8.   Valdes, J. G. (2008) *Pinochet's Economists: The Chicago School of Economics in Chile.* Cambridge University Press, Cambridge.

9.   Piñera, J. (2007) 'Milton Friedman and world freedom, a personal note. The Legacy of Milton Friedman', Manhattan Institute and *Wall Street Journal* Conference, January 29, 2007, University Club, New York, NY.

10. Huneeus, C. (2007) *The Pinochet Regime.* Lynne Rienner, London.

11. Valdes, J. G. (2008)

12. Piñera, J. (1995) 'Empowering workers: The privatisation of social security in Chile'. *Cato Journal*, vol. 15, no. 2. https://www.cato.org/sites/cato.org/files/serials/files/cato-journal/1995/11/cj15n2-3-1.pdf

13. Eatwell, J. (1999). 'The anatomy of the pensions "crisis"'. *Economic Survey of Europe*, no. 3. Economic Commission for Europe, United Nations, Geneva. http://mbz.net.pl/eftepe/Eatwell.pdf

14. *New York Times* (1988) 'Jamaican emigres bring thrift clubs to New York'. *New York Times*. https://www.nytimes.com/1988/06/19/nyregion/jamaican-emigres-bring-thrift-clubs-to-new-york.html

15. Bouman, F. J. A. (1995) 'ROSCA: On the origin of the species'. *Savings and Development*, vol. 19, no. 2, pp. 117–148. https://www.jstor.org/stable/25830410

16. Aizenman, A. (2017) How to buy a goat when you're really poor? Join a 'merry go round'. National Public Radio. https://www.npr.org/sections/goatsandsoda/2017/08/19/542436391/how-to-buy-a-goat-when-you-re-ultra-poor-join-a-merry-go-round

17. Rutherford, S. (2009) *The Poor and Their Money: Microfinance from a Twenty-first Century Consumer's Perspective.* Oxford University Press, New Delhi.

18. Collins, D., Morduch, J., Rutherford, S. and Ruthven, O. (2010) *Portfolios of the Poor: How the World's Poor Live on $2 a Day*. Princeton University Press, Princeton, NJ.

19. Ibid.

20. Kay, J. (2009) *The Long and Short of it: A Guide to Finance and Investment for Normally Intelligent People Who Aren't in the Industry*. Profile Books, London.

21. Gigerenzer, G., Swijtink, Z. G., Porter, T. M., Daston, L., Beatty, J. and Krüger, L. (1989). 'Ideas in context', in *The Empire of Chance: How Probability Changed Science and Everyday Life*. Cambridge University Press, Cambridge.

22. Spang, R. (2015) *Stuff and Money in the Time of the French Revolution*. Harvard University Press, Cambridge, MA.

23. Le Roy, S. F. and Singell, L. D. Jr. (1987) 'Knight on risk and uncertainty'. *Journal of Political Economy*, vol. 95, no. 2, pp.394–406 https://www.jstor.org/stable/1832078

24. Hacking, I. (2013) *The Emergence of Probability: A Philosophical Study of Early Ideas about Probability, Induction and Statistical Inference*. Cambridge University Press, Cambridge.

25. Ibid.

26. Velde, F. R. and Weir, D. R. (1992) 'The financial market and government debt policy in France, 1746–1793'. *Journal of Economic History*, vol. 52, no. 1, pp.1–39. https://www.jstor.org/stable/2123343

27. Spang, R. (2015)

28. Taylor, G. V. (1962) 'The Paris bourse on the eve of the French Revolution'. *American Historical Review*, vol. 67, no. 4, pp.951–957. https://www.jstor.org/stable/1845247

29. Velde, F. R. and Weir, D. R. (1992)

30. Kurlansky, M. (2002) *Salt: A World History*. Vintage, London.

31. Weir, D. R. (1989) 'Tontines, public finance and revolution in France and England, 1688–1789'. *Journal of Economic History*, vol. 49, no. 1, pp.95–124. https://www.jstor.org/stable/2121419

32. Sargent, T. J. and Velde, F. R. (1995) 'Macroeconomic features of the French Revolution'. *Journal of Political Economy*, vol. 103. no. 3, pp.474–518. https://www.jstor.org/stable/2138696

33. White, E. N. (1995) 'The French Revolution and the politics of government finance, 1770–1815'. *Journal of Economic History*, vol. 55, no. 2, pp.227–255. https://www.jstor.org/stable/2123552

34. Spang, R. (2015)

35. Ibid.

36. Goetzmann, W. N. (2016). *Money Changes Everything: How Finance Made Civilization Possible*. Princeton University Press, Princeton, NJ.

37. Poterba, J. M. (2004) 'Annuities in early modern Europe', in Goetzmann, W. N. and Rouwenhorst, K. G. (eds), *The Origins of Value: The Financial Innovations That Created Modern Capital Markets*. Oxford University Press, Oxford.

38. Spang, R. (2015)

39. Wigglesworth, R. (2018) 'Quant hedge funds set to surpass $1tn management mark'. *Financial Times* [online]. https://www.ft.com/content/ff7528bc-ec16-11e7-8713-513b1d7ca85a

40. Bossenga, G. (2010) 'The financial origins of the French Revolution', in Kaiser, T. E. and Van Kley, D. K. (eds), *From Deficit to Deluge: The Origins of the French Revolution*. Stanford University Press, Stanford, CA.

41. White, E. N. (1989) 'Was there a solution to the Ancien Régime's financial dilemma?' *Journal of Economic History*, vol. 49, no. 3, pp.545–568. https://www.jstor.org/stable/2122504

42. Ibid.

43. Ferguson, N. (2001) *The Cash Nexus*. Penguin Books, London.

44. Andritzky, J. R. (2012) Government bonds and their investors: What are the facts and do they matter? IMF working paper no. 12158. https://www.imf.org/external/pubs/ft/wp/2012/wp12158.pdf

45. Hohman, E. P. (1926) 'Wages, risk, and profits in the whaling industry'. *Quarterly Journal of Economics*, vol. 40, no. 4, pp.644–671. https://www.jstor.org/stable/1884458

46. Davis, L. E., Gallman, R. E. and Glitter, K. (1997) *In Pursuit of Leviathan: Technology, Institutions, Productivity and Profits in American Whaling, 1816–1906*. Chicago University Press, Chicago, IL.

47. Melville, H. (1851) *Moby-Dick*. Penguin, London.

48. *The Economist* (2016a) 'Fin-tech'. *The Economist* [online]. https://www.economist.com/finance-and-economics/2015/12/30/fin-tech

49. Superintendencia de administradoras de pensiones (2003) *The Chilean Pension System* (4th ed.). https://www.spensiones.cl/portal/institucional/594/w3-article-3523.html

50. Markowitz, H. (1952) 'Portfolio selection'. *Journal of Finance*, vol. 7, no. 1, pp.77–91. https://onlinelibrary.wiley.com/doi/abs/10.1111/j.1540-6261.1952.tb01525.x

51. Fabozzi, F. J., Modigliani F. P. and Jones, F. J. (2014) *Foundations of Financial Markets and Institutions*, 4th ed. Pearson, Harlow.

52. Delbecque, B. (2012) 'Key functions of asset management'. *VoxEU*. https://voxeu.org/article/key-functions-asset-management

53. *The Economist* (2016b) 'The perils of not saving'. *The Economist* [online]. https://www.economist.com/the-americas/2016/08/27/the-perils-of-not-saving

54. Schwed, F. (1960) *Where are the customers' yachts? Or a good hard look at Wall Street*. J. Magee, Spingfield, MA.

55. Rovnick, N. and Williams, A. (2016) 'How much do you really pay your money manager?' *Financial Times* [online]. https://www.ft.com/content/56243606-6614-11e6-a08a-c7ac04ef00aa

56. Money and Banking blog (2017) Moral hazard: A primer. https://www.moneyandbanking.com/commentary/2017/9/24/moral-hazard-a-primer

57. Bray, M. (1985) 'Rational expectations, information and asset markets: An introduction'. *Oxford Economics Papers*, new series, vol. 37, no. 2, pp.161–195. https://www.jstor.org/stable/2663195

58. Samuelson, P. A. (1973) 'Proof that properly discounted present values of assets vibrate randomly'. *Bell Journal of Economics and Management Science*, vol. 4, no. 2, pp.369–374. https://www.jstor.org/stable/3003046

59. Fama, E. F. (1970) 'Efficient capital markets: A review of theory and empirical work'. *Journal of Finance*, vol. 25, no. 2. https://www.jstor.org/stable/2325486

60. Fama, E. F. (1965) 'The behavior of stock-market prices'. *Journal of Business*, vol. 38, no. 1, pp. 34–105. https://www.jstor.org/stable/2350752

61. Fama, E. F. (1990) 'Stock returns, expected returns, and real activity'. *Journal of Finance*, vol. 45, no. 4, pp.1089–1108. https://www.jstor.org/stable/2328716

62. Malkiel, B. G. (1973, 4th ed. 1985) *A Random Walk Down Wall Street*. W. W. Norton, New York, NY.

63. Ibid.

64. Pastor, L. and Vorsatz, M. B. (2021) Mutual fund performance and flows during the COVID-19 crisis. NBER working paper no. 27551. https://www.nber.org/papers/w27551

65. Chevalier, J. and Ellison, G. (1996) Are some mutual funds managers better than others? Cross-sectional patterns in behavior and performance. NBER working paper no. 5852. https://www.nber.org/papers/w5852

66. Grossman, S. J. and Stiglitz, J. E. (1980) 'On the impossibility of informationally efficient markets'. *American Economic Review*, vol. 70, no. 3, pp.393–408. https://www.jstor.org/stable/1805228

67. Pedersen, L. (2015) *Efficiently Inefficient*. Princeton University Press, Princeton, NJ.

68. Kinder, T. (2017) 'The death of the "hedge fund"?' *Financial News* [online]. https://www.fnlondon.com/articles/the-death-of-the-hedge-fund-20170614

69. Mallaby, S. (2010) *More Money than God: Hedge Funds and the Making of a New Elite*. Bloomsbury, London.

70. Ibid.

71. Pedersen, L. (2015)

72. Ibid.

73. Fletcher, L. (2020) 'Why some big investors have had enough of hedge funds'. *Financial Times* [online]. https://www.ft.com/content/71b5478c-3d40-11ea-b232-000f4477fbca

74. Authers, J. and Childs, M. (2016) 'Hedge funds: Overpriced, underperforming'. *Financial Times* [online]. https://www.ft.com/content/9bd1150e-1b76-11e6-b286-cddde55ca122

75. Flood, C. (2019) 'Hedge fund fee model morphs from "two and 20" to "one or 30"'. *Financial Times* [online]. https://www.ft.com/content/7e4e2cdc-8c2a-34d4-a7e2-60c9db9e2a2d

76. Wigglesworth, R. (2019) 'Diminishing returns: Hedge funds look to keep it in the family'. *Financial Times* [online]. https://www.ft.com/content/47ba9fdc-201c-11e9-b126-46fc3ad87c65

77. Wigglesworth, R. (2021) *Trillions: How a Band of Wall Street Renegades Invented the Index Fund and Changed Finance Forever*. Penguin, London.

78. Wigglesworth, R. (2021) 'Global passive assets hit $15tn as ETF boom heats up'. *Financial Times* [online]. https://www.ft.com/content/7d5c2468-619c-4c4b-b3e7-b0da015e939d

79. Cassidy, J. (2010) 'Interview with Eugene Fama'. *New Yorker* [online]. https://www.newyorker.com/news/john-cassidy/interview-with-eugene-fama

80. Martin, A. and Ventura, J. (2011) 'Origins and macroeconomic implications of asset bubbles'. *VoxEU*. https://voxeu.org/article/asset-bubbles-origins-and-implications

81. Greenwood, R., Shleifer, A. and You, Y. (2017) *Bubbles for Fama*. Harvard University. https://scholar.harvard.edu/files/shleifer/files/bffs_20170217.pdf

82. Kindleberger, C. (2001) *Manias, Panics and Crashes: A History of Financial Crises*. Basic Books, New York, NY.

83. Bisonette, Z. (2015) *The Great Beanie Baby Bubble*. Penguin, London.

84. Jarvis, C. (2000) 'The rise and fall of Albania's pyramid schemes'. *Finance and Development*, vol. 37, no. 1. https://www.imf.org/external/pubs/ft/fandd/2000/03/jarvis.htm

85. Fama, E. F. (2013) Two pillars of asset pricing. Prize lecture, December 8, 2013. https://www.nobelprize.org/uploads/2018/06/fama-lecture.pdf

86. Giugliano, F. and Aglionby, J. (2013) 'Fama, Hansen and Shiller win Nobel Prize for Economics'. *Financial Times* [online]. https://www.ft.com/content/6f949e8c-34c1-11e3-8148-00144feab7de

87. Shleifer, A. (2000) *Inefficient Markets: An Introduction to Behavioural Finance*. Oxford University Press, Oxford.

88. Shiller, R. J. (1981) 'Do stock prices move too much to be justified by subsequent changes in dividends?' *American Economic Review*, vol. 71, no. 3, pp.421–436. https://www.jstor.org/stable/1802789

89. Shiller, R. J. (2003) 'From efficient markets theory to behavioural finance'. *Journal of Economic Perspectives*, vol. 17, no. 1, pp.83–104. http://www.econ.yale.edu/~shiller/pubs/p1055.pdf

90. Fox, J. (2009) *The Myth of the Rational Market*. Harriman House, Petersfield.

91. Shleifer, A. (2000)

92. Wigglesworth, R. (2021) 'Investors brace for "major shift" as momentum and value collide'. *Financial Times* [online]. https://www.ft.com/content/979714e5-f93b-4a4c-a445-8b2e8ccef80c

93. Pedersen, L. (2015)

94. Malkiel, B. G. (2003) 'The efficient market hypothesis and its critics'. *Journal of Economic Perspectives*, vol. 17, no. 1, pp.59–82. https://eml.berkeley.edu/~craine/EconH195/Fall_16/webpage/Malkiel_Efficient%20Mkts.pdf

95. Fama, E. F. (2013)

96. Malkiel, B. G. (2003)

97. *The Economist* (2016b)

98. Caputo, R. and Saravia, D. (2019) The monetary and fiscal history of Chile, 1960–2016. University of Chicago, Becker Friedman Institute for Economics Working Paper no. 2018-62. https://bfi.uchicago.edu/wp-content/uploads/The-Case-of-Chile.pdf

99. Huneeus, C. (2007)

100. Velasco, A. and Parrado, E. (2012) 'The political economy of fiscal policy: The experience of Chile', in *The Oxford Handbook of Latin American Political Economy*, Santiso, J. and Dayton-Johnson, J. (eds). Oxford University Press, Oxford.

101. *The Economist* (2019) 'Riots after a fare increase damage Chile's image of stability'. *The Economist* [online]. https://www.economist.com/the-americas/2019/10/20/riots-after-a-fare-increase-damage-chiles-image-of-stability

102. Winn, P. (ed.) (2004) *Victims of the Chilean Miracle: Workers and Neoliberalism in the Pinochet Era, 1973–2002*. Duke University Press, London.

103. Modigliani, F., and Brumberg, R. H. (1954) 'Utility analysis and the consumption function: An interpretation of cross-section data', in Kenneth K. Kurihara (ed.), *Post-Keynesian Economics*. Rutgers University Press, New Brunswick, NJ.

104. Deaton, A. (2005) Franco Modigliani and the life cycle theory of consumption. https://papers.ssrn.com/sol3/papers.cfm?abstract_id=686475

105. Barr, N. (2001) *The Welfare State as Piggy Bank: Information, Risk, Uncertainty and the Role of the State*. Oxford University Press, Oxford.

106. Rutherford, S. (2009)

107. Barr, N. (2020) *The Economics of the Welfare State*. Oxford University Press, Oxford.

108. Esping-Andersen, G. (1990) *The Three Worlds of Welfare Capitalism*. Polity, Cambridge.

109. Samuelson, P. A. (1958) 'An exact consumption-loan model of interest with or without the social contrivance of money'. *Journal of Political Economy*, vol. 66, no. 6, pp.467–482. https://www.jstor.org/stable/1826989

110. Barr, N. (2001)

111. OECD (2021) All-in average personal income tax rates at average wage by family type. https://stats.oecd.org/index.aspx?DataSetCode=TABLE_I6

112. Barr, N. and Diamond, P. (2006) 'The economics of pensions'. *Oxford Review of Economic Policy*, vol. 22, no. 1, pp.15–39. http://eprints.lse.ac.uk/2630/1/economics_of_pensions_final.pdf

113. Arrow, J. K. (1963) 'Uncertainty and the welfare economics of medical care'. *American Economic Review*, vol. 53, no. 5, pp.941–973. https://web.stanford.edu/~jay/health_class/Readings/Lecture01/arrow.pdf

114. Barr, N. and Diamond, P. (2016) 'Reforming pensions in Chile'. *Polityka Społeczna*, no. 1, 2016, pp.4–9. https://economics.mit.edu/files/12427

115. Crawford, R. and O'Brien, L. (2021) Understanding the gender pension gap. IFS Observation. https://www.ifs.org.uk/publications/15426

116. Mander, B. and Stott, M. (2020) 'Chile's famed pensions system faces an existential crisis'. *Financial Times* [online]. https://www.ft.com/content/3c25b7e0-b31f-4d5b-9845-3514af2970a3

117. Thomson, E. (2021) 'Chicago Boys' free market pension model is unraveling in Chile'. Bloomberg [online]. https://www.bloomberg.com/news/articles/2021-05-10/chicago-boys-free-market-pension-model-is-unraveling-in-chile

118. Mander, B. and Stott, M. (2021) 'Chile votes for radicals and independents to write new constitution'. *Financial Times* [online]. https://www.ft.com/content/263a45a7-a4bd-48d8-80cc-41c5b3ab4f44

10. What is the future of money?

1. Kazmin, A., Stacey, K. and Mundy, S. (2016) 'India scraps high-value banknotes in black economic clampdown'. *Financial Times* [online]. https://www.ft.com/content/97d44cee-a5d4-11e6-8b69-02899e8bd9d1

2.   Modi, N. (2016) Address to the nation by Prime Minister Narendra Modi, November 8, 2016.

3.   Kazmin, A. (2016) 'India: Narendra Modi's bonfire of the rupees'. *Financial Times* [online]. https://www.ft.com/content/0467b734-ac23-11e6-ba7d-76378e4fef24

4.   Banerjee, A. and Kala, N. (2019) 'The economic and political consequences of India's demonetisation'. *VoxDev*. https://voxdev.org/topic/institutions-political-economy/
economic-and-political-consequences-india-s-demonetisation

5.   Mundy, S., Kazmin, A. and Stacey, K. (2017) 'India demonetisation fails to purge black money'. *Financial Times* [online]. https://www.ft.com/content/7dbe0e14-8d8a-11e7-a352-e46f43c5825d

6.   Chodorow-Reich, G., Gopinath, G., Mishra, P. and Narayanan, A. (2018) Cash and the economy: Evidence from India's demonetisation. NBER working paper no. 25370. https://www.nber.org/papers/w25370

7.   BBC (2016) 'India rupees: Chaos at banks after "black money" ban'. BBC [online]. https://www.bbc.co.uk/news/world-asia-india-37933233

8.   Zhu, H., Gupta, A., Majumder, D. and Steinbach, S. (2017) Macro shocks and micro woes: Short-term effects of India's demonetisation on the poor. https://papers.ssrn.com/sol3/papers.cfm?abstract_id=3001396

9.   Parajuli, A. (2017) 'Has Narendra Modi's demonetisation gambit failed in India?' *Financial Times* [online]. https://www.ft.com/content/bf7cf078-8e47-11e7-a352-e46f43c5825d

10. *The Economist* (2019) 'Indians are switching to digital payments in droves'. *The Economist* [online]. https://www.economist.com/finance-and-economics/2019/06/08/indians-are-switching-to-digital-payments-in-droves

11. Stacey, K. (2016) 'India fintech groups look to cash in on banknote crunch'. *Financial Times* [online]. https://www.ft.com/content/3f31dc34-ab04-11e6-9cb3-bb8207902122

12. Tandon, S. (2016) 'In numbers: The advertising blitz that followed Modi's demonetisation decision'. *Quartz India* [online]. https://qz.com/india/866548/paytm-freecharge-co-the-advertising-blitz-that-followed-modis-shock-demon
etisation-decision

13. *The Economist* (2020) 'In bleak times for banks, India's digital payments system wins praise'. *The Economist* [online]. https://www.economist.com/finance-and-economics/2020/05/09/in-bleak-times-for-banks-indias-digital-payments-system-wins-praise

14. Guex, S. (2000) 'The origins of the Swiss banking secrecy law and its repercussions for Swiss federal policy'. *Business History Review*, vol. 74, no. 2, pp.237–266. https://www.jstor.org/stable/3116693

15. Varun, H. K. (2018) 'SC's Aadhaar verdict: Privacy vs identity'. *Deccan Herald* [online]. https://www.deccanherald.com/national/aadhaar-act-verdict-history-693614.html

16. Kocherlakota, N. R. (1998) 'Money is memory'. *Journal of Economic Theory*, 81, pp.232–251. http://citeseerx.ist.psu.edu/viewdoc/download?doi=10.1.1.361.3216&rep=rep1&type=pdf

17. Graeber, D. (2011). *Debt: The First 5,000 Years*. Melville House, Brooklyn, NY.

18. Jones, C. (2020) 'Is our money about to spout memories?' *FT Alphaville*. https://ftalphaville.ft.com/2020/06/24/1592991663000/Is-our-money-about-to-spout-memories

19. Cole, S. (2019) 'PayPal pulls out of Pornhub, hurting "hundreds of thousands" of performers'. *Vice* [online]. https://www.vice.com/en/article/d3abgv/paypal-pulls-out-of-pornhub-payments

20. Press Association (2018) 'PayPal bans Tommy Robinson from using service'. *Guardian* [online]. https://www.theguardian.com/uk-news/2018/nov/08/paypal-bans-tommy-robinson-from-using-service

21. Barr, A. (2012) 'Exclusive: PayPal backtracks on "obscene" e-book policy'. Reuters [online]. https://www.reuters.com/article/us-paypal-idUSBRE82C11C20120313

22. Addly, E. and Deans, J. (2011) 'WikiLeaks suspends publishing to fight financial blockade'. *Guardian* [online]. https://www.theguardian.com/media/2011/oct/24/wikileaks-suspends-publishing

23. Parkin, B. and Findlay, S. (2020) 'India: Is Modi's BJP introducing Big Brother?' *Financial Times* [online]. https://www.ft.com/content/c626fd96-4db3-11ea-95a0-43d18ec715f5

24. Stacey, K. (2018) 'India accused of creating identity card "Big Brother"'. *Financial Times* [online]. https://www.ft.com/content/53a2c11a-0b2f-11e8-8eb7-42f857ea9f09

25. Popper, N. (2016) *Digital Gold: The Untold Story of Bitcoin*. Penguin Books, London.

26. Dale, B. (2021) 'Crypto is the libertarian cheat code in the final battle over state coercion'. *Coindesk*. https://www.coindesk.com/crypto-is-the-libertarian-cheat-code-in-the-final-battle-over-state-coercion

27. Nakamoto, S. (2008) Bitcoin: A peer-to-peer electronic cash system. https://bitcoin.org/en/bitcoin-paper

28. Vigna, P. and Casey, M. J. (2016) *Cryptocurrency: The Future of Money?* Vintage, London.

29. Tapscott, D. and Tapscott, A. (2016) *Blockchain Revolution: How the Technology Behind Bitcoin and Other Cryptocurrencies is Changing the World*. Penguin Books, London.

30. Ammous, A. (2018) *The Bitcoin Standard: The Decentralized Alternative to Central Banking*. John Wiley & Sons, Hoboken, NJ.

31. Tapscott, D. and Tapscott, A. (2016)

32. Adriano, A. and Monroe, H. (2016) 'The internet of trust'. *Finance and Development*, vol. 53, no. 2. https://www.imf.org/external/pubs/ft/fandd/2016/06/adriano.htm

33. Nakamoto, S. (2008)

34. Sanderson, H. (2015) 'Digital currencies: A gold standard for bitcoin'. *Financial Times* [online]. https://www.ft.com/content/38d02382-f809-11e4-962b-00144feab7de

35. Eich, S. (2019) 'Old utopias, new tax havens: The politics of bitcoin in historical perspective', in *Regulating Blockchain: Techno-Social and Legal Challenges*, ed. P. Hacker, I. Lianos, G. Dimitropoulos, and S. Eich. Oxford University Press, Oxford.

36. Popper, N. (2016)

37. Ammous, A. (2018)

38. Tebble, A. (2021) Friedrich Hayek: Prophet of cryptocurrency? King's College London Centre for the Study of Governance and Society. https://csgs.kcl.ac.uk/friedrich-hayek-prophet-of-cryptocurrency

39. Hayek, F. A. (1974) *The Denationalisation of Money*. The Institute of Economic Affairs, London.

40. Popper, N. (2016)

41. Nakamoto, S. (2008)

42. Popper, N. (2016)

43. Eichengreen, B. (2019) From commodity to fiat and now to crypto: What does history tell us? NBER working paper no. 25426. https://www.nber.org/system/files/working_papers/w25426/w25426.pdf

44. Greeley, B. (2021) 'How can bitcoin become money if it is too valuable to spend?' *Financial Times* [online]. https://www.ft.com/content/b4023a49-2819-4a01-94f6-2a8f6dc77c18

45. Blockchain (2021) Cost per transaction. Blockchain.com. https://www.blockchain.com/charts/cost-per-transaction

46. Nakamoto, S. (2008)

47. Criddle, C. (2021) 'Bitcoin consumes "more electricity than Argentina"'. BBC [online]. https://www.bbc.co.uk/news/technology-56012952

48. Popper, N. (2016)

49. Odd Lots (2017) A human rights activist explains why bitcoin is so important to his work. https://podcasts.apple.com/us/podcast/human-rights-activist-explains-why-bitcoin-is-so-important/id1056200096?i=1000460530878

50. Cuen, L. (2019) 'Global protests reveal bitcoin's limitations'. Coindesk. https://www.coindesk.com/global-protests-reveal-bitcoins-limitations

51. BBC (2020) 'Cryptocurrencies: Why Nigeria is a global leader in bitcoin trade'. BBC [online]. https://www.bbc.co.uk/news/world-africa-56169917

52. Munshi, N. (2021) 'Nigerian crypto investors defy crackdown to ride bitcoin frenzy'. *Financial Times* [online]. https://www.ft.com/content/c139596c-92b7-45bd-88b9-175d7881604f

53. Kazeem, Y. (2020) 'How bitcoin powered the largest Nigerian protests in a generation'. *Quartz Africa* [online]. https://qz.com/africa/1922466/how-bitcoin-powered-nigerias-endsars-protests

54. Cuen, L. (2019)

55. Cornish, C., Fortado, L. Waters, R. and Wigglesworth, R. (2017) '"Crypto" hedge funds spring up in crowded field'. *Financial Times* [online]. https://www.ft.com/content/98031696-9e67-11e7-8cd4-932067fbf946

56. Gerard, D. (2020) *Libra Shrugged*. Kindle edition.

57. Murphy, H. (2019) 'Facebook unveils global digital coin called Libra'. *Financial Times* [online]. https://www.ft.com/content/af6b1d48-90cc-11e9-aea1-2b1d33ac3271

58. Favas, M. (2020) 'Payment systems: The financial world's nervous system is being rewired'. *The Economist* [online]. https://www.economist.com/special-report/2020/05/07/the-financial-worlds-nervous-system-is-being-rewired

59. Beioley, K. and Pickford, J. (2018) 'Bitcoin investors struggle to cash out new fortunes'. *Financial Times* [online]. https://www.ft.com/content/40c64992-f606-11e7-88f7-5465a6ce1a00

60. Libra white paper (2019) https://www.allcryptowhitepapers.com/facebook-libra-coin-whitepaper

61. Marcus, D. (2019) Testimony to the US Senate Committee on Banking, Housing and Urban Affairs. https://www.banking.senate.gov/download/marcus-tesimony-7-16-19

62. Gerard, D. (2020)

63. Hern, A. (2019) 'Libra: US Congress asks Facebook to pause development'. *Guardian* [online]. https://www.theguardian.com/technology/2019/jul/03/libra-us-congress-asks-facebook-pause-development-cryptocurrency

64. Partington, R. (2019) 'France to block Facebook's Libra cryptocurrency in Europe'. *Guardian* [online]. https://www.theguardian.com/technology/2019/sep/12/france-block-development-facebook-libra-cryptocurrency

65. Agnew, H. (2019) 'France says it will not support Libra's development in Europe'. *Financial Times* [online]. https://www.ft.com/content/6d414606-d549-11e9-a0bd-ab8ec6435630

66. Arner, D., Auer, R. and Frost, J. (2020) Stablecoins: Risks, potential and regulation. BIS working paper no. 905. https://www.bis.org/publ/work905.pdf

67. Libra white paper (2019)

68. Greeley, B. (2019) 'Facebook's Libra currency is wake-up call for central banks'. *Financial Times* [online]. https://www.ft.com/content/6960c7a4-f313-11e9-b018-3ef8794b17c6

69. Murphy, H. (2020) 'Facebook's Libra currency to launch next year in limited format'. *Financial Times* [online]. https://www.ft.com/content/cfe4ca11-139a-4d4e-8a65-b3be3a0166be

70. Stacey, K. and Murphy, H. (2020) 'How Facebook's Libra went from world changer to just another PayPal'. *Financial Times* [online]. https://www.ft.com/content/79376464-72b5-41fa-8f14-9f308acaf83b

71. Jones, C. (2019) 'Central bank plans to create digital currencies receive backing'. *Financial Times* [online]. https://www.ft.com/content/428a0b20-99b0-11e9-9573-ee5cbb98ed36

72. Sandbu, M. (2019) 'How Facebook's Libra fuelled push for central bank-run digital currencies'. *Financial Times* [online] https://www.ft.com/content/746808a0-d9f6-11e9-8f9b-77216ebe1f17

73. Mitchell, T., Yang, Y. and McMorrow, R. (2021) 'Jack Ma vs Xi Jinping: The future of private business in China'. *Financial Times* [online]. https://www.ft.com/content/751c2500-f50d-47c9-8f04-a28ad62285fd

74. Clark, D. (2016) *Alibaba: The House That Jack Ma Built*. Ecco, New York, NY.

75. McMorrow, R. and Yu, S. (2021) 'The vanishing billionaire: How Jack Ma fell foul of Xi Jinping'. *Financial Times* [online]. https://www.ft.com/content/1fe0559f-de6d-490e-b312-abba0181da1f

76. McMorrow, R. and Lockett, H. (2020) 'China halts $37bn Ant Group IPO, citing "major issues"'. *Financial Times* [online]. https://www.ft.com/content/c1ee03d4-f22e-4514-af46-2f8423a6842e

77. Gross, I., Perez, K. and Quah, B-L. (2020) 'Why hasn't Apple Pay replicated Alipay's success?' *Harvard Business Review* [online]. https://hbr.org/2020/09/why-hasnt-apple-pay-replicated-alipays-success

78. Yang, Y. (2020) 'Jack Ma rails against global financial rules ahead of $30bn Ant Group IPO'. *Financial Times* [online]. https://www.ft.com/content/66808017-59fd-49d1-9016-34684001c978

79. Feng, V. (2020) 'Jack Ma has lost 12 billion since China's internet clampdown'. Bloomberg [online]. https://www.bloomberg.com/news/articles/2020-12-29/jack-ma-has-lost-12-billion-since-china-s-internet-clampdown

80. McMorrow, R. and Mitchell, T. (2020) 'China plots "rectification" drive to bring Jack Ma's Ant Group to heel'. *Financial Times* [online]. https://www.ft.com/content/84d57797-4211-4658-ac54-ebdcb5146151

81. Davies, R. and Davidson, H. (2021) 'The strange case of Alibaba's Jack Ma and his three-month vanishing act'. *Guardian* [online]. https://www.theguardian.com/business/2021/jan/23/the-strange-case-of-alibabas-jack-ma-and-his-three-month-vanishing-act

82. Yang, Y. (2018) 'Does China's bet on big data for credit scoring work?' *Financial Times* [online]. https://www.ft.com/content/ba163b00-fd4d-11e8-ac00-57a2a826423e

83. Kobie, N. (2019) 'The complicated truth about China's social credit system'. *Wired* [online]. https://www.wired.co.uk/article/china-social-credit-system-explained

84. Yu, S. and Mitchell, T. (2021) 'China's central bank fights Jack Ma's Ant Group over control of data'. *Financial Times* [online]. https://www.ft.com/content/1dbc6256-c8cd-48c1-9a0f-bb83a578a42e

85. McMorrow, R. and Yang, Y. (2021) 'Jack Ma's Ant forced into arms of banks he once dubbed "pawnshops"'. *Financial Times* [online]. https://www.ft.com/content/80800888-dc13-4094-ac34-18b90e3aef03

86. Yu, S. and Mitchell, T. (2021) 'China's clampdown on Jack Ma's Ant boosts rivals'. *Financial Times* [online]. https://www.ft.com/content/02ecd3cc-40ee-4712-ae9a-d9b41427d6e9

87. Yang, Y. (2018)

88. Clover, C. (2016) 'China: When big data meets Big Brother'. *Financial Times* [online]. https://www.ft.com/content/b5b13a5e-b847-11e5-b151-8e15c9a029fb

89. Kobie, N. (2019)

90. Areddy, J. T. (2021) 'China creates its own digital currency, a first for major economy'. *Wall Street Journal* [online]. https://www.wsj.com/articles/china-creates-its-own-digital-currency-a-first-for-major-economy-11617634118

91. Sender, H. (2020) 'China's new digital currency takes aim at Alibaba and Tencent'. *Financial Times* [online]. https://www.ft.com/content/fec06de9-ac43-4ab8-81f3-577638bd3c16

92. Reuters (2019) 'China says new digital currency will be similar to Facebook's Libra'. Reuters [online]. https://www.reuters.com/article/us-china-crypto-currency-cenbank-idUSKCN1VR0NM

93. Eich, S. (2019)

94. Voreacos, D. (2019) 'US, South Korea bust giant child porn site by following a bitcoin trail'. Bloomberg [online]. https://www.bloomberg.com/news/articles/2019-10-16/giant-child-porn-site-is-busted-as-u-s-follows-bitcoin-trail

95. Murphy, H., McCormick, M. and Manson, K. (2021) 'Hacking group tied to cyber attack on US pipeline said to have shut down'. *Financial Times* [online]. https://www.ft.com/content/734f923a-c2eb-4709-93f7-98f9b1ebd178

96. Orwell, G. (1944) 'The Road to Serfdom by F.A. Hayek / The Mirror of the Past by K. Zilliacus'. *Observer*, April 9.

97. Jenkins, P. (2018) '"We don't take cash": Is this the future of money?' *Financial Times* [online]. https://www.ft.com/content/9fc55dda-5316-11e8-b24e-cad6aa67e23e

98. Sullivan, A. (2018) 'Times change but German obsession with cash endures'. Deutsche Welle [online]. https://www.dw.com/en/times-change-but-german-obsession-with-cash-endures/a-43718626

99. Devins, S. (2017) 'Handelsblatt explains: Why Germans are so private about their data'. *Handelsblatt* [online]. https://www.handelsblatt.com/english/handelsblatt-explains-why-germans-are-so-private-about-their-data/23572446.html

100. BankID (2021) This is BankID. https://www.bankid.com/en/om-bankid/detta-ar-bankid

101. Fulton, C. (2020) 'Sweden starts testing world's first central bank digital currency'. *Reuters* [online]. https://www.reuters.com/article/us-cenbank-digital-sweden-idUSKBN20E26G

102. Jones, C. (2021) 'Crackdown on Ant Group will be echoed elsewhere'. *FT Alphaville*. https://www.ft.com/content/51419af3-bee0-4167-9e95-0d7c-f38e9ec4

103. Jones, C. (2020) 'Does a digital euro challenge the dollar's global dominance?' *FT Alphaville*. https://www.ft.com/content/d492ac51-5016-4f7f-b2d6-29876fb57fd0

104. Bank for International Settlements (2021) Central bank digital currencies: Foundational principles and core features 1. https://www.bis.org/publ/othp33.pdf

105. Committee on Payments and Market Infrastructures (2018) Central bank digital currencies. Bank for International Settlements. https://www.bis.org/cpmi/publ/d174.pdf

106. Brainard, L. (2021) Private money and central bank money as payments go digital: An update on CBDCs. Consensus by CoinDesk 2021 Conference, May 24. https://www.federalreserve.gov/newsevents/speech/brainard202105 24a.htm

107. *The Economist* (2021) 'When central banks issue digital money'. *The Economist* [online]. https://www.economist.com/special-report/2021/05/06/when-central-banks-issue-digital-money

108. Douglas, P. B., Hamilton, E. J., Fisher, I., King, W. I., Graham, F. D. and Whittlesey, C. R. (1939) A program for monetary reform. https://faculty.chicagobooth.edu/amir.sufi/research/monetaryreform_1939.pdf

109. Brunnermeier, M. K., James, H. and Landau, J-P. (2019) The digitalization of money. https://scholar.princeton.edu/sites/default/files/markus/files/02c_digitalmoney.pdf

110. Kumhof, M. and Benes, J. (2012) The Chicago plan revisited. IMF working paper no. 12/202. https://www.imf.org/en/Publications/WP/Issues/2016/12/31/The-Chicago-Plan-Revisited-26178

111. Arnold, M. (2021) 'Europeans raise privacy concerns over digital currency'. *Financial Times* [online]. https://www.ft.com/content/661e066c-b41b-46e3-a9c0-275132039c1a

112. Manchini-Griffoli, T. (2021) Dear mom, forget the cash. https://www.imf.org/external/pubs/ft/fandd/2021/03/what-are-central-bank-digital-currencies-mancini-griffoli.htm

113. Murgia, M. (2017) 'WhatsApp row explained: Backdoors and bad guys'. *Financial Times* [online]. https://www.ft.com/content/8c8de3b8-12d0-11e7-80f4-13e067d5072c

114. Poitras, L., Rosenbach, M. and Stark, H. (2013) 'NSA monitors financial world'. *Der Spiegel* [online]. https://www.spiegel.de/international/world/how-the-nsa-spies-on-international-bank-transactions-a-922430.htm

11. Can money save the world?

1. Tooze, A. (2019) 'Why central banks need to step up on global warming'. *Foreign Policy* [online]. https://foreignpolicy.com/2019/07/20/why-central-banks-need-to-step-up-on-global-warming

2. Arnold, M. (2019) 'Christine Lagarde wants key role for climate change in ECB review'. *Financial Times* [online]. https://www.ft.com/content/61ef385a-1129-11ea-a225-db2f231cfeae

3. Khalaf, R. and Arnold, M. (2020) 'Lagarde puts green policy top of agenda in ECB bond buying'. *Financial Times* [online]. https://www.ft.com/content/f776ea60-2b84-4b72-9765-2c084bff6e32

4. Tucker, P. (2018) *Unelected Power: The Quest for Legitimacy in Central Banking and the Regulatory State*. Princeton University Press, Princeton, NJ.

5. Lagarde, C. (2021) Climate change and central banking. Keynote speech by Christine Lagarde, President of the European Central Bank, at the ILF Conference on Green Banking and Green Central Banking, Frankfurt am Main, 25 January. https://www.bis.org/review/r210127d.htm

6. *The Economist* (2019) 'The rights and wrongs of central bank greenery'. *The Economist* [online]. https://www.economist.com/leaders/2019/12/14/the-rights-and-wrongs-of-central-bank-greenery

7. Arnold, M. (2021) 'ECB stress test reveals economic impact of climate change'. *Financial Times* [online]. https://www.ft.com/content/7b734848-1287-4106-b866-7d07bc9d7eb8

8. Batten, S., Sowerbutts, R. and Tanaka, M. (2016) Let's talk about the weather: The impact of climate change on central banks. Bank of England staff working paper no. 603. https://www.bankofengland.co.uk/working-paper/2016/lets-talk-about-the-weather-the-impact-of-climate-change-on-central-banks

9. Brainard, L. (2019) Why climate change matters for monetary policy and financial stability. Remarks at The Economics of Climate Change. https://www.federalreserve.gov/newsevents/speech/files/brainard20191108a.pdf

10. Batten, S. (2018) Climate change and the macro-economy: A critical review. Bank of England staff working paper no. 706. https://www.bankofengland.co.uk/-/media/boe/files/working-paper/2018/climate-change-and-the-macro-economy-a-critical-review.pdf

11. Beattie, A. (2010) *False Economy*. Penguin, London.

12. Carney, M. (2015) Breaking the tragedy of the horizon – Climate change and financial stability. Speech at at Lloyd's of London, London, 29 September 2015. https://www.bis.org/review/r151009a.htm

13. Coase, R. H. (1960) 'The problem of social cost'. *Journal of Law and Economics*, vol, 3. https://www.law.uchicago.edu/files/file/coase-problem.pdf

14. Stern, N. (2008) 'The economics of climate change'. *American Economic Review*, vol. 98, no. 2, pp.1–37. https://www.jstor.org/stable/29729990

15. Baumol, W. J. (1972). 'On taxation and the control of externalities'. *American Economic Review*, vol. 62, no. 3, pp.307–322. https://www.jstor.org/stable/1803378

16. *The Economist* (2017) 'Getting serious about overfishing'. *The Economist* [online]. https://www.economist.com/briefing/2017/05/26/getting-serious-about-overfishing

17. Niccolo, G. D., Favara, G. and Ratnovski, L. (2012) Externalities and macro prudential policy. IMF staff discussion note. https://www.imf.org/external/pubs/ft/sdn/2012/sdn1205.pdf

18. Cecchetti, S. G. and Schoenholtz, K. L. (2015) Making driving safe. Money and Banking blog. https://www.moneyandbanking.com/commentary/2015/10/12/making-driving-safe

19. Edlin, A. S. and Karaca-Mandic, P. (2006) 'The accident externality from driving'. *Journal of Political Economy*, vol. 114, no. 5, pp.931–955. https://www.jstor.org/stable/10.1086/508030

20. Niccolo, G. D., Favara, G. and Ratnovski, L. (2012)

21. Farhi, E. and Werning, I. (2015) A theory of macro prudential policies in the presence of nominal rigidities. NBER working paper no. 19313. https://www.nber.org/papers/w19313

22. Network for greening the financial system (2021) Adapting central bank operations to a hotter world: Reviewing some options. https://www.ngfs.net/sites/default/files/medias/documents/ngfs_monetary_policy_operations_final.pdf

23. Baumol, W. J. and Oates, W. E. (1971) 'The use of standards and prices for protection of the environment'. *Swedish Journal of Economics*, vol. 73, no. 1, pp.42–54. https://www.jstor.org/stable/3439132

24. Carney, M. (2015)

25. Monnin, P. (2018) Central banks and the transition to a low carbon economy. Council on Economic Policies. https://www.cepweb.org/wp-content/uploads/2018/03/CEP-DN-Central-Banks-and-the-Transition-to-a-Low-Carbon-Economy.pdf

26. Berenguer, M., Cardona, M. and Evain, J. (2020) Integrating climate-related risks into banks' capital requirements. Institute for Climate Economics. https://www.i4ce.org/wp-core/wp-content/uploads/2020/03/Integrating Climate_EtudeVA.pdf

27. Money and Banking blog (2018) Understanding bank capital: A primer. https://www.moneyandbanking.com/commentary/2018/2/11/understanding-bank-capital-a-primer

28. Basel Committee on Banking Supervision (2020) Risk-basked capital requirements. BCBS. https://www.bis.org/basel_framework/standard/RBC.htm

29. Lucia, A., Ossola, E. and Panic, R. (2019) The Greenium matters: Greenhouse gas emissions, environmental disclosures, and stock prices. Working papers 2019-12, Joint Research Centre, European Commission. https://ideas.repec.org/p/jrs/wpaper/201912.html

30. FitchRatings (2021) Royal Dutch Shell plc. https://www.fitchratings.com/entity/royal-dutch-shell-plc-80891259 (AA-)

31. FitchRatings (2020) Saudi Arabian oil company. https://www.fitchratings.com/entity/saudi-arabian-oil-company-96540423

32. FitchRatings (2021) United States of America. https://www.fitchratings.com/entity/united-states-of-america-80442210

33. FitchRatings (2021) France. https://www.fitchratings.com/entity/france-80442195

34. Volkswagen AG (2021) Investor relations: ratings. https://www.volkswagenag.com/en/InvestorRelations/fixed-income/ratings.html

35. Basel Committee on Banking Supervision. (2020) Climate-related financial risks: A survey on current initiatives. https://www.bis.org/bcbs/publ/d502.pdf

36. Brunnermeier, M. K. and Langau, J-P. (2020) 'Central banks and climate change'. *VoxEU.* https://voxeu.org/article/central-banks-and-climate-change

37. Van Lerven, F. and Ryan-Collins, J. (2018) Adjusting banks' capital requirements in line with sustainable finance objectives. New Economics Foundation. https://www.ucl.ac.uk/bartlett/public-purpose/sites/public-purpose/files/briefing-note-capital-requirements-for-sustainable-finance-objectives.pdf

38. Miles, D., Yang, J. and Marcheggiano, G. (2011) Optimal bank capital. Bank of England external MPC unit discussion paper no. 31. https://www.bankofengland.co.uk/external-mpc-discussion-paper/2011/optimal-bank-capital

39. Dafermos, Y., Nikolaidi, M. and Galanis, G. (2018) Can green quantitative easing (QE) reduce global warming? Greenwich Political Economy Research Centre. https://www.feps-europe.eu/attachments/publications/feps%20gperc%20policybriefgreenqe.pdf

40. D'Amico, A. and Kaminska, I. (2019) Credit easing versus quantitative easing: Evidence from corporate and government bond purchase programs. Bank of England staff working paper no. 824. https://www.bankofengland.co.uk/-/media/boe/files/working-paper/2019/credit-easing-versus-quantitative-easing-evidence-from-corporate-and-government-bond-purchase.pdf

41. Ferrari, A. and Landi, V. N. (2020) Whatever it takes to save the planet? Central banks and unconventional green policy. ECB working paper no. 2500. https://www.ecb.europa.eu/pub/pdf/scpwps/ecb.wp2500~f7a50c6f69.en.pdf

42. De Santis, R. A., Geis, A., Juskaite, A. and Vaz Cruz, L. (2018) 'The impact of the corporate sector purchase programme on corporate bond markets and the financing of euro area non-financial corporations'. *ECB Economic Bulletin*, no. 3. https://www.ecb.europa.eu/pub/pdf/other/ecb.ebart201803_02.en.pdf

43. Jourdan, S. (2019) 'Green QE is about more than buying climate-friendly bonds'. *FT Alphaville.* https://www.ft.com/content/6b4a8875-4985-4c14-ad74-3b1885b84380

44. The IMF (2020) Mitigating climate change: the world economic outlook. https://www.imf.org/en/Publications/WEO/Issues/2020/09/30/world-economic-outlook-october-2020#Chapter%203

45. O'Connor, S. (2021) 'Not all blue-collar workers will find green-collar jobs'. *Financial Times* [online]. https://www.ft.com/content/6133f8d7-a8a8-4f7a-83b6-d063ea98e3b9

46. Robins, N., Dikau, S. and Volz, U. (2021) Net-zero central baking: A new phase in greening the financial system. Grantham Research Institute on Climate Change and the Environment Policy Report. https://eprints.soas.ac.uk/34895/1/Net%20zero%20central%20banking%20Weds%2010%20March.pdf

47. Ross, A. (2020) *Investing to Save the Planet: How Your Money Can Make a Difference*. Penguin Business, London.

48. Mooney, A. and Smith, P. (2018) 'As the climate changes, ESG investing powers into the mainstream'. *Financial Times* [online]. https://www.ft.com/content/3a9ddee9-83ef-365a-b1ed-db02a55f68e7

49. Mooney, A. (2021) 'New criteria for chiefs' bonuses: Diversity and climate change'. *Financial Times* [online]. https://www.ft.com/content/75849e75-d3c3-4c28-843e-04b7cdbfafd4

50. Ross, A. (2020)

51. Stiglitz, J. E. and Weiss, A. (1988) Banks as social accountants and screening devices for the allocation of credit. NBER working paper no. 2710. https://www.nber.org/papers/w2710

52. Davies, D. (2018) *Lying for Money*. Profile Books, London.

53. Storbeck, O., McCrum, D. and Palma, S. (2020) 'Wirecard fights for survival as it admits scale of fraud'. *Financial Times* [online]. https://www.ft.com/content/2581fda5-8c89-46b5-9acf-ba8a88d74d88

54. Sherman, H. D. and Young, S. D. (2017) 'The pitfalls of non-GAAP metrics'. *MIT Sloan Management Review*. https://sloanreview.mit.edu/article/the-pitfalls-of-non-gaap-metrics/

55. Ford, J. (2019) 'Accounting has become the opposite of useful for users'. *Financial Times* [online]. https://www.ft.com/content/e4b555f0-41c0-11e9-b896-fe36ec32aece

56. Mackintosh, J. (2018) 'Is Tesla or Exxon more sustainable? It depends who you ask'. *Wall Street Journal* [online]. https://www.wsj.com/articles/is-tesla-or-exxon-more-sustainable-it-depends-whom-you-ask-1537199931

57. Ehlers, T., Mojon, B. and Packer, F. (2020) 'Green bonds and carbon emissions: Exploring the case for a rating system at the firm level'. *BIS Quarterly Review*. https://www.bis.org/publ/qtrpdf/r_qt2009c.htm

58. Clapp, C. and Pilay, K. (2017) 'Green bonds and climate finance', in Markandya, A., Galarraga, I., and Rübbelke, D. (eds), *Climate Finance: Theory and Practice*. World Scientific Publishing Company, Singapore.

59. Allen, K. (2018) 'Schiphol becomes first European airport to sell green bond'. *Financial Times* [online]. https://www.ft.com/content/1fd66748-d5f4-11e8-a854-33d6f82e62f8

60. *The Economist* (2021) 'Sustainable finance is rife with greenwash, time for more disclosure'. *The Economist* [online]. https://www.economist.com/leaders/2021/05/22/sustainable-finance-is-rife-with-greenwash-time-for-more-disclosure

61. De Bruin, B., Herzog, L., O'Neill, M. and Sandberg, J. (2020) 'Philosophy of money and finance', in the *Stanford Encyclopaedia of Philosophy*, Zalta, E. N. (ed.). https://plato.stanford.edu/entries/money-finance/#SociRespInve

62. https://www.climatebonds.net/market/data/

63. Feyzioglu, T., Swaroop, V. and Zhu, M. (1998) 'A panel data analysis of the fungibility of foreign aid'. *World Bank Economic Review*, vol. 12, no. 1, pp.29–58. https://www.jstor.org/stable/3990208

64. Matikainen, S. (2017) Green doesn't mean risk-free: Why we should be cautious about a green supporting factor in the EU. LSE Grantham Institute. https://www.lse.ac.uk/GranthamInstitute/news/eu-green-supporting-factor-bank-risk

65. Wigglesworth, R. (2021) 'ESG rush opens opportunities for betting against the angels'. *Financial Times* [online]. https://www.ft.com/content/262f2dfa-82bc-4454-96aa-bc5c38f82cdd

66. Smart, J. J. C. and Williams, B. (1973) *Utilitarianism: For and Against.* Cambridge University Press, Cambridge. https://www.utilitarianism.com/utilitarianism-for-and-against.pdf

67. Riding, S. (2021) 'EU rules promise to reshape opaque world of sustainable investment'. *Financial Times* [online]. https://www.ft.com/content/87615a23-0105-4210-8e7f-ccf84370656e

68. *The Economist* (2020) 'What is the point of green bonds?' *The Economist* [online]. https://www.economist.com/finance-and-economics/2020/09/19/what-is-the-point-of-green-bonds

69. Khan, M. (2021) 'Brussels faces backlash over delay to decision on whether gas is green'. *Financial Times* [online]. https://www.ft.com/content/25177f38-f4c6-4f0c-9e01-399e51258f79

70. Coyle, D. (2014) *GDP: A Brief but Affectionate History.* Princeton University Press, Princeton, NJ.

71. Hodgson, C. and Nauman, B. (2021) 'How much is a tree worth? Investors seek to build a market for nature'. *Financial Times* [online]. https://www.ft.com/content/599675df-25f5-4846-860c-195faf91059e

72. Bureau of Economic Analysis (2008) Why does GDP include imputations? https://www.bea.gov/help/faq/488

73. Carbon Pricing Leadership Coalition (2017) Report of the high-level commission on carbon prices. https://static1.squarespace.com/static/54ff9 c5ce4b0a53decccfb4c/t/59244eed17bffc0ac256cf16/1495551740633/Carbon Pricing_Final_May29.pdf

74. Ember (2021) Daily EU ETS carbon market price. https://ember-climate. org/data/carbon-price-viewer

75. Helm, D. (2015) *Natural Capital: Valuing the Planet.* Yale University Press, New Haven, CT.

76. Pilling, D. (2021) 'Africa's green superpower: Why Gabon wants markets to help tackle climate change'. *Financial Times* [online]. https://www.ft.com/content/4f0579ac-409f-41d2-bf40-410d5a2ee46b

77. Sheppard, D., Dempsey, H. and Hollinger, P. (2021) 'EU industry calls for urgent carbon border tax as prices soar'. *Financial Times* [online]. https://www.ft.com/content/17e157b2-21ea-4e22-9278-35f157046e85

78. Carney, M. (2021) *Value(s): Building a Better World.* William Collins, London.

12. Has money made us unequal?

1. Jones, S. and Romei, V. (2020) 'Pandemic makes world's billionaires – and their advisers – richer'. *Financial Times* [online]. https://www.ft.com/content/ab30d301-351b-4387-b212-12fed904324b

2. Neate, R. (2020) 'Billionaires' wealth rises to $10.2tn amid Covid crisis'. *Guardian* [online]. https://www.theguardian.com/business/2020/oct/07/covid-19-crisis-boosts-the-fortunes-of-worlds-billionaires

3. Greenwald, D. L., Leombroni, M., Lustig, H. and Nieuwerburgh, S. V. (2021) Financial and total wealth inequality with declining interest rates. NBER working paper no. 28613. https://www.nber.org/papers/w28613

4. Zucman, G. (2019) 'Global wealth inequality'. *Annual Review of Economics*, vol. 11, pp.109–138. https://gabriel-zucman.eu/files/Zucman2019.pdf

5. Greenwald, D. L., et al. (2021)

6. Giles, C. (2014) 'Debate rages on quantitative easing's effect on inequality'. *Financial Times* [online]. https://www.ft.com/content/c630d922-586f-11e4-942f-00144feab7de

7. Powell, T. and Wessel, D. (2021) Why is the New Zealand government telling its central bank to focus on rising house prices? Brookings. https://www.brookings.edu/blog/up-front/2021/04/02/why-is-the-new-zealand-government-telling-its-central-bank-to-focus-on-rising-house-prices/

8. O'Connor, S. (2021) '"We are drowning in insecurity": Young people and life after the pandemic'. *Financial Times* [online]. https://www.ft.com/content/77d586cc-4f3f-4701-a104-d09136c93d44

9. Smyth, J. (2020) 'New Zealand wins plaudits for coronavirus approach'. *Financial Times* [online]. https://www.ft.com/content/7514ea27-aff7-4733-a827-6ae792364f75

10. Osnos, E. (2017) 'Doomsday prep for the super rich'. *New Yorker* [online]. https://www.newyorker.com/magazine/2017/01/30/doomsday-prep-for-the-super-rich

11. Harding, R. (2021) 'Central banks should not target house prices'. *Financial Times* [online]. https://www.ft.com/content/03348778-ec31-4120-a68e-098eea760440

12. Brooks, D. (2020) New Zealand weighs negative interest rates as COVID rages overseas. NikkeiAsia [online] https://asia.nikkei.com/Economy/New-Zealand-weighs-negative-interest-rates-as-COVID-rages-overseas

13. Goode, R. (1960) 'Imputed rent of owner-occupied dwellings under the income tax'. *Journal of Finance*, vol. 15, no. 4, pp.504–530. https://www.jstor.org/stable/2325629

14. Meen, G. and Whitehead, C. (2020) *Understanding Affordability: The Economics of Housing Markets*. Bristol University Press, Bristol.

15. Poteba, J. M. (1984) 'Tax subsidies to owner-occupied housing: An asset-market approach'. *Quarterly Journal of Economics*, vol. 99, no. 4, pp.729–752. https://www.jstor.org/stable/1883123

16. Miles, D. and Monro, V. (2019) UK house prices and three decades of decline in the risk-free real interest rate. Bank of England working paper no. 837. https://www.bankofengland.co.uk/working-paper/2019/uk-house-prices-and-three-decades-of-decline-in-the-risk-free-real-interest-rate

17. Meen, G. and Whitehead, C. (2020)

18. Hunt, E. (2021) '"Can you help me?": The quiet desperation of New Zealand's housing crisis'. *Guardian* [online]. https://www.theguardian.com/world/2021/mar/20/can-you-help-me-the-quiet-desperation-of-new-zealands-housing-crisis

19. Smyth, J. (2021) 'New Zealand tells central bank to consider housing in policy decisions'. *Financial Times* [online]. https://www.ft.com/content/0898db07-8ba5-43d7-a47a-de7bebad995e

20. Robertson, G. (2021) Reserve Bank to take account of housing in decision making. New Zealand Government. https://www.beehive.govt.nz/release/reserve-bank-take-account-housing-decision-making

21. Singleton, J., Grimes, A., Hawke, G. and Holmes, F. (2006) *Innovation in Central Banking: A History of the Reserve Bank of New Zealand*. Auckland University Press, Auckland.

22. Jones, C. (2021) 'The era of central bank convergence is over'. *FT Alphaville*. https://www.ft.com/content/7c56165b-5d6b-4eea-b663-07dac93dd28a

23. Harding, R. (2021)

24. Jordà, Ò., Schularick, M. and Taylor, A. M. (2014) Betting the house. NBER working paper no. 20771. https://www.nber.org/papers/w20771

25. Leamer, E. E. (2007) Housing IS the business cycle. NBER working paper no. 13428. https://www.nber.org/papers/w13428

26. Broadbent, B. (2014) Monetary policy, asset prices and distribution. Speech at the Society of Business Economists Annual Conference, 23 October. https://www.bankofengland.co.uk/-/media/boe/files/speech/2014/monetary-policy-asset-prices-and-distribution.pdf

27. Haldane, A. G. (2018) How monetary policy affects your GDP. Finch lecture, University of Melbourne, 10 April. https://www.bankofengland.co.uk/-/media/boe/files/speech/2018/how-monetary-policy-affects-your-gdp-speech-by-andy-haldane.pdf

28. Skidelsky, R. (2018) *Money and Government*. Penguin Books, London.

29. Smith, C. and Stubbington, T. (2021) 'The summer of inflation: Will central banks and investors hold their nerve?' *Financial Times* [online]. https://www.ft.com/content/414e8e47-e904-42ac-80ea-5d6c38282cac

30. Alabi, L. O., Hume, N. and Kasumov, A. (2021) 'US tech stocks tumble on nerves over inflation outlook'. *Financial Times* [online]. https://www.ft.com/content/cab2caee-60c9-40cb-a115-099287ab8bf4

31. Reserve Bank of New Zealand (2021) Loan-to-valuation ratio restrictions. https://www.rbnz.govt.nz/regulation-and-supervision/banks/macro-prudential-policy/loan-to-valuation-ratio-restrictions

32. Wind, B., Lersch, P. and Dewilde, C. (2016) 'The distribution of housing wealth in 16 European countries: Accounting for institutional differences'. *Journal of Housing and the Built Environment*, vol. 32, pp.625–647. https://link.springer.com/article/10.1007/s10901-016-9540-3

33. Sen, A. (1979) Equality of what? The Tanner Lecture on Human Values, May 22. https://www.ophi.org.uk/wp-content/uploads/Sen-1979_Equality-of-What.pdf

34. Coote, A. (2020) 'The case for universal basic services'. *New Economics Foundation*. https://neweconomics.org/2020/02/the-case-for-universal-basic-services

35. Cowell, F. A., Karagiannaki, E. and McKnight, A. (2013) Accounting for cross-country differences in wealth inequality. Centre for Analysis of Social Exclusion. https://sticerd.lse.ac.uk/dps/ case/cp/CASEpaper168.pdf

36. *The Economist* (2019) 'In Sweden, billionaires are surprisingly popular'. *The Economist* [online]. https://www.economist.com/briefing/2019/11/28/in-sweden-billionaires-are-surprisingly-popular

37. Bruenig, M. (2017) Nordic socialism is realer than you think. People's Policy Project. https://www.peoplespolicyproject.org/2017/08/05/nordic-socialism-is-realer-than-you-think/

38. Frick, J. R. and Grabka, M. M. (2013) 'Public pension entitlements and the distribution of wealth', in *Income Inequality*, Gornick, J. C. and Jäntti, M. (eds). Stanford University Press, Stanford, CA.

39. Domeij, D. and Klein, P. (2002) 'Public pensions: To what extent do they account for Swedish wealth inequality?' *Review of Economic Dynamics*, vol. 5, no. 1, pp.503–534. https://www.sciencedirect.com/science/article/abs/pii/S1094202502901572

40. Segal, P. (2020) Inequality as entitlements over labour. Working paper no. 43. International Inequalities Institute, London School of Economics and Political Science. http://eprints.lse.ac.uk/104083/

41. Nilsson, P. (2018) 'Swedish society's big division – in 6 charts'. *Financial Times* [online]. https://www.ft.com/content/3b9566e4-941a-11e8-b747-fb1e803ee64e

42. Dahlstedt, M. and Fejes, A. (2019*) Neoliberalism and Market Forces in Education: Lessons from Sweden*. Routledge, London.

43. Milne, R. (2018) 'Swedish angst grows over tensions in public–private model'. *Financial Times* [online]. https://www.ft.com/content/535c4e42-9b64-11e6-b8c6-568a43813464

44. Bender, G. (2018) A cautionary tale to be had from Swedish school reforms. Social Europe. https://socialeurope.eu/a-cautionary-tale-to-be-had-from-swedish-school-reforms

45. Bénabou, R. and Tirole, J. (2003) 'Intrinsic and extrinsic motivation'. *Review of Economic Studies*, vol. 70, no. 3, pp.489–520. https://www.jstor.org/stable/3648598

46. Gneezy, U. and Rustichini, A. (2000) 'A fine is a price'. *Journal of Legal Studies*, vol. 29, no. 1, pp.1–17. https://rady.ucsd.edu/faculty/directory/gneezy/pub/docs/fine.pdf

47. Elster, J. (1989) 'Social norms and economic theory'. *Journal of Economic Perspectives*, vol. 3, no. 4, pp.99–117. https://www.jstor.org/stable/1942912

48. Sandel, M. J. (2012) *What Money Can't Buy*. Penguin Books, London.

49. Roth, A. E. (2007) 'Repugnance as a constraint on markets'. *Journal of Economic Perspectives*, vol. 21, no. 3, pp.37–58. https://www.aeaweb.org/articles?id=10.1257/jep.21.3.37

50. Cheung, H. (2014) 'Surrogate babies: Where can you have them, and is it legal?' BBC [online]. https://www.bbc.co.uk/news/world-28679020

51. Fenton-Glynn, C. (2019) 'Surrogacy: Why the world needs rules for "selling" babies'. BBC [online]. https://www.bbc.co.uk/news/health-47826356

52. Atwood, M. (2012) *Payback: Debt and the Shadow Side of Wealth*. Bloomsbury, London.

53. Smith, A. (1776) *An Inquiry into the Nature and Causes of the Wealth of Nations*. Oxford University Press, Oxford.

54. Marçal, K. (2015) *Who Cooked Adam Smith's Dinner?* Portobello Books, London.

55. Sandel, M. J. (2012)

56. Hugo, V. (1862) *Les Misérables*. Penguin Books, London.

57. Lewin, T. (2015) 'Egg donors challenge pay rates, saying they shortchange women'. *New York Times* [online]. https://www.nytimes.com/2015/10/17/us/egg-donors-challenge-pay-rates-saying-they-shortchange-women.html

58. Thorn, R. (2016) 'The mothers secretly working as sex workers'. BBC [online]. https://www.bbc.co.uk/news/uk-38128523

59. Harding, R. and McGregor, R. (2013) 'Janet Yellen: The economist tipped to be the first lady at the Fed'. *Financial Times* [online]. https://www.ft.com/content/7c2d5430-216c-11e3-8aff-00144feab7de

60. Arnold, M. and Dombey, D. (2021) 'Women central bankers want action on "hidden barriers" to equality'. *Financial Times* [online]. https://www.ft.com/content/0d1d2d4d-8bb8-42ce-b263-9863a1f377ed

61. UK government (2021) Past Chancellors of the Exchequer. https://www.gov.uk/government/history/past-chancellors

62. *The Economist* (2017) 'Women and economics'. *The Economist* [online]. https://www.economist.com/christmas-specials/2017/12/19/women-and-economics

63. Weeden, A. K., Thébaud, S. and Gelbgiser, D. (2017) 'Degrees of difference: Gender segregation of US doctorates by field and program prestige'. *Sociological Science*, no. 4, pp.123–150. https://sociologicalscience.com/articles-v4-6-123/

64. Önder, A. S. and Hakan, Y. (2016) 'Thirty-five years of peer-reviewed publishing by North American economics PhDs: Quantity, quality, and beyond'. *SSRN Electronic Journal*. https://papers.ssrn.com/sol3/papers.cfm?abstract_id=277323

65. Bansak, C. and Starr, M. (2010). 'Gender differences in predispositions towards economics'. *Eastern Economic Journal*, vol. 36, no. 33. https://doi.org/10.1057/eej.2008.50

66. Ashcroft, R. E. (2011) 'Personal financial incentives in health promotion: Where do they fit in an ethic of autonomy?'. *Health Expect*, vol. 14, no. 2, pp.191–220. https://www.ncbi.nlm.nih.gov/pmc/articles/PMC3123700/

67. Bunce, L., Baird, A. and Jones, S. E. (2017) 'The student-as-consumer approach in higher education and its effects on academic performance'.

Studies in Higher Education, vol. 42, no. 11, pp.1958–1978. https://www.tandfonline.com/doi/full/10.1080/03075079.2015.1127908

68. Bell, T. (2020) 'When it comes to care workers, don't just applaud, pay them properly'. *Guardian* [online]. https://www.theguardian.com/commentisfree/2020/apr/19/when-it-comes-to-care-workers-dont-just-applaud-pay-them-properly

69. Benería, L. (1999) 'The enduring debate over unpaid labour'. *International Labour Review*, vol. 138, no. 3. https://library.fes.de/libalt/journals/swetsfulltext/17160677.pdf

70. Yi, Y. A. (2010) 'Margaret G. Reid: Life and achievements'. *Feminist Economics*, vol. 2, no. 3, pp.17–36. https://www.tandfonline.com/doi/abs/10.1080/13545709610001707746

71. Carney, M. (2021) *Value(s): Building a Better World*. William Collins, London.

72. Yea, J. Y. (2017) 'Money norms'. *Loyola, University Chicago Law Journal*, vol. 49. https://elibrary.law.psu.edu/cgi/viewcontent.cgi?article=1364&context=fac_works

73. Hart, K. (2005) 'Towards an anthropology of money'. *Kritikos*, vol. 2. https://intertheory.org/hart.htm

74. *Mad Men* (2007) Series 4, Episode 7, 'The Suitcase' [TV]. AMC, 5 September 2010.

75. Zelizer, V. A. (2017) *The Social Meaning of Money*. Princeton University Press, Princeton, NY.

76. Bohannan, P. (1955) 'Some principles of exchange and investment among the Tiv'. *American Anthropologist*, vol. 57, no. 1, pp.60–70. https://www.jstor.org/stable/665788

77. Sandel, M. (2012)

78. Jackson, G. (2017) 'Bank of England unveils plastic Jane Austen £10 note'. *Financial Times* [online]. https://www.ft.com/content/f4ec1836-6bc6-11e7-b9c7-15af748b60d0

79. Zelizer, V. A. (2017)

Index

Index